Readings
in
Curriculum Evaluation

Readings

in

Curriculum Evaluation

Peter A. Taylor

Social and Human Analysis Branch
DREE
161 Laurier Avenue West
Ottawa 4, Ontario
Canada

Doris M. Cowley

University of Toronto
Ontario, Canada

WM. C. BROWN COMPANY PUBLISHERS
Dubuque, Iowa

CREDITS

Cronbach, Lee J., "Course Improvement Through Evaluation," *The Record,* May, 1963, Vol. 64, No. 8, pp. 672-683, by permission of the author and The Teachers' College Record.

Atkin, J. Myron, "Some Evaluation Problems in a Course-Content Improvement Project," *Journal of Research in Science Teaching,* 1963, Vol. 1, pp. 129-132. By permission of author and publisher.

Eisner, Elliot W., "Educational Objectives—Help or Hindrance," *School Review,* Autumn, 1967, pp. 250-260, by permission of the author and The University of Chicago Press.

Scriven, Michael, "Methodology of Evaluation," in Tyler, Gagne, and Scriven, *Perspectives of Curriculum Evaluation,* © 1967 by Rand McNally & Company, Chicago.

Messick, Samuel, "The Criterion Problem in the Evaluation of Instruction: Assessing Possible, Not Just Intended Outcomes," in *Evaluation of Instruction: Issues and Problems,* edited by M. C. Wittrock and David Wiley; Holt, Rinehart and Winston, Inc., publisher. By permission of author and publisher.

Hastings, J. Thomas, "Evaluating Change," by permission of author.

Lortie, Daniel C., "The Cracked Cake of Educational Custom and Emerging Issues in Evaluation," in Evaluation of Instruction: Issues and Problems, edited by M. C. Wittrock and David Wiley; Holt, Rinehart and Winston, Inc., publisher. By permission of author and publisher.

Willems, Edwin P., "Implications of Viewing Educational Evaluation as Research in the Behavioral Sciences," by permission of the author.

Welty, Gordon, "Evaluation Research and Research Designs," by permission of the author.

Scriven, Michael, "An Introduction to Meta-Evaluation," by permission of the author. Credit to EPIE Institute and *Educational Product Report.*

Taylor, Peter A., and Maguire, Thomas O., "A Theoretical Evaluation Model," published in the *Manitoba Journal of Educational Research,* June, 1966, by permission of the publisher.

Stake, Robert E., "The Countenance of Educational Evaluation," *The Record,* by permission of the author and The Teachers' College Record.

Glass, Gene V., "Two Generations of Evaluation Models," by permission of the author.

Alkin, Marvin C., "Towards an Evaluation Model: A Systems Approach," by permission of the author.

Provus, Malcolm M., "The Discrepancy Evaluation Model," by permission of the author.

Welty, Gordon, "Evaluation and Planning in Education: A Community Concern." Used by permission.

Ambray, Edward J., "Evaluation for Environmental Education," by permission of the author and The New Jersey State Council for Environmental Education.

Lindvall, C. M., "The Task of Evaluation in Curriculum Development Projects: A Rationale and Case Study," School Review, Summer, 1966, pp. 159-167, by permission of the author and The University of Chicago Press.

Schutz, Richard M., "Experimentation Relating to Formative Evaluation." In Klausmeier, Herbert J., James L. Wardrop, Mary R. Quilling, Thomas A. Rhomberg, and Richard E. Schutz, Research and development strategies in theory refinement and educational improvement, Theoretical Paper No. 15 of the Wisconsin Research and Development Center for Cognitive Learning; University of Wisconsin, Madison, and the Southwest Regional Laboratory for Educational Research and Development, Englewood, California, 1968.

Grobman, Hulda, "The Place of Evaluation in a Curriculum Study," by permission of the author.

Ausubel, David P., "Crucial Psychological Issues in the Objectives, Organization and Evaluation of Curriculum Reform Movements," by permission of the author.

Knox, Alan B., "Continuous Program Evaluation." Used by permission.

Alkin, Marvin C., "Evaluating the Cost-Effectiveness of Instructional Programs." Used by permission.

Weiss, Carol H., "Utilization of Evaluation: Toward Comparative Study," by permission of the author.

Merriman, Howard O., "Evaluation of Planned Educational Change at the Local Education Agency Level," by permission of the author.

Hammond, Robert L., "Evaluation at the Local Level." Used by permission.

CONTENTS

Section 1. An Overview

Section 2. The Beginnings of a New Era: Some General Concerns & Issues

Section 3. Evaluation Models

Section 4. Application of the New Approaches to Evaluation

Instructors in any discipline usually encourage their students to read materials in addition to the basic textbook for the course. Most instructors provide reading lists of classical and currently relevant articles that deal with issues of concern to their field. Library facilities have not always been ideal, however, and so collections of papers known as "readings" have become an accepted and acceptable alternative.

The particular concern of curriculum evaluation had not even been blessed with a *textbook* of any recency until the appearance of Bloom, Hastings and Maddaus (1970). In the urgent need to meet practical demands on the evaluator's time, in the need to find methodological approaches appropriate to the new problems in curriculum evaluation, in the very definition of evaluation itself, there has been more discussion than writing and even fewer writings available in journal format. Much of what has been of impact in the theory and practice of evaluation has appeared as appendages to project reports, in theses, and in papers circulated to a limited audience. We have leaned on these latter papers as much as on the more readily available sources in making our selections.

Not all of the papers that we have included are what we would consider as representing our own point of view or even the current majority view of curriculum evaluation. We have deliberately included papers that represent different and even debatable viewpoints in order to stimulate further discussion. The readings are therefore a useful source of materials for seminar discussions; we particularly hope that they will be used in this fashion.

Another reason that several of the papers have been chosen is that they suggest areas for further research and study. Students should realize the space limitations of any volume such as this, and should be willing to pursue through the references and the bibliography any issue which is of particular interest to him. Many of the papers represent but initial thoughts on an attack to a particular problem; others can lead to considerations of applications and resolutions not apparent at the time of their publication. Careful reading will suggest many thesis topics and concerns for longer-term research.

The practically-oriented have not been entirely forgotten. We have tended to the theoretical side in our selection partly because this is approximately the current state of the art. There are simply not many good, pithy examples of evaluative activity in print. But we have tried to include a number of examples of a practical nature and have certainly been most sensitive in selecting theoretical papers that could find some application without too much effort.

Hopefully the papers will also provide a modicum of enjoyment for their own sake. We have included selections that illustrate the kinds of intellectual struggle that go on as any new field develops. The convergences and discrepancies that occurred during the sixties should be obvious enough.

Finally, the authors would like to express their appreciation to the several contributors who granted permission to reproduce their work. Not a few of these selections are in print for the first time and a number were reworked especially for us. To these people and to those reviewers who made helpful suggestions regarding the organization of this anthology—our thanks.

PETER A. TAYLOR
DORIS M. COWLEY

SECTION 1

AN OVERVIEW

CHAPTER 1

NEW DIMENSIONS OF EVALUATION

Peter A. Taylor
Doris M. Cowley

During the past decade, the previously disjointed practices of curriculum evaluators have gradually emerged as a formal technology. As this technology has emerged, changes in the philosophy underlying evaluation have also occurred. The essence of these changes has been supplementary rather than substitutive, reflecting a considerable increase in the domain considered as legitimate for investigation by the evaluator.

The history of curriculum evaluation can be divided—like all of Gaul—into three parts. Prior to the 1930's, evaluation was equated almost exclusively with the administration of standardized tests. Comparisons, when these were appropriate, were made between two groups or between a target group and a set of norms. This kind of evaluation stemmed from the preoccupation with content objectives that characterized education in the early part of this century—and from behavioral evidence that still is of primary concern to too many educators today. The activities of the pre-1930 period are of little interest here since they cannot properly be called evaluation in today's sense. The second era encompasses the interval between the Eight-Year Study and the beginning of the post-Sputnik subject-matter curriculum projects (that is, from about 1935 to 1957). This second era is important for the establishment, through trial in on-going projects, of a basic pattern of evaluation activities. This second wave was based in part on an increased concern for the higher-order cognitive and affective objectives and the consequent inappropriateness of comparative evaluation using either another group or norms as a comparison. The final, post-Sputnik era in evaluation may be characterized by attempts to formalize a paradigm that would be applicable across many programs and projects. This era is marked by the realization that the domain of evaluation must be extended beyond the mere measurement of outcomes to improvement of courses. Chief among the advocates of this change was Cronbach (1963).

Clearly the most significant contribution to evaluation made during the second era was accomplished using the model developed by Ralph Tyler and his associates. The first of the evaluations employing this approach was conducted by the evaluation staff of the Commission on the Relation of School and College (the Eight-Year Study). Tyler and his group (Smith and Tyler, 1941) devised and implemented a philosophy of evaluation that has formed the basis for almost all subsequent thought about evaluation. Five purposes of evaluation were identified by this group. The first was to make a periodic check on the effectiveness of an educational program and to indicate to the educators where changes should be made. The second was to validate the hypotheses upon which a school operates. (For example, if a school develops a program based upon a Pragmatic philosophy, one role of an evaluator would be to validate that philosophy.) A third purpose was to provide information basic to the disposition and guidance of individual students. Too often this single purpose has become the sole purpose of evaluation. A fourth purpose was to provide what might be termed a level of psychological security to parents, students and school staff, by supplying evidence as to whether or not the school was attaining the goals it had set for itself. Finally, evaluation was seen as providing a sound basis for what we would now call "public relations" by indicating the value of the school program.

In order to meet their five purposes, the evaluation staff of the Eight-Year Study formulated a set of guidelines for establishing evaluation programs. The guidelines consisted of seven steps necessary for effective education evaluation.

1. Formulating objectives. The pure Tylerian approach required the *a priori* behavioral specification of objectives. The Committee argued that

valid educational objectives are reached on the basis of considered judgment using evidence regarding the demands of society, the characteristics of the students, the potential contributions which various fields of learning might make, the social and educational philosophy of the school, and what we know from the psychology of learning about the possibility of attaining the various classes of objectives.

At one time, the primary purpose of formal education was to teach each generation all the knowledge accumulated by the previous generations. This concept has now been largely superseded by another: to train pupils in such a way that they are better able to satisfy their needs (Tyler, 1953, p. 216). The goals, then, of formal education stem from the needs of youth, yet the goals are not based on all the needs of youth since there are many agencies other than the school influential in the satisfaction of needs. To translate the pertinent needs into educational objectives one must identify the new patterns of behavior to be acquired in the acquisition of knowledge, development of understandings, attitudes, interests, verbal, numerical, and motor skills and abilities to perform. Of course, value judgments are involved in the selection and limiting of pertinent needs.

Objectives should be stated in a manner which is pupil-oriented. Teacher-oriented objectives are stated in terms of the activities the teacher is to perform, i.e., "What am *I* going to *do* in this lesson?" Such objectives emphasize subject-matter content and sequence of presentation. Pupil-oriented objectives, on the other hand, identify the new patterns of behavior to be acquired, and therefore must be stated in terms of expected pupil behavior. The teacher must consider a different type question: "What change in pupil behavior am I to bring about in this lesson?"

Over the years, increasing attention has been paid by educators to the problem of the formal statement of educational objectives. The NEA Commission on the Reorganization of Secondary Education (1918) produced "The Seven Cardinal Principles of Secondary Education": Health, Command of Fundamental Processes, Home, Vocation, Citizenship, Leisure, Character. The NEA Educational Polices Commission (1938) produced four objectives: Self-realization, Human relationships, Economic efficiency, Civic responsibility. Havighurst (1953, p. 2) defined objectives as "developmental tasks." The achievement of such tasks predicts happiness and success. Notice that the foregoing abbreviated objectives, worthy as they may be, indicate some of the goals and/or broad objectives of education but their formal statements are too general to specify the changes in behavior to be produced in the school situation.

A definite attempt to formally state objectives in terms of observable pupil behavior and to select those goals attainable by average children in their first fifteen years was made by the Mid-Century Committee on Outcomes in Elementary Education (Kearney, 1953) and in Secondary Education (French, et al., 1957). In elementary education, nine goals and four behavioral patterns were specified. The behavioral patterns were defined as: Knowledge and understandings, Skills and competences, Attitudes and interests, Action patterns. In secondary education, three goals were identified: Self-realization, Interpersonal relations, Effective membership or leadership; and four behavioral patterns: Intellectual, Cultural, Physical, Economic. Again, notice although general behavioral patterns are identified, the identification is still too general to specify the changes in behavior to be produced in the school situation.

Probably the most exhaustive attempt to classify educational objectives was made by Krathwohl, Bloom and Masia (1964), and Bloom (1956, pp. 201-207) who identified three domains of educational objectives, the cognitive, affective and psychomotor:

1. Cognitive (recall and development)
   A. Knowledge
   B. Understanding
      comprehension
      application
      analysis
      synthesis
      evaluation
2. Affective (interests, attitudes, values, appreciations)
   receiving
   responding
   valuing
   organization
   characterization
3. Psychomotor (motor skills)

2. Classifying objectives. The objectives resulting from step one were to be classified into ten major categories described by the Committee as follows:

1. The development of effective methods of thinking.
2. The cultivation of useful work habits and study skills.
3. The inculcation of social attitudes.
4. The acquisition of a wide range of significant interests.
5. The development of increased appreciation of music, art, literature and other esthetic experiences.
6. The development of social sensitivity.

7. The development of better personal-social adjustment.
8. The acquisition of important information.
9. The development of physical health.
10. The development of a consistent philosophy of life.

The utility of such a classification was justified on two counts: it suggested areas for emphasis, and it focussed attention on the evaluation instruments that were needed.

3. Defining objectives in terms of behaviors. As a third step in the evaluation process the Committee was insistent that the broad objectives be defined in behavioral terms. The formal statements of educational objectives so far have not mentioned the relative importance of objectives nor specific objectives for specific teaching-learning situations. These omissions are unavoidable since they result from the statement of common goals and the recognition that there are individual differences among pupils, teachers, schools, communities, etc. Thus the most prominent single person involved in the identification of educational objectives is the teacher in the classroom. Yet, if the teacher in the classroom is operating on objectives as general as those cited, he is faced with a problem of evaluation. How does one produce acquisition of knowledge, develop understandings, inspire appreciations, direct attitudes and interests, promote good citizenship, or produce critical thinkers, and how does one know when and to what extent the objective has been achieved? Teacher-derived objectives should be stated in specific terms of observable pupil behavior, for if the teacher can observe the change in behavior intended to be produced by his instruction, he is in a better position to objectively plan his instruction and to evaluate its results both during and after instruction.

Mager (1962, p. 12) proposes three basic steps for the formulation of behavioral objectives:

1. The objective must state explicitly the *kind* of behavior the pupil must be able to demonstrate in order to achieve the objective.
2. The conditions (supportive and restrictive) under which the pupil demonstrates his competence must be stated.
3. The criteria of acceptable performance must be specified by describing at least its lower limit.

For example: When provided with drawings of a variety of triangles (2), the pupil can correctly identify them by name (1) at least 90 percent of the time (3).

In formulating behavioral objectives, the task of Step (1) is considerably lightened if one uses the performance terms (action verbs) or their synonyms defined by the AAAS (1965). Some examples of the nine AAAS action verbs are "identify," "name," "construct," "describe," "order," "demonstrate." Romey (1968) has further clarified the formulating of behavioral objectives by proposing a taxonomic division of objectives into levels ranging from the affective domain to very sophisticated observable behavior:

Level "NO" —Affective domain: appreciate, know, understand, comprehend. . . .
Level 0 —Simple recall or rote memory objectives: recall, state, tell, list, define. . . .
Level 1 —Simple behavioral objectives: describe, measure, identify, classify. . . .
Level 2 —More complex behavioral objectives: apply, interpret, distinguish, prove, construct, plot, discriminate, analyze, estimate. . . .
Level 3 —Behavior showing that the student has acquired the major concept or shows original thought: generalize, infer, predict, reorganize, discover, formulate hypotheses, discuss critically. . . .

The phrase preceding all these verbs is of the type "After completing . . . unit of instruction, the student should be able to . . . to . . . criterion."

4. Suggesting situations in which achievement of objectives will be shown. The sub-committees, having described the broad objectives in terms of behavior, were then required to specify the situations in which such behaviors might be observed. Carefully detailed statements in step three made this task relatively easy.

In contrast, the *process* of evaluating changes in pupil behavior is extremely complex. Firstly, the evaluator must be knowledgeable in the subject matter of instruction, learning theory, developmental psychology and the methods of educational evaluation. The pupil must be given the opportunity of demonstrating his level of achievement of a particular goal within as natural a situation as possible; performance and paper-and-pencil tests are approximations to natural situations. Thus, as the teacher formulates objectives and plans his instruction, he should also select the appropriate method of evaluation and specify the experimental conditions, recognizing the assumptions he is making in the artificial measurement of the abilities of a pupil to perform in a natural situation. All appraisal thus far is relative to the stated goals; the concern is with how well the pupil achieves the intended objectives, in Scriven's (1967) terminology, "The estimation of goal achievement." However, one should also inquire as to what extent the objectives are worth achieving. Secondly, then, evaluation should provide for the evaluation of value judgments, especially the goals; that is, concern itself not only with intended outcomes but also with possible outcomes. Stake (1967) terms these two components of evaluation as "description," the effects of the treatment, and "judgment," a decision of acceptable standard of excellence. Dyer (1967) emphasizes that the evaluation of the *side* effects may be more important than that of the intended effects, indeed, that one may need first measure the outcomes before deciding what the objectives ought to be.

5. Selecting and trying promising evaluation methods. Since by the time the Eight-Year Study was being conducted there were many standardized measuring instruments on the market, schools were encouraged to experiment in their usage for providing useful evaluative information. In general, this was not a fruitful pursuit, as it was rare for the existing instruments to measure the specific goals of a particular program. This fact gave rise to steps six and seven:

6. Developing and improving appraisal techniques.

7. Interpreting results. In the final step, results were interpreted in terms of the objectives. That is, an assessment was made of the extent to which the stated objectives were attained. It was suggested that progress towards several goals should be considered simultaneously. It was by this type of analysis that one could suggest hypotheses for improving the program.

The evaluation committee of the Eight-Year Study suggested that in order to carry out an evaluation it is necessary to know the objectives of the program but that the task of content formulation falls to the program developers. The important point to note is that the evaluation of the objectives themselves was apparently not considered to be a concern of an evaluator.

As another example of evaluation in the second era, there was the Co-operative Study of Evaluation in General Education, carried out by the American Council on General Education under the direction of Paul Dressel and Lewis Mayhew (1954). Although the format of the study differed from the Eight-Year Study its underlying philosophy was essentially the same. In their study the ACE committee identified six possible purposes of education:

1. Clarification and possible redefinition of the objectives of general education.
2. Development of more adequate and reliable means of measurement.
3. Appraisal of the development of students.
4. Adaptation of courses and programs to the individual student.

5. Motivation of student learning through continual self-evaluation.
6. Improvement of instruction.

Interestingly, in historical perspective, the committee de-emphasized the importance of purposes (4) and (5), suggesting that they were of concern only after the completion of other phases. Purpose (6) was considered of paramount importance.

In short, important evaluation thought in the second of the three eras can be characterized by its stress on stating objectives behaviorally and a lack of stress on valuing the objectives themselves. Within the time context when such ideas as stating objectives behaviorally were being advocated there was a legitimate need for their forceful promotion, but a degree of sophistication has been reached in contemporary curriculum evaluation where attention can be directed to additional problems.

With the advent of large, governmentally-endowed curriculum projects, scholars from many disciplines have become interested in the problems of curriculum development and evaluation. Thus, the present era of curriculum evaluation can be characterized by an expansion of the evaluation domain brought about in part by the funding agencies for proof of results; in part by non-educationist curriculum developers who saw a need for more information and knowledge about the educational process; and in part by pressures from educationists themselves. An even more noticeable characteristic of the present era of evaluation has been the attempt by several writers to formulate a conceptual framework for curriculum evaluation. Notable among these attempts has been Scriven's (1967) *Methodology of Evaluation*.

In his paper, Scriven differentiated between the goals of evaluation and the roles of evaluation. According to Scriven, evaluation has as its goal the answering of product-oriented questions about education instruments. ("Instruments" was used in a broad sense to include programs, procedures, processes, personnel, equipment, etc., rather than in the psychometric sense meaning a measuring device.) Essentially, the kinds of questions to be answered concern the merit of the instrument, where merit was to be considered in both a comparative and absolute sense. The activities associated with evaluation were seen as involving the collection of data and the combining of data into goal scales, as well as the justification of goals.

The role of evaluation, on the other hand, referred (in Scriven's terms) to the use to which the evaluation is to be put, such as curriculum evaluation or making decisions about accepting or rejecting a given instrument for a given situation. Scriven's argument was that educators have sacrificed goals to roles, because individuals who are connected with the instrument become highly anxious when faced with attempts to assess the merit of the instrument with which they are associated. Evaluators (perhaps dishonestly) therefore tended to adopt the ploy of stressing the useful role that evaluation could play. This tactic evoked far less anxiety from the personnel involved but has led to the confusion of goals with roles with the result that questions of merit and value have been avoided. Scriven called for a reversal of this trend.

A second clarifying point made by Scriven was the distinction between formative and summative evaluation. These *roles* might be thought of as operating at two different times in the development of an educational instrument. Formative evaluation is the feedback of product information into the developmental process for the purpose of improving the product. Summative evaluation involves the collection of data concerning an already-operating program for the purpose of making judgments about the program. Of course, summative data may be used subsequently for formative purposes. The distinction was that certain steps must be taken to ensure that objective judgment was possible in the summative case whereas in the formative case, payoff might well come from persons involved in product-formation. In this view, the role of evaluative activity dictates the characteristics of the evaluator.

A third distinction made by Scriven was between payoff and intrinsic evaluation. Intrinsic evaluation involves an appraisal of the instrument itself; payoff evaluation is concerned more with the effects that the instrument has (for example, the effect that the new biology program has on the scientific literacy).

However, one of Scriven's most valuable contributions was an insistence that evaluation implies value judgments. Although he gave some credence to the Tylerian model of judging performance against goals, Scriven demanded that evaluation of any kind must include procedures for the assessment of the goals themselves. It was pointed out that people who design courses or who run schools are not infallible in their goal-selection and that much of the contemporary upheaval in school curricula is the direct result of dissatisfaction with previously held goals.

Following the theme of the Scriven pronouncements, Taylor and Maguire (1966) attempted to formulate a model of curriculum evaluation. Their model was based on the rational-sequential approach to curriculum development. The model was not a strong model, subject to empirical verification, but rather was a representation of curriculum development geared to curriculum evaluation which was intended to suggest variables to

be measured, judgments to be made and contingencies to be determined. Its validity as a mode of representation lies in whether an evaluator, aware of the model, attends to variables, judgments and contingencies that he would not have attended to otherwise.

The authors noted that evaluation activities have two components: a measurement component and a value-assessment component. In regard to the latter, it was suggested that the worth of objectives be judged in terms of their priority to the entire educational program; that the value of pedagogical strategies be judged in terms of their efficiency and adequacy for bringing about the set of desired student outcomes; and that judgments of the student outcomes not be confined to isolated achievement measures but that a determination be made of their goodness-of-fit to the objectives.

The Taylor-Maguire model is one illustration of the extended role that judgment has been given in current evaluative thought. A further example would be the model proposed by Stake (1967), in which a more general picture of evaluation was outlined. In the Stake model, data descriptive of three aspects of a program were seen as being pertinent: the antecedents, the transactions and the outcomes.

The three evaluative statements that have been described as being typical of evaluative thought in this, the third era, indicate a growing trend toward making an assessment of merit part of the evaluative process. Evaluation should, under no circumstances, be used as a synonym for achievement-testing. Collect all kinds of data and make from them the judgments of merit that are appropriate: judge the value or worth of the objectives themselves; the compatability of methods; the curriculum materials; the equipment; the psychological climate; the personnel; the cost-efficiency; as well as the students.

The growing trend toward making an assessment of the worth of objectives is reflected in the most recent definition of educational objectives by Eisner (1969). Eisner distinguishes between "instructional" and "expressive" objectives to comply with his view of the dual purpose school: to provide for the acquisition of skills and to provide for contributions to culture by the expansion of skills. Instructional objectives are specific, behavioral; the objective is stated, the activity selected and the extent of achievement evaluated, the expectancy being a homogeneous outcome. Expressive objectives are descriptions of educational encounters; the objective identifies a situation or problem but does not specify what is to be learned, what behavior to be acquired. Since the expectancy is a diversity of outcomes, one cannot evaluate by applying a common standard, but must evaluate the uniqueness and significance, an esthetic criticism, more or less. Eisner's distinction of objectives serves to confuse the measurement and judgment components of evaluation promoted in this paper. Popham's (1969, p. 22) criticism of expressive objectives is that they are not objectives but are "learning activities" and, as such, they are chosen with some degree of preconception as to outcomes.

The point is, then, that evaluation is not to be equated solely with testing. As a matter of fact, modern evaluative data includes test data as only a small portion of the whole—information from affective and psychomotor domains are regarded as equally important, as is a wide variety of antecedent ("background") data. A second critical dimension to modern evaluation, and a more complex one, is the judgmental aspect. The question of arriving at objectives and what they are intended to convey has been discussed at some length. In circumstances where individual differences are being more and more highly valued and provided for, attention must be given to the valuing of goals, both immediate and long-range.

REFERENCES

Ahmann, J. S. and Glock, M. D. *Evaluating Pupil Growth*. 3rd. ed. Boston: Allyn and Bacon, Inc., 1967.

American Association for the Advancement of Science. *Commission on Science Education Newsletter*, 1965.

Bloom, B. S. *Taxonomy of Educational Objectives: Cognitive Domain*. New York: David McKay Co., Inc., 1956.

Cardinal Principles of Secondary Education. *U.S. Office of Education Bulletin*, No. 35, 1918.

Cronbach, L. J. "Evaluation for Course Improvement," *Teachers College Record* 64(1963):676-683.

Dressel, P. L. and Mayhew, L. *General Education. Explorations in Evaluation*. Washington, D.C.: American Council on Education, 1954.

Dyer, H. S. The discovery and development of educational goals. *Proceedings of the 1966 Invitational Conference on Testing Problems*, 1967.

Educational Policies Commission. *The Purposes of Education in American Democracy*. Washington,

D.C.: National Education Association and the American Association of School Administrators, 1938.

Eisner, E. W. Instructional and expressive educational objectives: their formation and use in curriculum. *AERA Monograph Series on Curriculum Evaluation* #3. Chicago: Rand McNally & Co., 1969.

French, Will, et al. *Behavioral Goals of General Education in High School*. New York: Russell Sage Foundation, 1957.

Havighurst, R. J. *Human Development and Education*. New York: Longmans, Green and Co., Ltd., 1953.

Kearney, N. C. *Elementary School Objectives*. New York: Russell Sage Foundation, 1953.

Krathwohl, D. R., Bloom, B. S. and Masia, B. B. *Taxonomy of Educational Objectives: Affective Domain*. New York: David McKay Co., Inc., 1964.

Mager, R. F. *Preparing Instructional Objectives*. Palo Alto, Calif.: Fearon Publishers, 1962.

Messick, S. The criterion problem in the evaluation of instruction: assessing possible, not just intended outcomes. *Educational Testing Service Research Bulletin*, 69-86.

Popham, W. J. (in discussion of the Eisner paper). *AERA Monograph Series on Curriculum Evaluation* #3. Chicago: Rand McNally & Co., 1969.

Romey, W. D. *Inquiry Techniques for Teaching Science*. Englewood Cliffs, N.J.: Prentice-Hall, Inc., 1968.

Scriven, M. The methodology of evaluation. *AERA Monograph Series on Curriculum Evaluation*. #1. Chicago: Rand McNally & Co., 1967, 39-83.

Smith, E. R. and Tyler, R. W. *Appraising and Recording Student Progress*. New York: Harper & Row, Publishers, 1941.

Stake, R. E. "The Countenance of Educational Evaluation," *Teachers College Record* 68 (1967): 523-540.

Sullivan, H. J. Objectives, evaluation and improved learner achievement. *AERA Monograph Series on Curriculum Evaluation* #3. Chicago: Rand McNally & Co., 1969.

Taylor, P. A. and Maguire, T. O. A theoretical evaluation model. *Manitoba Journal of Educational Research* 1(1966):12-21.

Tyler, R. E. Adapting the secondary school program to the needs of youth. *Fifty-Second Yearbook National Social Studies Education*. Part 1. Chicago: University of Chicago Press, 1953.

THE BEGINNINGS OF A NEW ERA: SOME GENERAL CONCERNS & ISSUES

Until the late 1950's, the term "evaluation" was being used almost as a synonym for "testing." Most theories of testing had been developed on the assumption that the purpose of evaluation was to measure individual differences and to provide reliable descriptive indices for groups of people. The ideal evaluation instrument was one that was homogeneous in content and with a difficulty of about 50 percent. The Bloom and the Krathwohl **Taxonomies,** in particular, had drawn attention to the possibility of using conventional items to tap a wide array of human behaviors.

With the development of the new curricula that followed the appraisals of the immediate post-Sputnik years questions of relative and absolute effectiveness of the new products arose. The then-available tests and other evaluative instruments were not designed to furnish information about the relative effectiveness of courses and were found wanting for the task. With the provision of huge sums of money for developing programs for the disadvantaged child different kinds of effectiveness-questions arose. The standardized tests that had been available were of very little use in assessing the potential of children for whom the majority of concepts in those tests were both foreign and meaningless. And there was the general accountability question always not too far off. Innovation in education, like any other innovational process, is costly. Continual assessment of the product and process of the schools is needed to provide the data upon which judgments can be made about the worth of what the schools teach and the efficiency of their methods. The traditional tests were inadequate for assessing the efficacy of modern technological advances now commonly found in schools.

Further, the occupational patterns in society are constantly changing, requiring new and different evaluative techniques. The grossly physical occupations have lost ground steadily to those requiring intellectual activity and social sensitivity. Very few people who leave school at the end of an elementary school education can expect to find jobs. The task of the high school and the college has changed from providing for an intellectual elite to providing for a wide range of potential talent and enabling each of those talents to mature to their fullest. Tests for weeding-out all but the superior few are less in demand than tests for identifying aptitudes.

The evaluator, too, had new resources open to him. The same technological advances that created difficulties in their evaluation were able to be turned to the advantage of the evaluator himself. Computers, videotapes, and sound recordings, to mention but the more obvious, greatly increased the kinds of data that could be stored and utilized in the evaluative activity.

These, then, are the kinds of influences and problems that existed in the early sixties, and indeed are still with us today.

It is probably impossible to say where the precise stimulus to a resurgence of interest in evaluation came from. Each of these sources had its own influence—social, technical and disciplinary. But in a sense even they were not new. There had always been questions of which of several curricula was in some way "best"; there were always questions of selection and placement; there were always questions as to the efficacy of educational processes. Somehow they became more urgent because more money and more people were being involved in the curriculum projects—the academic rewards were again to be found in being interested in evaluation.

If one were attempting to indicate the start of the modern era in evaluation, with its widened horizons and greater responsibilities, it would be difficult not to suggest Cronbach's 1963 paper, "Course Improvement through Evaluaton" as deserving that honor. Yet that paper was itself the outcropping of years of concern and discussions, particularly those that had been going on at the University of Illinois under the leadership of J. Thomas Hastings. The Cronbach paper was certainly instrumental in focussing these discussions in print and for that reason alone deserves first place in an anthology such as this.

Cronbach's paper is not so much a complaint against the obvious constraints of traditional evaluation as a beginning of a new methodology of evaluation. In fact, it is to the everlasting credit of the pioneers of the new era of evaluation that they did not waste time in print by complaining about the inadequacies of conventional testing techniques, but set about rebuilding the philosophy and methodology of evaluation with purpose. The basic methodological suggestion made in Cronbach's paper is the use of unmatched experimental designs for gathering information on the educational achievement of groups. The wider issues he raised, about process and product evaluation and the need to state desired outcomes, were probably better handled by later writers, but unquestionably their stimulus came from this classical paper.

The "response," or simultaneous desire to raise related evaluation issues, centered around two broad issues. The first of these issues was the question of whether or not one should state the objectives of a course of study or any other educational endeavor, behaviorally and prior to the start of such a program. This question has raged since and has probably been more divisive than any other issue in evaluation. The more traditional view of Tyler, Lindquist, Bloom and others, was that the behavioral statement of objectives was the **sine qua non** of evaluation. As the new curriculum development projects began to employ scientists from the non-behavioral disciplines who couldn't, wouldn't (or both), understand the need for the prior behavioral statement of objectives, some practical middle path had to be found and in a pragmatic way it was discovered that perhaps the premise wasn't as compelling as it had always appeared. So there appeared opposition by way of articles such as those by Atkin and Eisner reproduced here. This debate has surely not ended. We have deliberately not provided a "balanced" selection here, advocating the behavioral statement of objectives, since it is hoped that the answers might be found in responding to the points raised by these authors. A useful "rounding out" reference is Popham, et al., **Instructional Objectives** (1969).

The second of the broad issues raised by Cronbach's paper was the general methodological one. Five papers have been included here that have each, in their own way, contributed to the methodological questions. More have been raised in the next section.

Of the articles that have been included, there can be little question that the most influential has been that by Scriven (1967). Though this paper did not appear in print until 1967 it had been available in mimeographed form for several years and had already led to the enrichment of the vocabulary of evaluation with such terms as "formative" and "summative" evaluation. The clarity and direction brought to evaluation by Scriven's contribution has been incalculable. It has not only given us a clarified vocabulary, but has directed the search for useful methodology and has kept questions of value constantly before us.

The papers by Messick, Hastings, Lortie and Willems each make more specific reference to methodological questions and issues. Lortie writes as a sociologist, Willems and Messick as psychologists and Hastings as an educational psychologist. Their perceptions reflect both their backgrounds and their contacts with the field. It is interesting to study what each sees as an issue in evaluation, and as a solution to the issue.

The final article in this section is a second paper by Scriven. It provides an easily-read introduction to the important question of meta-evaluation. The paper, though brief, is self-explanatory and provocative.

	CHAPTER 2
COURSE IMPROVEMENT THROUGH EVALUATION	Lee J. Cronbach

The national interest in improving education has generated several highly important projects to improve curricula, particularly at the secondary-school level. In conferences of directors of "course content improvement" programs sponsored by the National Science Foundation, questions about evaluation are frequently raised.* Those who inquire about evaluation have various motives, ranging from sheer scientific curiosity about classroom events to a desire to assure a sponsor that money has been well spent. While the curriculum developers sincerely wish to use the skills of evaluation specialists, I am not certain that they have a clear picture of what evaluation can do and should try to do. And, on the other hand, I am becoming convinced that some techniques and habits of thought of the evaluation specialist are ill suited to current curriculum studies. To serve these studies, what philosophy and methods of evaluation are required? And particularly, how must we depart from the familiar doctrines and rituals of the testing game?

Programmatic Decisions

To draw attention to its full range of functions, we may define "evaluation" broadly as the collection and use of information to make decisions about an educational program. The program may be a set of instructional materials distributed nationally, the instructional activities of a single school, or the educational experiences of a single pupil. Many types of decisions are to be made, and many varieties of information are useful. It becomes immediately apparent that evaluation is a diversified activity and that no one set of principles will suffice for all situations. But measurement specialists have so concentrated upon one process—the preparation of pencil-and-paper achievement tests for assigning scores to individual pupils—that the principles pertinent to that process have

somehow become enshrined as *the* principles of evaluation. "Tests," we are told, "should fit the content of the curriculum." Also, "Only those evaluation procedures should be used that yield reliable scores." These and other hallowed principles are not entirely appropriate to evaluation for course improvement. Before proceeding to support this contention, I wish to distinguish among purposes of evaluation and to relate them to historical developments in testing and curriculum making.

We may separate three types of decisions for which evaluation is used:

1. Course improvement: deciding what instructional materials and methods are satisfactory and where change is needed.
2. Decisions about individuals: identifying the needs of the pupil for the sake of planning his instruction, judging pupil merit for purposes of selection and grouping, acquainting the pupil with his own progress and deficiencies.
3. Administrative regulation: judging how good the school system is, how good individual teachers are, etc.

Course improvement is set apart by its broad temporal and geographical reference; it involves the modification of recurrently used materials and methods. Developing a standard exercise to overcome a misunderstanding would be course improvement, but deciding whether a certain pupil should work through that exercise would be an individual decision. Administrative regulation likewise is local in effect, whereas an improvement in

*My comments on these questions, and on certain more significant questions that *should* have been raised, have been greatly clarified by the reactions of several of these directors and of my colleagues in evaluation to a draft of this paper. J. Thomas Hastings and Robert Heath have been especially helpful. What I voice, however, are my personal views, deliberately more provocative than "authoritative."

a course is likely to be pertinent wherever the course is offered.

It was for the sake of course improvement that systematic evaluation was first introduced. When that famous muckraker Joseph Rice gave the same spelling test in a number of American schools, and so gave the first impetus to the educational testing movement, he was interested in evaluating a curriculum. Crusading against the extended spelling drills that then loomed large in the school schedule—"the spelling grind"—Rice collected evidence of their worthlessness so as to provoke curriculum revision. As the testing movement developed, however, it took on a different function.

The Turning Tides

The greatest expansion of systematic achievement testing occurred in the 1920's. At that time, the content of any course was taken pretty much as established and beyond criticism save for small shifts of topical emphasis. At the administrator's direction, standard tests covering the curriculum were given to assess the efficiency of the teacher or the school system. Such administrative testing fell into disfavor when used injudiciously and heavyhandedly in the 1920's and 1930's. Administrators and accrediting agencies fell back upon descriptive features of the school program in judging adequacy. Instead of collecting direct evidence of educational impact, they judged schools in terms of size of budget, student-staff ratio, square feet of laboratory space, and the number of advanced credits accumulated by the teacher. This tide, it appears, is about to turn. On many university campuses, administrators wanting to know more about their product are installing "operations research offices." Testing directed toward quality control seems likely to increase in the lower schools as well, as is most forcefully indicated by the statewide testing recently ordered by the California legislature.

After 1930 or thereabouts, tests were given almost exclusively for judgments about individuals —to select students for advanced training, to assign marks within a class, and to diagnose individual competences and deficiencies. For any such decisions, one wants precise and valid comparisons of one individual with other individuals or with a standard. Much of test theory and test technology has been concerned with making measurements precise. Important though precision is for most decisions about individuals, I shall argue that in evaluating courses we need not struggle to obtain precise scores for individuals.

While measurers have been well content with the devices used to make scores precise, they have been less complacent about validity. Prior to 1935, the pupil was examined mostly on fac-

tual knowledge and mastery of fundamental skills. Tyler's research and writings of that period developed awareness that higher mental processes are not evoked by simple factual tests, and that instruction that promotes factual knowledge may not promote—indeed, may interfere with—other more important educational outcomes. Tyler, Lindquist, and their students demonstrated that tests can be designed to measure such general educational outcomes as ability to comprehend scientific method. Whereas a student can prepare for a factual test only through a course of study that includes the facts tested, many different courses of study may promote the same general understandings and attitudes. In evaluating today's new curricula, it will clearly be important to appraise the student's general educational growth, which curriculum developers say is more important than mastery of the specific lessons presented. Note, for example, that the Biological Sciences Curriculum Study offers three courses with substantially different "subject matter" as alternative routes to much the same educational ends.

Although some instruments capable of measuring general outcomes were prepared during the 1930's, they were never very widely employed. The prevailing philosophy of the curriculum, particularly among "progressives," called for developing a program to fit local requirements, capitalizing on the capacities and experiences of local pupils. The faith of the 1920's in a "standard" curriculum was replaced by a faith that the best learning experience would result from teacher-pupil planning in each classroom. Since each teacher or each class could choose different content and even different objectives, this philosophy left little place for standard testing.

Tests as Training

Many evaluation specialists came to see test development as a strategy for training the teacher in service, so that the process of test-making came to be valued more than the test—or the test data— that resulted. The following remarks by Bloom[2] are representative of a whole school of thought.*

The criterion for determining the quality of a school and its educational functions would be the extent to which it achieves the objectives it has set for itself. . . . Our experiences suggest that unless the school has translated the objectives into specific and operational definitions, little is likely to be done about the objectives. They remain pious hopes and platitudes. . . . Participation of the teaching staff in selecting as well as constructing evaluation instruments has resulted in improved instruments on one hand

*Elsewhere, Bloom's paper discusses evaluation for the new curricula. Attention may also be drawn to Tyler's highly pertinent paper.[6]

and, on the other hand, it has resulted in clarifying the objectives of instruction and in making them real and meaningful to teachers. . . . When teachers have actively participated in defining objectives and in selecting or constructing evaluation instruments, they return to the learning problems with great vigor and remarkable creativity. . . . Teachers who have become committed to a set of educational objectives which they thoroughly understand respond by developing a variety of learning experiences which are as diverse and as complex as the situation requires.

Thus, "evaluation" becomes a local and beneficial teacher-training activity. The benefit is attributed to thinking about what data to collect. Little is said about the actual use of test results; one has the impression that when test-making ends, the test itself is forgotten. Certainly, there is little enthusiasm for refining tests so that they can be used in other schools, for to do so would be to rob those teachers of the benefits of working out their own objectives and instruments.

Bloom and Tyler describe both curriculum making and evaluation as integral parts of classroom instruction, which is necessarily decentralized. This outlook is far from that of "course improvement." The current national curriculum studies assume that curriculum-making can be centralized. They prepare materials to be used in much the same way by teachers everywhere. It is assumed that having experts draft materials, and revising these after tryout, produces better instructional activities than the local teacher would be likely to devise. In this context, it seems wholly appropriate to have most tests prepared by a central staff and to have results returned to that staff to guide further course improvement.

When evaluation is carried out in the service of course improvement, the chief aim is to ascertain what effects the course has—that is, what changes it produces in pupils. This is not to inquire merely whether the course is effective or ineffective. Outcomes of instruction are multidimensional, and a satisfactory investigation will map out the effects of the course along these dimensions separately. To agglomerate many types of post-course performance into a single score is a mistake, because failure to achieve one objective is masked by success in another direction. Moreover, since a composite score embodies (and usually conceals) judgments about the importance of the various outcomes, only a report that treats the outcomes separately can be useful to educators who have different value hierarchies.

The greatest service evaluation can perform is to identify aspects of the course where revision is desirable. Those responsible for developing a course would like to present evidence that their course is effective. They are intrigued by the idea of having an "independent testing agency" render a judgment on their product. But to call in the evaluator only upon the completion of course development, to confirm what has been done, is to offer him a menial role and to make meager use of his services. To be influential in course improvement, evidence must become available midway in curriculum development, not in the home stretch, when the developer is naturally reluctant to tear open a supposedly finished body of materials and techniques. Evaluation, used to improve the course while it is still fluid, contributes more to improvement of education than evaluation used to appraise a product already placed on the market.

Effects and Effectiveness

Insofar as possible, evaluation should be used to understand how the course produces its effects and what parameters influence its effectiveness. It is important to learn, for example, that the outcome of programmed instruction depends very much upon the attitude of the teacher; indeed, this may be more important than to learn that on the average such instruction produces slightly better or worse results than conventional instruction.

Hopefully, evaluation studies will go beyond reporting on this or that course and help us to understand educational learning. Such insight will, in the end, contribute to the development of all courses rather than just the course under test. In certain of the new curricula, there are data to suggest that aptitude measures correlate much less with end-of-course achievement than they do with achievement on early units.[4] This finding is not well confirmed, but it is highly significant if true. If it is true for the new curricula and only for them, it has one implication; if the same effect appears in traditional courses, it means something else. Either way, it provides food for thought for teachers, counselors, and theorists. Evaluation studies should generate knowledge about the nature of the abilities that constitute educational goals. Twenty years after the Eight-Year Study of the Progressive Education Association, its testing techniques are in good repute, but we still know very little about what these instruments measure. Consider "Application of Principles in Science." Is this in any sense a unitary ability? Or has the able student only mastered certain principles one by one? Is the ability demonstrated on a test of this sort more prognostic of any later achievement than is factual knowledge? Such questions ought to receive substantial attention, although to the makers of any one course they are of only peripheral interest.

The aim to compare one course with another should not dominate plans for evaluation. To be sure, decision makers have to choose between courses, and any evaluation report will be interpreted in part comparatively. But formally designed experiments, pitting one course against another, are rarely definitive enough to justify their cost. Differences between average test scores resulting from different courses are usually small relative to the wide differences among and within classes taking the same course. At best, an experiment never does more than compare the present version of one course with the present version of another. A major effort to bring the losing contender nearer to perfection would be very likely to reverse the verdict of the experiment.

Any failure to equate the classes taking the competing courses will jeopardize the interpretation of an experiment—and such failures are almost inevitable. In testing a drug, we know that valid results cannot be obtained without a double-blind control in which the doses for half the subjects are inert placebos; the placebo and the drug look alike, so that neither doctor nor patient knows who is receiving medication. Without this control, the results are useless even when the state of the patient is checked by completely objective indices. In an educational experiment, it is difficult to keep pupils unaware that they are an experimental group. And it is quite impossible to neutralize the biases of the teacher as those of the doctor are neutralized in the double-blind design. It is thus never certain whether any observed advantage is attributable to the educational innovation as such, or to the greater energy that teachers and students put forth when a method is fresh and "experimental." Some have contended that any course, even the most excellent, loses much of its potency as soon as success enthrones it as "the traditional method."

Weakness of Comparisons

Since group comparisons give equivocal results, I believe that a formal study should be designed primarily to determine the post-course performance of a well described group with respect to many important objectives and side effects. Ours is a problem like that of the engineer examining a new automobile. He can set himself the task of defining its performance characteristics and its dependability. It would be merely distracting to put his question in the form, "Is this car better or worse than the competing brand?" Moreover, in an experiment where the treatments compared differ in a dozen respects, no understanding is gained from the fact that the experiment shows a numerical advantage in favor of the new course. No one knows which of the ingredients is responsible for the advantage. More analytic ex-

periments are much more useful than field trials applying markedly dissimilar treatments to different groups. Small-scale, well controlled studies can profitably be used to compare alternative versions of the same course; in such a study, the differences between treatments are few enough and well enough defined that the results have explanatory value.

The three purposes—course improvement, decisions about individuals, and administrative regulation—call for measurement procedures having somewhat different qualities. When a test will be used to make an administrative judgment on the individual teacher, it is necessary to measure thoroughly and with conspicuous fairness; such testing, if it is to cover more than one outcome, becomes extremely time consuming. In judging a course, however, one can make satisfactory interpretations from data collected on a sampling basis, with no pretense of measuring thoroughly the accomplishments of any one class. A similar point is to be made about testing for decisions about individuals. A test of individuals must be conspicuously fair and extensive enough to provide a dependable score for each person. But if the performance will not influence the fate of the individual, we can ask him to perform tasks for which the course has not directly prepared him, and we can use techniques that would be prohibitively expensive if applied in a manner thorough enough to measure each person reliably.

Evaluation is too often visualized as the administration of a formal test, an hour or so in duration, at the close of a course. But there are many other methods for examining pupil performance, and pupil attainment is not the only basis for appraising a course.

It is quite appropriate to ask scholars whether the statements made in the course are consistent with the best contemporary knowledge. This is a sound and even a necessary procedure. One may go on to evaluate the pedagogy of the new course by soliciting opinions, but here there is considerable hazard. If the opinions are based on some preconception about teaching method, the findings will be controversial and very probably misleading. There are no theories of pedagogy so well established that one can say, without tryout, what will prove educative.

Systematic Observation

One can accept the need for a pragmatic test of the curriculum and still employ opinions as a source of evidence. During the tryout stages of curriculum-making, one relies heavily on the teachers' reports of pupil accomplishment—"Here they had trouble"; "This they found dull"; "Here they needed only half as many exercises as were provided," etc. This is behavior observation even though unsystematic, and it is of great value. The reason for shifting to systematic observation is that this is more impartial, more public, and sometimes more penetrating. While I bow to the historian or mathematician as a judge of the technical soundness of course content, I do not agree that the experienced history or mathematics teacher who tries out a course gives the best possible judgment on its effectiveness. Scholars have too often deluded themselves about their effectiveness as teachers—particularly, have they too often accepted parroting of words as evidence of insight—for their unaided judgment to be trusted. Systematic observation is costly, and introduces some delay between the moment of teaching and the feedback of results. Hence, systematic observation will never be the curriculum developer's sole source of evidence. Systematic data collection becomes profitable in the intermediate stages of curriculum development, after the more obvious bugs in early drafts have been dealt with.

The approaches to evaluation include process studies, proficiency measures, attitude measures, and follow-up studies. A process study is concerned with events taking place in the classroom, proficiency and attitude measures with changes observed in pupils, and follow-up studies with the later careers of those who participated in the course.

The follow-up study comes closest to observing ultimate educational contributions, but the completion of such a study is so far removed in time from the initial instruction that it is of minor value in improving the course or explaining its effects. The follow-up study differs strikingly from the other types of evaluation study in one respect. I have already expressed the view that evaluation should be primarily concerned with the effects of the course under study rather than with comparisons of courses. That is to say, I would emphasize departures of attained results from the ideal, differences in apparent effectiveness of different parts of the course, and differences from item to item; all these suggest places where the course could be strengthened. But this view cannot be applied to the follow-up study, which appraises effects of the course as a whole and which has very little meaning unless outcomes can be compared with some sort of base rate. Suppose we find that 65 per cent of the boys graduating from an experimental curriculum enroll as scientific and technical majors in college. We cannot judge whether this is a high or low figure save by comparing it with the rate among boys who have not had the course. In a follow-up study, it is necessary to obtain data on a control group equated at least crudely to the experimental cases on the obvious demographic variables.

Despite the fact that such groups are hard to equate and that follow-up data do not tell much about how to improve the course, such studies should have a place in research on the new curricula, whose national samples provide unusual opportunity for follow-up that can shed light on important questions. One obvious type of follow-up study traces the student's success in a college course founded upon the high-school course. One may examine the student's grades or ask him what topics in the college course he found himself poorly prepared for. It is hoped that some of the new science and mathematics courses will arouse greater interest than usual among girls; whether this hope is well founded can be checked by finding out what majors and what electives these ex-students pursue in college. Career choices likewise merit attention. Some proponents of the new curricula would like to see a greater flow of talent into basic science as distinct from technology, whereas others would regard this as potentially disastrous; but no one would regard facts about this flow as lacking significance.

Measuring Meanings

Attitudes are prominent among the outcomes with which course developers are concerned. Attitudes are meanings or beliefs, not mere expressions of approval or disapproval. One's attitude toward science includes ideas about the matters on which a scientist can be an authority, about the benefits to be obtained from moon shots and studies of monkey mothers, and about depletion of natural resources. Equally important is the match between self-concept and concept of the field: What roles does science offer a person like me? Would I want to marry a scientist? And so on. Each learning activity also contributes to attitudes that reach far beyond any one subject, such as the pupil's sense of his own competence and desire to learn.

Attitudes can be measured in many ways; the choices revealed in follow-up studies, for example, are pertinent evidence. But measurement usually takes the form of direct or indirect questioning. Interviews, questionnaires, and the like are quite valuable when not trusted blindly. Certainly, we should take seriously any *un*desirable opinion expressed by a substantial proportion of the graduates of a course (e.g., the belief that the scientist speaks with peculiar authority on political and ethical questions, or the belief that mathematics is a finished subject rather than a field for current investigation).

Attitude questionnaires have been much criticized because they are subject to distortion, especially where the student hopes to gain by being less than frank. Particularly if the questions are asked in a context far removed from the experimental course, the returns are likely to be trustworthy. Thus, a general questionnaire administered through homerooms (or required English courses) may include questions about liking for various subjects and activities; these same questions administered by the mathematics teacher would give much less trustworthy data on attitude toward mathematics. While students may give reports more favorable than their true beliefs, this distortion is not likely to be greater among students who take an experimental course than among those who do not. In group averages, many distortions balance out. But questionnaires insufficiently valid for individual testing can be used in evaluating curricula, both because the student has little motive to distort and because the evaluator is comparing averages rather than individuals.

Process and Proficiency

For measuring proficiency, techniques are likewise varied. Standardized tests are useful. But for course evaluation it makes sense to assign different questions to different students. Giving each student in a population of 500 the same test of 50 questions will provide far less information to the course developer than drawing for each student 50 questions from a pool of, say, 700. The latter plan determines the mean success of about 75 representative students on every one of the 700 items; the former reports on only 50 items.[5] Essay tests and open-ended questions, generally too expensive to use for routine evaluation, can profitably be employed to appraise certain abilities. One can go further and observe individuals or groups as they attack a research problem in the laboratory or work through some other complex problem. Since it is necessary to test only a representative sample of pupils, costs are not as serious a consideration as in routine testing. Additional aspects of proficiency testing will be considered below.

Process measures have especial value in showing how a course can be improved because they examine what happens during instruction. In the development of programmed instructional materials, for example, records are collected showing how many pupils miss each item presented; any piling up of errors implies a need for better explanation or a more gradual approach to a difficult topic. Immediately after showing a teaching film, one can interview students, perhaps asking them to describe a still photograph taken from the film. Misleading presentations, ideas given insufficient emphasis, and matters left unclear will be identified by such methods. Similar interviews can disclose what pupils take away from a laboratory activity or a discussion. A process study

may turn attention to what the teacher does in the classroom. In those curricula that allow choice of topics, for example, it is worthwhile to find out which topics are chosen and how much time is allotted to each. A log of class activities (preferably recorded by a pupil rather than the teacher) will show which of the techniques suggested in a summer institute are actually adopted and which form "part of the new course" only in the developer's fantasies.

I have indicated that I consider item data to be more important than test scores. The total score may give confidence in a curriculum or give rise to discouragement, but it tells very little about how to produce further improvement. And, as Ferris[4] has noted, such scores are quite likely to be mis- or overinterpreted. The score on a single item, or on a problem that demands several responses in succession, is more likely than the test score to suggest how to alter the presentation. When we accept item scores as useful, we need no longer think of evaluation as a one-shot, end-of-year operation. Proficiency can be measured at any moment, with particular interest attaching to those items most related to the recent lessons. Other items calling for general abilities can profitably be administered repeatedly during the course (perhaps to different random samples of pupils) so that we can begin to learn when and from what experiences change in these abilities comes.

In course evaluation, we need not be much concerned about making measuring instruments fit the curriculum. However startling this declaration may seem, and however contrary to the principles of evaluation for other purposes, this must be our position if we want to know what changes a course produces in the pupil. An ideal evaluation would include measures of all the types of proficiency that might reasonably be desired in the area in question, not just the selected outcomes to which this curriculum directs substantial attention. If you wish only to know how well a curriculum is achieving its objectives, you fit the test to the curriculum; but if you wish to know how well the curriculum is serving the national interest, you measure all outcomes that might be worth striving for. One of the new mathematics courses may disavow any attempt to teach numerical trigonometry, and indeed, might discard nearly all computational work. It is still perfectly reasonable to ask how well graduates of the course can compute and can solve right triangles. Even if the course developers went so far as to contend that computational skill is no proper objective of secondary instruction, they will encounter educators and laymen who do not share their view. If it can be shown that students who come through the new course are fairly proficient in computation despite the lack of direct teaching, the doubters will be reassured. If not, the evidence makes clear how much is being sacrificed. Similarly, when the biologists offer alternative courses emphasizing microbiology and ecology, it is fair to ask how well the graduate of one course can understand issues treated in the other. Ideal evaluation in mathematics will collect evidence on all the abilities toward which a mathematics course might reasonably aim; likewise in biology, English, or any other subject.

Ferris states that the ACS Chemistry Test, however well constructed, is inadequate for evaluating the new CBA and CHEM programs because it does not cover their objectives. One can agree with this without regarding the ACS test as inappropriate to use with these courses. It is important that this test not stand alone, as the sole evaluation device. It will tell us something worth knowing, namely, just how much "conventional" knowledge the new curriculum does or does not provide. The curriculum developers deliberately planned to sacrifice some of the conventional attainments and have nothing to fear from this measurement, completely interpreted (particularly if data are examined item by item).

Security, Content, Terms

The demand that tests be closely matched to the aims of a course reflects awareness that examinations of the usual sort "determine what is taught." If questions are known in advance, students give more attention to learning their answers than to learning other aspects of the course. This is not necessarily detrimental. Wherever it is critically important to master certain content, the knowledge that it will be tested produces a desirable concentration of effort. On the other hand, learning the answer to a set question is by no means the same as acquiring understanding of whatever topic that question represents. There is, therefore, a possible advantage in using "secure" tests for course evaluation. Security is achieved only at a price: One must prepare new tests each year and consequently cannot make before-and-after comparisons with the same items. One would hope that the use of different items with different students, and the fact that there is less incentive to coach when no judgment is to be passed on the pupils and the teachers, would make security a less critical problem.

The distinction between factual tests and tests of higher mental processes, as elaborated for example in the *Taxonomy of Educational Objectives*,[1] is of some value in planning tests, although classifying items as measures of knowledge, application, original problem solving, etc., is difficult and often impossible. Whether a given response represents

rote recall or reasoning depends upon how the pupil has been taught, not solely upon the question asked. One may, for example, describe a biological environment and ask for predictions regarding the effect of a certain intervention. Students who have never dealt with ecological biology will be more likely to succeed, reasoning from specific principles; and those who have lived in such an ecology or read about it may answer successfully on the basis of memory. We rarely, therefore, will want to test whether a student "knows" or "does not know" certain material. Knowledge is a matter of degree. Two persons may be acquainted with the same facts or principles, but one will be more expert in his understanding, better able to cope with inconsistent data, irrelevant sources of confusion, and apparent exceptions to the principle. To measure intellectual competence is to measure depth, connectedness, and applicability to knowledge.

Too often, test questions are course-specific, stated in such a way that only the person who has been specifically taught to understand what is being asked for can answer the question. Such questions can usually be identified by their use of conventions. Some conventions are commonplace, and we can assume that all the pupils we test will know them. But a biology test that describes a metabolic process with the aid of the $\geqq$ symbol presents difficulties for students who can think through the scientific question about equilibrium but are unfamiliar with the symbol. A trigonometry problem that requires use of a trigonometric table is unreasonable, unless we want to test familiarity with the conventional names of functions. The same problem in numerical trigonometry can be cast in a form clear to the average pupil entering high school; if necessary, the tables of functions can be presented along with a comprehensible explanation. So stated, the problem becomes course-independent. It is fair to ask whether graduates of the experimental course can solve such problems, not previously encountered, whereas it is pointless to ask whether they can answer questions whose language is strange to them. To be sure, knowledge of certain terminology is a significant objective of instruction, but for course evaluation, testing of terminology should very likely be separated from testing of other understandings. To appraise understanding of processes and relations, the fair question is one comprehensible to a pupil who has not taken the course. This is not to say that he should know the answer or the procedure to follow in attaining the answer, but he should understand what he is being asked. Such course-independent questions can be used as standard instruments to investigate any instructional program.

Pupils who have not studied a topic will usually be less facile than those who have studied it. Graduates of my hypothetical mathematics course will take longer to solve trigonometry problems than will those who have studied trig. But speed and power should not be confused; in intellectual studies, power is almost always of greater importance. If the course equips the pupil to deal correctly, even though haltingly, with a topic not studied, we can expect him to develop facility later when that topic comes before him frequently.

Two Types of Transfer

The chief objective in many of the new curricula seems to be to develop aptitude for mastering new materials in the field. A biology course cannot cover all valuable biological content, but it may reasonably aspire to equip the pupil to understand descriptions of unfamiliar organisms, to comprehend a new theory and the reasoning behind it, and to plan an experiment to test a new hypothesis. This is transfer of learning. It has been insufficiently recognized that there are two types of transfer. The two types shade into one another, being arranged on a continuum of immediacy of effect; we can label the more immediate pole applicational transfer, and speak of slower-acting effects as gains in aptitude.[3]

Nearly all educational research on transfer has tested immediate performance on a partly new task. We teach pupils to solve equations in x, and include in the test equations stated in a or z. We teach the principles of ecological balance by referring to forests, and as a transfer test, ask what effect pollution will have on the population of a lake. We describe an experiment not presented in the text, and ask the student to discuss possible interpretations and needed controls. Any of these tests can be administered in a short time. But the more significant type of transfer may be the increased ability to learn in a particular field. There is very likely a considerable difference between the ability to draw conclusions from a neatly finished experiment, and the ability to tease insight out of the disorderly and inconsistent observations that come with continuous laboratory work on a problem. The student who masters a good biology course may become better able to comprehend certain types of theory and data, so that he gains more from a subsequent year of study in ethnology; we do not measure this gain by testing his understanding of short passages in ethnology. There has rarely been an appraisal of ability to work through a problem situation or a complex body of knowledge over a period of days or months. Despite the practical difficulties that attend an attempt to measure the effect of a course on a person's subsequent learning, such

"learning to learn" is so important that a serious effort should be made to understand how they may be fostered.

The techniques of programmed instruction may be adapted to appraise learning ability. One may, for example, test the student's rate of mastery of a self-contained, programmed unit on the physics of heat or some other topic not studied. If the program is truly self-contained, every student can master it, but the one with greater scientific comprehension will hopefully make fewer errors and progress faster. The program can be prepared in several logically complete versions, ranging from one with very small "steps" to one with minimal internal redundancy, on the hypothesis that the better educated student could cope with the less redundant program. Moreover, he might prefer its greater elegance.

Toward Deeper Understanding

Old habits of thought and long established techniques are poor guides to the evaluation required for course improvement. Traditionally, educational measurement has been chiefly concerned with comparing score averages of competing courses. But course evaluation calls for description of outcomes. This description should be made on the broadest possible scale, even at the sacrifice of superficial fairness and precision.

Course evaluation should ascertain what changes a course produces and should identify aspects of the course that need revision. The outcomes observed should include general outcomes ranging far beyond the content of the curriculum itself— attitudes, career choices, general understandings and intellectual powers, and aptitude for further learning in the field. Analysis of performance on single items or types of problems is more informative than analysis of composite scores. It is not necessary or desirable to give the same test to all pupils; rather, as many questions as possible should be given, each to a different, moderate sized sample of pupils. Costly techniques, such as interviews and essay tests, can profitably be applied to samples of pupils, whereas testing everyone would be out of the question.

Asking the right questions about educational outcomes can do much to improve educational effectiveness. Even if the right data are collected, however, evaluation will have contributed too little if it only places a seal of approval on certain courses and casts others into disfavor. Evaluation is a fundamental part of curriculum development, not an appendage. Its job is to collect facts the course developer can and will use to do a better job, and facts from which a deeper understanding of the educational process will emerge.

References

1. Bloom, B. S. (ed.) *Taxonomy of Educational Objectives*. New York: Longmans, Green and Co., Ltd., 1965.
2. Bloom, B. S. Quality control in education. *Tomorrow's Teaching*. Oklahoma City: Frontiers of Science Foundation, 1961. pp. 54-61.
3. Ferguson, G. A. On learning and human ability. *Canadian J. Psychol.* 8(1954):95-112.
4. Ferris, F. L., Jr. "Testing in the New Curriculums: Numerology, Tyranny, or Common Sense?" *School Rev.* 70(1962):112-131.
5. Lord, F. M. Estimating norms by item-sampling. *Educ. psychol. Measmt.* 22(1962):259-268.
6. Tyler, R. W. The functions of measurement in improving instruction. In *Educational Measurement*, edited by E. F. Lindquist, pp. 47-67. Washington, D.C.: American Council of Education, 1951.

CHAPTER 3

J. Myron Atkin

SOME EVALUATION PROBLEMS IN A COURSE CONTENT IMPROVEMENT PROJECT

Those who suggest that curriculum be modified have the responsibility for demonstrating the desirability as well as the feasibility of the modifications they suggest. This truism, to the extent that it is accepted, protects the schools from poorly conceived innovations, from dealing with each and every fashionable novelty. Thus those who aspire to influence curriculum decisions broadly are expected to report suitably objective evidence about the effectiveness of their work. But it is possible that this expectation, while essential, sometimes may be limiting.

It is not the purpose here to deprecate the standards that have come to be accepted for educational evaluation. Few would deny their usefulness for many educational purposes. Rather it is the contention here that inadequate attention has been given to certain evaluation problems in the broad area of curriculum development, particularly in a period of radical modification of course content such as we see today in mathematics and science, and that a few of the problems are only dimly recognized.

Specialists in evaluation may detect traces of pre-knowledge bias in what follows. The paper makes no pretext of being authoritative. However, certain evaluational rubrics seem deeply ingrained in educational practice, and if a small body of researchers is challenging some of the older guidelines, their influence is not yet broad enough to have had an appreciable impact on curriculum evaluation.

It is hoped that some of the evaluation problems can be delineated in this paper, and they will be outlined in the context of a single course improvement activity, the University of Illinois Elementary-School Science Project. This Project which received its initial support from the National Science Foundation in September, 1960, has had as its major purpose from the inception the production of astronomy materials for children—materials that are sound astronomically, that reflect the structure of the subject as it is viewed by astronomers of stature, and that can be handled by teachers and children in actual classrooms. Thus, the Project reflects a trend characteristic of several of the current mathematics and science curriculum activities: a delineation of content is required that reveals a potent hierarchy of conceptual schemes, a few ideas with considerable intellectual mileage that help the learner understand in the most economical manner possible a given discipline as it is perceived by its senior practitioners.

Hence "new" content must be identified. It must be presented effectively to the children and teachers. It must be revised based on field trial. The revisions must conform to the content standards established by the scientists while they are adapted to the abilities of children and teachers. For such evaluation in the early stages of a curriculum project, there is usually heavy reliance on opinion. Teacher comments are solicited. Extensive observations are made of student and teacher behavior. Scientists instrumental in the development of the new curriculum materials typically work with children themselves. This semi-systematic type of evaluation is thought to be appropriate in the early stages of a course improvement activity. Feasibility, after all, is a necessary condition for curriculum innovation. A multitude of evaluation problems are still present in these early stages, problems that can and should occupy scores of well-trained people. Sampling questions

*Dr. Atkin, who is Co-Director of the Illinois Elementary-School Science Project, has long been interested in the evaluation of learning materials and, in particular, the evaluation of the new curricula in science. In this article he brings into sharp focus one of the important issues of the day: the related questions of when, how, and by whom learning goals should be stated in curriculum building and the suitability of traditional procedures for evaluating them.

and feedback procedures are just two examples of areas that need further work.

But it is in the intermediate stages of curriculum development that evaluation problems are most obvious. It is a fact, and to this writer a fortunate one, that prime movers in the large high school curriculum projects have moved ahead with a certain brashness in suggesting curriculum modifications. They have insisted on working on new curriculum and its implementation in its entirety and immediately, often recognizing but choosing to postpone some tough evaluational questions rather than to accept a reductionist approach and work primarily on the more readily solvable subsidiary problems. The scientists and mathematicians in these projects seem to have had few doubts about their ability to recognize valid curriculum materials and effective teaching. However, few curriculum developers schooled primarily in elementary and secondary education feel confident enough about their own taste to place strong reliance on rather "unsystematic" attempts at evaluation once feasible materials have been produced. There exists a pronounced expectation for the accumulation of objective evidence to ascertain the success of the materials in achieving specified aims.

The comprehension of content per se by the children represents one type of evaluation problem. Generally, curriculum developers are aware of a range of possible outcomes other than recall of specific information, e.g., application, comprehension of major principles. Test makers, among others, have made ingenious attempts to construct methods of measuring a multitude of content outcomes.

A major evaluation difficulty relates to the assessment of certain outcomes that may not be specific to a particular course but the outgrowth, hopefully, of many courses. Most of those engaged in science curriculum development consider the materials they produce to influence children's attitudes about science and scientists—in addition to extending understanding of certain concepts that reflect the structure of the discipline. Further, it is the hope of some that new curriculum materials will lead to a comprehension of certain broad scientific ideas—randomness, symmetry, arbitrariness, proportionality, successive approximation, reference frame, discreteness—that are tangential to the sequence of conceptual schemes within a given discipline. Few evaluation specialists seem to have directed attention to such broad questions; yet the total effect of a sequence of courses over a number of years seems to be a rather crucial educational outcome.

Still another difficulty lies in the fact that those engaged in curriculum development are exhorted to assess learning in terms of readily observable and measurable behaviorable change in the students. Since psychologists in recent decades have found it most useful to employ some sort of behavioral change model when studying human learning, and since few would want to question the effectiveness of such models as antidotes to solely verbal learning, and since the models have been markedly effective for mechanical and technical applications like learning how to operate a radar set, the models of learning as behavioral change have achieved a firm place in virtually all curriculum research. (A few extremists deny that verbal learning is behavioral.) However, under this rubric rather short-term behavioral change usually is identified and measured, few investigators having the patience or the inclination to plan long-term studies. In most of the curriculum projects, there is a suspicion that rather higher order intellectual abilities than those readily observable and measurable in terms of immediate behavioral change are achieved, or at least sought. There is the fear that a preoccupation with short-term goals may obscure the long-term ones.

More profoundly, it is suspected that the ability of certain senior scientists radically to restructure their disciplines in a manner that is aesthetically as well as intellectually pleasing and potent has outdistanced the ability of many educational evaluators to understand completely the import of this restructuring for purposes of curriculum. "Define your objectives," says an evaluator, "and I will help you to determine your degree of success." But there is a real danger that the objectives are not understood even when enunciated, or at least their implications not appreciated. Clever men for centuries have been helping to build our conception of science. There is some danger of achieving less than the possible in curriculum revision if insights into science must be subordinated to the state of development of the field of educational evaluation.

The curriculum developer is urged, at the start, to formulate clear statements of anticipated behaviors. The possibility that such behaviors may be identified later in a new curriculum activity seems like too slipshod a procedure to certain evaluators. Of possibly greater significance is the fact that too early a statement of objectives may obscure potentially significant outcomes that do not become apparent until later because they are seldom anticipated. This statement, of course, applies to negative outcomes as well as positive ones. Scientists, as a rule, are not particularly articulate about listing the objectives of a course of study with which they are pleased. They sense the appropriateness of the course; when they enumerate their reasons, they can be expected to overlook a few of the most significant ones.

Evaluation activity in the University of Illinois Elementary-School Science Project has centered around more readily ascertainable information such as the following:

(1) To what extent do children comprehend the content of the astronomy materials? We make assessments of the knowledge of astronomical ideas before and after each of the books is used. We try to avoid solely recall items. Every attempt is made to gauge the ability of the children to apply the major ideas in fresh contexts and comprehend major relationships. Here we have had assistance from able test makers, and although our problems in this realm are far from solved, we believe that patterns are apparent that will make our tests increasingly valid and reliable.

(2) To what extent does our delineation of content reflect a major and potent sequence of astronomical ideas? Here we rely on the community of astronomers plus certain physical scientists who work in related areas. These scientists are asked to review our materials as well as to help write them. In general, our "story line" is perceived as a potentially powerful one. Suggested modifications are sometimes crucial but seldom extensive.

(3) What modifications in approach are suggested by teachers? Our materials are being tried by about 350 teachers. Each teacher is asked to submit a reaction sheet on every chapter in each book. The teacher is asked to report the amount of preparation and teaching time required, his estimate of appropriateness of the content for his class, his estimate of children's interest, and his suggestions for improvement of the materials. In addition, an increasing number of teachers join our writing conference during the summer. As a further check on the validity of written teacher reactions, extensive observations of the use of Project materials are made by the central Project staff. Numerous conferences are held with participating teachers.

We also ask each participating teacher to submit a personal information sheet reporting formal science and mathematics background, age, and number of years of teaching experience.

From these data, we are able to determine a few relationships:

What is the relationship between the formal science and mathematics background of the teacher and the success of his children with our books, success as measured by our tests?

What is the relationship between success with our materials and participation by children in "new" math programs?

What is the relationship between the teacher's estimate of children's interest and teacher estimate of appropriateness of content?

These examples indicate just a few of the potentially revealing interconnections that are being sought from the data collected. They are informative of course. They are frequently useful. Probably they are necessary.

But it is the hope of Project personnel that our goals, if not our accomplishments, transcend these more measurable outcomes, that there is a long-term intellectual and aesthetic element for which we strive that is difficult even to identify, much less measure. Such pretensions are not particularly appealing in the precise literature of educational research. Yet, as indicated, we feel that some of our more significant accomplishments potentially are in the realm of a realization of the full import of new content identification, however difficult the definitive assessment of such aims.

One approach now being developed in the Project to overcome some of the limitations of evaluational procedures used to date is to make use of a type of classroom and student observation that, in one sense, is only loosely structured. On the assumption that the books developed for children are valid astronomically—i.e., they contain an astronomical "story line" embodying a potent and carefully sequenced series of ideas, and they are teachable—but that it is difficult to anticipate all the outcomes that may result from the course, Project personnel are beginning a series of classroom observations in an attempt to identify unexpected behavioral changes in students. In the customary method of course development and evaluation, such a procedure seems backward. The standard practice is to identify the changes desired in the students, then see if the course is effective in producing the changes. Instead we are observing classes for the purpose of identifying changes that are not predicted or recognized at the start. A child makes a remark about an insight into equilibrium based on a particular section of one book, an insight that was not expected by the authors of the book. Another child exhibits an appreciation of symmetry embedded in the development of the concept of the median. Through such observation, though time consuming and sometimes unproductive, we are succeeding in identifying post hoc some "objectives" of the astronomy materials.

It is universally accepted that evaluation should be central to course improvement. But only when evaluation is seen as facilitating rather than limiting function will it be utilized more effectively by curriculum developers. To achieve this end, a flexible approach to the role of evaluation must be fostered by evaluation specialists themselves; there must be a willingness to question some of the conventional wisdom that has been accepted for decades, possibly with little analysis of the appropriateness today of the basic assumptions.

	CHAPTER 4
EDUCATIONAL OBJECTIVES: HELP OR HINDRANCE?[1]	Elliot W. Eisner

If one were to rank the various beliefs or assumptions in the field of curriculum that are thought most secure, the belief in the need for clarity and specificity in stating educational objectives would surely rank among the highest. Educational objectives, it is argued, need to be clearly specified for at least three reasons: first, because they provide the goals toward which the curriculum is aimed; second, because once clearly stated they facilitate the selection and organization of content; third, because when specified in both behavioral and content terms they make it possible to evaluate the outcomes of the curriculum.

It is difficult to argue with a rational approach to curriculum development—who would choose irrationality? And, if one is to build curriculum in a rational way, the clarity of premise, end or starting point, would appear paramount. But I want to argue in this paper that educational objectives clearly and specifically stated can hamper as well as help the ends of instruction and that an unexamined belief in curriculum as in other domains of human activity can easily become dogma which in fact may hinder the very functions the concept was originally designed to serve.

When and where did beliefs concerning the importance of educational objectives in curriculum development emerge? Who has formulated and argued their importance? What effect has this belief had upon curriculum construction? If we examine the past briefly for data necessary for answering these questions, it appears that the belief in the usefulness of clear and specific educational objectives emerged around the turn of the century with the birth of the scientific movement in education.

Before this movement gained strength, faculty psychologists viewed the brain as consisting of a variety of intellectual faculties. These faculties, they held, could be strengthened if exercised in appropriate ways with particular subject matters.

Once strengthened, the faculties could be used in any area of human activity to which they were applicable. Thus, if the important faculties could be identified and if methods of strengthening them developed, the school could concentrate on this task and expect general intellectual excellence as a result.

This general theoretical view of mind had been accepted for several decades by the time Thorndike, Judd, and later Watson began, through their work, to chip away the foundations upon which it rested. Thorndike's work especially demonstrated the specificity of transfer. He argued theoretically that transfer of learning occurred if and only if elements in one situation were identical with elements in the other. His empirical work supported his theoretical views, and the enormous stature he enjoyed in education as well as in psychology influenced educators to approach curriculum development in ways consonant with his views. One of those who was caught up in the scientific movement in education was Franklin Bobbitt, often thought of as the father of curriculum theory. In 1918 Bobbitt published a signal work titled simply, *The Curriculum.*[2] In it he argued that educational theory is not so difficult to construct as commonly held and that curriculum theory is logically derivable from educational theory. Bobbitt wrote in 1918:

The central theory is simple. Human life, however varied, consists in its performance of specific activities. Education that prepares for life is one that prepares definitely and adequately for these specific activities. However numerous and diverse they may be for any social class, they can be discovered. This requires that one go out into the world of affairs and discover the particulars of which these affairs consist. These will show the abilities, habits, appreciations, and forms of knowledge that men need. These will be the objectives of the curriculum. They will be numerous, definite, and particularized. The curriculum will then be that series of experiences which childhood and youth must have by way of attaining those objectives.[3]

In *The Curriculum*, Bobbitt approached curriculum development scientifically and theoretically: study life carefully to identify needed skills, divide these skills into specific units, organize these units into experiences, and provide these experiences to children. Six years later, in his second book, *How To Make a Curriculum*,[4] Bobbitt operationalized his theoretical assertions and demonstrated how curriculum components—especially educational objectives—were to be formulated. In this book Bobbitt listed nine areas in which educational objectives are to be specified. In these nine areas he listed 160 major educational objectives which run the gamut from "Ability to use language in all ways required for proper and effective participation in community life" to "Ability to entertain one's friends, and to respond to entertainment by one's friends."[5]

Bobbitt was not alone in his belief in the importance of formulating objectives clearly and specifically. Pendleton, for example, listed 1,581 social objectives for English, Guiler listed more than 300 for arithmetic in grades 1-6, and Billings prescribed 888 generalizations which were important for the social studies.

If Thorndike was right, if transfer was limited, it seemed reasonable to encourage the teacher to teach for particular outcomes and to construct curriculums only after specific objectives had been identified.

In retrospect it is not difficult to understand why this movement in curriculum collapsed under its own weight by the early 1930's. Teachers could not manage fifty highly specified objects, let alone hundreds. And, in addition, the new view of the child, not as a complex machine but as a growing organism who ought to participate in planning his own educational program, did not mesh well with the theoretical views held earlier.[6]

But, as we all know, the Progressive movement too began its decline in the forties, and by the middle fifties, as a formal organization at least, it was dead.

By the late forties and during the fifties, curriculum specialists again began to remind us of the importance of specific educational objectives and began to lay down guidelines for their formulation. Rationales for constructing curriculums developed by Ralph Tyler[7] and Virgil Herrick[8] again placed great importance on the specificity of objectives. George Barton[9] identified philosophic domains which could be used to select objectives. Benjamin Bloom and his colleagues[10] operationalized theoretical assertions by building a taxonomy of educational objectives in the cognitive

domain; and in 1964, Krathwohl, Bloom, and Masia[11] did the same for the affective domain. Many able people for many years have spent a great deal of time and effort in identifying methods and providing prescriptions for the formulation of educational objectives, so much so that the statement "Educational objectives should be stated in behavioral terms" has been elevated—or lowered—to almost slogan status in curriculum circles. Yet, despite these efforts, teachers seem not to take educational objectives seriously—at least as they are prescribed from above. And when teachers plan curriculum guides, their efforts first to identify over-all educational aims, then specify school objectives, then identify educational objectives for specific subject matters, appear to be more like exercises to be gone through than serious efforts to build tools for curriculum planning. If educational objectives were really useful tools, teachers, I submit, would use them. If they do not, perhaps it is not because there is something wrong with the teachers but because there might be something wrong with the theory.

As I view the situation, there are several limitations to theory in curriculum regarding the functions educational objectives are to perform. These limitations I would like to identify.

Educational objectives are typically derived from curriculum theory, which assumes that it is possible to predict with a fair degree of accuracy what the outcomes of instruction will be. In a general way this is possible. If you set about to teach a student algebra, there is no reason to assume he will learn to construct sonnets instead. Yet, the outcomes of instruction are far more numerous and complex for educational objectives to encompass. The amount, type, and quality of learning that occurs in a classroom, especially when there is interaction among students, are only in small part predictable. The changes in pace, tempo, and goals that experienced teachers employ when necessary and appropriate for maintaining classroom organization are dynamic rather than mechanistic in character. Elementary school teachers, for example, are often sensitive to the changing interests of the children they teach, and frequently attempt to capitalize on these interests, "milking them" as it were for what is educationally valuable.[12] The teacher uses the moment in a situation that is better described as kaleidoscopic than stable. In the very process of teaching and discussing, unexpected opportunities emerge for making a valuable point, for demonstrating an interesting idea, and for teaching a significant concept. The first point I wish to make, therefore, is that the dynamic and complex process of instruction yields outcomes far too numerous to be specified in behavioral and content terms in advance.

A second limitation of theory concerning educational objectives is its failure to recognize the constraints various subject matters place upon objectives. The point here is brief. In some subject areas, such as mathematics, languages, and the sciences, it is possible to specify with great precision the particular operation or behavior the student is to perform after instruction. In other subject areas, especially the arts, such specification is frequently not possible, and when possible may not be desirable. In a class in mathematics or spelling, uniformity in response is desirable, at least insofar as it indicates that students are able to perform a particular operation adequately, that is, in accordance with accepted procedures. Effective instruction in such areas enables students to function with minimum error in these fields. In the arts and in subject matters where, for example, novel or creative responses are desired, the particular behaviors to be developed cannot easily be identified. Here curriculum and instruction should yield behaviors and products which are unpredictable. The end achieved ought to be something of a surprise to both teacher and pupil. While it could be argued that one might formulate an educational objective which specified novelty, originality, or creativeness as the desired outcome, the particular referents for these terms cannot be specified in advance; one must judge after the fact whether the product produced or the behavior displayed belongs in the "novel" class. This is a much different procedure than is determining whether or not a particular word has been spelled correctly or a specific performance, that is, jumping a 3-foot hurdle, has been attained. Thus, the second point is that theory concerning educational objectives has not taken into account the particular relationship that holds between the subject matter being taught and the degree to which educational objectives can be predicted and specified. This, I suppose, is in part due to the fact that few curriculum specialists have high degrees of intimacy with a wide variety of subject matters and thus are unable to alter their general theoretical views to suit the demands that particular subject matters make.

The third point I wish to make deals with the belief that objectives stated in behavioral and content terms can be used as criteria by which to measure the outcomes of curriculum and instruction. Educational objectives provide, it is argued, the standard against which achievement is to be measured. Both taxonomies are built upon this assumption since their primary function is to demonstrate how objectives can be used to frame test items appropriate for evaluation. The assumption that objectives can be used as standards by which to measure achievement fails, I think, to distinguish adequately between the application of a standard and the making of a judgment. Not all—perhaps not even most—outcomes of curriculum and instruction are amenable to measurement. The application of a standard requires that some arbitrary and socially defined quantity be designated by which other qualities can be compared. By virtue of socially defined rules of grammar, syntax, and logic, for example, it is possible to quantitatively compare and measure error in discursive or mathematical statement. Some fields of activity, especially those which are qualitative in character, have no comparable rules and hence are less amenable to quantitative assessment. It is here that evaluation must be made, not primarily by applying a socially defined standard, but by making a human qualitative judgment. One can specify, for example, that a student shall be expected to know how to extract a square root correctly and in an unambiguous way, through the application of a standard, determine whether this end has been achieved. But it is only in a metaphoric sense that one can measure the extent to which a student has been able to produce an aesthetic object or an expressive narrative. Here standards are unapplicable; here judgment is required. The making of a judgment in distinction to the application of a standard implies that valued qualities are not merely socially defined and arbitrary in character. The judgment by which a critic determines the value of a poem, novel, or play is not achieved merely by applying standards already known to the particular product being judged; it requires that the critic—or teacher—view the product with respect to the unique properties it displays and then, in relation to his experience and sensibilities, judge its value in terms which are incapable of being reduced to quantity or rule.

This point was aptly discussed by John Dewey in his chapter on "Perception and Criticism" in *Art as Experience*.[13] Dewey was concerned with the problem of identifying the means and ends of criticism and has this to say about its proper function:

The function of criticism is the reeducation of perception of works of art; it is an auxiliary process, a difficult process, of learning to see and hear. The conception that its business is to appraise, to judge in the legal and moral sense, arrests the perception of those who are influenced by the criticism that assumes this task.[14]

Of the distinction that Dewey makes between the application of a standard and the making of a critical judgment, he writes:

There are three characteristics of a standard. It is a particular physical thing existing under specifiable conditions; it is *not* a value. The yard is a yard-stick, and the meter is a bar deposited in Paris. In the second place, standards are measures of things, of lengths, weights, capacities. The things measured are not values, although it is of great social value to be able to measure them, since the properties of things in the way of size, volume, weight, are important for commercial exchange. Finally, as standards of measure, standards define things with respect to *quantity*. To be able to measure quantities is a great aid to further judgments, but it is not a mode of judgment. The standard, being an external and public thing, is applied *physically*. The yard-stick is physically laid down upon things to determine their length.[15]

And I would add that what is most educationally valuable is the development of that mode of curiosity, inventiveness, and insight that is capable of being described only in metaphoric or poetic terms. Indeed, the image of the educated man that has been held in highest esteem for the longest period of time in Western civilization is one which is not amenable to standard measurement. Thus, the third point I wish to make is that curriculum theory which views educational objectives as standards by which to measure educational achievement overlooks those modes of achievement incapable of measurement.

The final point I wish to make deals with the function of educational objectives in curriculum construction.

The rational approach to curriculum development not only emphasizes the importance of specificity in the formulation of educational objectives but also implies when not stated explicitly that educational objectives be stated prior to the formulation of curriculum activities. At first view, this seems to be a reasonable way to proceed with curriculum construction: one should know where he is headed before embarking on a trip. Yet, while the procedure of first identifying objectives before proceeding to identify activities is logically defensible, it is not necessarily the most psychologically efficient way to proceed. One can, and teachers often do, identify activities that seem useful, appropriate, or rich in educational opportunities, and from a consideration of what can be done in class, identify the objectives or possible consequences of using these activities. MacDonald argues this point cogently when he writes:

Let us look, for example, at the problem of objectives. Objectives are viewed as directives in the rational approach. They are identified prior to the instruction or action and used to provide a basis for a screen for appropriate activities.

There is another view, however, which has both scholarly and experiential referents. This view would state that our objectives are only known to us in any complete sense after the completion of our act of instruction. No matter what we thought we were attempting to do, we can only know what we wanted to accomplish after the fact. Objectives by this rationale are heuristic devices which provide initiating

consequences which become altered in the flow of instruction.

In the final analysis, it could be argued, the teacher in actuality asks a fundamentally different question from "What am I trying to accomplish?" The teacher asks "What am I going to do?" and out of the doing comes accomplishment.[16]

Theory in curriculum has not adequately distinguished between logical adequacy in determining the relationship of means to ends when examining the curriculum as a *product* and the psychological processes that may usefully be employed in building curriculums. The method of forming creative insights in curriculum development, as in the sciences and arts, is as yet not logically prescribable. The ways in which curriculums can be usefully and efficiently developed constitute an empirical problem; imposing logical requirements upon the process because they are desirable for assessing the product is, to my mind, an error. Thus, the final point I wish to make is that educational objectives need not precede the selection and organization of content. The means through which imaginative curriculums can be built is as open-ended as the means through which scientific and artistic inventions occur. Curriculum theory needs to allow for a variety of processes to be employed in the construction of curriculums.

I have argued in this paper that curriculum theory as it pertains to educational objectives has had four significant limitations. First, it has not sufficiently emphasized the extent to which the prediction of educational outcomes cannot be made with accuracy. Second, it has not discussed the ways in which the subject matter affects precision in stating educational objectives. Third, it has confused the use of educational objectives as a standard for measurement when in some areas it can be used only as a criterion for judgment. Fourth, it has not distinguished between the logical requirement of relating means to ends in the curriculum as a product and the psychological conditions useful for constructing curriculums.

If the arguments I have formulated about the limitations of curriculum theory concerning educational objectives have merit, one might ask: What are their educational consequences? First, it seems to me that they suggest that in large measure the construction of curriculums and the judgment of its consequences are artful tasks. The methods of curriculum development are, in principle if not in practice, no different from the making of art—be it the art of painting or the art of science. The identification of the factors in the potentially useful educational activity and the organization or construction of sequence in curriculum are in principle amenable to an infinite number of combinations. The variable teacher, student, class group, require artful blending for the educationally valuable to result.

Second, I am impressed with Dewey's view of the functions of criticism—to heighten one's perception of the art object—and believe it has implications for curriculum theory. If the child is viewed as an art product and the teacher as a critic, one task of the teacher would be to reveal the qualities of the child to himself and to others. In addition, the teacher as critic would appraise the changes occurring in the child. But because the teacher's task includes more than criticism, he would also be responsible, in part, for the improvement of the work of art. In short, in both the construction of educational means (the curriculum) and the appraisal of its consequences, the teacher would become an artist, for criticism itself when carried to its height is an art. This, it seems to me, is a dimension to which curriculum theory will someday have to speak.

Notes

1. This is a slightly expanded version of a paper presented at the fiftieth annual meeting of the American Educational Research Association, Chicago, February, 1966.
2. Franklin Bobbitt, *The Curriculum* (Boston: Houghton Mifflin Co., 1918).
3. *Ibid.*, p. 42.
4. Franklin Bobbitt, *How To Make a Curriculum* (Boston: Houghton Mifflin Co., 1924).
5. *Ibid.*, pp. 11-29.
6. For a good example of this view of the child and curriculum development, see *The Changing Curriculum, Tenth Yearbook*, Department of Supervisors and Directors of Instruction, National Education Association and Society for Curriculum Study (New York: Appleton-Century-Crofts Co., 1937).
7. Ralph W. Tyler, *Basic Principles of Curriculum and Instruction* (Chicago: University of Chicago Press, 1951).
8. Virgil E. Herrick, "The Concept of Curriculum Design," *Toward Improved Curriculum Theory*, ed. Virgil E. Herrick and Ralph W. Tyler (Supplementary Educational Monographs, No. 71 [Chicago: University of Chicago Press, 1950]), pp. 37-50.
9. George E. Barton, Jr., "Educational Objectives: Improvement of Curriculum Theory about Their Determination," *ibid.*, pp. 26-35.
10. Benjamin Bloom *et al.* (ed.), *Taxonomy of Educational Objectives, Handbook I: The Cognitive Domain* (New York: Longmans, Green & Co., 1956).
11. David Krathwohl, Benjamin Bloom, and Bertram Masia, *Taxonomy of Educational Objectives, Handbook II: The Affective Domain* (New York: David McKay, Inc., 1964).
12. For an excellent paper describing educational objectives as they are viewed and used by elementary school teachers, see Philip W. Jackson and Elizabeth Belford, "Educational Objectives and the Joys of Teaching," *School Review*, LXXIII (1965), 267-91.
13. John Dewey, *Art as Experience* (New York: Minton, Balch & Co., 1934).
14. *Ibid.*, p. 324.
15. *Ibid.*, p. 307.
16. James B. MacDonald, "Myths about Instruction," *Educational Leadership*, XXII, No. 7 (May, 1965), 613-14.

CHAPTER 5

Michael Scriven

THE METHODOLOGY OF EVALUATION

Introduction

Current conceptions of the evaluation of educational instruments (e.g., new curricula, programmed texts, inductive methods, individual teachers) are still inadequate both philosophically and practically. This paper attempts to exhibit and reduce some of the deficiencies. Intellectual progress is possible only because newcomers can stand on the shoulders of giants. This feat is often confused with treading on their toes, particularly but not only by the newcomer. I confess a special obligation to Professor Cronbach's work,[1] and to valuable discussions with the personnel of CIRCE at the University of Illinois.

Outline

The main focus of this paper is on curricular evaluation but almost all the points made transfer immediately to other kinds of evaluation. Section headings are reasonably self-explanatory and occur in the following order:

1. Outline.
2. Goals of Evaluation versus Roles of Evaluation.
3. Arguments for and against Formative and Summative Evaluation.
4. Evaluation versus Process Studies.
5. Evaluation versus Estimation of Goal Achievement.
6. Instrumental versus Consequential Evaluation.
7. Comparative versus Non-Comparative Evaluation.
8. Comparative Evaluation—The Criteria of Educational Achievement.
9. Values and Costs.
10. Another Kind of Evaluation — "Explanatory Evaluation."
11. Conclusions.

The discussion in the earlier sections is relatively elementary and etiological, progressing to an occasionally more difficult and generally more practical level in later sections.

Goals of Evaluation versus Roles of Evaluation

The aims of evaluation may be thought of in two ways. At the general level, we may talk of the *goals* of evaluation; in a particular educational context, of the roles of evaluation.

In general, we may say that evaluation attempts to answer certain *types of questions* about certain *entities*. The types of questions include questions of the form: "*How well* does this instrument perform (with respect to such-and-such criteria)?" "Does it perform *better* than this other instrument?" "What does this instrument do (i.e., what variables from the group in which we are interested are significantly affected by its application)?" "Is the use of this instrument *worth* what it's costing?" Evaluation is itself a logical activity which is essentially similar whether we are trying to evaluate coffee machines or teaching machines, plans for a house or plans for a curriculum. The activity consists simply in the gathering and combining of performance data with a weighted set of goal scales to yield either comparative or numerical ratings.

But the *role* which evaluation has in a particular educational context may be enormously various; it may form part of a teacher training activity, of the process of curriculum development, of a field experiment connected with the improvement of learning theory, of an investigation preliminary to a decision about purchase or rejection of materials; it may be a data-gathering activity for

1. "Evaluation for Course Improvement," *Teachers' College Record* Vol. 64, No. 8, May, 1963, reprinted in *New Curricula*, edited by R. Heath, pp. 231-248. New York: Harper & Row, Publishers, 1964); references in this paper are to the latter version.

supporting a request for tax increases or research support, or a preliminary to the reward or punishment of people as in an executive training program, a prison, or a classroom. Failure to make this rather obvious distinction between the roles and goals of evaluation, not necessarily in this terminology, is one of the factors that has led to the dilution of the process of evaluation to the point where it can no longer serve as a basis for answering the questions which are its goal. This dilution has sacrificed goals to roles. One can only be against evaluation if one can show that it is improper to seek for an answer to questions of the above kind, and this involves showing that there are *no* legitimate activities (roles) in which these questions can be raised, an extraordinary claim. Obviously the fact that evaluation is sometimes used in an inappropriate role hardly justifies the conclusion that we *never* need to know the answers to the goal questions.

One role that has often and sensibly been assigned to evaluation is as an important part of the process of curriculum *development*. Obviously such a role does not preclude evaluation of the *final* product of this process. Evaluation can obviously play several roles. Yet it is clear from the treatment of evaluation in some of the recent literature and in a number of recent research proposals involving several million dollars that the assumption is being made that one's obligations in the direction of evaluation are fully discharged by having it appear *somewhere* in a project. Not only can it have several roles with respect to one educational enterprise, but with respect to each of these it may have several goals. Thus, it may have a role in the improvement of the curriculum and with respect to this role several types of question (goals) may be raised, such as "Is the curriculum at this point really getting across the distinction between prejudice and commitment?" "Is it taking too large a proportion of the available time to make this point?" etc. In another role, the evaluation process may be brought to bear on the question of whether the entire finished curriculum, refined by use of the evaluation process in its first role, represents a sufficiently significant advance on the available alternatives to justify the expense of adoption by a school system.

One of the reasons for the tolerance or indeed encouragement of the confusion between roles and goals is the well-meaning attempt to allay the anxiety on the part of teachers that the word "evaluation" precipitates. By stressing the constructive part evaluation may play in non-threatening activities (roles) we slur over the fact that its goals are always the same—the estimation of merit, worth, value, etc. which all too clearly serves in another role as part of the evaluation of personnel and courses. It is unfortunate that we should be tackling anxiety about evaluation by reducing its importance and confusing its presentation; the loss in efficiency is too great. Business firms can't keep executives or factories on when they know they are not doing good work and a society shouldn't have to retain textbooks, courses, teachers and superintendents that do a poor job when a better performance is possible. The appropriate way to handle anxiety of this kind is by finding tasks for which a better prognosis is possible for the individual in question. Failure to evaluate pupils' performance leads to the gross inefficiencies of the age-graded classroom, and failure to evaluate teachers' performances leads to the correlative inefficiency of incompetent instruction. A little toughening of the moral fibre is required if we are not to shirk the social responsibilities of the educational branch of our culture. Thus, it may even be true that "the greatest service evaluation can perform is to identify aspects of the course where revision is desirable" (Cronbach, p. 236), though it is not clear how one would establish this, but it is certainly also true that there are other extremely important services which must be done for almost any given project. And there are many contexts in which calling an evaluator in to perform a final evaluation of the project or person is an act of proper recognition of responsibility to the person, product or taxpayers. It therefore seems a little excessive to refer to this as simply "a menial role," as Cronbach does. It is obviously a great service if this kind of terminal evaluation (we might call it *summative* as opposed to *formative* evaluation) can demonstrate that a very expensive textbook is not significantly better than the competition, or that it is enormously better than any competitor. In more general terms it may be possible to demonstrate that a certain type of approach to e.g., mathematics, is not yielding significantly better pupil performance on any dimension that mathematicians are prepared to regard as important. This would certainly save a great deal of expenditure of time and money and constitute a valuable contribution to educational development, as would the converse, favorable, result. Thus there seem to be a number of qualifications that would have to be made before one could accept a statement asserting the greater importance of formative evaluation by comparison with summative. ("Evaluation, used to improve the course while it is still fluid, contributes more to improvement of education than evaluation used to appraise a product already placed on the market." Cronbach, p. 236) Fortunately we do not have to make this choice. Educational projects, particularly curricular ones, clearly must attempt to make best use of evaluation in both these roles.

Now any curriculum reformer is *automatically* engaged in formative evaluation, except on a very strict interpretation of "evaluation." He is presumably doing what he is doing because he judges that the material being presented in the existing curriculum is unsatisfactory. So as he proceeds to construct the new material he is constantly evaluating his own material as better than that which is already current. Unless entirely ignorant of his shortcomings as a judge of his own work, he is presumably engaged in field-testing the work while it is being developed, and in so doing he gets feedback on the basis of which he again produces revisions; this is of course formative evaluation. He is usually involved with colleagues, e.g., the classroom teacher or peers, who comment on the material as they see it—again, this is evaluation and it produces changes which are allegedly for the better. If the recommendation for formative evaluation has any content at all, it presumably amounts to the suggestion that a *professional* evaluator should be added to the curriculum construction project. There certainly can be advantages in this, but it is equally clear from practical experience that there can be disadvantages. But this argument is clearly not the same as the argument about summative evaluation. We devote part of the next section to a discussion of the pros and cons of formative evaluation.

Arguments for and against Formative and Summative Evaluation

The basic fact is that the evaluator, while a professional in his own field, is usually not a professional in the field relevant to the curriculum being reformed or, if he is, he is not committed to the particular development being undertaken. This leads to clashes and failures to communicate of a kind which are all too familiar to project directors today.

From these "failures of communication" between evaluators and teachers or curriculum makers there have sprung some unfortunate overreactions. The total anti-evaluation line is all too frequently a rationalization of the anxiety provoked by the presence of an external judge, not identified with or committed to (or perhaps even understanding) the ideals of the project. The equally indefensible opposite extreme is represented by the self-perceived tough-minded operationalist evaluator, all too likely to say "If you can't tell me what variables you are affecting, in operational terms, they can't be tested, and as long as they haven't been tested you haven't any reason for thinking you are making a contribution."

In order to develop a fair treatment of these views let us consider the difference between a contemporary educational project involving the development of a new curriculum or teaching method, and the co-authoring of a new ninth-grade algebra text by two or three teachers in the late 1930's. In the first place, the present projects are typically supported from government funds on a very large scale. The justification of this expenditure calls for some kind of objective evidence that the product was valuable. Moreover, future support for work in this area or by these same workers requires some objective evidence as to their merit at this kind of job. Since there are not sufficient funds to support all applicants, judgements of comparative merit are necessary; and objective bases for this are trivially superior to mere person-endorsements by peers, etc. Finally, the enormous costs involved in the adoption of such products by school systems commit another great slice of taxpayers' money and this kind of commitment should presumably be made only on the basis of rather substantial evidence for its justification. In this context, summative evaluation is an inescapable obligation on the project director, and an obvious requirement by the sponsoring agency, and a desideratum as far as the schools are concerned. And since formative evaluation is part of a rational approach to producing good results on the summative evaluation, it can hardly be wholly eschewed; indeed, as we have shown, its occurrence is to some degree guaranteed by the nature of the case. But the separate question of whether professional evaluators should be employed depends very much upon the extent to which they do more harm than good—and there are a number of ways in which they can do harm.

They may simply exude a kind of skeptical spirit that dampens the creative fires of a productive group. They may be sympathetic but impose such crushing demands on operational formulation of goals as to divert too much time to an essentially secondary activity. ("Secondary" in the sense that there cannot be any evaluation without a curriculum.) The major compromise that must be effected is to have the evaluator recognize it as partly his responsibility to uncover and formulate a testable set of criteria for the course. He may be substantially helped by the fact that the project has explicitly espoused certain goals, or rejected others, and he will certainly be aided by their criticism of his formulations. However, the exchange has to be a two-way one; curriculum writers are by no means infallible, and often extremely prejudiced in describing their actual tendencies. Evaluators, on the other hand, are handicapped so long as they are less than fully familiar with the subject matter being restructured, and less than fully sympathetic with the aims of the creative group. Yet once they become identified with those aims, emotionally as well as economically, they lose something of great importance to an objective evaluation—their independence. For this reason the formative evaluators should be very sharply distinguished from the summative evaluators, with whom they may certainly work in developing an acceptable summative evaluation schema, but they should of course exclude themselves from any judgemental role.

There are other problems about the intrusion of evaluation into education, and the intrusion of an evaluator into the curriculum-making process. Several of these have been admirably expressed by J. Myron Atkin.[2] Some of them are taken up elsewhere in this paper, but some mention of two of them should be made here. The first suggestion is that testing for learning of certain rather delicate and pervasive concepts may be itself destructive, in that it makes the student too self-conscious about the role of a concept at too early a stage, thereby preventing its natural and proper development. The problem is that with respect to some of these concepts, e.g., symmetry, equilibrium and randomness, it might be the case that very little accretion occurs in the understanding of a child during any particular course or indeed any particular year of his education, but that tiny accretion may be of very great importance in the development of good scientific understanding. It would not show up on tests, indeed it might be stultified by the intrusion of tests, in any given year, but it has to be in the curriculum in order to produce the finished product that we desire. In this case, evaluation seems to be both incompetent and possibly destructive.

Such a possibility should serve as an interesting challenge to the creative curriculum-maker. While not dismissing it, he would normally respond by attempting to treat it more explicitly, perhaps at a somewhat later stage in the curriculum than it is normally first mentioned, and see whether some significant and satisfactory accretion of comprehension cannot be produced by this direct attack. Only if this failed would he turn to the evaluator and demand a considerably more sensitive instrument. Again, it would also be possible to deliberately avoid testing for this during all the early years of its peripheral introduction, and test only in the senior year in high school, for example. We can acknowledge the *possibility* that concerns Atkin and allow some extra material in the curriculum to handle it even without any justification from the early feedback from tests. Errors of excess are much less significant than errors of commission or omission, in curriculum-making.

Just as there are dangers from having a curriculum-making group discuss the present curriculum with teachers who are experienced in its use—

although there are also possible advantages from this—so there are dangers and advantages in bringing the evaluator in too early. In such situations, some ingenuity on the part of the project director will often make the best of both worlds possible; for example, the evaluator may be simply introduced to the materials produced, but not to the people producing them, and his comments studied by the director with an eye to feeding back any fundamental and serious criticisms, but withholding the others until some later stage in the curriculum development activities where, for example, an extensive process of revision is about to begin. But these are practical considerations; there remain two more fundamental kinds of objection that should be mentioned briefly, of which the first is central to Atkin's misgivings.

No one who has been involved in the field-testing of a new curriculum has failed to notice the enormous variability in its appeal to students, often unpredictable from their previous academic performance. The child already interested in bird-watching will find one approach to biology far more attractive than another. Similarly, for some children the relevance of the material to problems with which they are familiar will make an enormous difference to their interest, whereas for others the properties of the hexaflexagon or the Moebius strip are immediately fascinating. More fundamentally, the structuring of the classroom situation may wholly alter the motivation for different students in different ways; the non-directive style of treatment currently regarded as desirable, partly for its supposed connection with the inductive approach, is totally unstimulating for some children, although an aggressive, competitive, critical interaction will get them up and running. In the face of this kind of variation, we are often committed to the use of the very blunt evaluation instrument of the performance, on tests, of the class as a whole. Even if we break this down into improvements in individual performances, we still have not fully exploited the potentialities of the material, which would be manifested only if we were to select the right material *and* the right instructional technique for a child with a particular background, attitudes, interests and abilities. Perhaps, the evaluation skeptic suggests, it is more appropriate to place one's faith in the creative and academically impeccable curriculum maker, using the field tests simply to make sure that it is *possible* to excite and teach students with the material, under appropriate circumstances. That is, our criterion should be markedly improved performance by *some*, even by a *sub-*

2. "Some Evaluation Problems in a Course Content Improvement Project," *Journal of Research in Science Teaching* 1 (1963): 129-132.

stantial number, rather than by the class as a whole. To this the evaluator must reply by asking whether one is to disregard possibilities such as serious lack of comprehensibility to students at this age-level, a marked deterioration of performance in some of the students more than offsetting the gains, the possibility that it is the pedagogical skill or enthusiasm of the teacher that is responsible for the success in the field tests and not the materials? The material is to go out to other teachers; it must be determined whether it will be of any use to them. To answer these questions—and indeed for the field tests themselves—a professional job in evaluation is necessary.

We can learn something important from this criticism, however. We must certainly weigh seriously the opinions of the subject matter expert as to the flavor and quality of the curriculum content. Sometimes it will be almost all we have to go on, and sometimes it will even be enough for some decisions. It should in any event be seriously considered and sometimes heavily weighted in the evaluation process, for the *absence* of supporting professional consensus of this kind is often adequate grounds for complete rejection of the material.

Finally, there is the objection that hovers in the background of many of these discussions, the uneasy feeling that evaluation necessitates making value judgements, and that value judgements are essentially subjective and not scientific. This is about as intelligent a view as the view that statements about oneself are essentially subjectives and hence incapable of rational substantiation. Some value judgments are essentially assertions about fundamental personal preferences and as such are factual claims which can be established or refuted by ordinary (though sometimes not easy) procedures of psychological investigation. But the process of establishing them does not show that it is right or wrong to hold these values; it only shows that it is true that somebody does or does not hold them. Another kind of value judgement is the assessment of the merit or comparative merit of some entity in a clearly defined context where this amounts to a claim that its performance is good or better than another's on clearly identifiable and clearly weighted criterion variables. With respect to value judgements of this kind, it is not only possible to find out whether or not they are believed by the individuals who assert them, but it is also possible to determine whether it is right or wrong to believe them. They are simply complex conflations of various performance ratings and the weightings of the various performances; it is in this sense that we can correctly assert that the Bulova Accutron is the best wrist chronometer currently available or that a particular desk dictionary is the best one for some-

body with extensive scientific interests. Finally, there are value judgements in which the criteria themselves are debatable, a type of value judgement which is only philosophically the most important of all and whose debatability merely reflects the fact that important issues are not always easy ones. Examples of this would be the assertion that the most important role of evaluation is in the process of curriculum writing, or that the I.Q. test is an unfortunate archaism, or that the Copenhagen interpretation of quantum physics is superior to any alternative. In each of these cases, the disputes turn out to be mainly disputes about what is to count as good, rather than to be arguments about the straightforward "facts of the situation," i.e., what is in fact good. It is immature to react to this kind of judgement as if it is contaminated with some disgusting disease; the only proper reaction is to examine the reasons that are put forward for them and see if and how the matter may be rationally discussed.

It is sometimes thought that in dealing with people, as we must in the field of education, we are necessarily involved in the field of *moral* value judgements, and that *these* really are essentially subjective. But in the first place value judgements about people are by no means necessarily moral, since they may refer to their health, intelligence and achievements; and secondly, even if they are moral, we are all presumably committed to one moral principle (the principle of the equality of rights of men) and by far the greater part of moral discourses takes place within the framework of this assumption, and is simply a rational elaboration of it in combination with complicated judgements about the consequences of alternatives. So, unless one is willing to challenge this axiom, or to provide rational support for an alternative, even moral value judgments are within the realm of rational debate. And even if one does challenge this axiom, a strong case can be made for its rational superiority over any alternatives. But whatever the outcome of such a discussion, the facts that some evaluation is moral evaluation and that some moral evaluation is controversial, do not conjointly imply the least degree of support for the conclusion that curricular evaluation is less than a fully objective activity of applied science.

Evaluation versus Process Studies

In the course of clarifying the concept of evaluation it is important not to simplify it. Although the *typical* goals of evaluation require judgements of merit and worth, when somebody is asked to evaluate a situation or the impact of certain kinds of materials on the market, then what is being called for is an analytical description of the process, usually with respect to certain possible causal connections. In this sense it is not inappropriate to regard some kinds of process investigation as evaluation. But the range of process research only overlaps with and is neither subsumed by nor equivalent to that of evaluation. We may conveniently distinguish three types of process research, as the term is used by Cronbach and others.

1. The non-inferential study of what actually goes on in the classroom. Perhaps this has the most direct claim to being called a study of the process of teaching (learning, etc.). We might for example be interested in the amount of time that the teacher talks, the amount of time that the students spend in homework for a class, the proportion of the dialogue devoted to explaining, defining, opining, etc. (B. O. Smith & Milton Meux). The great problem about work like this is to show that it is worth doing, in *any* sense. *Some* pure research is idle research. The Smith and Meux work is specifically mentioned because *it* is clearly original and offers promise in a large number of directions. It is difficult to avoid the conclusion, however, that most process research of this kind in education, as in psychotherapy, is fruitful at neither the theoretical nor the applied level.

2. The second kind of process research involves the investigation of causal claims ("dynamic hypotheses") about the process. Here we are interested in such questions as whether an increase of time spent on class discussions of the goals of a curriculum at the expense of time spent on training drills leads to improved comprehension in (a) algebra, (b) geography, etc. This kind of hypothesis is of course a miniature limited-scope "new instrument" project. Another kind looks for the answer to such questions as, Is the formation of sub-group allegiance and identification with the teacher facilitated by strong emphasis on pupil-teacher dialogue? The identifying feature of this sub-group of process hypotheses is that the dependent variables are either ones which would not figure amongst the set of criteria we would use in a summative evaluation study (though we might think of them as important because of their bearing on improved teaching techniques) or they are only a sub-group of such a set.

Process hypotheses of this second kind are in general about as difficult to substantiate as any "outcome" hypothesis, i.e., summative evaluation. Indeed they are sometimes harder to substantiate because they may require identifying the effects of only one of several independent variables that are present, and ordinary matching techniques to take care of the others are extremely hard—though usually not impossible—to apply. The advantage of some summative evaluation is that it is concerned with evaluating the effects of a whole teacher-curriculum package and has no need to identify the specific agent responsible for the overall improvement or deterioration. That advantage lapses when we are concerned to identify the variance due to the curriculum as opposed to the teacher.

3. Formative Evaluation. This kind of research can be called process research, but it is of course simply outcome evaluation at an intermediate stage in the development of the teaching instrument. The distinction between this and the first kind of dynamic hypothesis mentioned above is twofold. There is a distinction of role; the role of formative evaluation is to discover deficiencies and successes in the intermediate versions of a new curriculum; the role of dynamic hypothesis investigation is terminal; it is to provide the answer to an important question about the mechanism of teaching. And there is a distinction in the extent to which it matters whether the criteria used are an adequate analysis of the proper goals of the curriculum. The dynamic hypothesis study has no obligation to this; the formative evaluation does. But the two types of study are not always sharply distinct. They both play an important role in good curriculum research.

Now of course it is true that anybody who does an experiment of any kind at all should at some stage evaluate his results. It is even true that the experiment itself will usually be designed in such a way as to incorporate within itself procedures for evaluation of the results—e.g., by using an "objectively validated" test, which has a certain kind of built-in comparative evaluation in the scoring key. None of this shows that most research is evaluation research. In particular, even process research is not all evaluation research. That interpretation of data can be described as evaluation of results does not show that the interpretations (and the explanations) are about the *merit* of a teaching instrument. They may be about the temporal distribution of various elements of the instrument, etc. Such points are obvious enough, but a good deal of the comment pro and con evaluation research betokens considerable lack of clarity about its boundaries, whose admitted imprecision is really quite slight.

Evaluation versus Estimation of Goal Achievement

One of the reactions to the threat of evaluation, or perhaps to the use of over-crude evaluative procedures, was the extreme relativization of evaluation research. The slogan became "How well does the course achieve its goals?" instead of "How good is the course?" It is of course obvious that if the goals aren't worth achieving then it is uninteresting how well they are achieved. The success of this kind of relativism in the evaluation field rests entirely upon the premise that judgements of goals are value judgements of a non-objective kind. No doubt some of them are; but this in no way indicates that the field is one in which objectivity is impossible. An American History curriculum, K-14, which consisted of the memorization of names and dates would be absurd —it could not possibly be said to be a good curriculum, no matter how well it attained its goals. Nor could one which led to absolutely no recall of names and dates.

A "Modern Math" curriculum for general use which produced high school graduates largely incapable of reliable addition and multiplication would be simply a disgrace, no matter what else it conveyed. This kind of value judgement about goals is not beyond debate, but *good* arguments to the contrary have not been forthcoming so far. These are value judgements with excellent backing. Nor is their defensibility due to their lack of specificity. Much more precise ones can be given just as excellent backing; a physics curriculum which does not discuss the kinetic theory at any stage would be deficient, no matter how well it achieved whatever goals it had. And so on.

Thus evaluation proper must include, as an equal partner with the measuring of performance against goals, proceduers for the evaluation of the goals. That is, if it is to have any reference to goals at all. In the next two sections we will discuss procedures of evaluation that involve reference to goals and procedures which short-circuit such reference. First it should be pointed out that there is a complete difference between maintaining that judgement of goals is part of evaluation, i.e., that we cannot just accept anyone's goals, and maintaining that these goals should be the same for every school, for every school district, for every teacher, for every level, etc. It is entirely appropriate that a school with primarily vocational responsibilities should have somewhat different goals from those of a school producing 95 percent college-bound graduates. It just does not follow from this that the people who give the course or run the school or design the curriculum can be regarded as in any way immune from criticism in setting up their goals. A great deal of the energy behind the current attempts to reform the school curriculum springs straight out of the belief that the goals have been fundamentally wrong, that life-adjustment has been grossly overweighted, etc. To swing in the opposite direction is all too easy, and in no way preferable.

The process of relativization, however, has not only led to over-tolerance for over-restrictive goals, it has also led to incompetent evaluation of the extent to which these are achieved. Whatever one's views about evaluation, it is easy enough to demonstrate that there are very few professionally competent evaluators in the country today. The U.S. Office of Education's plans for Research and Development Centres, relatively modest in terms of the need, are probably unfulfillable because of the staffing problem, and the heavily financed evaluation projects already in existence are themselves badly understaffed in the evaluation side, even on the most conservative view of its role. Moreover the staff are themselves very well aware of their limitations, and in-service training projects for them are badly needed. The very idea that every school system, or every teacher, can today be regarded as capable of meaningful evaluation of their own performance is as absurd as the view that every psychotherapist today is capable of evaluating his work with his own patients. Trivially, they can learn something very important from carefully studying their own work; indeed they can identify some good and bad features about it. But if they or someone else need to know the answers to the important questions, whether process or outcome, they need skills and resources which are conspicuous by their absence at the *national* level.

Instrumental versus Consequential Evaluation

Two basically different approaches to the evaluation of a teaching instrument are possible. If you want to evaluate a tool, an instrument of another kind, say an axe, you might study its head design, the arguments for the weight distribution used, the steel alloy in the head, the grade of hickory in the handle, etc., or you might just study the kind and speed of the cuts it makes. (In either case, the evaluation may be either summative or formative, for these are roles of evaluation, not procedures for doing evaluation.)

The first approach involves an appraisal of the instrument itself; in the case of a particular course, this would involve evaluation of the content, goals, grading procedures, teacher attitude, etc. We shall call this kind of approach *instrumental* evaluation. The second approach proceeds via an examination of the effects of the teaching instrument on the pupil, and these alone. It involves an appraisal of the differences between pre- and post-tests, between experimental group tests and control group tests, etc., on a number of criterial parameters. We can call this *consequential* evaluation. Referring to the debates between Christians about the foundations of their faith, adherents of the second approach might be inclined to refer to it as the fundamentalist approach, by comparison with the theological approach of the first alternative. Defenders of the second alternative would support this kind of labelling by arguing that all that really counts are the effects of the course on the pupils and appeal to the evaluation of goals and content is defensible only insofar as are evaluations of these really correlates with consequential evaluations. Since these correlations are largely a priori in our present state of knowledge, the fundamentalist argues, the theologian is too much an armchair evaluator. The "theologian," on the other hand, is likely to counter by talking about values that do not show up in the outcome study to which the fundamentalist restricts himself, and the importance of these in the overall assessment of teaching instruments; he is likely to exemplify this claim by reference to qualities of a curriculum such as elegance, modernity, integrity, etc., which can best be judged by the academic experts in the fields in question.

The possibility arises that an evaluation involving some weighting of instrumental criteria and some of consequential criteria might be a worthwhile compromise. There are certain kinds of evaluation situations where this will be so, but before any assessment of the correct relative weighting is possible it is necessary to look a little further into the difficulties with the two alternatives. In this section we will look at the basic requirements on an instrumental study, in the next examine a currently important disagreement about two types of consequential study, and in the light of our conclusions there we shall be able to say something about the relative merits of instrumental and consequential evaluations.

To recapitulate, it was maintained in the preceeding section that evaluation in terms of goal-achievement is typically a very poor substitute for good summative evaluation. If we are going to evaluate in a way that brings in goals at all, then we shall typically have some obligation to evaluate the goals. As the fundamentalist reminds us, summative evaluation does not necessarily involve any reference to the goals at all, if we do it his way. Indeed, one of the charms of the fundamentalist's case is the *lack* of charm, indeed the messiness, of an adequate instrumentalist design.

A major difficulty with goal-mediated evaluation, which we shall take as the principal example of an instrumentalist approach, lies in the formulation of the goals. In the first place the espoused goals of a curriculum-maker are often not the implicit goals of his curriculum. Moreover, it is not always the case that this kind of error should be corrected in favor of the espoused goals by revising the curriculum, or in favor of the implicit goals by revising the espoused goals. How do we decide which should receive precedence? Even if we were able to decide this, there is the perennial headache of translating the decription of the goals that we get from the curriculum-maker or the curriculum-analyst into testable terms. Many a slip occurs between this cup and that lip.

In addition to this, there is the problem already mentioned, that pressure on a writer to formulate his goals, to keep to them, and to express them in testable terms, may enormously alter his product in ways that are certainly not always desirable. Perhaps the best way of handling this third problem is to give prospective curriculum-builders an intensive course in evaluation techniques and problems prior to their commencing work. Such a course would be topic neutral, and would thereby avoid the problems of criticism of one's own "baby." Interaction with a professional evaluator can then be postponed substantially and should also be less anxiety-provoking. Short courses of the kind mentioned should surely be available for subsidized attendance every summer at one or two centers in the country. Ignoring any further consideration of the problem of in-group harmony, and this proposal for improving formative evaluation, we can turn to the main difficulty.

Practical Suggestions for Goal-Mediated Evaluation

Any curriculum project has some kind of objectives at the very beginning. Even if these are only put in terms of producing a more interesting, or more up-to-date treatment, there has to be some kind of grounds for dissatisfaction with the present curriculum in order to provide a concept of the project as a worthwhile activity. Usually something rather more specific emerges in the course of planning discussions. For example, the idea of a three-track approach, aimed at various kinds of teacher or student interest, may emerge out of a rather explicit discussion of the aims of the project, from which it becomes clear that three equally defensible aims can be formulated which will lead to incompatible requirements on the curriculum. The fact that these aims can be seen as incompatible makes clear that they must have fairly substantial content. Another typical content presupposition refers to *coverage;* it is recognized from the beginning that at least certain topics should be covered, or if they are not then there must be some compensatory coverage of other topics.

At this early stage a member or members of the project team must be appointed to the task of goal-formulation. Many of the objections to this kind of activity stem from reactions to over-rigid requirements on the way in which goals can be formulated at this stage. Any kind of goal on which the group agrees, or even those which they agree should be considered seriously as a possibility in the developing stage, should be listed at this point, but none of them should be regarded as absolute commitments in any way—

simply as reminders. It is not possible to overlook the unfortunate examples of projects in which the creative urge has outdistanced reality restraints; it has to be faced from the beginning that too gross a divergence from a certain minimum coverage is going to make the problem of adoption insuperable. If, on the other hand, the risk of negligible adoptions is tolerable, then the goals of the project should be formulated so as to make this clear. Having market-type goals such as substantial adoption on the list is in no way inappropriate: one can hardly reform education with curricula that never reach the classroom.

As the project develops, three types of activities centering around the formulation of goals should be distinguished and encouraged. In the first place the goals as so far formulated should be regularly re-examined and modified in the light of changes in the actual activities, where it is felt that these changes have led to other, more valuable results. Even if no modification seems appropriate, the re-examination will always serve the useful purpose of reminding the writers of overall goals. Secondly, work should be begun on the construction of a test-question pool. Progress tests will be beginning, and the items in these can be thrown into this pool. The construction of this pool is the construction of the operational version of the goals. Consequently it should be scrutinized at the same time as re-examination of goals occurs. Even though the project is only at the stage of finishing the first unit of a projected ten-unit curriculum, it is entirely appropriate to be formulating questions of the kind that it is proposed to include in the final examination on the final unit, or for that matter, in a follow-up quiz. It is a commonplace that in the light of formulating such questions, the conception of the goals of the course will be altered. It is undesirable to require that substantial time be given to this activity, but it is typically not "undue influence" to encourage thinking about course goals in terms of "What kind of question would tap this learning achievement in the final examination or in a follow-up test?"

At times the answer to this will rightly be "None at all!" for not all values in a course manifest themselves in the final or later examinations. But where they do *not* thereby manifest themselves, some indication should be given of the time of manner in which they might be expected to be detectable, as in career choices, adult attitudes, etc.

The third activity that should commence at some intermediate stage is that of getting some external judgement as to the cohesiveness of the alleged goals, the actual content, and the test-question pool. There is no need at all for the individual judge at this task to be a professional evalu-

ator, and professional evaluators are frequently extremely bad at this. A good logician, an historian of science, a professional in the subject-matter field, an educational psychologist, or a curriculum expert, may be good at this or again they may not. The necessary skill, a very striking one when located, is not co-extensive with any standard professional requirement. This is an area where appointments should not be made without trial periods. It is worth considering whether the activities of this individual, at least in a trial period, may be best conducted without face-to-face confrontation with the project team. A brief written report may be adequate to indicate the extent of possible useful information from the source at this stage. But at some stage, and the earlier the better, this kind of activity is essential if gross divergences between (a) espoused, (b) implicit, and (c) tested-for goals are to be avoided. Not only can a good analyst prevent sidetracking of the project by runaway creative fervor, misconceptions of its actual achievement, etc., but he can provide a valuable stimulus to new lines of development. Ultimately, the justification of psychotherapy does not lie in the fact that the analyst felt he was doing the patient some good, but in the fact that he was; and the same applies to curricular research. Supposing that this procedure is followed throughout, we will end up with an oversize question pool which should then be examined for comprehensiveness as well as specificity. That is, one should be prepared to say that any significant desired outcome of the course will show up on the answers to these questions; and that what does show up will (normally) only come from the course. Possession of this pool has various important advantages. In the first and second place, it is an operational encapsulation of the goals of the course, if the various cross-checks on its construction have been adequate, which can be used to give the students an idea of what is expected of them as well as to provide a pool from which the final examinations can be constructed. In the third place it can be used by the curriculum-developer to get an extremely detailed picture of his own success (and the success of the cross-checks on pool construction) by administering a different random sample of questions from this pool to each student in a curriculum-check, instead of administering a given random sample to every student as justice requires in a final examination.[3]

What has been described is the bare bones of an adequate mediated evaluation. Now we have made some reference to content characteristics as one of the types of goals, because it is frequently the case that a particular curriculum group argues

3. See Cronbach, ibid., p. 242.

that one of the merits of its output is its superiority as a representation of contemporary advanced thinking about the subject. The natural way to test this is to have the course read through by some highly qualified experts in the field. It is obvious that special difficulties arise over this procedure. For the most that we can learn from this is that the course does not contain any lies, any distortions of the best contemporary views, or gross deficiencies with respect to them. There remains the question, as the fundamentalist would be the first to point out, of the extent to which the material is being communicated. Even a course with gross oversimplifications, professionally repugnant though it may be to the academic expert, may be getting across a better idea of the truth than its highbrow competitor. The amount of transferred material we infer from the elaborate apparatus of the final test, follow-ups, attitude inventories etc., some details of which are elaborated in a later section. The real advantage of the preceding methodology is to provide a means for making it possible to convert a set of results on the tests into an absolute evaluation, by making reasonably sure that the tests test the goals, one of which may be professional modernity, which may be partly judged by expert reports on the text material, insofar as the tests show this to be transferred fairly uniformly.

A number of further refinements on the above outline are extremely desirable, and in any serious study necessary. Essentially, we need to know about the success of three connected matching problems; first, the match between goals and course content, second, the match between goals and examination content, and third, the match between course content and examination content. Technically we only need to determine two of these in order to be able to evaluate the third; but in fact there are great advantages in attempting to get an estimate of each independently, in order to reduce the error range. We have talked as if one person or group might make each of these matching estimates. It is clearly most desirable that they should all be done independently, and in fact duplicated by independent workers. Only in this way are we likely to be able to track down the real source of disappointing results. Even the P.S.S.C. study, which has been as thoroughly tested as most recent curriculum projects, has nowhere approached the desirable level of analysis indicated here.

In general, of course, the most difficult problem in tests and measurement theory is the problem of construct validity, and the present problem is essentially an exercise in construct validity. The problem can be ignored, but only by someone who is prepared to accept immediately the consequence that their supposed goals cannot be regarded as met by the course, or that their examinations do not test what the course teaches, or that the examinations do not test the values/materials that are supposed to be imparted by the course. There are, in practice, many ways in which one can implement the need for comparisons here described; the use of Q-sorts and R-sorts, matching and projective tests for the analysts, etc. In one way or another the job has to be done—if we are going to do a mediated evaluation.

The Possibility of Bypassing Goal Evaluation

The pure consequentialist, the "fundamentalist," tends to watch the intricacies of this kind of experimental design with glee, for he believes that the whole idea of bringing in goal- or content-assessment is not only an irrelevant but an extremely unreliable procedure for doing the job of course evaluation. In his view it isn't very important to examine what a teacher says he is doing, or what the students say he is doing (or they are learning), or even what the teacher says in class; the only important data is what the student says (does, believes, etc.) at the end of the course that he wouldn't have said at the beginning (or, to be more precise, would not have said at the end if he had not taken this course). In short, says the fundamentalist, let's see what the course does, and let's not bother with the question of whether it had good intentions.

But the fundamentalist has difficulties of his own. He cannot avoid the construct validity issue entirely, that is, he cannot avoid the enormous difficulties involved in correctly describing *at a useful level of generality* what the student has learned. It is easy enough to give the exact results of the testing in terms of the percentage of the students who gave certain answers to each specific question: but what we need to know is whether we can say, in the light of their answers, that they have a *better* understanding of the elements of astronomy, or the chemical-bond approach to chemistry, or the ecological approach to biology. And it is a long way from data about answers to questions, to that kind of conclusion. It is not *necessary* for the route to lie through a discussion of goals—the fundamentalist is quite right about this. But if it does *not* lie through a discussion of goals, then we shall not have available the data that we need (a) to distinguish between importantly different explanations of success or failure, (b) to give reasons for using the new text or curriculum to those whose explicit aim *is* the provision of better understanding of the chemical-bond approach. For example, if we attempt a fundamentalist approach to evaluating a curriculum, and discover that the material retained and regurgitated by the student is regraded as grossly inadequate by the subject-matter specialists, we have no idea whether this is due to an inadequacy in the goals of the curriculum-makers, or to imperfections in their curriculum with respect to these goals, or to deficiencies in their examinations with respect to either of the preceding. And thus we cannot institute a remedial program —our only recourse is to start all over. Fundamentalism can be a costly simplification.

Suppose that we follow a fundamentalist approach and have the students' performance at the end of the course, and only this, rated by an external judge. Who do we pick for a judge? The answer to that question will apparently reveal a commitment on our own part to certain goals. The evaluator will have to relate the students' performance to *some* criterion, whether it is his conception of an adequate *professional* comprehension, or what he thinks it is reasonable to expect a *tenth-grader* to understand, or what somebody should understand who will *not* continue to college, etc. The fundamentalist is right in saying that we can dispense with any discussion of goals and still discover exactly what students have learnt, and right to believe that the latter is the most important variable; but he is mistaken if he supposes that we can in general give the kind of description of what is learnt that is valuable for our purposes without any reference to goals. At some stage, someone is going to have to decide what counts as adequate comprehension for students at a particular level, for a particular subject, and then apply this decision to the non-evaluative descriptions of what the students have learnt, in order to come up with the overall evaluation. At this stage of the debate between the supporter of fundamental and mediated evaluation, the latter would seem to be having the best of it, particularly since there are certain goals that can be (a) incorporated into a course (b) judged as worth incorporating by subject-matter authorities, but which (c) are not such as to show up in an appropriate kind of final examination at the end of a particular year. But the issue is not so one-sided; the fundamentalist is performing an invaluable service in reminding us of the potential irresponsibility of producing "elegant," "up-to-date," "rigorous" curricula if these qualities are not coming through to the students. We can take them on faith insofar as they are recognized as being the frosting on the cake; but we can't take the food-value of the cake on faith. The *amount* of goal analysis that is absolutely necessary in order to provide a summative evaluator with the basis for a value-judgement about the curriculum is very, very little compared with the amount that a thorough mediated evaluation involves. It is, after all, more important to put time and money

into deciding whether what the student has acquired is a misconception of the nature of electric current than whether the curriculum-writer has inadvertently incorporated some minor misconception of it into his curriculum. The real alternative which the fundamentalist presents is the use of an academic evaluator who is asked to look at the exact performance of the class on each question and at the pool from which the questions were drawn, and from these directly assess the adequacy of the course to the subject as he sees it. Such an evaluator makes his evaluations by reference to a criterion of *merit,* but this is not the same as saying that he presupposes something about the goals of the course. He may think it *unlikely* that a course should be much good (in terms of his criteria) unless it had his criteria as explicit or implicit goals, but he is not at all committed to such a claim. He *is* committed to the view that certain goals are or would be *desirable,* but they may be goals that no course-maker has ever employed. So there is no contradiction in the fundamentalist view that we do not have to have or evaluate goals in order to evaluate a course, and he is certainly right in believing that bringing them in makes for an invalid or very complex design. Yet *sometimes we have good practical reasons for doing so.*

In conclusion, it should be clear that a strong case can be made for incorporating the procedure described above as part of any good curriculum project, whether or not we use mediated evaluation. Doing so will of course help to make a good mediated evaluation feasible. In addition, however, it should be noted that an equally thorough analysis is required of the *results* of the students' tests, and not only of the course content. It is not at all adequate to go to great trouble setting up and cross-analyzing the goals, tests, and content of a curriculum and then attempt to use a percentage figure as the indication of goal achievement (unless the figure happens to be pretty close to 100% or 0%). This kind of gross approach is no longer acceptable as evaluation. The performance of the students on the final tests, as upon the tests at intermediate stages, must be analyzed in order to determine the exact locations of shortcomings of comprehension, shortages of essential facts, lack of practice in basic skills, etc. Percentages are not very important. It is the *nature* of the mistakes that is important in evaluating the curriculum, and in rewriting it. The technique of the large question pool provides us with an extremely refined instrument for locating deficiencies in the curriculum. But this instrument can only be exploited fully if evaluation of the results is itself handled in a refined way, with the same use of independent judges, putative generalizations about the nature of the mistakes being cross-matched, etc. It should be clear that the task of proper evaluation of curriculum materials is an enormous one. The use of essay type questions, the development and use of novel instruments, the use of reports by laboratory-work supervisors, the colligation of all this material into specially developed rating schemata, all of this is expensive and time-consuming. In a later section some consideration of the consequences of this picture of the scale of evaluation activities will be undertaken. At this point, however, it becomes necessary to look into a further and final divergence of approaches.

Comparative versus Non-Comparative Evaluation

The history of attempts to evaluate recent curricular reforms has been remarkably uniform; comparing students taking the old curriculum with students taking the new one, it usually appears that students using the new curriculum do rather better on the examinations designed for that curriculum and rather worse on those designed for the old curriculum, while students using the old curriculum perform in the opposite way. Certainly, there is a remarkable absence of striking improvements on the same criteria (with some exceptions, of which the most notable is the performance of students in studies of good programmed texts). Initially, one's tendency is to feel that the mountain has laboured and brought forth a mouse—and that it is a positive mouse and not a negative one entirely depends upon the evaluation of the goals (and hence of the examinations). A legitimate reaction is to look very seriously into the question of whether one should not weight judgement of content and goals by subject-matter experts as being a great deal more important than small differences in level of performance on these criteria. If we do this, then relatively minor improvements in performance, on the right goals, become very valuable, and in these terms the new curriculum looks considerably better. Whether this alteration of weights can really be justified is a matter that needs very serious investigation; it requires a rather careful analysis of the real importance to the understanding and use of contemporary physics, as it is seen by physicists, of the missing elements in the old curriculum. It is all too tempting to feel that the re-weighting must be correct because one is so thoroughly convinced that the new course is better.

Another legitimate reaction is to wonder whether the examinations are really doing a good job testing the depth of understanding of the people trained on the new curriculum. Here the use of the over-size question pool becomes extremely important. Cronbach speaks of a 700-item pool (without flinching!) and this is the kind of order

of magnitude that makes sense in terms of an exhaustive evaluation of a one or two-year curriculum. Whether this reaction reveals a legitimate basis for increasing the measure of importance of the difference between the students groups using the new and old curricula will depend upon the results of further tests using a thoroughly justified and much enlarged pool. Again, it is going to be tempting to put items into the pool that reflect mere differences of terminology in the new course, for example. Of course if the pool consists mainly of questions of that kind, the new curriculum-students will do much better. But their superiority will be entirely illusory. Cronbach warns us against this risk of course-dependent terminology, although he goes too far in segregating understanding from terminology (this point is taken up below). So here, too, we must be certain to use external evaluators in the construction or assessment of the question pool.

Other illegitimate reactions run from the charming suggestion that such results simply demonstrate the weaknesses of evaluation techniques, to a more interesting suggestion implicit in Cronbach's paper. He says:

Since group comparisons give equivocal results, I believe that a formal study should be designed primarily to determine the post-course performance of a well-described group, with respect to many important objectives and side-effects.[4]

Notice that Cronbach is not producing an alternative to mediated evaluation, in the way that the fundamentalist is; Cronbach explicitly includes reference to pre-evaluated objectives, i.e., *important* objectives. He is apparently about to suggest a way in which we can avoid comparison, not with goals or objectives, but with another group, supposedly matched on relevant variables. What is this non-comparative alternative procedure for evaluation? He continues:

Ours is a problem like that of the engineer examining a new automobile. He can set himself the task of defining its performance characteristics and its dependability. It would be merely distracting to put his question in the form: "Is this car better or worse than the competing brand?"

It is perfectly true that the automobile engineer *might* just be interested in the question of the performance and dependability of the new automobile. But no automobile engineer ever has had this pure interest, and no automobile engineer ever will have it. Objectives do not become "important" except in a practical context. *Unrealistic* objectives are *not* important. The very measures of the performance and dependability of an automobile and our interest in them spring *entirely*

4. This and the succeeding quotation are from p. 238.

from knowledge of what has and has not so far proved possible, or possible within a certain price-class, or possible with certain interior space, or with a certain overall weight, etc. The same applies in the field of curriculum development. We already have curricula aimed at almost every subject known to man, and there isn't any real interest in producing curricula for curricula's sake; to the extent that there is, there isn't any interest in evaluating them. We are interested in curricula because they may prove to be better than what we now have, in some important way. We may assign someone the task of rating a curriculum on certain variables, without asking them simultaneously to look up the performance of other curricula on these variables. But when we come to *evaluate* the curriculum, as opposed to merely describing its performance, then we inevitably confront the question of its superiority or inferiority to the competition. To say it's a valuable contribution, a desirable or useful course, even to say—in the usual context—that it's very good, is to imply relative merit. Indeed the very scales we use to measure its performance are often percentile scales or others with a built-in comparison.

There are even important reasons for putting the question in its comparative form immediately. Comparative evaluations are often very much easier than non-comparative evaluations, because we can often use tests which yield differences instead of having to find an absolute scale and then eventually compare the absolute scores. If we are discussing chess-teaching courses, for example, we might match two groups for background variables, and then let them play each other off in a round-robin tournament. Attempting to devise a measure of skill of an absolute kind would be a nightmare, but we might easily get consistent and significant differences from this kind of comparative evaluation. Cronbach is not making the fundamentalist's mistake of thinking that one can avoid reference to goals; but he is proposing a kind of neo-fundamentalism which underestimates the implicit comparative element in any field of social engineering including automobile assessment and curriculum evaluation.

Cronbach continues in this paragraph with a line of thought about which there can be no disagreement at all; he points out that in any cases of comparisons between importantly different teaching instruments, no real understanding is gained from the discovery that one of them is notably superior to the other: "No one knows which of the ingredients is responsible for the advantages." But understanding is not our *only* goal in evaluation. We are also interested in questions of support, encouragement, adoption, reward, refinement, etc. And these extremely important questions can be given a useful though in some cases not a complete answer by the mere discovery of superiority. It will be recalled that in an earlier section we argued that the fundamentalist position suffers by comparison with the supporter of mediated evaluation in that his results will not include the data we need in order to locate sources of difficulty, etc. Here Cronbach is arguing that his non-comparative approach will be more likely to give us the data we need for future improvement. But this is not in any way an advantage of the non-comparative method as such. It is simply an advantage of methods in which more variables are examined in more detail. If we want to pin down the exact reasons for differences between programs, it is quite true that "small-scale, well-controlled studies can profitably be used to compare alternative versions of the same course" whereas the large-scale overall comparison will not be so valuable. But that in no way bears on the question whether we have any alternative to comparative studies at some point in our evaluation procedures. In short this is simply an argument that one needs more control groups, and possibly more short-run studies in order to get explanations, than one needs for overall evaluation. It is incontestible; but it does not show that for the purposes of overall evaluation we can or should avoid overall comparison.

One might put the point in terms of the following analogy: in the history of automobile engine design there have been a number of occasions when a designer has turned out an engine that was quite inexplicably superior to the competition—the Kettering GM V8, the Coventry Climax and the Weslake Ford Conversions are well-known examples. At least thirty variables are involved in the design of any new engine and for a long time after these had been in production nobody, including the designer, knew which of them had been mainly responsible for the improvement. But the decision to go into production, the decision to put the further research into the engine that led to finding out what made it great, indeed the beginning of a new era in engine design, required *only the comparative evaluation.* You set a great team to work and you hope they are going to strike gold; after that you stake your claim and start trying to work out the configuration of the lode. This is the way we have to work in any field where there are too many variables and too little time.

*Practical Procedure in
Control-Group Evaluation*

It is a major theme of Cronbach's that control group comparisons in the curriculum game are not really very suitable. We have just seen how this attempt to provide a positive alternative does not develop into a realistic answer in the context of typical evaluation enquiries. It is now appropriate for us to attempt to meet some of the objections that he raises to the control group method if we are to recommend that this be left in possession of the field.

The suggestion that gross comparisons yield only small differences must be met, as indicated above (and as he recommends elsewhere), by increasing the power of the microscope—that is, by increasing the number of items that are being tested, increasing the size of the group in order to get more reliability into differences that do appear, and developing new and more appropriate tests where they seem to be the weakness. But once all this has been said, the fact remains that it is probably the case that we shall have to proceed in terms of rather small differences; that producing large differences will probably require a multiple-push approach, attacking not only the curriculum but the student-grouping procedures, the teacher presentation, the classroom time allocation, and above all the long-term effects that an attack on every subject in the school curriculum will eventually produce for us, a general increase in the level of interest and preparedness. This is not too depressing a prospect, and it is exactly paralleled in that other field in which we attempt to change human behaviour by applying pressure on the subjects for a few hours a week over a period of one or several years—the field of psychotherapy. We are perhaps too used to the discovery of miracle drugs or technological breakthroughs in the aero-space field to realize how atypical this is of progress in general. In the automobile engineering field, to stay with Cronbach's example, it is well known that developing a good established design yields better results than introducing a radical and promising new design in about twice as many cases as engineers under forty are willing to believe. What one may reasonably expect in the way of progress is not great leaps and bounds, but steady improvement. Cronbach says that "formally designed experiments pitting one course against another are rarely definitive enough to justify their cost" but this is just the kind of knowledge that we need to have. If we have really satisfied ourselves that we are using good tests of every criterion variable that matters (and of course we usually have a number in the follow-up series that make this kind of conclusion impossible for a few years) then to discover parity of performance *is* to have discovered something extremely informative.

Of course, we cannot conclude from this that all the techniques involved in the new curriculum are worthless improvements. We must go on to make the micro-studies that will enable us to see whether any one of them is worthwhile. But we have discovered something very significant. Doing the gross comparative study is going to cost the same whatever kind of results we get, and we have to do it. The real question is whether we stop after discovering an insignificant difference, or continue in the direction of further analytical research, as Cronbach enthusiastically recommends (or incorporate the refinements in the original design which will give us the further answer). The impact of his article is to suggest the unimportance of the control group study, whereas the case can only be made for its inadequacy as a *total* approach to *the whole of* curriculum research.[5] We shall here try to provide some practical suggestions for experimental designs that will yield more than a gross comparative evaluation.

A significant part of the reason for Cronbach's despair over comparative studies lies in his recognition that we are unable to arrange for double-blind conditions. "In an educational experiment it is difficult to keep people unaware that they are an experimental group. And it is quite impossible to neutralize the biases of the teacher as those of the doctor are neutralized in the double-blind design. It is thus never certain whether any observed advantage is attributable to the educational innovation as such, or to the greater energy that teachers and students put forth when a method is fresh and 'experimental'" (p. 237). But Cronbach despairs too quickly. The analogy in the medical field is not with drug studies, where we are fortunate enough to be able to achieve double-blind conditions, but with psychotherapy studies where the therapist is obviously endowed with enthusiasm for his treatment, and the patient cannot be kept in ignorance of whether he is getting some kind of treatment. If Cronbach's reasoning is correct, it would not be possible to design an adequate psychotherapy outcome study. But it *is* possible to design such a study, and the way to do it—as far as this point goes—is to make comparisons between a number of therapy groups, in each of which the therapist is enthusiastic, but in each of which the method of therapy is radically different.[6] As far as possible, one should employ forms of therapy in which directly incompatible procedures are adopted. There are already a number on the market which meet this condition in several dimensions, and it is easy enough to develop pseudotherapies which would be promising enough to be enthusiasm-generating for some prac-

---

5. Yet he does agree with the necessity for making the practical decisions between textbooks and similar instructional materials (p. 232), for which nothing less than a valid comparative study is adequate.

6. Other difficulties are discussed in more detail in "The Experimental Investigation of Psychoanalysis" in *Psychoanalysis, Scientific Method and Philosophy*, edited by S. Hook. New York: NYU Press, 1959.

titioners (e.g., newly graduated internists inducted into the experimental program for a short period). The method of differences plus the method of concomitant variations will then enable us to draw straightforward conclusions about whether enthusiasm is the (or a) major factor in therapeutic success, even though double-blind conditions are unobtainable. Nor is this the only kind of design which can do this; many other devices are available, and ingenious experimenters will doubtless think of still more, to enable us to handle this kind of research problem. There is nothing indispensable about the double-blind study.

Now the curriculum field is even more difficult than the psychotherapy field, because, although the average intelligent patient will accept almost any nonsense as a form of therapy, thanks to the witchdoctor tradition, need to be healed, etc., it is not equally easy to convince students and teachers that they are receiving and giving instruction in geometry unless what is going on really is a kind of geometry that makes some sense. And if it is, then interpretation of one of the possible outcomes is ambiguous, i.e., if the two groups do about as well, it may be because enthusiasm does the trick, or because the content is about equally valuable. However, comparative evaluation is still well worthwhile, because if we find a very marked *difference* between the groups, and are able to arrange for enthusiasm on the part of the teachers and students in both cases, we may be reasonably sure that the difference is due to the curriculum content.

Now it is not particularly difficult to arrange for the enthusiasm matching. Corresponding to the cut-rate therapy comparison group, where the therapy procedures are brainstormed up in a day or two of wild free-associating by the experimenters assisted by a lot of beer and some guilt-ridden eclectic therapists, we set up some cut-rate new curricula in the following way. First, we get two bright graduate students or instructors in (let us suppose) economics, give them a vocabulary list for the tenth grade and pay them $500 a chapter for a translation of Samuelson's text into tenth grade language, encouraging them to use their originality in introducing the new ideas. They could probably handle the whole text in a summer and so for a few thousands dollars, including costs of reproducing pilot materials, we have something we could set up against one of the fancier economics curriculum, based on a great deal of high-priced help and laborious field-testing. Then we find a couple of really bright college juniors, majoring in economics, from different colleges, and give *them* a summer to turn their recent experience at the receiving end of introductory economic courses, and their current direct acqaintance with the problems of concept grasp-

ing in the field, into a curriculum outline, not centered around any particular text, filled in as much as possible, of a brief introduction to economics for the tenth grade. And for a third comparison group we locate some enthusiasts for one of the current secondary school texts in "economics" and have them work on a revision of it with the author(s) and in the light of some sampling of their colleagues reactions to the text in class use.

Preferably using the curriculum-makers as teachers (pace State Departments of Education) we then turn them loose on matched comparison groups, in school systems geographically well removed from the ones where we are running the tests on the high-priced spread. We might toss in a little incentive payment in the way of a pre-announced bonus for these groups if they don't get significantly out-scored by the super-curriculum. Now then, if we *still* get a big difference in favor of the super-curriculum, we have good reason for thinking that we have taken care of the enthusiasm variable. Moreover we don't have to pull this stunt with every kind of subject matter, since enthusiasm is presumably reasonably (though definitely not entirely) constant in its effects across subject matter. At any rate, a modest sampling should suffice to check this.

One of the nice things about this kind of comparative study is that even if we get the ambiguous negligible-difference result, which will leave us in doubt as to whether a common enthusiasm is responsible for the result, or whether a roughly comparable job in teaching economics is being done by all curricula, we get a nice economic bonus. If we can whomp up new curricula on a shoestring which are going to produce pretty good results, so much the better: we can do it often and thereby keep up the supply of enthusiasm-stoked project directors, and increase the chances of hitting on some really new big-jackpot approach from a Newton of curriculum reform.

Moreover, still on a shoestring, we can settle the question of enthusiasm fairly quickly even in the event of a tie between the various curricula, by dumping them into the lap of some antagonistic and some neutral teachers to use during the next school term, while on the other hand arranging for the original curriculum-makers to lovingly train a small group of highly selected and innovation-inclined teachers to do the same job. Comparisons between the performance of these two new groups and that of the old ones should enable us to pin down the role of enthusiasm rather precisely, and in addition the no-doubt variable immunity of the various curricula to lack of enthusiasm.

A few obvious elaborations of the above procedures, including an opportunity for the novice curriculum-makers to spend a couple of afternoons on field-testing early sections of their new curriculum, to give them some 'feel' for the speed at which students at this level can grasp new concepts, the use of some care in selecting teachers for their conservatism or lethargy, using self-ratings plus peer-ratings plus attitude inventories, would immediately suggest themselves in the case of an actual study.

The enthusiasm "difficulty" here is simply an example of what we might call *disturbance effects,* of which the placebo effect in medicine and the Hawthorne effect in industrial and social psychology are well-known instances. In each case we are interested in finding out the effects of a certain factor, but we cannot introduce the factor into the experimental situation without producing a disturbance which may itself be responsible for the observed changes. In the drug field, the disturbance consists in the act of giving the patient something which he considers to be a drug, something which does not ordinarily happen to him, and consequently may produce effects of its own, quite apart form the effects of the drug. In the Hawthorne effect, the disturbance is the disruption of, e.g., conditions of work which may suggest to the worker that he is the subject of special study and interest, and *this* may lead to improved output, not the physical changes in the environment that are the intended parameters under study.

The cases so far mentioned are all ones where the beliefs of the subjects are the mediating factor between the disturbance and the ambiguous effects. This is characteristic in the field of psychology, but—as the term "disturbance effect" indicates—the situation is not essentially different from that occurring in technological research where we face problems such as the absorption of heat by a thermometer which thereby alters the temperature that it is supposedly measuring. That is, some of the effect observed (which is here the eventual length of the mercury column) is due to the fact that in order to get the effect at all you have to introduce another physical object into proximity with the measured object, the instrument itself having a certain heat capacity, a factor in whose influence you are not interested in order to find out what you do need to know you eventually have to make an estimate of the magnitude of the disturbance effect. The ingenious double-blind design is only appropriate in certain circumstances, and is only one of many ways in which we can compensate for disturbance effects. It therefore seems unduly pessimistic of Cronbach to suppose that the impossibility of a double-blind in curriculum work is fatal to comparative evaluation. Indeed, when he comes to discuss follow-up studies, he agrees that comparative work is essen-

tial (p. 240). The conclusion seems obligatory that comparative evaluation, whether mediated or fundamental, is the method of choice for evaluation problems.

Comparative Evaluation—The Criteria of Educational Achievement

We may now turn to the problem of specifying in more detail the criteria which should be used in evaluating a teaching instrument. We may retain Bloom's[7] convenient trichotomy of cognitive, affective and motor variables, though we shall often refer to the last two as motivational and physical or non-mental variables, but under the first two of these we shall propose a rather different structure, especially under the knowledge and understanding subdivisions of the cognitive field. It should be stressed at the beginning that the word "knowledge" *can* be used to cover understanding (or comprehension) and even affective conditions, but that it is here used in the sense in which it can be *contrasted* with comprehension and experience or valuation, i.e., in the sense in which we think of it as "mere knowledge." Comprehension or understanding, by contrast, refers to a psychological state involving knowledge, not of one item, nor of several separate items, but of a field. A field or structure is a set of items related in a systematic way, knowledge of the field involving knowledge not only of the items but of their relations. A field is often open-ended in the sense of having potential reference or applicability to an indefinite number of future examples. In this latter case, comprehension involves the capacity to apply to these novel cases the appropriate rule, rubric or concept. A field may be a field of abstract or practical knowledge, of thought or of skills.

With respect to any field of knowledge we can distinguish between a relatively abstract or *conceptual* description of the parameters (which are to occupy the role of dependent variables in our study) and a *manifestation* description, the latter being the next stage towards the specification of the particular tests to be used, which we may call the *operational* description. It is appropriate to describe the criteria at all three levels, although we finally apply only the third, just as it is appropriate to give the steps of a difficult proof in mathematics, because it shows us the *reasons* for adopting the particular final step proposed.

I have followed the usual practice here in listing positive goals (with the possible exception of the example in five) but a word of caution is in order. Although most negatively desired effects

7. B. S. Bloom et al., *Taxonomy of Educational Objectives,* Vols. I, II, and III (forthcoming).

are the absence of positively desired effects, this is not always true, and more generally it is often true that one may wish to alter the weighting of a variable when it drops below a certain level. For example, we may not be worried if we get no change on socialization with a course that is working well in the cognitive domain, and we may give small credit for large gains in this dimension. But if it produces a marked rise in sociopathic behaviour we may regard this as fatal; similarly with respect to forgetting or rejection of material in other subject areas, etc. Another example is discussed below.

A word about originality; this may be manifested in a problem-solving skill, an artistic skill (which combines motor and perceptual and perhaps verbal skills) and in many other ways. It does not seem desirable to make it a separate criterion.

In general, I have tried to reduce the acknowledged overlap amongst the factors identified in Bloom's analysis, and am prepared to pay a price for this desideratum, if such a price must be paid. There are many reasons for avoiding overlap, of which one of the more important and perhaps less obvious ones is that when the comparative weighting of criteria is undertaken for a given subject, independence greatly simplifies the process, since a straight weighting by merit will overweight the hidden loading factors.

There is still a tendency in the literature to regard factual recall and knowledge of terminology with disdain. But for many subjects, a very substantial score on that dimension is an absolutely necessary condition for adequate performance. This is not the same as saying that a sufficiently high score on that scale will compensate for lack of understanding, even where we use a single index compounded from the weighted scores. There are other subjects, especially mathematics and physics, where knowing the terminology requires and hence guarantees a very deep understanding and terminology-free tests are just bad tests. (cf Cronbach, p. 245.)

Conceptual Description of Educational Objectives

1. *Knowledge,* of
   a. Items of specific information including definitions of terms in the field.
   b. Sequences or patterns of items of information including rules, procedures or classifications for handling or evaluating items of information (we are here talking about mere knowledge of the rule and not the capacity to apply it).
2. *Comprehension or Understanding,* of
   a. Internal relationships in the field,[8] i.e., the way in which some of the knowledge claims

are consequences of others and imply yet others, the way in which the terminology applies within the field; in short what might be called understanding of the intrafield syntax of the field or sub-field.
   b. Inter-field relations, i.e., relations between the knowledge claims in this field and those in other fields; what we might call the inter-field syntax.
   c. Application of the field or the rules, procedures and concepts of the field to appropriate examples, where the field is one that has such applications; this might be called the semantics of the field.
3. *Motivation.* (Attitude/values/affect)
   a. Attitudes towards the course, e.g., acoustics.
   b. Attitudes towards the subject, e.g., physics.
   c. Attitudes towards the field, e.g., science.
   d. Attitudes towards material to which the field is relevant, e.g., increased skepticism about usual advertising claims about "high fidelity" from miniature radios (connection with 2c above).
   e. Attitudes towards learning, reading, discussing it, enquiring in general, etc.
   f. Attitudes towards the school.
   g. Attitudes towards teaching as a career, teacher status, etc.
   h. Attitudes towards (feelings about, etc.) the teacher as a person.
   i. Attitude towards class-mates, attitude towards society (obvious further sub-headings).
   j. Attitude towards self, e.g., increase of realistic self-appraisal (which also involves cognitive domain).
4. *Non-Mental Abilities.*
   a. Perceptual.
   b. Psycho-motor.
   c. Motor, including, e.g., some sculpting skills.
   d. Social skills.
5. *Non-Educational Variables.*
   There are a number of non-educational goals, usually implicit, which are served by many courses and even new courses, and some of them are even justifiable in special circumstances as, e.g., in a prison. The crudest example is the "keeps 'em out of mischief" view of schooling. It is realistic to remember that these criteria may be quite important to parents and teachers even if not to children.

---

8. Typically, "the field" should be construed more widely than "the subject" since we are very interested in transfer from one subject to related ones and rate a course better to the extent it facilitates this. In rating applications, we can range very far, e.g., from a course on psychology to reactions to commercials showing white-coated men.

Manifestation Dimensions of
Critical Variables

1. *Knowledge* (in the sense described above) is evinced by
   a. Recital skills.
   b. Discrimination skills.
   c. Completion skills.
   d. Labelling skills.

   Note: Where actual performance changes are not discernible, there may still be some subliminal capacity, manifesting itself in a reduction in re-learning or in future learning to criterion.

2. *Comprehension* is manifested on some of the above types of performance and also on:
   a. Analyzing skills, including laboratory analysis skills, other than motor, as well as the verbal analytic skills, exhibited in criticism, précis, etc.
   b. Synthesizing skills.
   c. Evaluation skills.
   d. Problem-solving skills (speed-dependent and speed-independent).

3. *Attitude* manifestations usually involve simultaneous demonstration of some cognitive acquisition. The kinds of instruments involved are questionnaires, projective tests, Q-sorts, experimental choice situations, and normal lifetime choice situations (choice of college major, career, spouse, friends, etc.). Each of the attitudes mentioned is characteristically identifiable on a passive to active dimension (related to the distinctions expounded on in Bloom, but disregarding extent of systematization of value system which can be treated under meta-cognitive skills).

4. *The Non-Mental Abilities* are all exhibited in performances of various kinds, which again can be either artificially elicited or extracted from life-history. A typical example is the capacity to speak in an organized way in front of an audience, to criticize a point of view not previously heard in an effective way, etc. (this again connects with the ability conceptually described under 2c).

Follow-Up

The time dimension is a crucial element in the analysis of performance and one that deserves an extensive independent investigation. Retention, recall, depth of understanding, extent of imprinting, can all be tested by reapplications of the tests or observations used to determine the instantaneous peak performance, on the dimensions indicated above. However, some follow-up criteria are not repetitions of earlier tests or observations; eventual choice of career, longevity of marriage, extent of adult social service, career success, are relevant

and important variables which require case history investigation. But changes of habits and character are often not separate variables, being simply long-term changes on cognitive and affective scales.

Secondary Effects

A serious deficiency of previous studies of new curricula has been a failure to adequately sample the teacher population. When perfecting a teaching instrument, we cannot justify generalizing from pilot studies unless not only the students but the teachers are fair samples of the intended population. This is one reason for the importance of the studies of interference effects. Just as generalizing has been based upon inadequate analysis of the teacher sample, so criterion discussions have not paid sufficient attention to teacher benefits. It is quite wrong to evaluate a teaching instrument without consideration of the effects on the operator as well as on the subjects. In an obvious sense, the operator *is* one of the subjects.

We may divide secondary effects (i.e., those on others than the students taking the course) into two categories. Direct secondary effects are those arising from direct exposure to the material, and only the teachers and teachers' helpers can be affected in this way. Indirect secondary effects are those effects mediated by someone who exhibits the primary effects.

Effects on the Teacher. A new curriculum may have very desirable effects on up-dating a teacher's knowledge, with subsequent pay-off in various ways including the better education of other classes at a later stage, in which he/she may be using either the old curriculum or the new one. Similarly, it may have very bad effects on the teacher, perhaps through induction of fatigue, or failing to leave her any feeling of status or significant role in the classroom, etc.

It is easy to itemize a number of such considerations, and we really need a minor study of the taxonomy of these secondary effects under each of their several headings. In particular, what I have called the interference effects, e.g., those due to enthusiasm, can be directly valued, as I think they should be—if we include secondary effects in the criteria. Very often the introduction of new curriculum material is tied to teacher in-service training institutes or special in-service training interviews. These of course have effects on the teacher herself with respect to status, self-concept, pay, interests, etc., and indirectly on later students. Many of these effects on the teacher show up in her other activities; at the college level there will normally be some serious reduction of research time resulting from association with an experimental curriculum, and this may have results for promotion expectations in either the positive or the negative direction, depending upon departmental policy. All of these results are effects of the new curriculum, at least for a long time, and in certain circumstances they may be sufficiently important to count rather heavily against other advantages. Involvement with curricula of a highly controversial kind may have such strongly damaging secondary effects as to raise questions as to whether it is proper to refer to it as a good curriculum for schools in the social context in which these secondary effects are so bad.

Indirect Effects on Teacher's Colleagues. Indirect secondary effects are the effects on people other than those directly exposed to the curriculum: once again they may be highly significant. A simple example of an indirect secondary effect involves other members of the staff who may be called upon to teach less attractive courses, or more courses, or whose load may be reduced for reasons of parity, or who may be stimulated by discussions with the experimental group teachers, etc. In many cases, effects of this kind will vary widely from situation to situation, and such effects may then be less appropriately thought of as effects of the curriculum (although even the primary effects of this, i.e., the effects on the students, will vary widely geographically and temporally) but there will sometimes be constancies in these effects which will require recognition as characteristic effects of this particular teaching instrument. This will of course be noticeable in the case of controversial experimental courses, but it will also be significant where the course bears on problems of school administration, relation of the subject to other subjects, and so on. Good evaluation requires some attempt to identify effects of this kind.

Indirect Effects on Other Students. Another indirect secondary effect, only partly covered in the effect of the curriculum on the teacher, is the effect on other students. Just as a teacher may be improved by exposure to a new curriculum, and this improvement may show up in benefits for students that she has in other classes, or at a later period using the old curriculum, etc., so there may be an effect of the curriculum on students *not* in the experimental class through the intermediary of students who are. Probably more pronounced in a boarding school, the communication between students is still a powerful enough instrument in ordinary circumstances for this to be a significant influence. The students may of course be influenced in other ways; there may be additions to the library as a result of the funds available for the new course that represent values for the other students, etc. All of these

are educationally significant effects of the course adoption.

Effects on Administrators. The college administrators may be affected by new teaching instruments in various ways; their powers of appointment may be curtailed, if the teaching instrument's efficiency will reduce faculty, they may acquire increased prestige (or nuisance) through the use of the school as an experimental laboratory, they may find this leads to more (or less) trouble with the parents, the pay-off through more national scholarships may be a value to them, either intrinsically or incidentally to some other end, etc. Again, it is obvious that in certain special cases this variable will be a very important part of the total set that are affected by the new instrument, and evaluation must include some recognition of this possibility. It is not so much the factors common to the use of novel material, but the course-specific effects that particularly require estimation and almost every new science or social studies course has such effects.

Effects on Parents. Effects on the parents are of course well known, but they tend to be regarded as nuisance-generating effects. On the contrary, many such effects should be regarded as part of the adult education program in which this country is remarkably lacking. In some subjects, e.g., Russian, this is unlikely to have a very significant effect, but in the field of problems of democracy, elementary accounting, and literature, this may be a most important effect.

Effects on the School or College. Many of these are covered above, particularly under the heading of effects on the administrator, but there are of course some effects that are more readily classified under this heading, such as improvement in facilities, support, spirit, applicants, integration, etc.

Effects on the Taxpayer. These are partly considered in the section on costs below, but certain points are worth mentioning. We are using the term taxpayer and not rate-payer here to indicate a reference to the total tax structure, and the most important kinds of effects here are the possibility of very large-scale emulation of a given curriculum reform project, which in toto, especially with evaluation on the scale envisioned here, is likely to add a substantial amount to the overall tax burden. For the unmarried or childless taxpayer, this will be an effect which may with some grounds be considered a social injustice. Insofar as evaluation of a national armament program must be directly tied to questions of fair and unfair tax loads, the same must be applied in any national considerations of very large-scale curriculum reforms.

Values and Costs

Range of Utility

No evaluation of a teaching instrument can be considered complete without reference to the range of its applicability and the importance of improvement of education in that range. If we are particularly concerned with the underprivileged groups, then it will be a value of considerable importance if our new teaching instrument is especially well adapted for that group. It may not be very highly generalizable, but that may be offset by the social utility of the effects actually obtained. Similarly, the fact that the instrument is demonstrably usable by teachers with no extra training, sharply increases its short-term utility. Indeed it may be so important as to make it one of the goals of instrument development, for short-run high-yield improvements.

Moral Considerations

Considerations of the kind that are normally referred to as moral have a place in the evaluation of new curricula. If the procedures for grading, or treating students in class, although pedagogically effective, are unjust, then we may have grounds for judging the instrument undesirable which are independent of any directly testable consequences. If one conceives of morality as a system of principles founded upon the maximizing of extreme long-run social utility, based on an egalitarian axiom, then moral evaluations should show up somewhere else on the criteria given above, as primary or secondary effects. But the time lag before they do so may be so long as to make it appropriate for us to introduce this as a separate category. There are a number of other features of teaching instruments that may be reacted to morally; "the dehumanizing influence of teaching machines" is a description often used by critics who are partly affected by moral considerations; whether misguidedly or not is another question. Curricula stressing the difference in performance on the standardized intelligence tests of Negro and white children have been attacked as morally undesirable, and the same has been said of textbooks in which the role of the United States in world history has been viewed somewhat critically. Considerations like this will of course show up on a content-mediated approach to evaluation but they deserve a separate entry because the reaction is not to the truth or insight provided by the program, but to some other consequences of providing what may well be truths or insights, namely the consequences involving the welfare of the society as a whole.

Costs

The costing of curriculum adoption is a rather poorly researched affair. Enthusiasts for new curricula tend to overlook a large number of secondary costs that arise, not only in the experimental situation, but in the event of large-scale adoption. Evaluation, particularly of items for purchase from public funds, has a strong committment to examination of the cost situation. Most of the appropriate analysis can be best obtained from an experienced industrial accountant, but it is perhaps worth mentioning here that even when the money has been provided for the salaries of curriculum-makers and field-testers and in-service training institutes there are a number of other costs that are not easily assessed, such as the costs of re-arrangements of curriculum, differential loads on other faculty, diminished availability for supervisory chores of the experimental staff (and in the long run, where the instrument requires more of the teacher's time than the one it replaces, this becomes a permanent cost), the "costs" of extra demands on *student time* (presumably at the expense of other courses they might be taking), and of energy drain on the faculty as they acquire the necessary background and skills in the new curriculum, and so on through the list of other indirect effects, many of which have cost considerations attached, whether the cost is in dollars or some other valuable.

Another Kind of Evaluation— "Explanatory Evaluation"

Data relevant to the variables outlined in the preceding section are the basic elements for almost all types of evaluation. But sometimes, as was indicated in the first section, evaluation refers to *interpretation* or *explanation* in a different sense. While not considering this to be a primary or even a fully proper sense, it is clear from the literature that there is some tendency to extend the term in this direction. It seems to be preferable to distinguish between evaluation, and the attempt to discover an explanation of certain kinds of result, even when both are using the same data. Explanation-hunting is sometimes part of process research and sometimes part of other areas in the field of educational research. When we turn to considerations of this kind, data of a quite different variety is called for. We shall, for example, need to have information about specific skills and attitudes of the students who perform in a particular way, we shall call upon the assistance of experts who, or tests which, may be able to demonstrate that the failure of a particular teaching instrument is due to its use of an inappropriately advanced vocabulary, rather than to any lack of comprehensible organization. Evaluation of this kind, however, is and should be secondary to evaluation of the kinds discussed previously, for the same reason that therapy is secondary to diagnosis.

Conclusions

The aim of this paper has been to move one step further in the direction of an adequate methodology of curriculum evaluation. It is clear that taking this step involves considerable complication of the model of adequate evaluation study, by comparison with what has passed under this heading all too frequently in the past. Further analysis of the problem may reveal even greater difficulties that must be sorted out with an attendant increase in complexity. Complex experiments on the scale we have been discussing are very expensive in both time and effort. But it has been an important part of the argument of this paper that no substitutes will do. If we want to know the answers to the questions that matter about new teaching instruments, we have got to do an experiment which will yield those answers. The educational profession is suffering from a completely inappropriate conception of the cost scale for educational research. To develop a new automobile engine or a rocket engine is a very, very expensive business despite the extreme constancy in the properties of physical substances. When we are dealing with a teaching instrument such as a new curriculum or classroom procedure, with its extreme dependence upon highly variable operators and recipients, we must expect considerably more expense. The social payoff is enormously more important, and this society can, in the long run, afford the expense. At the moment its deficiency is trained manpower, so that short-term transition to the appropriate scale of investigation is possible only in rare cases. But the long-term transition must be made. We are dealing with something more important and more difficult to evaluate than an engine design, and we are attempting to get by with something like one percent of the cost of developing an engine design. The educational profession as a whole has a primary obligation to recognize the difficulty of good curriculum development, with its essential concomitant evaluation, and to begin a unified attack on the problem of financing the kind of improvement that may help us towards the goal of a few million enlightened citizens on the earth's surface, even at the expense of one on the surface of Mars.

CHAPTER 6

THE CRITERION PROBLEM IN THE EVALUATION OF INSTRUCTION: ASSESSING POSSIBLE, NOT JUST INTENDED OUTCOMES[1]

Samuel Messick

This paper will discuss two major classes of criterion variables that should be taken into account in the evaluation of instruction—namely, cognitive styles and affective reactions. I emphasize these two types of variables because of the kinds of questions I think should be asked in evaluation studies—questions that stem from particular views about the diversity of human performance and about the role of values in educational research.

Individual Differences in Response to Educational Treatments

Traditional questions in education and psychology have frequently spawned answers that are either downright wrong, in that they summarize findings "on the average" in situations where a hypothetical "average person" doesn't exist, or else are seriously lacking in generality, in that they fail to take account of the multiplicity of human differences and their interactions with environmental circumstances.

Consider the kind of "horse race" question typical of much educational research of past decades: Is textbook A better than textbook B? Is teacher A better than teacher B? Or, more generally, is treatment A better than treatment B? Such questions are usually resolved empirically by comparing average gains in specific achievement for students receiving treatment A with average gains for students receiving treatment B. But suppose treatment A is better for certain kinds of students and treatment B better for other kinds of students. Depending upon the mix of students in the two groups, the two treatments might exhibit negligible differences on the average when they actually produce wildly different effects upon individuals. A completely different evaluation of the treatments might have resulted if some other questions had been asked, such as "Do these treatments interact with personality and cognitive characteristics of the students or with factors in their educational history or family background to produce differential effects upon achievement? Do certain student characteristics correlate with gains in achievement differently in one treatment than in the other?"

From the vantage point of differential psychology, it would appear that educational researchers frequently fail to take proper account of consistent individual differences. They tend to assess treatment effects on the average, presuming that variations in performance around the average are unstable fluctuations rather than expressions of stable personal characteristics. Developmental psychologists, on the other hand, survey essentially the same arena with their own limited purview. They not only frequently make the same assumption about individual variation but the obverse one about environmental variation as well. They seek to uncover general laws of learning and cognition for the generic human being—at best a small number of different laws for assorted idealized types of individuals—and to map the course of mental development *on the average*, where now the average is taken over all the differential educational experiences and environmental impacts that might interact with current psychological status to moderate change.

To evaluate educational treatments in terms of their effects upon individual students requires not only the assessment of variables directly related to the specific goals of the treatment, such as achievement level, but also the assessment of those personal and environment variables that may moderate the learning. Similarly, to understand how a cognitive or personality characteristic develops from one time to another, i.e., to formulate the psychology of its development over a fixed period, may require not only information about individual differences in the trait in relation to other traits at the two times, but also information about the educational treatments and environmental variations accompanying the change and perhaps even information about the course of the trait's previous development and about the personal, social, and environmental factors associated with prior growth.

If concerns about personal characteristics and concerns about social and environmental characteristics were systematically combined with concerns about the effects of educational treatments, a conceptual framework for educational and psychological research would result from which questions about interactions among these components would flow naturally—questions such as "What dimensions of educational experience are associated with growth on dimensions of cognitive functioning or with changes in attitude or affective involvement, and what social and environmental factors moderate these effects?" The need for such a multivariate interactional approach derives from the view that we are dealing in education and psychology with a complicated *system* composed of differentiated subsystems and that even in research on presumably circumscribed issues it is important to recognize the interrelatedness of personal, social, environmental, and educational factors. In such a system it is possible that compensating trade-offs among variables will occur under different conditions to produce similar effects and that particular outcomes will frequently be multiply-determined and sometimes over-determined. This is not to say that overall main effects due to specific education treatments will not occur or that no personal characteristics will prove to be general over situations, but rather that interactions between treatment variables and personal or environmental factors are likely and should be systematically appraised in evaluating treatment effects.

The major thrust of this approach is that evaluations of the significance of changes in performance or attitude over a given time period as a presumed function of a specific instructional program should take into account other changes in human characteristics also transpiring during the same period and other environmental influences active at the same time. Educational growth should not be viewed as independent of human growth, and the effects of instructional experiences should not be viewed as independent of other life experiences.

These multiple influences upon behavior should not only be considered at the grand level of systems analysis, but at much simpler levels as well —such as in developing and evaluating a measure of academic achievement—where we sometimes forget that even specific responses are frequently complexly determined and buffeted by many en-

vironmental influences. Consider a researcher who attempts to assess quantitative reasoning in a lower class, culturally disadvantaged child by inquiring, "If you had seven apples and I asked you for two, how many would you have left?" The answer comes quickly and triumphantly— "Seven!" Hopefully, of course, we would never use such loose phrasing in any of our questions, but it serves to illustrate the point. We often fail to appreciate the extent to which the respondent's affect will be engaged by the content of a question and the extent to which personal, social, and economic factors will focus his attention upon problems quite different from the ones we thought we had posed.

When the efficacy of instruction is evaluated in such a multivariate framework, cognitive styles and affective reactions assume particular interest in three ways: (1) as personal characteristics that may interact with treatment variables to moderate learning, retention, and transfer; (2) as dispositions to be monitored to detect any possibly undesirable side effects of instruction; and (3) as qualities to be fostered either directly as specific objectives of the instructional program or indirectly as by-products of other efforts. This latter possibility of fostering stylistic and affective qualities appears to be consonant with general educational aims as far as affects are concerned, for who would dispute the desirability of developing positive attitudes toward school or learning or subject matter or self. But with respect to cognitive styles there is much less consensus, for we are not sure whether to emphasize particular styles or flexibility in the use of multiple styles, nor are we sure what the options are for changing styles. This problem will be discussed in more detail later after we have had an opportunity to consider the nature of cognitive styles and some reasons why individual differences in characteristic modes of cognition are relevant to educational practice.

The Role of Values in the Science of Education

To suggest that cognitive styles and affects might serve as additional criteria in the evaluation of instruction is of course to make a value judgment. But value judgments abound in the evaluation process, as its name implies, and appear to be made with hesitancy only at the end of the enterprise when a decision about the worth of the program is required. Value judgments are usually made explicitly when the specific goals of the instructional program are outlined and when particular standards of excellence are accepted for judging success, but they are also made, usually implicitly, when criterion instruments are selected to assess the intended outcomes, when additional criterion measures are chosen to appraise side effects, when particular teaching methods or media or materials are scrutinized during the course of instruction, when certain types of transactions between the student and other persons are observed[2]—in short, whenever a subset of the possible alternatives is marked for special attention. The selection of a subset from the range of possibilities implies priorities, that some things are more important to assess than others. But it is not enough to label such decisions "value judgments" and then proceed with the assessment. If it were, evaluation would be a straightforward affair indeed: We could specify the goals of the instructional program as we intend them and select criterion measures to assess those outcomes that seem directly relevant to the stated objectives. This is what Scriven has called "estimation of goal achievement" in contradistinction to evaluation proper. All appraisal in this case is relative to the stated goals, and the concern is with how well the program achieves its intended objectives. In addition, however, we should inquire to what extent the objectives are worth achieving and, in general, should endeavor to include in the evaluation process provisions for evaluating the value judgments, especially the goals.[3]

An important step in this direction is to exhibit concern about *possible* outcomes and not just *intended* outcomes. Evaluation comprises two major functions—one is to ascertain the nature and size of the effects of the treatment and the other is to decide whether the observed effects attain acceptable standards of excellence. These two components have been termed "description" and "judgment" by Stake.[4] The point here is that the descriptive phase of evaluation should be as complete as our art and resources can make it. In this instance the evaluation specialist should be, in Bruner's words, a "diviner and delineator of the possible"—he should "provide the full range of alternatives to challenge society to choice."[5] This attempt to describe the full range of possible effects of instruction is an important prerequisite for the judgmental phase of evaluation, since it might unearth alternatives that ought to be weighed in reaching the final appraisal. As Henry Dyer has emphasized, "Evaluating the *side* effects of an educational program may be even more important than evaluating its intended effects." Dyer also pointed out that such broad assessment of the possible effects of an educational program should contribute to an evaluation of the goals of the program. Inverting the customary prescription that one must determine the objectives of instruction before one can develop mea-

sures of instructional outcomes, Dyer suggested that it may not be possible to decide what the objectives ought to be until one has first measured the outcomes.[6]

In practice, of course, evaluation studies rarely approach completeness. We in fact include in any feasible assessment program only a selection of criterion variables—those that reflect our current view of priorities (or our attempt to represent several diverse viewpoints). But again it is not enough just to admit that practical considerations force us to be selective. If we are to develop a science of evaluation, we should endeavor to justify these value judgments on rational grounds not only in terms of the specific objectives of the instructional program in question but in terms of goals of education in American society that transcend the particular course.[7] In this exercise it is important not only to explicate the separate value judgments implicit in the choice of each criterion variable, but also to consider interrelations among them. Values rarely exist in isolation. They are typically part of organized frameworks called ideologies that provide characteristic ways of thinking about man and society. In considering the assortment of variables to be assessed in a particular evaluation study and the goals that the instruction might potentially serve, we should inquire to what extent do the possible outcomes reflect divergent value systems that "need to be reconciled or compromised and to what extent do they represent simply different frames of reference for compatible goals."[8]

Incidentally, the particular teaching methods chosen for use in an instructional program should also be evaluated for their compatibility with muliple goals and values. It sometimes happens that even though two goals are reasonably compatible, the method of instruction selected tends to foster one aim and hinder the other. Wallach, for example, has expressed concern that modern methods of teaching, especially those using programmed materials and teaching machines, so emphasize accuracy of responding that the student is likely to acquire a generalized intolerance of error, with a consequent decline in his originality of thinking. Some other method or combination of methods might be used instead that would develop facility in the analysis of logical implications, as desired, but would not at the same time diminish fluency in the generation of conceptual possibilities.[9]

Since educational values derive from broader systems of social values, it is appropriate to evaluate goals and criteria for instruction not only in terms of specific educational implications but also in terms of more general social implications. The suggestion in the present instance that cognitive styles and affective reactions be used as criterion variables in the evaluation of instruction, for example, should be upheld in precisely such terms, but a consideration of the educational and social implications of these dimensions must await a more detailed discussion of the nature of the variables themselves.

Cognition, Affect, and Personality

In recent years several dimensions of individual differences in the performance of cognitive tasks have been isolated that appear to reflect consistencies in the manner or form of cognition, as distinct from the content of cognition or the level of skill displayed in the cognitive performance.[10] These dimensions have been conceptualized as *cognitive styles,* which represent a person's typical modes of perceiving, remembering, thinking, and problem solving. Some examples of these dimensions are:

1. *Field independence vs. field dependence*—"an analytical, in contrast to a global, way of perceiving (which) entails a tendency to experience items as discrete from their backgrounds and reflects ability to overcome the influence of an embedding context."[11]

2. *Scanning*—a dimension of individual differences in the extensiveness and intensity of attention deployment, leading to individual variations in the vividness of experience and the span of awareness.[12]

3. *Breadth of categorizing*—consistent preferences for broad inclusiveness, as opposed to narrow exclusiveness, in establishing the acceptable range for specified categories.[13]

4. *Conceptualizing styles*—individual differences in the tendency to categorize perceived similarities and differences among stimuli in terms of many differentiated concepts, which is a dimension called *conceptual differentiation,*[14] as well as consistencies in the utilization of particular conceptualizing approaches as bases for forming concepts (such as the routine use in concept formation of thematic or functional relations among stimuli as opposed to the analysis of descriptive attributes or the inference of class membership[15]).

5. *Cognitive complexity vs. simplicity*—individual differences in the tendency to construe the world, and particularly the world of social behavior, in a multidimensional and discriminating way.[16]

6. *Reflectiveness vs. impulsivity*—individual consistencies in the speed with which hypotheses are selected and information processed, with impulsive subjects tending to offer the first answer that occurs to them, even though it is frequently incorrect, and reflective subjects tending to ponder various possibilities before deciding.[17]

7. *Leveling vs. sharpening*—reliable individual variations in assimilation in memory. Subjects at the leveling extreme tend to blur similar memories and to merge perceived objects or events with similar but not identical events recalled from previous experience. Sharpeners, at the other extreme, are less prone to confuse similar objects and, by contrast, may even judge the present to be less similar to the past than is actually the case.[18]

8. *Constricted vs. flexible control*—individual differences in susceptibility to distraction and cognitive interference.[19]

9. *Tolerance for incongruous or unrealistic experiences*—a dimension of differential willingness to accept perceptions at variance with conventional experience.[20]

Stylistic consistencies have also been observed in the differential tendencies of individuals to err by omission or by commission on memory tasks.[21] In addition, several dimensions deriving from the work of Thurstone, Cattell, and Guilford, although usually considered to fall within the purview of intellectual abilities, also reflect such potential exemplars of style or mode of cognition as speed, flexibility, divergence, convergence, and fluency.

Cognitive styles, for the most part, are information-processing habits. They are characteristic modes of operation which, although not necessarily completely independent of content, tend to function across a variety of content areas. Before considering some possible implications of cognitive styles for educational practice, let me discuss one of them in more detail to give you some feeling for their generality and breadth of operation. For these purposes, the dimension of analytic vs. global attitude offers the best example, since it has been extensively studied in various forms for over twenty years, primarily by H. A. Witkin and his colleagues but also in other laboratories around the globe.

Witkin's early work emphasized individual differences in the characteristic ways in which people perceive both the world and themselves. One of the test situations used was a tilted room in which the subject, seated in a tilted chair, must adjust his body to the true upright. Reliable individual differences were found in the ability to do this; i.e., some individuals were reliably more susceptible than others to the influence of the surrounding tilted room. In another test, the subject was seated in a completely dark room and confronted with a luminous rod surrounded by a luminous picture frame; his task was to set the rod to the true vertical position while the frame was set aslant. Again, reliable individual differences were found in the ability to do this, and a substantial correlation was noted between the two tests: the subjects who had difficulty withstanding the influence of the surrounding room while adjusting their body to the upright also had difficulty withstanding the influence of the surrounding frame while adjusting the rod to the upright. These individual differences were initially conceptualized in terms of a differential reliance upon visual cues obtained from the external field as opposed to kinesthetic cues obtained from the subject's own body.

This interpretation of field vs. body orientation was extended to a more general dimension of perceptual analysis, however, when it was found that subjects who had difficulty overcoming the influence of the tilted room and the tilted frame also had difficulty overcoming the influence of superimposed complex designs when asked to find hidden simple forms in an embedded-figures test. This extended conception of the dimension was now termed "field dependence vs. field independence": the perception of relatively field-dependent subjects is dominated by the overall organization of the field, whereas relatively field-independent subjects readily perceive elements as discrete from their backgrounds. Sex differences have been repeatedly obtained on the measures of this dimension, with females being relatively more field dependent and males relatively more field independent.[22]

Since many correlates for these perceptual scores have been subsequently uncovered in several areas of intellectual and personality functioning, field independence vs. field dependence is now viewed as the perceptual component of a broader dimension of *articulated vs. global cognitive style*. For example, with the possible relation of field independence to intelligence was investigated, substantial correlations were obtained with some subtests of the Wechsler intelligence scales but not with others. The subtests of the Wechsler scales cluster into three major factors—a verbal dimension composed of the Vocabulary, Information, and Comprehension subtests; an attention-concentration dimension composed of the Digit Span, Arithmetic, and Coding subtests; and an analytic dimension, composed of the Block Design, Object Assembly, and Picture Completion subtests. The measures of field independence were found to correlate substantially with the dimension of analytic intelligence but not with the other two. Thus field-independent subjects exhibited a marked advantage on analytical intelligence tasks, but they could not be characterized as being superior in verbal intelligence or, in a meaningful way, as being superior in general intelligence.[23]

Children with a relatively articulated mode of cognitive functioning have also been found to have relatively articulated body concepts, as inferred from figure drawings; i.e., when asked to draw human figures, these children display more realistic body proportions, more details, and more sex and role characteristics than children with a relatively global mode of functioning. Global subjects also tend to lack a developed sense of separate identity, as reflected in their relative reliance upon others for guidance and support, the relative instability of their self-view, their suggestibility, and their susceptibility to social influence in forming and maintaining attitudes and judgments.[24]

Developmental studies have indicated that mode of cognitive functioning becomes progressively more articulated, and perception more field independent, with age up to late adolescence. At the same time, however, a child's relative level of articulation vis-à-vis his peers is quite stable. From age 10 to 14, the test-retest reliability of the perceptual index score of field independence was .64 for a group of 30 boys and .88 for a group of 30 girls, and from age 14 to 17 it was .87 for the boys and .94 for the girls.[25]

In an effort to uncover the possible origins of this cognitive style, Witkin and his colleagues studied patterns of maternal child-rearing practices and mother-child relations. On the basis of interview data, the mothers were classiifed into two groups: those who fostered the child's differentiation from herself and who helped him develop a sense of separate identity, and those who did not. In general, this classification of the mothers was found to be significantly related to the performance scores of the children, with the children of the mothers judged to have fostered differentiation being more independent and cognitively articulated.[26]

Differences have been noted in the type of defense mechanisms likely to be adopted by subjects at the two extremes of articulated and global cognitive style when confronted by conflict and stress. Articulated subjects are more likely to utilize specialized defenses, such as intellectualization and isolation, and global subjects are more likely to utilize primitive defenses, such as denial and repression. No general relation has been found, however, between the degree of articulation of the cognitive style and the degree of personal adjustment or psychopathology. Rather, as with the defenses, when psychological disturbances occur, there are differences in the kinds of pathology that are likely to develop at the two extremes of the style. Psychopathology in articulated persons is more likely to involve problems of overcontrol, overideation, and isolation; in severe pathological states, delusions are more likely to develop. Pathology in global persons, on the other hand, is more likely to involve problems of dependence, with symptoms such as alcoholism, obesity, ulcers, and asthma; in severe states hallucinations are more likely to develop.[27]

Such findings highlight the fact that styles of intellectual and perceptual functioning are part of the total personality and are intimately interwoven with affective, temperamental, and motivational structures. In some cases for example, "The general style of thinking may be considered a matrix . . . that determines the *shape* or *form* of symptom, defense mechanism, and adaptive trait."[28] In other cases the form-determining matrix may not be a mode of cognition but perhaps a type temperament or character structure or neurosis—the cognitive style would then be more derivative and would reflect but one component of a broader personality structure that permeates several areas of psychological functioning.

Although in most of this discussion one probably gets the impression that articulated, field-independent subjects have the advantage over their field-dependent peers, situations do exist where a more dependent reliance upon the external field, and particularly a reliance upon social stimuli for guidance and support, pays off in the accrual of incidental information. Field-dependent subjects have been found to be significantly better than field-independent subjects, for example, in their memory for faces and social words, even though their incidental memory for nonsocial stimuli is not generally superior.[29] The fact that certain types of problem situations and certain types of subject matter favor field-dependent subjects over field-independent subjects and vice versa (just as other types of problems might favor broad categorizers over narrow categorizers or levelers over sharpeners, and vice versa) is extremely important, since it highlights the relativity of value of the opposing extremes of each cognitive style. Unlike conventional ability dimensions, one end of these stylistic dimensions is not uniformly more adaptive than the other.

The perceptual and intellectual consistencies just discussed have been interpreted in stylistic terms, which implies, for example, that an individual spontaneously and habitually applies his particular degree of analytic or articulated field approach to a wide variety of situations. Even though a relatively global individual may appear typically global in most situations, however, when confronted with a situation that patently demands analysis, it is conceivable that he might be able to analyze with acceptable skill. Yet in the measurement of this cognitive style, it is usually presumed that subjects who characteristically display an analytic approach will in fact perform better on tasks requiring analysis (such as finding a simple figure in a complicated one) than will subjects who characteristically display a more global approach. Accordingly, most measures of analytic attitude are cast in an ability or maximum performance framework: if a subject does well at the task,

he is assumed to have performed analytically and if he does poorly, he is assumed to have performed more globally (or to be inadequately applying an unfamiliar, atypical analytic approach). In order to buttress the stylistic interpretation, it would be of interest to relate such maximum performance scores to measures of the spontaneous tendency to articulate the field in a task that ostensibly does not demand analysis.

In one attempt to develop such a task, subjects were required to learn to identify by name (a nonsense syllable) ten complex visual designs, each consisting of a large dominant figure, composed of elements, against a patterned background. In learning to identify these designs, the subject does not have to articulate the component parts, although the instructions do encourage analysis. The subjects are then told that each design was a member of a family of similar designs and that the names they had learned were family names. They are now presented with variations of the original designs (such as the element alone, the form alone, and the form composed of different elements) and asked to identify them in terms of the appropriate family name. In this strategy of test design, it was assumed that subjects who spontaneously articulated the designs during the learning process would be able to identify more variations than subjects who learned to identify the designs in a more global fashion. The total number of variations correctly identified, however, did not turn out to correlate significantly with the embedded-figures test. But this was because individuals differed consistently not only in the degree to which they articulated the original designs but in the type of figural component articulated, and the articulation of only one of these components was associated with embedded-figures performance. A factor analysis of variation scores uncovered two major dimensions representing two distinct modes of stimulus analysis, one emphasizing the articulation of discrete elements and the other of figural forms. A third mode reflecting the utilization of background information was substantially correlated with the other two. A significant relation was obtained between embedded-figures performance and the element articulation factor but not the form articulation factor. Although on the one hand element and form articulation are distinct dimensions of stimulus analysis and exhibit different personality correlates, on the other hand they are significantly correlated with each other and combine, along with the background information factor, to form a second-order dimension.[30]

These findings underscore the fact that the generality of the articulated vs. global cognitive style appears at a higher-order level in the factor-analytic sense. Another illustration of this point occurs in a study that attempted to extend Thurstone's perceptual closure factors into the verbal and semantic domains. Thurstone's factor of flexibility of perceptual closure, which is measured by tests like embedded figures, deals with the ability to break one closure in order to perceive a different one and thereby depends upon the capacity to analyze a highly organized perceptual field. Thurstone's factor of speed of perceptual closure deals with the ability to assemble discrete parts into an integrated, meaningful whole and thereby reflects the capacity to structure a relatively unorganized perceptual field.[31] The concept of an articulated mode of perception implies facility in both analysis and structuring,[32] thereby requiring that the two closure factors be correlated, which usually tends to be the case. When several experimental closure tests were constructed using single words and meaningful discourse as the stimulus fields, factors were also uncovered for both speed and flexibility of verbal closures and for both speed and flexibility of semantic closure, in addition to the two perceptual closure factors. The concept of a general articulated vs. global cognitive style requires that all of these closure factors be mutually intercorrelated, which also tends to be the case, although the level of correlation is certainly not uniform. Indeed, some limitation on the generality of the style appeared in a second-order factor analysis, which revealed two relatively independent articulation dimensions, one involving the analysis and structuring of figural materials and the other the analysis and structuring of symbolic materials. In addition, a separate second-order factor of general analytical reasoning was also obtained.[33]

Studies of other cognitive styles, particularly scanning and breadth of categorizing, have revealed a similar range of involvement in areas of personality and psychopathology. Silverman, for example, found that paranoid schizophrenics exhibited significantly more extensive scanning behavior and utilized significantly narrower categories than nonparanoid schizophrenics.[34] Gardner and Long reported that extreme scanning was marginally related to ratings of isolation, projection, and generalized delay on the Rorschach.[35] This latter finding that scanning behavior tends to be associated with two different defense mechanisms suggests the possibility that extensive scanning may serve different purposes under different circumstances or, perhaps, that there may be two distinct types of scanning. The association with isolation, which is a preferred defense mechanism of obsessives, suggests that the scanning may occur in the service of information seeking, as reflected in the obsessive's concern with exactness to offset doubt and uncertainty. The association with projection, which is a preferred defense mechanism of paranoids, suggests that the scanning may occur in the service of signal detection, particularly danger-signal detection, as reflected in the paranoid's concern with accuracy to offset suspicion and distrust. Some current research now in progress at Educational Testing Service attempts to differentiate empirically between these two possible types of scanning. This is being done using perceptual search tasks in which the subject is required to locate stimuli (signals) embedded in meaningfully organized visual fields, e.g., to locate faces camouflaged in pictorial scenes or four-letter words embedded in sentences. Upon completion of the search task, the stimulus materials are removed, and the subject is then asked specific questions about the content of the scenes or the meaning of the set of sentences. Subjects who incidentally take in information about the field in the process of scanning can thus be differentiated from those whose concern is apparently limited to detecting the signals.

With this brief characterization of cognitive styles in mind, let us now consider some of their possible implications for educational practice and evaluation. To begin with, cognitive styles, by embracing both perceptual and intellectual domains and by their frequent implication in personality and social functioning, promise to provide a more complete and effective characterization of the student than could be obtained from intellectual tests alone. These stylistic dimensions offer us new types of process variables to appraise that extend the assessment of mental performance beyond the crystallized notion of achievement levels to a concern with patterns of cognitive functioning. These stylistic characteristics should have relevance, although direct research evidence is admittedly very scanty, not only for the course of individual learning in various subject matter areas, but also for the nature of teacher-pupil interactions and of social behavior in the classroom.

Thus, cognitive styles, by virtue of their widespread operation, appear to be particularly important dimensions to assess in the evaluation of instruction. Yet, the very pervasiveness that underscores their importance at the same time interferes with the measurement of other important personal characteristics, such as dimensions of specific aptitude. This is because cognitive styles operate in testing situations as well and frequently interact with test formats and test conditions to influence the examinee's score. Consider, for example, the possibility that the five-alternative multiple-choice form of quantitative aptitude tests may favor subjects who prefer broad categories on category-width measures. Quick, rough approximations to the quantitative items might appropriately be judged by these subjects to be "close enough" to a given alternative, whereas "narrow range" subjects may require more time-consuming exact solutions before answering. Significant correlations between category preferences and quantitative aptitude tests have indeed been found, but the level of the correlation turns out to vary widely as a function of the spacing of alternatives on multiple-choice forms of the quantitative items. Scores for breadth of categorizing were found to be substantially correlated with quantitative aptitude scores derived from a multiple-choice form having widely-spaced alternatives, marginally correlated with scores on a free-response quantitative test, and negligibly correlated with scores derived from a narrowly-spaced form. This suggests that wide spacing of alternatives enhances, and narrow spacing disrupts, the "approximation" strategy that broad categorizers tend to employ on multiple-choice quantitative tests.[36] Such findings suggest that we should consider the "fairness" of our aptitude and achievement tests not only for different cultures and different sexes, but for individuals having different stylistic propensities. Thus, it is quite possible that cognitive styles are already being reflected in standard evaluation devices, but their operation under these circumstances is not being assessed for evaluation purposes but serves to contaminate the interpretation of other measures.

Information about cognitive styles offers several possibilities for instructional practice, but choices among them depend upon the results of much needed empirical research. For example, as soon as we are able to assess the cognitive styles of students, we have the possibility of placing them in classrooms in specified ways, perhaps in homogeneous groupings or perhaps in particular mixes or combinations. At this point it is by no means clear which particular placements will foster learning for individuals, just as it is by no means clear that homogeneous ability grouping is uniformly beneficial. Similarly, if we can assess the cognitive styles of students, we could also assess the cognitive styles of teachers and consider the possibility of assigning teachers to students to obtain particular combinations of styles that would optimally foster learning. We could also consider selecting particular teaching methods that would be especially appropriate for certain cognitive styles and certain subject matters. As yet, of course, there is very little research to guide us on these points. But in even considering the possibility of matching the student to the teacher or the teaching method and remembering that with our present assignment procedures some students are in effect so matched while others are not, we should ponder what the criterion of success in this enterprise should be. Should it be the maximal learning of content skills and information?

Consider as a possibility that, in the sciences at least, students with an articulated field approach, and perhaps reflective students as well, might learn better with an inductive or "discovery" method of teaching, since it would probably capitalize upon their propensities for analysis and careful consideration of alternatives. More global and more impulsive students, on the other hand, might learn content information better with a directed method of teaching in which rules and principles are specified rather than induced. Consider the likelihood, however, that in our efforts to optimize the learning of subject matter we may so solidify the global child's cognitive style that he may never learn to discover anything in his entire school career. This possibility suggests that teaching to produce maximal learning of subject matter is not enough. We should also be concerned with the student's manner of thinking. One possibility here is that we should attempt to foster alternative modes of cognition and multiple stylistic approaches to problem solving.

Such a goal will not be easily attained, however, since there are many cognitive and personality dimensions that could interact with properties of teaching methods to produce negligible or adverse results. It makes a difference, for example, when and to whom and to what subject matter an inferential discovery method of teaching is applied. Kagan warns us, as an instance, that "Impulsive children are apt to settle on the wrong conclusion in the inferential method and become vulnerable to developing feelings of inadequacy. . . . Since these impulsively derived hypotheses are apt to be incorrect, the impulsive child encounters a series of humiliating failures and eventually withdraws involvement from school tasks."[37]

The success of attempts to develop multiple modes of cognition in the individual will depend to a large extent upon the degree to which cognitive styles are malleable. Cognitive styles, as usually conceived, are habits that are spontaneously applied without conscious choice in a wide variety of situations. The possibility being considered here is that through manipulation of educational experience we might convert cognitive *styles* into cognitive *strategies,* by which I mean to imply a conscious choice among alternative modes of perceiving, remembering, thinking, and problem solving as a function of the conditions of particular situations. If the cognitive styles are relatively mutable, such efforts at change and multiple development might be feasible at all levels of the educational sequence. If the cognitive styles, or at least some of them, are relatively immutable, it may be necessary to focus attention on the early years and attempt to foster multiple modes of cognition before particular styles crystallize and become predominant. This latter possibility of predominant cognitive styles may be inevitable, regardless of our educational efforts, but we might at least be able to increase somewhat the power of alternative cognitive modes in the hierarchy, thereby reducing to some extent the preemptiveness of habitual thought. As always, however, we must also consider and evaluate the potential dangers in such an enterprise: our efforts to foster multiple modes of cognition in a child may prevent him from soaring in the unfettered application of his preferred style in a particular field.

I have not discussed affective variables at length because most educators, at least when pressed, affirm the importance of enhancing curiosity and of implanting in the student massive and enduring positive affects toward learning and subject matter. Most of us would agree, therefore, that even when an instructional program does not attempt to enhance positive attitudes directly, these variables should still be monitored if possible in the evaluation of the program to guard against unintended decreases in interest or involvement. In the measurement of these affective reactions, however, it seems to me unfortunate that evaluation studies rely so heavily upon the engineering model, which relates inputs and outputs, for there is a marked tendency to assess student achievement and attitudes only at the beginning and the end of the course. As Scriven has emphasized, the medical model is the appropriate paradigm for educational research,[38] and one derivative from that model should be an explicit attempt in evaluating a program to take account of the student's attitudes and feelings about the course of the treatment and not just the end result.

I wish to close by underscoring the importance of affect for learning and hence the importance of assessing affect in the evaluation of instruction. This point has been elegantly summarized by John Barth in his novel, *The Sot-Weed Factor:*

. . . of the three usual motives for learning things— necessity, ambition, and curiosity—simple curiosity was the worthiest of development, it being the "purest" (in that the value of what it drives us to learn is terminal rather than instrumental), the most conducive to exhaustive and continuing rather than cursory or limited study, and the likeliest to render pleasant the labor of learning. . . . this sport of teaching and learning should never become associated with certain hours or particular places, lest student and teacher alike . . . fall into the vulgar habit of turning off their alertness, as it were, except at those times and in those places, and thus make by implication a pernicious distinction between learning and other sorts of natural human behavior.[39]

FOOTNOTES

1. The preparation of this paper was supported in part by the National Institute of Mental Health under Research Grant MH-4186.

2. Stake, R. E. "The Countenance of Educational Evaluation." *Teachers College Record* 68(1967): 523-540.

3. Scriven, M. The methodology of evaluation. *American Educational Research Association Monograph Series on Curriculum Evaluation*, No. 1.

4. Stake, op. cit.

5. Bruner, J. S. *Toward a theory of instruction.* Cambridge: Harvard University Press, 1966.

6. Dyer, H. S. The discovery and development of educational goals. *Proceedings of the 1966 Invitational Conference on Testing Problems.* Princeton, N. J.: Educational Testing Service, 1967. pp. 12-24.

7. Scriven, op. cit.

8. *Proposal for a Research and Development Center for Measurement and Evaluation in Education.* Princeton, N. J.: Educational Testing Service, 1965.

9. Wallach, M. A. Creativity and the expression of possibilities. In *Creativity and learning*, edited by J. Kagan, pp. 36-57. Boston: Houghton Mifflin Co., 1967.

10. Thurstone, L. L. A factorial study of perception. *Psychometric Monograph No. 4.* Chicago: University of Chicago Press, 1944. Also, Witkin, H. A.; Lewis, H. B.; Hertzman, M.; Machover, K; Meissner, P. B.; & Wapner, S. *Personality through perception.* New York: Harper & Row, Publishers, 1954. Also, Witkin, H. A.; Dyk, R. B.; Faterson, H. F.; Goodenough, D. R., & Karp, S. A. *Psychological differentiation.* New York: John Wiley & Sons, Inc., 1962. Also, Gardner, R. W.; Holzman, P. S.; Klein, G. S.; Linton, H. B.; & Spence, D. Cognitive control: a study of individual consistencies in cognitive behavior. *Psychological Issues*, 1959, 1, Monograph 4. Also, Gardner, R. W.; Jackson, D. N., & Messick, S. Personality organization in cognitive controls and intellectual abilities. *Psychological Issues*, 1960, 2, Monograph 8.

11. Witkin, H. A., et al., op cit., 1962.

12. Holzman, P. S. Scanning: a principle of reality contact. *Perceptual and Motor Skills* 23 (1966): 835-844. Also, Schlesinger, H. J. Cognitive attitudes in relation to susceptibility to interference. *Journal of Personality* 22 (1954): 354-374. Also, Gardner, R. W., and Long, R. I. Control, defense, and centration effect: a study of scanning behaviour. *British Journal of Psychology* 53 (1962): 129-140.

13. Pettigrew, T. F. The measurement and correlates of category width as a cognitive variable. *Journal of Personality* 26 (1958): 532-544. Also, Bruner, J. S., and Tajfel, H. Cognitive risk and environmental change. *Journal of Abnormal and Social Psychology* 62 (1961): 231-241. Also, Kogan, N., and Wallach, M. A. *Risk Taking.* New York: Holt, Rinehart & Winston, Inc., 1964.

14. Gardner, R. W., and Schoen, R. A. Differentiation and abstraction in concept formation. *Psychological Monographs*, 1962, 76, No. 41. Also, Messick, S., and Kogan, N. Differentiation and compartmentalization in object-sorting measures

of categorizing style. *Perceptual and Motor Skills* 16 (1963): 47-51.

15. Kagan, J., Moss, H. A., and Sigel, I. E. Conceptual style and the use of affect labels. *Merrill-Palmer Quarterly* 6 (1960): 261-278. Also, Kagan, J., Moss, H. A., and Sigel, I. E. Psychological significance of styles of conceptualization. In basic cognitive processes in children, edited by J. C. Wright and J. Kagan, *Monograph of Society for Research in Child Development* 28 (1963): 73-112.

16. Kelly, G. A. *The psychology of personal constructs.* Vol. I. New York: W. W. Norton & Co., Inc., 1955. Also, Bieri, J. Complexity-simplicity as a personality variable in cognitive and preerential behavior. In *Functions of varied experience,* edited by D. W. Fiske & S. R. Maddi. Homewood, Ill.: Dorsey Press, 1961. Also, Bieri, J.; Atkins, A. L.; Scott, B.; Leaman, R. L.; Miller, H.; and Tripodi, T. *Clinical and social judgment: The discrimination of behavioral information.* New York: John Wiley & Sons, Inc., 1966. Also, Scott, W. A. Conceptualizing and measuring structural properties of cognition. In *Motivation and social interaction,* edited by O. J. Harvey. New York: The Ronald Press Co., 1963. See also the closely related work on abstractness-concreteness of conceptual systems: Harvey, O. J., Hunt, D. E., and Schroder, H. M. *Conceptual systems and personality organization.* New York: John Wiley & Sons, Inc., 1961.

17. Kagan, J.; Rosman, B. L.; Day, D.; Albert, J.; and Phillips, W. Information processing in the child: significance of analytic and reflective attitudes. *Psychological Monographs,* 1964, 78, Whole No. 58. Also, Kagan, J. Reflection-impulsivity and reading ability in primary grade children. *Child Development* 36 (1965): 609-628.

18. Holzman, P. S. The relation of assimilation tendencies in visual, auditory, and kinesthetic time-error to cognitive attitudes of leveling and sharpening. *Journal of Personality* 22 (1954): 375-394. Also, Holzman, P. S., and Klein, G. S. Cognitive system-principles of leveling and sharpening: individual differences in assimilation effects in visual time-error. *Journal of Psychology* 37 (1954): 105-122. Also, Gardner, R. W., et al., op. cit., 1959.

19. Klein, G. S. Need and regulation. In *Nebraska Symposium on Motivation,* edited by M. R. Jones, pp. 225-274. Lincoln: University of Nebraska Press, 1954. Also, Gardner, R. W., et al., op. cit., 1959.

20. Klein, G. S., Gardner, R. W., and Schlesinger, H. J. Tolerance for unrealistic experiences: a study of the generality of a cognitive control. *British Journal of Psychology* 53 (1962): 41-55.

21. McKenna, V. *Stylistic factors in learning and retention.* Princeton, N. J.: Eduactional Testing Service, Research Bulletin, 1967.

22. Witkin, H. A., et al., op. cit., 1954.

23. Goodenough, D. R., and Karp, S. A. Field dependence and intellectual functioning. *Journal of Abnormal and Social Psychology* 63 (1961): 241-246. Also, Witkin, H. A., et al., op. cit., 1962.

24. Witkin, H. A., et al., op. cit., 1962. Also, Linton, H. B., and Graham, E. Personality correlates of persuasibility. In *Personality and Persuasibility,* edited by I. L. Janis et al. New Haven: Yale University Press, 1959.

25. Witkin, H. A., et al., op. cit., 1962. Also, Witkin, H. A.; Goodenough, D. R., and Karp, S. A. Stability of cognitive style from childhood to young adulthood. *Journal of Personality and Social Psychology* 7 (1967): 291-300.

26. Ibid. Also, Dyk, R. B., and Witkin, H. A. Family experiences related to the development of differentiation in children. *Child Development* 36 (1965): 21-55.

27. Witkin, H. A. Psychological differentiation and forms of pathology. *Journal of Abnormal Psychology* 70 (1965): 317-336.

28. Shapiro, D. *Neurotic Styles.* New York: Basic Books, Inc., Publishers, 1965.

29. Messick, S., and Damarin, F. Cognitive styles and memory for faces. *Journal of Abnormal and Social Psychology* 69 (1964): 313-318. Also, Fitzgibbons, D., Goldberger, L., and Eagle, M. Field dependence and memory for incidental material. *Perceptual and Motor Skills* 21 (1965): 743-749.

30. Messick, S., and Fritzky, F. J. Dimensions of analytic attitude in cognition and personality. *Journal of Personality* 31 (1963): 346-370. Also, Messick, S. *Cognitive interference and flexible control.* Princeton, N. J.: Educational Testing Service Research Bulletin, in preparation.

31. Thurstone, L. L., op. cit., 1944.

32. Dyk, R. B., and Witkin, H. A., op. cit., 1965.

33. Messick, S., and French, J. W. Dimensions of closure in cognition and personality. Paper delivered at the American Psychological Association meetings, Washington, D.C., 1967.

34. Silverman, J. Scanning-control mechanism and "cognitive filtering" in paranoid and nonparanoid schizophrenia. *Journal of Consulting Psychology* 28 (1964): 385-393.

35. Gardner, R. W., and Long, R. I., op. cit., 1962.

36. Messick, S., and Kogan, N. Category width and quantitative aptitude. *Perceptual and Motor Skills* 20 (1965): 493-497.

37. Kagan, J. Personality and the learning process. In *Creativity and Learning,* edited by J. Kagan, pp. 153-163. Boston: Houghton Mifflin Co., 1967. Also, Kagan, J., Pearson, L., and Welch, L. Conceptual impulsivity and inductive reasoning. *Child Development* 37 (1966): 583-594.

38. Scriven, M. Student values as educational objectives. *Proceedings of the 1965 Invitational Conference on Testing Problems.* Princeton, N. J.: Educational Testing Service, 1966. pp. 33-49.

39. Barth, J. *The Sot-Weed Factor.* New York: Grosset & Dunlap, Inc., 1964. p. 17.

	CHAPTER 7
EVALUATING CHANGE	J. Thomas Hastings

Some bright, perceptive, and knowledgeable person thought up the title for the presentation in this Assembly. I cannot claim the honor; the title was handed to me. I say *bright* because he used a two-word title instead of a course outline run together. I say *perceptive* because he discriminated nicely—and consciously, I'll assume—between the word endings *tion* and *ting*. And I say *knowledgeable* because he chose the ending which emphasizes the continuing quality of any meaningful and sincere attempts at either *change in education* or *assessment and judgment* of such change. Far too many people express—whether they admit it or not—a concept of evaluating an educational effort which is parallel to their view of setting a price on a house: One does it *after* the house is built; it is based upon a rather tricky mixture of fact, subjective values, and wishful thinking; and —with the exception of giving a point or two— when it's done, it's done. Our title-writer saw a job having less finality. I hope that I can present a picture of "evaluating" which has a less entangled mixture of fact, subjective value, and wishful thinking—although fact and subjective value *are* the essence.

Most of this presentation will focus on evaluation in the larger setting of "national" curriculum projects. The issues and the concepts can be demonstrated on these, but the ideas apply equally well to other educational change and to less global educational settings.

Everyone does evaluate, you know—ongoing educational programs and especially changes in education. Furthermore, quite seriously, *almost* everyone uses both descriptive data (observables) and values (privately or publicly held.) Have *you* ever made an evaluative statement about a new curriculum in arithmetic, a new method of engendering inquiry, a new technique for teaching reading, a change in organizational plan from age-grades to ungraded arrangements? Did *you* use

some good, solid descriptive material along with some personal (however common with the group) values? Did you ever hear a parent (in or out of PTA) spin out evaluative conclusions regarding a proposed or adopted program? Your students? A businessman? A taxi driver? Yes, even a U.S. Navy Admiral and a University of Illinois historian! Seriously, with evaluation so rampant and universal, why do we hear bright people making conscientious suggestions that we should "get some real evaluation going"? Or suggestions that we "learn *how* to evaluate"?

I contend that even if we could take some gigantic poll concerning any one new development and in this poll collect all of the evaluations of teachers, parents, administrators, students (et cetera)—even if we could do that poll and the collating in a systematic way, we still would be unhappy. I further suggest that this negative feeling would stem from three things: (1) It would be apparent that we couldn't extricate the judgments from the descriptive data. (2) This would put us in a position of not being able to establish the locus of conflicts, i.e., do differences lie in having looked at different data? (3) The summed pronouncements (pooled evaluations) would result in such extreme generalizations—good-bad, better-poorer, useful-harmful—that the result would be almost, if not completely, irrelevant to bringing about desired change. Very few of us, if any, would claim that evaluation should be vote counting.

The intended import of this discussion of "pooled evaluations"—from many sources is to indicate that we (all of us) do know some of the guidelines which we want and which are necessary in the act of usefully evaluating educational things. To attempt to cover—or touch upon—all aspects, all guidelines, all criteria of educational evaluation in the time this Assembly has would be obviously foolish, which is as follows: My main intent is to give us pegs on which we can hang our reactions and discussion—a sampling of the issues, arguments, concepts, and examples. In the remainder of this paper I shall start by describing some of my notions of what evaluation is or is not; then go on to citing some of the problems, issues, and current concepts in evaluation; and then briefly describe a few examples of what I believe are useful current attacks on evaluation. Then the floor will belong to the Reactors and you under the guidance of the Chairman. I am making no attempt to be all inclusive in any of these things, but I do hope that the pieces I have picked will raise questions for various ones of you or suggest new ways to thinking about evaluating change.

The ideas and practices developed by Tyler and associates in the 1930's pushed brand new light into many dark corners. Certain aspects of those ideas continue to be a revelation to many who enter or skirt the field. The central concepts of that Tylerian model were reinforced in the 1950's by the publication of the *Taxonomy of Educational Objectives,* edited by Bloom. The ideas generated immense power and usefulness. I say this because recently I have caught some mumblings which suggest that we can forget the old—now that we have the truth. Sure, we can now forget Dewey because we have Bruner! Paraphrasing a statement by Michael Scriven in a paper on the "methodology of evaluation," intellectual progress is possible only because newcomers step on the shoulders of giants—not because they tread on their toes.

Until less than a decade ago most evaluation efforts were centered on somewhat limited concerns: the classroom of the individual teacher—or at most the school system; on an innovation by and for a relatively small audience; on evaluation of a specific curricular arrangement in one institution—such as the Dressel et al. studies at Michigan State University. Such limited fields are not, per se, easier to evaluate—nor are they less worth evaluating—than are the larger, more visible projects and movements of today.

In the last eight to ten years a number of forces—not unrelated—have combined to put the focus on evaluation on the larger scene and to make the act more visible among different groups of professionals and scholars. You are familiar with the various forces—the Sputnik fever starting in October, 1957, the interest of scholars in structuring their disciplines, the dollars available for educational effort. At this point I have no interest in sorting out the causes. My point here is, as these things happened, the picture of evaluation shifted to a larger and more complex-appearing scene. People from more diverse specialities got into the act. The curriculum specialist in education and the educational-measurement personnel

are no longer alone. The scholar in learning or developmental psychology; the philosopher (not only of education but of science, of history); the specialist in nuclear physics; and the leader in human ecology—all of these and others have become involved in evaluating change. This has brought about some different questions to be answered, some added possibilities of data, some different concepts of the act.

With all this ferment, evaluation remains a logical activity directed at answering certain types of questions about education through examination of the contingencies among input, treatment, objectives, and outcomes with a value-weighted interpretation. Basically, the questions concern feasibility, cost, and change in performance. The most general idea is fairly simple; the execution of the acts themselves is extremely complex and the way is ladened with booby traps.

One of the main points, I wish to make is that evaluation has to do with many different purposes. Evaluation is brought into play by the question of whether some person likes or feels comfortable with the program or the change. This question is generally trivial, but it is conceivable for it to be of use in a larger context of teacher-training or a problem of public support. A more complicated question might deal with the appropriateness of the cost of a new technique of teaching in relation to the amount of gain in a given competence. Such a question probably requires some fairly sophisticated research design with reasonably complicated data handling. An equally complicated question is one which has to do with the relative value of including various concepts in a particular field of study at a given learning level. This question can be attacked rationally (one of my later examples will describe a start), but the special skills of scholar and philosopher become important in answering the question. There has been too great a tendency on the part of far too many to equate educational evaluation with the one question of the extent to which a given program meets objectives in terms of student behaviors. This isn't a bad question. Quite contrary, it's excellent. But many arguments stem from failing to see that it is not the only question.

I warned you that I would speak to the idea of what evaluation is not. Evaluation is not equivalent to testing. It is not equivalent to giving and scoring tests and then interpreting them in normative terms. At the very best the acts of giving, scoring, and reporting data-reduction on tests are of some use in the descriptive part of evaluation. Although the tests were developed or selected with value judgments playing a large role, the descriptive presentations of the results of tests add nothing to the judgment side of evaluation. The main reason that I am emphasizing this point is that many people seem to confuse the idea that tests of certain techniques and materials of testing are useful in some phases of evaluation with the idea that testing *is* evaluation. In the current issue of *Look* entitled "Testing Versus Your Child," is an article by Senior Editor, George B. Leonhard. It is somewhat in the mode of Benesh Hoffman's *The Tyranny of Testing* except that Leonhard's article takes in a little more territory. My interpretation of what he says is that we can blame almost all or any of the ills of schools, teachers, education, and our children's miseries on the liberal use of tests. In the presentation I am presently making it matters little whether Leonhard in his *Look* magazine article is correct or not. What really matters to me is that several people have approached me with the comment that this particular article on testing certainly knocks the evaluators in the head. So, once again, evaluation is not school testing.

Now, for some of the current problems and issues in evaluation. Once again, please remember that this is not a review; it is only an attempt to focus on some issues which may serve as pegs for the ensuing discussion. Let me start with some of the problems which have become apparent in the use of tests. In a 1963 article in *Teachers College Record,* Cronbach raises some questions as to whether the usual test scores were really appropriate for curriculum evaluation. For years, the test maker's art and his science have been directed toward developing instruments which will discriminate individual differences most effectively. Many of the characteristics which have been stressed as necessary for "good tests" are necessary only when the focus is on the question of how much one student differs from another. In educational evaluation directed at curricula, materials, and methods, we have far less concern with differences between students than we do with central tendency or range differences from one method to another. Cronbach suggested that the giving of one test to all students in a given curriculum might be far less efficient than the giving of different sub-groups of items to different sub-groups of students.

Another rather obvious problem has arisen in the use of tests for comparison studies. If one wishes to get information on the comparability of the outcomes of Curriculum A to the outcomes of Curriculum B, a common method demands the selection of a published test or the development of a new one and the administration of the test to students who were under Treatment A and to those under Treatment B. I suspect that I need not expand this example very far. The more sophisticated members of the audience will apply covariance techniques to solve the problem. If the test you use has items in it appropriate to Treatment A but not to B, or vice-versa, the results are impeccable—but irrelevant to the question. If, on the other hand, you devised some items which are relevant to Treatment A and others relevant to Treatment B, all in the same tests, then you really have a problem in arriving at comparability. If you make up a test which measures only those things which are common to Treatment A and Treatment B when you know that A and B were intended to be different, you certainly have fouled up the intent of comparing the two. I realize that all of this may sound like frightfully unnecessary admonitions to quite a number of you. If so, please go look at the articles in the journals.

Now to an issue which those of us in the Center for Instructional Research and Curriculum Evaluation have encountered recently. We have been assuming that the amassing of quantities of more precise and relevant descriptive data, on which rational and overt decisions by school administrators could be based, would be an unquestioned boon to educational change. In discussing a sociologist at the University of Chicago, we have discovered that our viewpoint needs questioning. For instance, Lortie seems to suggest that in our society made up of innumerable points of view, the institutional leaders who make rational, public decisions about given programs for specific objectives may run into difficulties. Perhaps one of the strong features in our system of public education is stating public objectives in extremely generalized terms and not making open decisions on specific objectives. From this we may have our freedom for change. Perhaps our picture of total evaluation including rational and open decisions on programs has missed some of the consequences. In citing this example of an issue, I am trying to point out that we need to look at the endeavor from the viewpoints of various disciplines. My thesis is that the more different viewpoints, the better—but we must expect real issues to be developed.

Another series of issues was raised some thirty months ago—and not satisfactorily answered as yet —by J. Myron Atkin. As many of you know, he has been co-director of a well known elementary-science curriculum project supported by MSF; and he has faced both evaluation and the evaluators. I wish to mention only one of the issues which he raised. In his attempts to learn more about evaluation, Atkin kept being told that the first basic principle was to begin with stating the objectives in behavioral terms. This is certainly one of the most quoted facets of the Tylerian model. In an article in Volume 1 of the *Journal of Research in Science Teaching,* Atkin sets forth the proposition that requiring statements of objectives in behavioral terms of senior scientists in a discipline (for example, the eminent astronomers who are writing materials for his projects) may indeed restrict unnecessarily and harmfully the kinds of materials being developed. He suggests that using this approach may tend to identify only short-term behavioral change and that, as a consequence, the developers of the materials may put their creative work on those short-term objectives which they have been requested to enunciate. Atkin proposed that the scholar who is innovating should be allowed the freedom of *not* having to state explicit objectives—at least in the beginning. At some point the behavioral scientist attempts to discover what skills and abilities are developing.

So much for some of the current issues and problems in the business of evaluating change. It is rather interesting to note that for the most part each of these issues and many others have been articulated for the first time in the professional literature published or unpublished during the past three years or so. The new-found urgency for evaluating and the new-found money for conducting appropriate studies and for inducing the appropriate scholars to have a look may well index the beginning of the coming of age of evaluation.

Now for some of the concepts which are currently being used in attempts to develop models for evaluation. Michael Scriven has suggested quite a number. Perhaps the one which has had the greatest take has been his differentiation of formative and summative evaluation. Formative evaluation is that which is carried on during the developmental stages of a curriculum project. Its main purpose is to give feedback to the innovator while he is working on or revising the materials. Summative evaluation, on the other hand, has to do with that kind of evaluation which is conducted after a project is "fully developed." Such evaluation ordinarily is executed for the purpose of letting others know the usefulness (and hopefully the shortcomings) of the developed program. Scriven seems well aware that many facets of a formative evaluation—tryout runs of small parts of new materials—can also be of real use in evaluating the final product. The real power, however, of this particular concept lies in the fact that it helps clarify purposes and therefore clarifies the kinds of data and the kinds of relationships among data which are needed.

Cronbach in his 1963 article elaborates on a concept of using evaluation to uncover durable relationships among teaching-learning variables for the purpose of guiding future educational changes. The implication of this concept is that evaluators should consider carefully the inclusion of a large number of behavioral science variables which cover more than the stated objectives of the program materials. Cronbach also has presented the concept of examining courses—particularly at the elementary and secondary levels—as though they were designed to develop readiness of further learnings in the discipline and in related areas. If evaluators would take his ideas into account, we might have some truly significant longitudinal studies which would be of real help in furthering educational change.

Robert E. Stake has proposed a series of concepts which call for looking at the descriptive data to be gathered as falling into three classes: antecedents, transactions, and outcomes. He then divides each of these into intended and observed categories and further connects them by means of congruence measures from intended to observed categories. I am not suggesting that this is the only model which should be used in looking at descriptive data, but I am insisting that such concepts as these should give the evaluator greater power for generalization—and should make his reports more meaningful to the intended consumer of the developed program.

And now for a few examples of ongoing evaluation studies. It is not my intent to describe in detail any one of them but rather to flavor the kind of concern and the types of data being gathered. Nor have I chosen studies because I believe they are exemplary (a word made famous in requirements for Title III proposals!)—although some of them may fit that category. My intent is to present variety.

A study conducted by Peter A. Taylor, at the University of Illinois, is concerned with the development of a methodology whereby the value judgments of appropriate individuals concerning the importance of various concepts in a given discipline can be more meaningfully described and inter-related than has been possible previously. He is using groups defined by roles in our educational establishment: teachers, subject-matter specialists, authors. He is using a number of different psychometric methods to collect his data and models of multi-dimensional scaling to treat the data collected. If the methods work, and it appears that they will, we should find ourselves with a new and useful technique for attacking a long-standing, troublesome problem. Earlier in this paper I spoke of the need for answering the question of relative value of including various concepts in a particular course at a given level. Taylor's work will certainly help in the processing of judgments of appropriate judges—the systematic sorting out of arguments and conflicts.

A number of studies currently being conducted around materials from the Biological Sciences Curriculum Study afford a range of questions and techniques which could have a broadening influence on the practice of evaluation. Ira Gordon and Arthur Combs (Florida) are collecting data concerning changes in the behavior and perceptions of students with low academic aptitude and the use of the new Special Materials from BSCS. There is no simple study of knowledge acquisition gains; it involves student self-perception, attitudes of teachers toward such students, students' attitudes toward schooling in general, and teacher treatment of material in the classroom—among other variables. Another study of a complex but intriguing order is being conducted by Paul Hurd (Stanford) and Mary Rowe (Columbia T.C.). It is built around special laboratory materials which require group work and variables of the students. It is asking questions about types of objectives which are too often left at the mention-and-forget level. James J. Gallagher is doing a study, using BSCS classrooms for the setting, which focusses upon definable characteristics of classroom interaction. The method is based upon a model which he and Aschner developed for identifying classroom strategies and certain relations among them. From the standpoint of evaluating change, such studies may well lead to improved possibilities of describing and judging materials-teacher-student interactions. This type of investigation certainly helps round out in practice the middle part of the model which Stake set forth in terms of *antecedents, transactions,* and *outcomes.* BSCS, one of the largest of the national curriculum projects, has discovered that evaluation is important but that it is very complex. It takes the studies I have mentioned and many more to begin to evaluate change meaningfully.

An extremely large and complex study spoken of as the Oak Leaf Project—from the name of the elementary school which is being studied—is being conducted by the Learning Research and Development Center at Pittsburgh under the direction of Robert Glaser. The focus of the study is on individualization of instruction, with a heavy use of programmed materials, in an ungraded setting. This is not a study of a particular curriculum development, but it certainly provides descriptive data and, we hope, judgments of an important and current educational change. For me it is an example of Cronbach's concept of evaluation studies which will be beneficial in future curriculum development.

My last example is one with which you are familiar and which has elicited a considerable amount of very public controversy—some of which demonstrates nicely the concern I mentioned as being discussed by the sociologist, Lortie. The study is the National Assessment Project being directed by Tyler. It exemplifies four things which I believe are important. First, the study is aimed at a meaningful description of the outcome aspects of American education as a whole—as opposed to assessing pieces and parts. Secondly, it certainly affords the basis for a continuing, longitudinal study of change. Third, it should give us much good experience with the techniques and methodology of using tests which are aimed at a problem different from the standard psychometric problem of individual differences. And, finally, the results of the study—or I should say studies—will give us a Texas hatful of real questions and hypotheses concerning educational change.

Evaluating change is a great big, burly, Paul Bunyan sort of topic. I have tried to peck away at some of the more recent issues and concepts—many of which are just developing. Obviously, I chose the pieces which are interesting to me. Probably your tastes differ at least somewhat from mine. Possibly you would have preferred one large bite. At any rate, the floor now belongs to the Reactors and *you* . . .

CHAPTER 8	
Daniel C. Lortie	THE CRACKED CAKE OF EDUCATIONAL CUSTOM AND EMERGING ISSUES IN EVALUATION

The changes taking place in American public schools today have a familiar ring. Contact replaces isolation as new social groups (business, federal agencies) engage themselves in school affairs. Heterogeneity displaces homogeneity when school staffs expand to include people from different occupations (social work, psychology, library work) and teachers are more diverse in social and educational backgrounds.[1] A hierarchical, paternalistic authority system is challenged by subordinates who clamor for a say in decision-making. Interaction within the sub-system quickens as new kinds of buildings and work patterns (team teaching for example) take out the walls separating fellow teachers and fellow students. Age-old pedagogical conventions are discarded as students are turned loose to teach themselves with the help of complicated, expensive machines. All these juxtapositions have been witnessed before by anthropologists and sociologists studying cultural and social change; the analogy to processes of modernizing societies is striking. In Walter Bagehot's phrase, "The cake of custom is cracking."[2]

Cultural and social change involves shifts in how people assign value to various parts of their world; ambiguities arise as old certainties melt. This paper explores this process as educational evaluation confronts a system in transition; it focuses on issues which arise as a consequence of change.[3] Such analysis requires more than mere assertion that changes are taking place—the trick is to trace their specific effects. There is the temptation, often yielded to by sensational journalists, to see a revolution in every protest rally. Conservatism seems indicated. I shall, therefore, limit my observations to trends which are already visible and, in sketching out probable effects, eschew long lines of inference. It is, in fact, very doubtful whether social science theory permits us to gauge anything more than such first order

effects. Yet it is interesting that the implications of current educational change are such that even a prudent approach produces a set of rather complicated possibilities.

Organizational Trends and Evaluation

Using the local school district as our point of reference, we can classify organizational trends occurring today as "external" and "internal." We begin with events taking place in the external system. There seems little doubt that the augmented roles of the federal government, business corporations and universities will have important effects on the public schools.

The activities of the federal government erode educational tradition. We can see this as the government legitimates and diffuses that set of ideas symbolized by the phrase "research and development." This conception of educational practice stresses a core idea of rationality in governance—it applies scientific ways of thinking to the appraisal of alternatives and to the making of decisions. This viewpoint is not new to university professors. Yet as a statement of official government policy, backed by public tax monies, it is novel for the public schools. The research and development viewpoint has migrated from universities and industry to school boards justifying their claims for federal grants. It becomes part of the working reality of school officials because it is built into the rhetoric of applying for funds and undergirds the logic of allocation used by federal agencies. We need not argue that school officials understand it fully to argue that it influences their actions. Thoughtways can affect organizational behavior even where understanding is incomplete.[4] It is becoming routine for federal agencies supporting new programs to require recipients to build in evaluation procedures. Such requirements force compliance to the new ideology and undermine belief in tradition as the warrant for educational practice.

Federal activities in education are conducted by a variety of agencies featuring a variety of primary objectives.[5] It seems that once an agency takes on the foundation function, its officials begin to act like foundation men; they prefer to back undertakings which are original and, if possible, dramatic. Thus new funds, coupled with diverse sponsors with a bent toward the novel, produce an increased number of institutional options and thereby add to the alternatives confronting decision-makers in local school districts. Such an increase in options reinforces notions of rationality conveyed by the research and development ideology. The necessity to make choices forces people to attend to the grounds for choice. The larger the number of alternatives, furthermore, the more those who would prefer to "stand pat" must defend their inactivity as a choice in and of itself. This is not to say that the availability of options carries assurance that all or even most will be adopted by local school officials. But when we recall the potency of incentives possessed by the federal government (i.e., large amounts of new monies, a capacity to give national publicity to selected school systems), it seems reasonable to expect at least some of the new approaches to enter school decision-making. It is theoretically possible, moreover, that some highly innovative school systems will make radically divergent initial choices (e.g., Pittsburgh commitment to educational parks) and, constrained in the selection of subsequent solutions, will branch into ultimately highly divergent overall solutions. It is probably too early for us to conduct empirical studies of radical branching, but it is a possibility well worth keeping in mind.

Business corporations dealing with educational matters will add to the number and range of instructional practices and solutions; individual firms, in fact, will do so or go out of business. The new firms combining publishing and electronic resources, moreover, frequently have vast financial resources available for development, production and sales. Competition between firms is likely to be fierce, particularly as each battles to get and hold as large a share of the market as possible. Recall as well that when businessmen talk about "merchandising," they are describing effective techniques for disseminating practices. If we can assume that no single firm or coalition of firms monopolizes sales, the outcome will be further differentiation among school systems as patterns of purchasing and implementation vary.

It is many years since Veblen showed that universities act like business corporations in struggling for prestige, wealth and influence.[6] They, like business organizations, are under pressure to come up with differentiated "products for the educational market." Universities have their own resources in countering competition from government and business; they export highly trained persons as well as ideas. Graduates of a particular university can be uniquely competent in implementing and refining an approach developed at their institution; professors acting as consultants widen the institution's sphere of influence. Competition between universities is, of course, softened by cooperation among specialists from different institutions, (e.g., the professor developed curricula), but the net effect is similar for local school officials. They confront not only diverse university programs but demands for more and more student time issued by competing bands of university scholars. Professors engaged in public school affairs produce alternatives which must be considered by those governing school districts.

Changes in the external system, then, point to greater pressures on local decision-makers to deal with ever-more possible lines of action. School officials will probably look for ways to reduce those pressures; inquiry would probably reveal that structures are being constructed now to filter and contain innovative forces.[7] Yet the external system, primarily because it is external and largely outside the power system of local officials, can stay with its self-appointed function of generating new ways to keep school. School officials, whether they wish change or prefer continuity, will have little choice but to examine an expanding number of instructional approaches in the years ahead.

The examination of new alternatives will require considerable increases in the amount of evaluative activity carried on by school personnel. The justification of a particular choice requires comparisons between alternatives and the explication of general grounds for choice; effects on students, and the rating of effects as more or less desirable, will be difficult to avoid. Thoughtful school board members, administrators and teachers will be skeptical of claims made by sponsors of any given approach. Less thoughtful colleagues may find that the public expects them to appear as if they are giving careful consideration to new possibilities. One does not need to be a specialist in evaluation to realize that tradition is no guide in choosing between competing novelties.

The evaluative load will increase most dramatically where school systems undertake large-scale changes. The simultaneous introduction of innovations creates a special and demanding evaluative problem, for one must take account of local circumstance and of interaction effects among innovations. For example, a school system might decide to combine educational parks with com-

puter-assisted instruction. What affective outcomes flow from impersonalities associated with
man-machine systems and sharp increases in the
number of fellow students? Situations of this sort
do not permit local officials to apply evaluations
developed elsewhere; they must do their own
digging.

Two major trends are taking place in the internal system of public schools and both are
likely to have serious implications for the conduct
of evaluation. The first, functional differentiation,
develops quietly and may go unnoticed. The second, "teacher militancy," hits the headlines almost
daily. Both trends, however, seem to share a
common effect. They weaken familistic and paternalistic conceptions of authority relationships
among people working in schools.

The history of American school organization is
largely the story of increasing specialization in
the knowledge to be transmitted and in the tasks
of those engaged in transmitting that knowledge.
Contrast, for example, the one-room schoolhouse
of the nineteenth century with its modern coun-
terpart, the rural regional school. Grades, subjects and teaching tasks have all been sub-divided.
Today specialists counsel students, supervise their
health, store and distribute books, purchase and
distribute audio-visual equipment and visit families with problems. These specialists, moreover,
have separate occupational associations concerned
with "professionalizing" each sub-field. One influential spokesman has called for the creation
of a national system of specialty boards for various categories of teachers.[8]

Yet the division-of-labor we see today may prove
to be but pale prologue to much greater differentiation in the future. Functional differentiation
among school professionals has, so far, tended to be
differentiation among equals. But now we see new
forms of stratification being introduced as specialists of lower or higher status are hired. Some
school systems, for example, are employing teacher
aides whose credentials make it very unlikely that
they will ever move into teacher ranks.[9] Team
teaching arrangements in some places, on the other
hand, involves higher status for team leaders and
senior teachers.[10] New technologies bring specialists, sometimes of higher rank, in their wake; we
now have television teachers, programmers of instruction and computer experts. Similar things are
happening in central offices where superintendents look for men to specialize in relationships
with the federal government, experts in collective
bargaining and men who can design program
budgets. The pace of role differentiation is quick-
ening.

Problems of communication and conflicts in orientation occur more readily when systems become
internally differentiated.[11] Occupational differen-

tiation produces specialisms not only of skill but
of perspective, of moral outlook.[12] Additional lay-
ers of authority in organizations complicate communication within by producing more blockages
in the flow of information and affect.[13] Thus we
can look ahead to schools and school systems
where people of diverse outlook and rank find
it harder to agree on instructional matters. We
expect that mechanisms will be developed to cope
with this problem. Building such mechanisms, however, requires considerable time and it is debatable whether they ever attain the easy consensus associated with earlier social homogeneity.

Perhaps "teacher militancy" is a special case
of role differentiation; in any event, it is clear
that teacher demands are producing controversy
over instructional matters as well as salaries and
working conditions. The New York City strike is
a recent example. There the union bargained hard
and long over whether the More Effective Schools
Program would receive additional financing. Nor
is New York unique, for state after state is making legal provision for the participation of teacher
groups in setting school policy.[14] Other categories
of school workers are also agitating for more influence in instructional matters.[15] It is ironic that
the external system should begin to produce increased options at that point when overt conflict
on instructional policies emerges within the internal system.

Evaluation will undergo alterations where instructional policy-making is colored by conflict.
Spirited advocacy by opponents will make policy
deliberations more like courtroom trials and legis-
lative battles. Protagonists, eager to cloak their
positions in the garb of educational superiority,
will buttress their beliefs with evaluations.[16] Overt
conflict may lead to debates in which discrepant
evaluations of the same program are presented.
Since judgments made by contending parties can
affect the interests and prestige of combatants,
the process of evaluation could itself become embedded in controversy. Should this occur, the public and its representatives, confused by competing
claims, will call for clarification, for disinterested
and objective assessments upon which they can
rely. Controversy makes it essential that some
evaluators be regarded as men of probity and
objectivity. The educational system must find a
way to solve the problem of integrity-trust in the
performance of the evaluative function.

Processes of Innovation and Evaluation

Two facets of the current emphasis on change
deserve attention in our consideration of emerging issues in evaluation. The first is the sheer fact
of the ferment itself, of the interest in finding
and carrying out new ways of instructing chil-

dren. The second has to do with the scope of changes now under way, with the emergence of large-scale, structural changes. Both aspects of the innovative thrust have important consequences for the conduct of evaluation.

In the decades immediately preceding 1950, public education was characterized by a relatively slow rate of change. Despite the ideological concerns of the twenties and thirties, the principal chronicler of that period does not point to consequences which followed in the actual conduct of school affairs.[17] Callahan argues, in fact, that school practice was heavily influenced by a simplistic conception of business efficiency.[18] Although one can find changes in curricula, textbooks, teacher training and the like during this period, it is difficult to identify significant structural changes.[19] The energies of American school men and women were absorbed in constructing a vast system of public education along previously conceived lines; the years between World War I and 1950 were years of extending rather than reorganizing a social form.

Although it is difficult to be certain (we lack empirical studies on the conduct of evaluation during this period), evaluation appears to have been part of a system of decision-making adapted to slow rather than rapid change. The thirties and forties saw the emergence of "Democratic Administration," of a preoccupation with winning the support of diverse groups for school activities. The superintendent, by this doctrine, should "involve" a wide variety of publics in school affairs and "harmonize" them to a trouble-free consensus.[20] The curriculum committee is symbolic of this ideology. The composition of that body might include citizens-at-large, teachers, parents, professors, representatives of special interest groups, etc. Curriculum was not an area for the application of esoteric knowledge and research skills. One might, of course, consult an expert in evaluation or curriculum, but the basic mechanism in resolving issues was the vote rather than recourse to "professional opinion."

Whatever the strengths and weaknesses of the participatory model may have been, it cannot be effectively argued that it fostered rapid change. Its very composition and organization conforms to those bodies which Blau describes as least likely to act with dispatch.[21] The emphasis on consensus did nothing to advance techniques of evaluation. One gains the impression, in fact, that considerably more effort was expended in verbalizing objectives than in operationalizing them. Robert Wood was led to comment, rather in exasperation, that "Public education is a continuing constitutional convention."[22]

Change begets more change. For as social systems shift to new and different ways, solutions to problems produce new problems demanding new solutions. Inasmuch as education is engaged in serious change, pressures for more expeditious evaluation will mount. School officials, pressed for more rapid action, will skirt cumbersome participatory methods and favor rapidly obtainable expert advice. Other factors make it likely that evaluation will become defined as an area for expert treatment. The diffusion of the research and development orientation, coupled with increasing public awareness of statistics and behavioral science as fields in their own right, will help to define evaluation as "specialized" work. I consider it extremely probable that the expert, highly trained evaluator will come into his own.

Some instructional changes taking place today alter student experience in much greater ways than in the past. Most evaluative work has concentrated on differences between one more-or-less similar component and another; one measured for example, the efficacy of a given French curriculum over another. Large-scale changes, however, disturb aspects of student experience and socialization which, previously constant, could be reasonably ignored. Since we did not propose to alter them, they did not matter. But large-scale changes make previously latent functions relevant to evaluative actions, for to change them without considering the effects on students may be to alter socialization in unintended ways. We can illustrate this process with concrete examples.

The serious introduction of team teaching is manifestly a major change in collegial and student-teacher relationships. Yet our grasp of the meaning of the change for student socialization is limited by our ignorance of the latent functions served by the self-contained classroom pattern. Is Parsons right, for example, in implying that it requires a relationship to one nurturant teacher to move the student from the ascriptive world of the family to the achievement world of the higher grades and work?[23] Could evaluators make initially positive reports on teaming in the early grades and miss effects which become observable, let us say, only during adolescence? What are the latent effects in grading children by age and having them move, almost regardless of ability, at the same rate as their age cohorts? Will self-paced study and non-graded arrangements, in increasing the performance gap between those of the same age, augment or diminish net self-esteem among school children? It would not be hard to produce a long list of such questions, questions which point to our lack of knowledge about the functions of existing arrangements. How effectively can we assess serious change in light of our weak grasp on present learning structures?

Social forms used in instruction can "contain" some values and exclude others apart from the explicit content communicated within the form. A given learning structure, I submit, may "instruct" persons in values considered important by the society yet not be explicitly planned nor consciously evaluated. Note, for example, how different professions use different forms in their professional schools without explicit theoretical justification.[24] Graduate departments in arts and science "automatically" rely on seminars and laboratories, military academies cling to recitation long after other institutions have forsaken it, schools of architecture organize instruction around student projects, and medical schools elevate the importance of the clinic and operating room. Are such choices merely "technical" or "accidental?" Could it not be that the selected forms inculcate, by the very rules which obtain within them, implicit conceptions of occupationally appropriate beliefs on such questions as the relationship between knowledge and action or action and rank? What underlying assumptions about structure and values lead graduate students, asked to design single-purpose schools, to repeatedly link loyalty induction to strict hierarchical organization or creativity as a goal, to structural looseness and equality?[25] Breer and Locke have shown that temporary, experimental involvement in divergent task configurations tends to change attitudes in divergent directions.[26] Is it not likely that protracted engagement in particular learning structures has considerably greater effect on student attitudes and values?

The state of knowledge on interpersonal structures and socialization outcomes forces us to raise questions rather than cite propositions. Yet the probability that structures influence students in as yet unknown ways is, to my view, great enough to have significance for evaluators. To the extent that alternative social forms actualize different values, evaluating "pedagogical means" turns out to be, in fact, the evaluation of "educational ends." Evaluators claiming to assess the effects of large-scale changes should examine functions in depth and decipher effects on latent as well as manifest levels. To ignore such value implications, perhaps by using such single dimensions as cognitive learning, could result in missing unintended and perhaps undesired effects. Large-scale changes make it inappropriate for evaluators to adopt a narrowly technical conception of their role, for such changes add moral complexities to the work of the evaluator.

Broader Goals and Evaluative Expertise

Schooling is more and more a matter of broad societal concern; today the specification of educational objectives includes references to wider social, political and economic problems. The school-

house is no longer an isolated establishment holding interest only for its students, teachers and parents; the issues which arise there arouse excitement in many sectors of our society.

Examples of the newly perceived closeness between schools and society-at-large are easy to find. The writer recalls that his undergraduate professors of economics depicted education as a luxury, as an activity using up scarce goods to economically questionable ends. Today economists pay close attention to the role of education in developing societies and urge heavy investment in it; Schultz and others argue that education contributes directly to human capital formation.[27] Time-worn phrases about "equality of opportunity" take on pungency when the federal government commissions James Coleman to measure departures from that ideal in the conduct of public education.[28] The report that resulted affects our view of educational goals and processes; we are now more likely to concentrate on the output of self-confidence and the relative contribution to institutions (e.g., the family) outside the formal educational apparatus. Education is involved deeply in other questions of our time, from structural unemployment to crime prevention, from producing more scientists to early identification of emotionally disturbed children.

It is not difficult for educators in convention to write statements outlining education's manifold responsibilities. It is quite another matter, however, to calibrate specific instructional choices with particular social or economic or political goals. Past practice has been based on the general idea that mastery of conventional knowledge and/or training in a particular trade would result in students prepared for adult life. What happens when the boundaries of conventional knowledge explode? Or what decisions must be made when traditional occupational lines melt under the impact of automation? Such events make the design of study programs extremely problematic and complicate the evaluative criteria to be used. The educator must become expert in gauging events outside of school affairs, in predicting what knowledge will prove basic, what core skills will have generality in the labor market, what educative experiences will prove to be of persisting value.

The verbal broadening of educational objectives will make no discernible impact until specific instructional practices are aligned with specific social goals. Should demands for such refined interconnections develop, acts of evaluation will take on new dimensions of substantive expertise. Evaluators familiar only with procedures organized around in-school events will find themselves puzzled in translating tests or whatever into meaningful indices of relevance to those demands. The question is, what substantive knowledge will prove vital in such assessments? Should that knowledge prove to be various and broad, educational evaluation, as a field of expert study and practice, may itself break down into a series of sub-specialties organized around substantive fields and particular societal problems.

Some Notes and Questions

It is clear that the writer believes evaluative functions will become more critical in the years ahead; rational decision-making will hinge largely on whether they can be performed in an effective way. I wish to conclude this paper somewhat unsystematically by making additional comments on emerging issues and by raising a few questions which deserve the close attention of educators. The aim is not to design a general evaluative scheme, but to stimulate thought and discussion in the hope that those responsible for governing schools will begin work on needed solutions.

(1) We noted that there will be more options available to school personnel. There are forces at work which will enhance the role of evaluators and move evaluation toward greater expertise and specialization. Yet we must not overlook the great likelihood that *all* persons working in schools will be affected by the presence of more options. Administrators, teachers and specialists will perceive more personal possibilities in their respective roles; the public-at-large, long exposed to claims of professionalism, will expect educators to be ready with informed judgments on alternatives. Scarcities in highly trained personnel make it unlikely that there will be enough specialized evaluators around to relieve other educators of all such pressures. Effective evaluation, furthermore, will proceed only as those who are not specialized come to understand enough about assessment problems and techniques to initiate useful questions and make sensible use of findings.

We may see a collision between the proliferation of options and the subculture of those working in public schools. There is, to my knowledge, no tradition of tough-minded empirical evaluation among American teachers and administrators. Their subculture seems to stress the merits of intuitive judgment based upon experience.[29] Yet experience is of little use in predicting the potential costs and benefits of novel alternatives. How will school people react to problems they cannot resolve through experience? One possibility is firm and unyielding attachment to the status quo. Another, likely to occur where pressures for change are powerful, is the arbitrary adoption of what appear to be politic programs of action. The writer is willing to wager that such fadism will increase in the years ahead.

Those who have a special concern with evaluation, then, face allocative dilemmas in making the best use of scarce teaching resources in their field. Granted that some upgrading of teacher and administrator knowledge of evaluative basics is needed, what weight should be assigned to that need in comparison to the production of able specialists? Given the massiveness of the educational establishment and the extreme improbability of reaching two million teachers and administrators, which groups have the greatest potential for furthering effective evaluation? Presuming that resources will never be sufficient to find and train "enough" specialized evaluators, how can specialists be deployed to attain maximum effectiveness? In view of the long lead-time required to create new resources of high skill, early attention to such questions seems indicated.

(2) The quantity of evaluative work is likely to make it a routine rather than occasional activity of local school districts. It is also highly probable that evaluators will become key members of the administrative group which concerns itself with policy recommendations. Evaluators will need considerable influence if they are to perform well, for they will need control over how innovations are instituted and conducted in order to generate reliable data. Thus evaluators will take part in setting up record-keeping systems, experimental controls, etc., in order to ensure relevant and dependable feedback on programs and their effects.

Constructing evaluative systems is no novelty to American businessmen and government officials. In business, we find elaborate and precise accounting systems, production records, sales statistics, merchandising data, etc., integrated into overall statements which are highly useful in executive decision-making. The "art" of business management is more and more the "art" of interpreting quantitative data and making inferences about their meaning for corporate action.[30] Federal agencies frequently possess complex machinery for evaluation and control of operations.[31] The diffusion of rational modes of decision-making in public schools will also require the development of feedback systems useful to decision-making.

Moving to the rational model is not without complications, however, and this is especially true in education. Business and government systems occur where there is little dispute over the propriety of hierarchical authority and organization—both tend to emphasize centralized decision-making. The introduction of effective evaluative controls in education could, in fact, centralize decision-making without that being anyone's intention; Rourke believes that this is currently taking place in universities as a consequence of the administrative use of computers.[32] Ironically, demands for careful evaluation are arising in education at the point where monolithic and bureaucratic forms of administration are coming under attack from teacher associations, professors and others.

It would ill-suit evaluators with their passion for objective assessment to prejudge an issue as complex as the relative merits of centralized and decentralized decision-making in schools. They had best step gently in designing and implementing systems of data gathering and program control. This problem raises particularly vexing and subtle questions about designing evaluative systems for studying school programs; it looks as if special ingenuity in design will have to be accompanied by special understanding of the dynamics of organization and decision-making.

(3) Unchecked controversy over the conduct of educational evaluation could result in the loss of public confidence. Ways should be found to limit conflicts over the evaluative process itself. The issue of integrity-trust may require considerable attention in the years ahead.

The problem arises from the principle that persons and organizations cannot be trusted to act as judges in their own case.[33] This rule controls financial accountability in our society. No matter how intricate the system of internal audits or how secure the reputation of officials, corporate bodies employ outside accountants to review and report on their financial status. By analogy, we cannot expect protagonists in policy disputes or members of the general public to accept a school system's self-appraisals without question.

Are existing organizational resources adequate to solve the integrity issue, or are new social forms needed? It may be, for example, that critical evaluations will occur infrequently and will be sufficiently independent of university interests so that professors can serve where outside, expert judgments are needed. On the other hand, the volume of work and the consequent necessity for regular "audits" may strain readily available resources in universities and research centers.

What of models from other fields? Medicine, for example, has impressive controls based largely upon the work of pathologists in reviewing surgical tissue and diagnoses through post mortem examinations. But medicine is organized on the basis of sharp autonomy from public inspection linked to a high degree of internal, collegial control, a debatable model for schools which are part of local government. The role of the certified public accountant is more suggestive. A fee-for-service professional, he reports in standard ways understandable to those who choose to learn the elements of accounting rhetoric. Assuming that enough work would be available to give them autonomy from any single client, fee-for-

service evaluators could be employed by school boards or, in some cases, dissident groups, to render a public and disinterested accounting. Such an arrangement might forestall pointless controversies where arguments center on the fact of the case rather than issues of policy.

(4) Issues of moral complexity stemming from ends-means ambiguities are difficult to resolve by examining models outside education. It seems that other fields can use simple dichotomies (profit-loss; sick-healthy) which would be gross oversimplifications in education.

Could evaluative reporting, however, pay closer attention to this question of moral complexity by reporting empirical results in several ways? What I am wondering is whether alternative value schemes could be represented by statistical weighting schemes. Thus a single report might review the data gathered from several perspectives and in terms of several generally recognizable educational positions. The reader would be free to introduce his own dichotomies if he chose; the evaluator would, on the other hand, avoid sacrificing complexity for "a clear answer."

I can see several problems in this approach. Considerable work would be needed to find and express moral positions which are meaningful to the key publics involved in public education. Open identification would undoubtedly stir up debate which is currently minimized by fuzzy statements of both goals and outcomes. But might the long-terms gains in the quality of public discourse justify short-term conflicts? There is risk in the present course of overlooking value conflicts; evaluation may eventually suffer "whiplash" from publics who realize later that they do not *really* want *that* particular set of values.

An adequate system of evaluation, whatever its formats for reporting, will have to cope with shifts in the latent functions of instructional forms. But does current knowledge and research permit us to undertake such analysis with confidence? How much does current social psychology tell us about relationships between socialization and educational structures? If it tells us too little, what basic research is needed, and what responsibility do evaluators have in furthering such research?

(5) Broadened educational goals raise the question of evaluator expertise. To what extent should evaluators working outside the traditional domains of education (the economy, crime prevention, race relations) possess substantive knowledge which is especially relevant to the problem area?

This is delicate territory for those who, like myself, lack expertise in evaluative methodology. How generally applicable are models used in the field? Has the historic link to educational psychology institutionalized data-gathering techniques and analytic habits better suited to in-school than out-school considerations? Can evaluators absorb specialized knowledge about new sectors and problems rapidly enough to practice on a variety of fronts?

Those who have intimate knowledge of the field are better equipped than I to answer these questions. The possibility of specialization within evaluation is, however, an issue which should receive very careful thought. Should such specialization prove desirable, it would have important implications for the training of evaluative specialists and would point toward greater exposure to a wide variety of university-based disciplines.

Speculative analyses are high-risk undertakings; there is no assurance that the method, no matter how prudent, discerns the truly vital issues. But I can conclude with one certainty. To crack the cake of educational custom is to release forces which, by comparison, make the occupants of Pandora's box appear to be docile, innocent and amusing creatures.

ENDNOTES

1. A national survey of teachers conducted by the NEA disclosed that teachers come close to a representative sample of Americans in general, in terms of the social class status of their parents. Many observers believe that this represents a broadening of the teacher base. Undergraduate schooling today is considerably more diverse than it was several decades ago; today there are relatively few beginning teachers who have been trained in "single purpose" institutions. See National Education Association, Research Division, "The American Public School Teachers, 1960-61," Research Monograph 1963-M2.
2. Bagehot, Walter. *Physics and Politics*. New York: Alfred A. Knopf, Inc., 1948.
3. "Evaluation" and "assessment" are given broad definition in this paper, for evaluative acts are intertwined with most educational decisions. The writer assumes, however, that technical evaluation involves some measurement of effects of programs, etc., on students. I have omitted references to the evaluation of personnel since I see it as a somewhat different kind of administrative function.
4. Callahan, Raymond E. *Education and the Cult of Efficiency*. Chicago: University of Chicago Press, 1962.
5. Compare, for example, the preoccupations of the National Science Foundation with those of the Office of Economic Opportunity.
6. Veblen, Thorstein. *The Higher Learning in America*. New York: Sagamore Press, 1957.
7. One might, for example, review the activities of the Education Commission of the States from this perspective.
8. Lieberman, Myron. *The Future of Public Education*. Chicago: University of Chicago Press, 1960.
9. Leggatt, Timothy W. "The Use of Non-Professionals in Public Education," Unpublished doctoral dissertation, Department of Sociology, University of Chicago, 1966.
10. Shaplin, J. and Olds, H., eds. *Team Teaching*. New York: Harper & Row, Publishers, 1964.
11. Several sociologists of note have made this point. Emile Durkheim was among the most prominent, as in his *The Division of Labor*. Glencoe, Illinois: Free Press, 1947.
12. One of the earliest statements of this is found in Hughes, E. C. "Personality and the Division of Labor," In *Men and Their Work*, E. C. Hughes. Glencoe, Illinois: Free Press, 1958.
13. Gardner, B. and Moore, D. *Human Relations in Industry*. Homewood, Illinois: Richard D. Irwin, Inc., 1955.
14. The author recently heard a report on this topic by James Guthrie presented at the Annual Social Science Institute of the University of California, Berkeley.
15. There are indications that principals may become a special interest group. In Michigan, for example, they find themselves caught in cross-pressures of bargaining and are considering the possibility of forming their own professional association.
16. The New York City teachers' union was undoubtedly hampered by the somewhat negative report on the M.E.S. program submitted by the Center on Urban Education. One presumes that next time, they will present evaluative studies of their own!
17. Cremin, L. *The Transformation of the School*. New York: Alfred A. Knopf, Inc., 1961.
18. Callahan, R., op. cit.
19. A possible exception is the introduction of the junior high school.
20. Practically any textbook in educational administration published during the period will serve as an example. See, for example, Hunt, H. and Pierce, P. *The Practice of School Administration*. Boston: Houghton Mifflin Co., 1958, for a recent instance.
21. Blau, Peter. *Bureaucracy in Modern Society*. New York: Random House, Inc., 1956.
22. I heard Robert Wood make this statement in a public address in Cambridge, Massachusetts around 1959.
23. Parsons, Talcott. "The Classroom as a Social System," *Harvard Educational Review*, Fall, 1959.
24. These observations are based on a pilot study conducted by the author of some twenty fields in which vocational training occurs in universities.
25. I have asked students, sub-divided into groups of four or five members, to design the curriculum and structure of a school system dedicated to one major purpose, e.g., induction of piety, cognitive master, creativity in the arts, etc. This has been done four times, and on each occasion students moved toward similar structures for the same overall purposes.
26. Breer, Paul and Locke, Edwin. *Task Experience as a Source of Attitudes*. Homewood, Illinois: Dorsey Press, 1965.

27. Schultz, T. W. *The Economic Value of Education.* New York: Columbia University Press, 1963.

28. Coleman, James, et. al. *Equality of Educational Opportunity.* U.S. Department of Health, Education and Welfare, Office of Education. Washington, D. C.: U.S. Government Printing Office, 1966.

29. This impression is based on interviews conducted as part of the writer's research on teaching as an occupation.

30. The Harvard Business School, long associated with case instruction, recently augmented the amount of quantitative material to be taught their master's students. There was also a special program instituted to train faculty members in the newer quantitative techniques.

31. Kaufman, Herbert. *The Forest Ranger: A Study in Administrative Behavior.* Baltimore: The John Hopkins Press, 1960.

32. Rourke, Francis E. "Computers and University Administration," *Administrative Science Quarterly,* March, 1967.

33. Parsons, T. "Some Ingredients of a General Theory of Formal Organization." In *Administrative Theory in Education,* edited by Andrew Halpin. Chicago: Midwest Administration Center, University of Chicago, 1958.

CHAPTER 9

IMPLICATIONS OF VIEWING EDUCATIONAL EVALUATION AS RESEARCH IN THE BEHAVIORAL SCIENCES

Edwin P. Willems

Under a flood of public financial support and pressure toward innovation, experimentation, and change, resulting in a concern about short-term and long-range effects of unusual support and change, *evaluation* has become a distinctive password in education circles.[1] As with many passwords, it is easy to hope for too much from evaluation, and to infuse it with magic and power that it does not have. There should be some advantage in stripping the concept of its unintended and undeserved attributes and preserving its more realistic and workable ones.

First, evaluation says nothing about what the goals of education ought to be. The generating and articulating of goals, hopes, and ideals come from community consensus and society's norms. Rather, evaluation is a process of gathering evidence that will form the basis for the most accurate statements possible about particular institutions, strategies, sequences, and styles of educational practice. While the resulting statements may focus on the extent to which goals and hopes are realized, evaluation itself is the process by which one uses the best skills and techniques available to make reasonable statements, that is, to answer questions about education.

Second, evaluation as such is neutral as to the level at which the questions are asked and answers sought. At one time, the question might be, "To what extent does school system A meet certain standards of economic efficiency?" At another time, one might ask, "Is teaching style Z enhancing the reading speed of intellectually marginal students?" Furthermore, evaluation as such is neutral as to the time perspective of the questions asked. That is, one might wonder about a portion of a particular class session or about lifelong effects.

Viewing evaluation as the process by which persons use the best skills and means available to answer questions makes it equivalent to another set of human activities called *research*. Research has also become a password, and as a result, there are varying opinions about its power and usefulness. It is also common to infuse research with too much magic and power, and to circumscribe it with overly strict boundaries. For example, Kerlinger says, "It should be clear then, that the ideal of science (research)[2] is the controlled experiment . . . the controlled experiment is the desired model of science (research)."[3] No particular method or technique represents the model of research. The model of research is the process by which a person or group of persons use the best skills or means available to gather evidence to answer their questions. Thus, evaluation and research are similar, if not equivalent, processes.

Assuming, as Kerlinger does, that one particular method or technique represents the model of evaluation or research has two subtle but pervasive by-products: (a) Every issue or question about education or behavior must be tailored to fit that method. (b) When the issues or questions do not fit that method, they are not amenable to evaluation or research. This is putting the cart before the horse. Tools and methods must be chosen by persons to suit their problems and questions.

Viewing evaluation as equivalent to, or as a special case of, research and viewing research as a personal, human process of seeking answers to questions, have many implications, some of which will be discussed below. However, one distinction

1. Gene Atkinson and David A. Knickel, "Evaluation of Educational Programs: An Exploration." (Paper prepared for Gulf Schools Supplementary Education Center, Pearland, Texas, 1966.)

2. Present author's insertion.

3. F. N. Kerlinger. *Foundations of Behavioral Research: Educational and Psychological Inquiry.* New York: Holt, Rinehart & Winston, Inc., 1964. p. 291.

must be made clearly at the outset, the distinction between "personal" and "private." Research is a personal activity, subject to many human foibles, mistakes, and weaknesses. However, research is also an explicit, documented process, open to public scrutiny, so that another person can independently repeat the process and independently verify or refute the resulting statements. A private, undocumented process for generating statements is a mysterious one that cannot be independently repeated and checked. Such a private process is not research. The issue here is the general issue of the grounds for evidence. Whenever someone makes statements in the evaluation of education, it should be possible to assess independently whether his statements are justified. If the process of arriving at his statements is private, the accuracy of his statements cannot be assessed.

Methodology in Behavioral Research

The argument can be taken a step further by viewing evaluation as a special case of research in the social or behavioral sciences. That is, evaluation is research on institutions, organizations, large and small social groups, and individual abilities and predispositions, i.e., the interplay among physical, economic, and social environment and individual behavior and experience. The distinct advantage of viewing evaluation as social and behavioral research is that there exists an extensive literature on the issues, problems, strategies, techniques, and guidelines of such research. This literature is too far ranging to review here; however, authors such as Gage,[4] Kerlinger (mentioned above), Selltiz et al.,[5] Festinger and Katz,[6] and Webb et al.,[7] have provided excellent treatments of research methodology. A great number of books and articles on educational and psychological testing are also available. In other words, the process of obtaining data to answer questions, together with the precautions and guidelines required for making statements based on the data, have been thoroughly described and documented. However, in spite of this extensive literature, there remains one special problem for education evaluation that has not been treated extensively enough and in enough detail. This problem has to do with what one is studying and the conditions under which one is studying it in the typical, workaday exercise of education evaluation.

Two Strategies of Research

One way to evaluate an educational program, or a part of an educational program, is to construct a paradigm case and study its outcomes, that is, to conduct an explicitly arranged experiment. This strategy has the great advantages of any controlled experiment, such as carefully isolating and controlling the conditions and it increases the possibility of making clear statements on what leads to what. Laboratory schools and experimental educational groups, in which students are carefully selected and assigned to groups and in which teaching conditions and environmental circumstances can be varied or held constant at will, are examples of this evaluative strategy. A further advantage of this strategy, here called *experimental evaluation*, is that the rationale and guidelines for it have been discussed so carefully by writers such as Campbell and Stanley,[8] Shaw,[9] Festinger,[10] and Kerlinger (mentioned earlier), who offer strong and reasonable arguments favoring the experimental approach.

Granting the advantages and strengths of experimental evaluation, the major problem in adopting it as a strategy is that in the usual evaluation of an educational program, whether by a participant in the program or by an outside person or agency, that which is being evaluated is an already existing, intact program. By its very nature, the typical, workaday process of evaluation involves what is here called *naturalistic evaluation* or *naturalistic research* wherein the evaluator or researcher does not have manipulative, experimental control over the events he is studying.[11] In contrast to experimental research, there is a relative lack of careful, thoughtful literature that discusses the strengths, rationale, and guidelines for naturalistic research. In other words, despite a few

4. Nathaniel L. Gage, ed. *Handbook of Research on Teaching.* Chicago: Rand McNally & Co., 1963.
5. Claire Selltiz, et al. *Research Methods in Social Relations.* New York: Holt, Rinehart & Winston, Inc., 1961.
6. Leon Festinger and Daniel Katz, eds. *Research Methods in the Behavioral Sciences.* New York: Holt, Rinehart & Winston, Inc., 1953.
7. Eugene J. Webb, et al. *Unobtrusive Measures: Nonreactive Research in the Social Sciences.* Chicago: Rand McNally & Co., 1966.
8. Donald T. Campbell and Julian C. Stanley. "Experimental and Quasi-Experimental Designs for Research on Teaching." In *Handbook of Research on Teaching,* edited by Nathaniel L. Gage, pp. 171-246. Chicago: Rand McNally & Co., 1963.
9. M. E. Shaw. "Social Psychology and Group Processes." *Experimental Methods and Instrumentation in Psychology,* edited by J. B. Sidowski, pp. 607-643. New York: McGraw-Hill Book Company, 1966.
10. Leon Festinger. "Laboratory Experiments." In *Research Methods in the Behavioral Sciences,* edited by Leon Festinger and Daniel Katz, pp. 136-172. New York: Holt, Rinehart & Winston, Inc., 1953.
11. The following paper discusses some of the differences between the experimental and naturalistic strategies:
    Edwin P. Willems. Toward an explicit rationale for naturalistic research methods. *Human Development* 10 (1967): 138-154.

exceptions,[12] there is a comparative lack of material dealing with the kind of research methods that the typical evaluative process calls for.

Dimensions of Naturalistic Research

Because of the relative lack of detailed material on naturalistic research, some space will be devoted to the rationale and reasons for such methods.

Inventory of educational phenomena. Handbooks and encyclopedias of the physical sciences agree in saying that potassium ranks seventh in order of abundance of elements, and constitutes 2.59 percent of the igneous rocks of the earth's crust; that potassium compounds are widely distributed in the primary rocks, the oceans, the soil, plants, and animals; and that soluble potassium salts are present in all fertile soils. Such findings on the distribution of potassium in nature are extremely helpful to persons who are evaluating occurrences of potassium and its compounds and effects. In other words, physical scientists and engineers have detailed information on the frequency and range of occurrence of the things with which they deal. It is odd that apart from the occasional, spotty educational census, the norms of a few tests, and some selective service summaries, the engineers, planners, and evaluators of educational programs and behavior know so little about how their phenomena are distributed in nature. They know relatively little about the frequency, range, and classification of teaching styles, problem-solving, succeeding, failing, aspiring, cooperating, accepting responsibility, playing, being valued, conflict, etc. In other words, in the evaluation of programs for optimizing and arranging human resources, there is no handbook, inventory, or periodic table which will put specific findings into perspective. The process of generating such a handbook of education-related behavior calls for a tremendous amount of naturalistic research or the observation and classification of intact, naturally-occurring educational situations. Evaluation, if viewed and conducted as serious research, could aid in filling this need.

Problem of yield. It is often thought that naturalistic research, the kind of research involved in evaluating existing programs, is inefficient in that a disproportionately small amount of information is gleaned from the investment of time and money. Experimental evaluation is often viewed as being more efficient, in that the information yield is greater.

The problem of ratio of effort to yield occurred in a study by Gump and Kounin,[13] who had been studying how disciplinary techniques directed at one child affected the other children in classrooms. Extending their studies to public camps, they observed camp leaders and campers. In the

written narratives describing 46 hours of the behavior of campers, only one incident of the type they were studying occurred for every 18 pages of narrative. This was extremely low yield from a naturalistic study. However, Kounin reported another study in which the yield was disappointingly low from a piece of experimental evaluation.[14] Kounin was again assessing effects of disciplinary techniques upon nontarget children, but this time he wanted to assess their effects upon children who ranged from high to low on commitment to the tasks. After carefully training his experimental teachers, he arranged for a sample of adolescents to come to the laboratory school during the summer, for pay, to serve as experimental students. Kounin was unable to induce low commitment in any of these experimental students, while in intact, naturally-occuring classrooms, he was able to find such students. The implication is that the problem of economy of effort is not unique to naturalistic evaluation.

Artificiality. Perhaps more important than the question of yield is the likelihood of artificiality in experimental evaluation. Artificiality refers to educational arrangements and situations that students and teachers never confront in their intact, everyday experiences. Two published studies illustrate the problem of artificiality.

Gump and Kounin (mentioned above) wanted again to assess the effects of disciplinary techniques by teachers upon nontarget students, this time in college classrooms. They arranged for student accomplices to come late to classes, and they trained teachers to sometimes try supportive, friendly reactions and sometimes threatening, punitive reactions on the late arrivals. In this experimental arrangement, they found that punitive, as compared to friendly, reactions resulted in lower ratings of the teachers' competence, likableness, and fairness by nontarget students. However, the

12. Roger G. Barker. "Observation of Behavior: Ecological Approaches." *Journal of Mt. Sinai Hospital* 31 (1964): 268-284.

Roger G. Barker. Explorations in ecological psychology. *American Psychologist* 20 (1965): 1-14.

Paul V. Gump and Jacob S. Kounin. Issues raised by ecological and classical research efforts. *Merrill-Palmer Quarterly* 6 (1959-1960): 145-152.

Edwin P. Willems. An ecological orientation in psychology. *Merrill-Palmer Quarterly* 11 (1965): 317-343.

Edwin P. Willems. Toward an explicit rationale for naturalistic research methods. *Human Development* 10 (1967): 138-154.

Edwin P. Willems and H. L. Raush, eds. *Naturalistic Viewpoints in Psychological Research.* New York: Holt, Rinehart & Winston, Inc., 1969.

13. Paul V. Gump and Jacob S. Kounin. Issues raised by ecological and classical research efforts. *Merrill-Palmer Quarterly.* 6 (1959-1960): 145-152.

14. Jacob S. Kounin. Dimensions of Adult-Child Relationships in the Classroom. Paper read at Topology Meeting, New York, August, 1961.

investigators found through later questionnaires that the students were surprised that one of their college teachers would make a point of taking time out from class to correct and respond to a late arrival. In their attempts to create a neat experimental evaluation, Gump and Kounin had taken a phenomenon out of its everyday context and produced an arrangement that was not customary for the students.

Gump and Sutton-Smith studied the reactions and behavior of poorly skilled boys when they were assigned to more or less difficult roles in games.[15] In the experimental game, a boy who was *It* worked in the center of a rectangular playing field and attempted to tag other players who ran to and from safe areas at each end of the field. High power was given to the *It* role by having the boy who was *It* call the turns; he dictated when others could run. In the low power condition, the other players could run whenever they chose. Preselected slow runners were assigned to the two *It* conditions. In the low power as compared to the high power *It* conditions, poorly skilled boys experienced more tagging failures, uttered more comments indicating defeat and distress, and were teased and combined against more frequently. However, when the investigators adopted the naturalistic strategy and observed what happened in gyms, camps, and playgrounds, where they had not arranged and manipulated the game conditions, they found that poorly skilled boys seldom got into difficult games. If they did get involved, they avoided or were excluded from the difficult roles. The experimental evaluation created conditions that were artificial and unusual for the boys. The naturalistic evaluations pointed out in what ways the experiment failed to match the everyday event.

There are several implications of these examples of artificiality. There is certainly nothing inherently wrong with experimental evaluations. In fact, experiments are often ideal for testing hunches and theories. On the other hand, it is clear that naturalistic evaluation is not a weak second cousin of experimental evaluation. In fact, it is the only choice of strategies when one wishes to evaluate intact, already existing educational arrangements. Finally, as a later section will suggest, naturalistic evaluation can often point out specifically those ways in which experimental educational research has generated artificial, restricted conditions.

Repeatability. Reference was made earlier to a distinction between personal and private activities, and the point was made that private activities have no place in research or, therefore, in evaluation. One characteristic of evaluation that takes it out of the private domain and brings it into the acceptable research domain is repeatability. An evaluation is repeatable when the same evalu-

ator or another evaluator can use the same techniques or observe the same conditions a second or third time and end up with the same results. If two persons evaluate the same phenomenon, supposedly using the same techniques of observation and assessment, and get discrepant results, the evaluative processes they have used should be open to question as containing too many private, unrepeatable aspects. Naturalistic research, the type typically required for evaluating existing educational conditions, is often criticized on the grounds that it is not repeatable. Fortunately, repeatability is not a matter for pure speculation and argument to decide; it can be decided on the basis of what persons actually find. One example will illustrate the point.

In the face of a strong movement to consolidate high schools in Kansas, a group of psychologists sought to evaluate the effects of school size upon the experience and behavior of students.[16] One subpart of this program of research, which is still in progress, sought to assess how school size related to the development of sense of obligation to school activities, or social responsibility, in the students. Two studies, four years apart, involving different samples of students, yielded almost identical results: students in small schools reported much more sense of social obligation than students in large schools. Several studies independently obtained corroborating results. The point here is that all of these studies involved naturalistic methods of evaluation, and they yielded repeatable, nonprivate results.

Generalizing. Much of the preceding discussion is relevant to what is perhaps the most important rationale for naturalistic evaluation, or naturalistic research. It is probably a truism that persons who are evaluating an educational arrangement wish to make general concluding statements about the arrangement and perhaps others like it. Several examples will illustrate how naturalistic research sometimes disagrees with experimental research and will suggest how naturalistic evaluation serves a uniquely important function. The examples may appear to range far afield from direct educational applications, but their implications are rather direct and important.

S. L. Washburn, the anthropologist, reports that baboons have been studied frequently in experimental research, as in primate laboratories, and in captivity, as in zoos.[17] When two or more baboons are confined together, it is common to find

15. Paul V. Gump and B. Sutton-Smith. "The It Role in Children's Games." *The Group* 17 (1955): 3-8.

16. Roger G. Barker and Paul V. Gump. *Big School, Small School: High School Size and Student Behavior.* Stanford: Stanford University Press, 1964.

17. Sherwood L. Washburn, Phi Beta Kappa Lecture, University of Kansas, 1963.

that one emerges as the leader, which is not surprising in itself. Under these conditions, the leaders emerge and maintain their leadership through physical intimidation and comparative brute power. Washburn goes on to report the results of observations of baboons in their natural habitats, and one set of findings is of special interest. Leaders also emerge in the wild, but they appear not to emerge by physical intimidation and brute power. Superior cunning, sexual expertise, and attractiveness seem to be the route to leadership among baboons in the wild.

The work of Beecher on pain relieving drugs also suggests the important contribution of naturalistic research.[18] Beecher's findings suggest that laboratory experiments on pain and pain-relieving drugs contribute little to the understanding of pain and analgesia as they occur outside the laboratory. Compounds that seem to relieve pain in the controlled laboratory conditions often fail to do so in the wards of hospitals, while substances which, by laboratory experiment would seem to be ineffective, frequently are highly effective in the clinical situation. In other words, the picture of drugs and pain relief would be incomplete without naturalistic evaluation.

Hall and Williams, two psychologists, recently reported a fascinating study of how groups handle conflict and solve problems.[19] They compared the performances of 20 established, intact groups of management trainees to 20 contrived groups, groups with no history as groups before the individuals came to the laboratory. The established groups differed markedly from the contrived groups, especially in the way they dealt with conflict. In other words, Hall and Williams found that it is precarious business to generalize from contrived laboratory groups to established, naturally occurring groups.

The implications of these examples for educational evaluation are clear. It is seductively easy to be content with the results obtained in controlled experimental research and to assume that caution is the only requirement for generalizing these findings and making them applicable to the real life situation. The examples suggest that caution is not the only requirement, and that naturalistic research performs a uniquely required function. Not only is naturalistic research not a second-rate adjunct to experimental research, but it is very important in ascertaining the generalizability of experimental research. In other words, naturalistic evaluation promises to perform an important function in educational research.

Summary of naturalistic evaluation. A significant amount of space has been devoted to the rationale for naturalistic evaluation, and parts of the discussion appear propagandistic. This is so by intent, for two reasons. First, evaluation is a special case of research. The kind of research represented by the evaluation of intact, already existing situations can and should be seen as falling inside the main body of educational research. Second, the distinct advantages and strengths that naturalistic evaluation bring the research domain should be recognized by all those who take educational research seriously.

Advantages and Implications

In behavioral research, the investigator must have a clear idea of what he wants to study. In evaluation, one must have a correspondingly clear idea of what one is evaluating. In both research and evaluation, the investigator seeks to make statements that document the occurrence of something or that document that one thing leads to another. In all these efforts, the investigator or evaluator attempts to gather information or data to form a basis for his statements. One advantage of viewing evaluation as a special case of research is that other persons engaged in research have learned certain critical lessons from the process of gathering data. These lessons have been well-documented, and should also be taken into account in evaluation.

Reliability. One such important lesson concerns the reliability of the ways, means, and techniques used to gather information. Tests, firsthand observations, questionnaires, interviews, tabulations from school records, and reports of students and teachers are all examples of techniques that might be used for gathering evaluative information, and they constitute what researchers call measures, or data-gathering techniques. If one administered an achievement test twice to the same group of students, under standard conditions and found that students' scores fluctuated widely from one time to the next, one should question the ability of the test to measure anything. This is one example of lack of reliability. Authors of published tests usually study reliability as a matter of course. However, it is easy to forget that any technique for gathering information is a measuring instrument whose reliability should be assessed directly.

18. The following references summarize some of Beecher's research:

Henry K. Beecher. Relationship of significance of wound to pain experienced. *Journal of the American Medical Association* 161 (1956): 1609-1613.

Henry K. Beecher. Generalization from pain of various types and origins. *Science* 130 (1959): 267-268.

Henry K. Beecher. *Measurement of Subjective Responses.* New York: Oxford, 1959.

Henry K. Beecher. Increased stress and effectiveness of placebos and active drugs. *Science* 132 (1960): 91-92.

19. Jay Hall and Martha S. Williams. A comparison of decision-making performances in established and *ad hoc* groups. *Journal of Personality and Social Psychology* 3 (1966): 214-222.

If a technique or measuring instrument fails the test of reliability, then the answer to the critical question, "Does my technique measure anything?" must be cast in doubt.

The problem of reliability is not critical in measures of such things as weight, height, hair color, and sex, but measures of the kinds of things educational evaluation seeks to assess usually involve very complicated problems of reliability. If a zoologist has difficulty arriving at reliable measures of how many chimpanzees cross paths in a small jungle area,[20] it seems likely that evaluation of education will have difficulty arriving at reliable measures of such phenomena as self-actualization or "a full grasp of the opportunities for preparing for a productive life."[21] Furthermore, it will not do for persons involved in evaluation to deemphasize and criticize those who worry about reliability, because reliability is fundamentally involved in what constitutes acceptable evaluative evidence.

Validity. Reliability focuses on the question, "Do I have a measure at all?" Assuming reliability, the next critical question is, "Does my technique measure what I *think* it measures?" The latter is a question of validity, a question that has been thoroughly probed in the literature on research.[22] By way of analogy, suppose one were informed that school A had beaten school B by a score of 14 to 10 in football. The scores would undoubtedly represent valid measures of the number of times the teams scored touchdowns, extra points, and field goals; however, they would probably represent increasingly *invalid* measures of team ability, quality of coaching, and quality of football in the regions from which the schools came. Likewise, data on how often students are absent are probably a valid measure of attendance, but their validity as a measure of student initiative or sense of responsibility is much more questionable.

Validity is directly involved in the grounds or basis for making evaluative statements, and the question, "Do his data measure what he thinks they measure?" probably lies at the heart of many controversies that arise over evaluation.

Control groups. Closely related to the problem of validity is the importance of control groups, another lesson learned the hard way by persons involved in research. Campbell and Stanley, in the paper cited earlier, discuss the usefulness and importance of control groups in detail, so that only enough space will be devoted to them here to suggest their relevance to evaluation. One detailed example will suffice.

Sense of responsibility, commitment, loyalty, or sense of obligation, all refer to something that parents, teachers, and group leaders commonly hope children will acquire during their develop-

ment. Several years ago some studies were conducted to assess the relation between high school size and students' sense of obligation to school activities.[23] For present purposes, the exact details are less important than the findings. Students in small high schools reported a strong sense of obligation to activities, much stronger than their counterparts in a large school. However, the small schools were located in small rural towns, while the large school was located in an urban area, a circumstance that made it impossible to attribute the differences in sense of obligation to school size instead of rural-urban differences. In this case, another study served the function of a control group.[24] The second study compared students in schools that varied in size but which were all located in relatively small towns, and obtained the same results for school size. Taking into account this control study, the impact of school size upon sense of obligation could be evaluated more clearly. In other words, rather than controlling anything in the usual sense, control groups, when properly chosen and used, allow one to attribute effects where they should be attributed, a very important consideration in educational evaluation.

Only three implications, in the form of lessons to be learned, that follow from viewing evaluation as a special case of research have been discussed in detail. The three areas discussed, reliability, validity, and control groups, deal with the process of gathering defensible information, and are perhaps the most fundamental. Other lessons learned from research also have their im-

20. Adriaan Kortlandt. Chimpanzees in the Wild. *Scientific American* 206 (1962): 128-140.

21. Henry S. Dyer. "The Pennsylvania Plan." *Science Education* 50 (1966): 242-248.

22. Validity is one of the most common topics in the literature on educational, psychological, and social research. The following is just one example of such discussions:

Lee J. Cronbach. *Essentials of Psychological Testing.* 2nd ed. New York: Harper & Row, Publishers, 1960.

23. The following papers summarize the research on sense of obligation:

Edwin P. Willems. "Forces Toward Participation in Behavior Settings." In *Big School, Small School: High School Size and Student Behavior,* edited by Roger G. Barker and Paul V. Gump, pp. 115-135. Stanford: Stanford University Press, 1964.

Edwin P. Willems. "Participation in Behavior Settings in Relation to Three Variables: Size of Behavior Settings, Marginality of Persons, and Sensitivity to Audiences." Unpublished doctoral dissertation, University of Kansas, 1965.

Edwin P. Willems. Sense of obligation to high school activities as related to school size and marginality of student. *Child Development* 38 (1967): 1247-1260.

24. W. J. Campbell. "Some Effects of High School Consolidation." In *Big School, Small School: High School Size and Student Behavior,* edited by Roger G. Barker and Paul V. Gump, pp. 139-153. Stanford: Stanford University Press, 1964.

plications, and will only be mentioned. Such specific evaluative problems as construction and use of questionnaires and tests, proper sampling of circumstances and persons, interview techniques, and useful, informative statistical techniques for summarizing and presenting the information gathered in evaluation all have their own unique problems and have all been treated extensively in the literature.[25]

Simplifying in Evaluation

The reasons for, and advantages and implications of, viewing evaluation as a special case of behavioral research discussed so far focus on factors that might usefully be taken into account in the actual exercise and activity of evaluating. One of the earmarks of research and, therefore, of evaluation, is that evaluative problems be refined, narrowed, and simplified into manageable size so that reasonable, defensible information can be gathered. No one to date has satisfactorily evaluated education per se; every attempt at evaluation selects some aspect or aspects of the educational process as being of special interest or particular importance. Sometimes, insidiously, the selection is made according to the kinds of observational and measuring tools that happen to be available. No matter what the reasons for the selection, the typical approach to educational evaluation is a *simplifying* one, where simplifying means arbitrary untying, dismantling, and selecting from the complex phenomena of education. The arguments in favor of simplifying are compelling, but simplifying also has major drawbacks. Just one such drawback, common to research in general and to evaluation in particular, is the very strong human tendency toward faddishness. In behavioral research and in evaluation it is tempting to invest the piece of work one is doing with too much value and representativeness, and assume that what one is observing and studying represents, or *is*, education. In the overall effort called evaluation, not only is there room for, but there should be explicit attention given to widening, complicating, and enriching the scope and complexity of the set of things and occurrences to be evaluated. In other words, there is also a need for just the opposite of simplifying, for at least three reasons.

The first such reason is the common tendency to develop stereotypes about what education is. One such stereotype might view education as the circumstances that produce creative problem-solving in students. Stereotypes have the advantage of leading to crucial, clear-cut evaluations, for example, measures of creative problem-solving on students from different schools and classrooms. However, stereotypes can also be translated into exclusive educational goals, whereby, for example, one might assume that if a little creative problem-solving is good and useful, more should be better.

In addition to the tendency to stereotype education itself, a second reason for guarding against premature simplifying is a common tendency in research, called "the law of the hammer."[26] The law of the hammer goes as follows: If you give a child a hammer, things to be pounded become the most important things around. Likewise, it is too often true that if one gives the researcher or educational evaluator a standardized achievement test, achievement *as that test measures it* becomes the most important aspect of education to be evaluated. Of course, the same can happen when the evaluator has a pet way of measuring self-actualization, leadership, social responsibility, ego-strength, student satisfaction, problem-solving, and so on, but the tendency encourages premature simplifying.

The third reason for avoiding premature simplifying focuses on the admirable but misleading little phrase: "Let's look at the facts." The directive to "look at the facts" can often cut away much of the polemic and controversy in educational evaluation, but the response to it can also be subtly misdirected. As a case in point, the Department of Education of the State of Kansas published a comprehensive educational survey of Kansas schools in the late 1950's, and the survey itself stated that any evaluation of the recommendations of the survey, without knowledge of the facts on which they were based, would be of little value. From the sizes, curricula, programs, and administrative organizations of Kansas schools, the survey concluded that the schools were suffering from educational malnutrition. Unfortunately, the survey did *not* provide the factual basis for a diagnosis of malnutrition, which should have included careful examination of the children who partook of the fare provided. To provide the factual basis, a group of psychologists at the University of Kansas undertook a series of studies of Kansas schools (see Barker and Gump, mentioned earlier), and found that when the experience and performance of the students were considered, some of the survey's conclusions were unfounded. These psychologists took seriously the dictum, "Let's look at the facts," indicated the ways in which the picture painted by the survey was prematurely simplified, and strengthened the picture by complicating it.

25. See, for example, *Handbook of Research on Teaching*, edited by Gage and mentioned above, and various chapters in:
　Gardner Lindzey, ed. *Handbook of Social Psychology*. Reading, Massachusetts: Addison-Wesley Publishing Co., Inc., 1954.
26. From a personal conversation with Professor Egon Guba.

A second case in point is the history of attempts in psychology to evaluate the effectiveness of various types of psychotherapy. In the early 1950's, the cry went up, "Let's just look at the facts," and various types of psychotherapy were evaluated in terms of simple discharge rates.[27] These early attempts were completely inconclusive, and it is only now, many years later, that the complexity of evaluating psychotherapy and guidelines for evaluating it are taking useful shape.[28]

All evaluation requires some simplification and choice. However, keeping in mind (a) the common tendency to enshroud the concept of education in stereotypes, (b) the common tendency to define education by the available measuring tools, and (c) how misleading the call to "Look at the facts" can be, might prevent premature and overly narrow simplification.

Evaluation and Everyday Practice

All that has been said so far has been directed toward the implications of viewing evaluation as research and the special contributions that evaluation can make to educational research in general. Little has been said about the relation between evaluation, or the persons engaged in evaluation, and the actual, day-to-day practice of education in the hands of school boards, administrators, teachers, and students. In the eye of the day-to-day practitioner, evaluation, especially when it is done by third persons and outsiders, is often seen as nosiness, intrusion, criticism, and recommended change. Perhaps, viewing evaluation as research will intensify such feelings. However, advocating a view of evaluation as research in no way implies a position that is incompatible with day-to-day practices, commitments, and traditional wisdom.

If, over the years, many different approaches of the practice of education have been tried, if some approaches have worked better than others, and if those that have worked better have, to some extent, been more persistently practiced by their originators, or imitated by others, or taught to apprentices, then the practices that have emerged may represent a valuable and tested portion of all possible practices. However, the bases for selecting and pruning among practices are very imprecise in the day-to-day process. Sometimes, what survives is a product of chance, or whim, or habit. Explicit evaluation, perhaps by an outsider, enters here as a means for sharpening the selection process. Explicit evaluation is not a source of ideas that are necessarily contradictory with day-to-day, accumulated wisdom, but is rather a refining process, or an aid to the refining process, supplementary to and sometimes superimposed upon accumulated wisdom. Thus, everyday accumulated practice and evaluation are *both* products of accumulation, remaining from experiences from which much has been weeded out. Evaluation as viewed here is one source of evidence for making decisions, and is not itself a policy-planning activity.

27. H. J. Eyesnck. The effects of psychotherapy: an evaluation. *Journal of Consulting Psychology* 16 (1952): 319-324.

28. D. J. Kiesler. Some myths of psychotherapy research and the search for a paradigm. *Psychological Bulletin* 65 (1966): 110-136.

CHAPTER 10

EVALUATION RESEARCH AND RESEARCH DESIGNS*

Gordon Welty

Americans are vitally concerned for the improvement of the quality of education. President Nixon recently rejected the notion of "more dollars for the same old programs without making the urgent new reforms that are needed." He went on to propose "a new and searching look at our American school system."[1] A critical aspect of the educational community's ability to meet the President's challenge is its ability to mount a viable program evaluation effort. To date, educational evaluation has been most notable in its failure.[2]

Speaking of evaluation in general, the American philosopher Clarence Irving Lewis points out that actions could not attain success except that there are *evaluations,* which are essentially predictions.[3] "Whether the action is performed or not will depend upon evaluations made."[4] In terms of general system theory, Lewis is emphasizing the necessity of *feedback* in any action scheme.

Action is an attempt to control the future, as far as is possible, for our own benefit. Action is based in the present, in the given situation; it is intentional behavior directed towards realizing desirable states-of-affairs and avoiding undesirable states-of-affairs.[5] The movement is from the reality of the present to a chosen future. Lewis continues that "the principal function of empirical knowledge is that of an instrument enabling transition from the one to the other."[6]

Feedback of evaluative reports to decision makers is a necessity in the rationally managed school system, if it is viewed as a system. On the revision of ongoing educational programs, for instance, J. T. Hastings has stated that "without such feedback, either the decision to revise or the decision not to revise—and most certainly the decision of how to revise—must be based upon feeling tones and the arguments of personal preference."[7] It has been frequently maintained that the demand for evaluative feedback is incompatible with the classical experimental design. For

example, consider Dean Egon Guba's statement that "the application of conventional experimental design to evaluation situations . . . conflicts with the principle that evaluation should facilitate the continuous improvement of a program."[8] A requirement of invariance of treatment and control are sufficient on Guba's argument to preclude program change. Thus, these conditions are sufficient to preclude evaluation feedback for managerial decision-making, because "treatments cannot be altered if the data about differences between treatments are to be unequivocal."[9]

Guba considers this a problem of "evaluation methodology." As such, it is a problem of paramount importance to the development of evaluation theory. If the dissemination of evaluative findings is not permitted to preserve the experimental design, then evaluation loses its value to

*This is a revised version of a paper presented in Division D, AERA 1969 Annual Meeting, February 7, 1969, Los Angeles, California.

1. Quoted in the *New York Times*, January 27, 1970.

2. Cf. Gordon A. Welty, "Educational Evaluation and Evolutionary Operation," *School Review* (1970). The shortcomings of program evaluation are hardly unique to education. The reader is invited to examine the Comptroller General's Report to the Congress (B-132900), *Need for Better Coordination Among, and Guidance of, Management Evaluation Groups in the Department of Defense* (Washington, D. C.: U. S. General Accounting Office, January 2, 1970) for a rather surprising comment on program evaluation in the Department of Defense, long considered a stronghold of rationality and efficiency.

3. C. I. Lewis, *An Analysis of Knowledge and Valuation* (1946), pp. 371-372.

4. Ibid. p. 4.

5. Ibid. ch. XII, esp. p. 367f.

6. Ibid. p. 4.

7. J. T. Hastings, "Curriculum Evaluation." *Journal of Educational Measurement* 9 (1969): 35.

8. Egon Guba, "The Failure of Educational Evaluation." *Educational Technology* 9 (1969): 35.

9. Guba, ibid.

the decision-maker. On the other hand, if experimental design is to be abandoned, serious problems await evaluators in the development of alternatives. We find, however, that these contentions are not valid. It is not the case that treatment must remain invariant. Corrective action by program managers, in light of evaluative feedback, can take place concurrent with an evaluation in the framework of an experimental design.

Of crucial importance is what Guba intends by *treatment alteration*. Suppose that quantitative change is a change of the value of a given variable (whether an intensive or extensive measurement); then it is convenient to let qualitative change be a change of a variable or dimension itself. Could not the latter be Guba's intent? Let us, then, consider as a possible meaning of qualitative change that a variable or dimension is simply added or deleted from the analysis, as the program manager adds or subtracts from the program, and treatment alterations correspond to this.

The Principle of Dimensional Homogeneity states that for a given equation, all the dimensions or variables in the equation can be categorized in terms of a collection of fundamental measures. For example, if volume occurs in an equation, the dimensions of volume are categorized in terms of length. The principle also states that the dimensionality of the variables (the dimensionality of volume for instance is 3) on the right- and left-hand side of the equation, by fundamental measure, must be equal. This is known as the π Theorem. For example, velocity is distance per time. The fundamental measures for velocity are two, length and time. Dimensionality is 1 and −1, respectively. As this also is the case for distance divided by time, the formula is dimensionally homogeneous. If it were otherwise, the introduction or deletion of either fundamental measures or dimensionally across the equation would be a case of *ad hoc* theorizing, however subtle.[10]

So it is not possible, as a methodological point, for there to be qualitative change in the sense of adding or deleting variables. Hence, we consider here only the case of treatment variance which is both a rational response to evaluative feedback and also treated as dimensionally homogeneous, and indicate how this is compatible with experimental design.

My colleague, Alfred Beradino and I have recently provided a proof that an experimental design and the feedback of action research findings are compatible.[11] This provides sufficient conditions for the falsity of Guba's methodological argument.

The question now can be raised whether a precedent exists in the literature for the use of experimental designs in this fashion. In the writings of Sir Ronald Fisher, we find sufficient conditions for the methodological (not practical) arguments for the use of experimental designs in evaluative research.

In his classic *Design of Experiments*, Fisher proposes to "examine the physical conditions of the experimental technique." After mentioning that *matching of conditions* across treatment levels in the experimental design is a formal condition for minimizing errors, Fisher argues it is impossible to realize this condition in fact, since "uncontrolled causes which may influence the result are always strictly innumerable."[12] With regards matching of conditions, the assumption that "refinements constitute improvements to the experiment" is dismissed on the basis of cost considerations. Since matching is a sufficient but not a necessary condition, control of errors in the experiment can and must be realized by other means. The cost of complete matching across treatment levels would be (quite strictly) infinite, and since "an essential characteristic of experimentation is that it is carried out with limited resources," Fisher proposes *randomization* as an alternative. This is a procedure by which the experiment "may be guaranteed against corruption by the causes of disturbance which have not been eliminated."[13] More precisely, random assignment of subjects to treatment levels permits a precise estimate of error. Thus there are two and only two sufficient conditions for experimental control; hence, one of the two is always necessary. Irrelevant variables are eliminated in effect either by matching of conditions, that is, "eliminated in the field," or by randomization. Fisher emphasizes the sufficiency of the latter technique when he argues that "it is apparent that the random choice of the objects to be treated in different ways would be a complete guarantee of the validity of the test of significance, if these treatments were the last in time of the stages in the physical history of the objects which might affect their experimental reaction."[14] This is to say that randomization is sufficient in the *absence* of treatment variation, to which Guba would undoubtedly agree.

10. For a further discussion of Dimensional Analysis, cf. Percy W. Bridgman's article, "Dimensional Analysis," *Encyclopedia Britannica* (1962 edition) Vol. VII.

11. Cf. Gordon Welty and Alfred Beradino, "Structural Models and Dynamic Organizational Research: A Possibility Theorem." Presented at the 1970 Annual Meeting of the Eastern Psychological Association, April 2, 1970, Atlantic City, New Jersey.

12. R. A. Fisher, *Design of Experiments*, 8th ed. New York: Hafner Publishing Co., Inc., 1966. pp. 17-18.

13. Fisher, op. cit., p. 19. Cf. also Frederic M. Lord, Statistical adjustments when comparing pre-existing groups. *Psychological Bulletin* 72 (1969): 336-337; and Herbert Walberg, "Curriculum Evaluation." *Teachers College Record* 71 (1970): esp. pp. 564-565.

14. Fisher, op. cit., p. 20.

In evaluation or action research, a new aspect is added. Because of the various institutional contingencies, it is usually an unacceptable policy to randomly choose subjects for treatment. It would be possible, for instance, to take the lower two-fifths of the students, as ranked by a standardized achievement test. This group could then have remedial treatment provided, by random assignment, to one half, which would amount to one-fifth of the total population. However, it is usually policy to take the lowest fifth, and administer treatment to them as a group. Thus no "control group" is available. This is, however, an institutional contingency, hence not a methodological problem *per se*. Randomization is still a possibility, hence Fisher's discussion of randomization is relevant to the methodology of evaluation.

Fisher generalizes his argument at this point by emphasizing that variance in treatment *subsequent* to randomization presents no "practical inconvenience." He states "subsequent causes of differentiation, if under the experimenter's control . . . can either be predetermined before the treatments have been randomized, or, if this has not been done, can be randomized on their own account."[15] The first alternative here is merely the recognition that the rational decision maker's response to evaluative feedback is program change. The second alternative is excluded from our discussion, as randomly distributed response by a program manager is not conducive to systematic pursuit of policy.

At this point, we can discuss three possible sources of error: first, consequences of differences already randomized: these are accounted for by the initial randomization; second, natural consequences of the difference in treatment levels: since the null hypothesis argues there will be no treatment effect, there can be no consequences of this effect; and third, effects supervening by chance, independent of treatment levels: because of random assignment, estimates of deviance from

a specified distribution across all treatment levels for these effects can be given. Any *systematic* variance will have been eliminated by the initial randomization.

The dissemination of evaluation findings to the rational program manager[16] will produce program change. As a corollary of the Principle of Management by Exception, we know that if a defect in the program is noted and reported, given adequate program resources, the defect will be corrected by the rational manager. Thus both the corrective action of the manager, and the adequacy of resources are determinate. As such, the variance of treatment as a function of evaluative feedback can in Fisher's terms, be "predetermined."

Hence, we see that, contrary to the contentions of Guba, it is *possible* to implement a rigorous experimental design, and also provide feedback for managerial decision-making, in the context of action research. Whether *practical* concerns, such as the competence of the researcher, or the resources and administrative support available to him, do in fact militate against his ability to implement a rigorous design, is not a methodological issue, and not under consideration here. On the other hand, if the manager is oblivious to feedback, or responds to feedback with random and affective behavior rather than systematic and rational action, this is a psychological issue, and not under consideration here. But the methodological "problem," posed by Guba, can be considered ill-conceived and non-existent.

15. Ibid.
16. Guba, op. cit. p. 35, questions the value of the rational model and notes the incrementalist model as offering more utility. We have elsewhere discussed problems of the rational model. Cf. G. E. Lundin and G. A. Welty, "Relevance of a Managerial Decision-Model to Educational Administration." Presented in Division A, AERA 1970 Annual Meeting, March 6, 1970, Minneapolis, Minnesota. Suffice it to say that the rational model can be viewed as a limiting case of the incremental model. Cf. Gordon Welty, "Reply to the Reluctant Consultant." *School Review* 78 (1969): 117-121.

CHAPTER 11

Michael Scriven

AN INTRODUCTION
TO META-EVALUATION

Meta-evaluation is second-order evaluation, i.e., evaluation of evaluation. Theoretically, meta-evaluation involves the methodological assessment of the role of evaluation; practically, it is concerned with the evaluation of specific evaluative performances. Both facets will be dealt with here.

Evaluation is one of the most important, and from many theoretical as well as practical points of view, *the* most important function of science. The arguments for keeping science value free are in general extremely bad, but in the applied sciences these arguments have never even been significant, since it was always conceded that "instrumental evaluation" (i.e., evaluating alternative means of accomplishing given ends) was legitimate. Evaluation of educational products or processes is obviously a case of applied evaluation. Why, then, has there been much reluctance to undertake it in a straightforward and tough-minded way? Remember that this is a period in the history of the social sciences when tough-mindedness, in the form of empiricism, positivism and operationalism, has been regarded with much favor in the methodological sphere.

There are two explanations. The creditable one is that in the educational area achieving *general agreement* about the aims of education is not easy. The discreditable reason is known by the non-technical name of chicken-heartedness. A lot of people are threatened by evaluations of their products just as they are threatened by evaluation of their own performance, and they often take or threaten strong countermeasures, as was demonstrated by the much discussed battery additive case several years ago.

But the general and more creditable objection, often said to be "realistic," is equally indefensible. It is, of course, unbelievably hard to get people to agree about the "aims of education," and indeed it may be foolish even to attempt this. But that point is almost completely irrelevant to the one at issue. It is extremely difficult to get people to agree on a formulation of the goals of man's existence, or of morality, but this doesn't mean that we have difficulty in agreeing that kicking little children to death because they irritate one is morally indefensible.

An educational evaluation of "our schools" does indeed get into the area of debatable goals, though even then there is enough overlap between differing judgments of the goals of education to enable a very widely acceptable and strongly negative case to be made against the performance of the schools. But when we get down to specific issues, like the evaluation of overhead projectors, for example, or the evaluation of two programmed texts in multiplication for a specific age level and state curriculum, then the sting of this general difficulty is almost completely lost. We are, in fact, simply into the area of *Consumer Reports,* and anybody who thinks that what they're doing is logically or methodologically illicit needs his head examined. Of course, their evaluators sometimes make mistakes with respect to the criteria as well as with respect to the experimental design, but that happens to be the heritage of science and hardly an exclusive sign of sin.

It should be clearly recognized that attacking evaluative enterprises in the applied areas on the grounds that they are evaluative and hence simply matters of opinion or taste is not merely wrong-headed, but in many areas highly antisocial. The difficulties which EPIE had when it began are strictly comparable to those which beset Consumers Union in *its* early days, because of producers who did not wish to have their products evaluated. It is hoped that we have seen the last of that kind of outrage. For business enterprises, in a society which provides them with immense subsidies and support in the taxation and legal areas and which is committed explicitly to free speech and free enterprise with reasonable constraints, to attack a serious attempt at objective verification of their claims and publication of the result is to attack the basic axioms of free speech and fair play which support these enterprises.

In the educational field such attacks are particularly antisocial as most of the expenditure here comes from the public purse, and as attempts to evaluate these products are in the public interest. To put the whole matter in a different way, I think it should be continually stressed in the field of education, as in many other fields of research in the social studies, that any attempt to avoid evaluation should be viewed with suspicion, as probably a sign of methodological muddleheadedness or of a lack of social consciousness. The burden of proof for avoiding evaluation with all its dependent difficulties and risks must be upon those who wish to do so. The present debates about grading students' work on the campus and in the schools are typical examples of a combination of muddleheadedness and chicken-heartedness. It is perfectly clear that a great deal of the grading that goes on is superficial and unreliable and used as a substitute for pedagogically more satisfactory procedures. It is equally clear that the role of grading as (a) providing feedback to the student on his progress towards the intended goals, (b) providing feedback to the instructor on his success in communicating learning, and (c) a basis for selective distribution of positions in specialist classes and types of reward or remedy is *absolutely indispensable* to the educational process in most areas and at most levels.

Evaluation does not begin at the point when the customer announces the values he wishes you to use as bench marks, except in a chronological sense. Methodologically and morally, evaluation absolutely requires that the evaluator investigate the justification for these "initial" criteria. Any evaluator who has substantial practical experience will know that frequently a project will be ruined by the discovery that the initially announced criteria turn out—when their consequences are realized—not to be the "true" criteria of the customer. The time to find this out, at least to the considerable extent that one can do this, is before investing heavily in the experimental design. And there are many ways to investigate both the phenomenological relative strength and the logical relative strength (i.e., defensibility) of the benchmark criteria.

Turning to the practical applications of meta-evaluation, let us consider the specific assessment of "A System for Analyzing Social Science Curricula" by W. W. Stevens Jr. and Irving Morrissett, *The EPIE Forum* (Vol. 1, Nos. 4 and 5).

The basic defects of the Curricula Analysis System are defects of clarity and presentation rather than defects of comprehensiveness. But these defects reflect a lack of clarity on the part of the constructors about the most important methodological distinctions to be made in evaluation, and unless they are corrected they will continue to result in deep-seated reactions by the consumers, who call the system "unwieldly in its present form" ("two/thirds of one clinic using it," p. 15). This system is a pretty good example of exactly what a programed text writer learns to avoid very quickly. It should have been presented in alternative simple forms, e.g., with the major sections in various order. Most of the complexities have probably developed because the constructors of the system have followed the practice of gradually developing their own jargon and distinction. This is pedagogically bad since there are no reasons to suppose that these distinctions or this jargon are natural for the ordinary language user; consequently he has to acquire this new, and in my view, perverse language before he can use the system. Common though this situation is in the educational field, it is long overdue for radical reform, especially as the reform is not particularly difficult. Without personally doing the field-testing, I can only speculate about alternative terminology, etc. But as a critique of an evaluative procedure, the main point I want to make is the one above—that field testing of preliminary, simplified forms are absolutely essential if one is not to develop an excessively metaphysical system.

The first question to ask is, "What does the consumer most want to know?" There is clear evidence on this presented in the article (p. 15) and the evidence makes it obvious that knowledge of rationale and objectives is the primary concern of the consumer. Therefore it should be the first section and not the second. It would probably be a good idea if a very brief introductory summary occupying not more than a paragraph and containing in the last sentence a summary of the overall evaluation was to lead off the entire analysis. We could then go to the more detailed subheadings under "Rationale and Objectives."

Having transposed the first two sections we now find that the original opening section, which is called "Descriptive Characteristics" is obviously mistitled. It is clearly a description of a curriculum to give its objectives and rationale. Indeed "Subject Area and Content" is a subheading under the original "Descriptive Characteristics." We may dispense with this in the revised order, and retitle the original Section 1 "Product Characteristics." We should then retitle Section 3 ("Antecedent Conditions"), "User Characteristics." Section 4 "Content," should be called "Details of Content," since a very good idea of the content was given by the "Objectives," and 1.8 "Subject

Area and Content," subsection. And then we can wind up by rechristening Section 6 (Overall Judgments"), "Evaluative Data," since it is not just judgments but data.

Under the new sequencing and titling, we have a much more plausible developmental sequence, but a number of the subsections need to be shifted around. Without going into immense detail, let me mention one or two examples where the present location illustrates a methodological misconception—in my view. We notice, for example, that subsection 1.7 "Performance Data Availability" is put in under "Descriptive Characteristics." But it's clear that this is simply evaluative data, and ought to go into that section. Of course it's also descriptive, because there is no significant distinction between description and evaluation in general. But in a particular context we make that distinction all the time, and the location for this section is clearly in the section stating the basis for the overall evaluation.

The use of the term "articulation" as the heading for 3.5 is an example of typical jargonistic performance. This is not the proper use of the term, and it is totally unnecessary to introduce a technical term at all at this point, since the heading "Relation to Other Curricula" completely covers the specific descriptions.

The real problem is in the detailed description of content for Section 4, where we find a distinction between the two subheadings one being called "Cognitive Structure" and the other being "Affective Content." As we read the detailed description we discover that the authors are committed to the view that values are not cognitive. This is a striking example of the contamination of evaluative schema by a dubious set of methodological prejudices. At an even simpler level, it is entirely inappropriate to identify affective content with values. Affect is feeling; values are theoretical constructs extracted from and causing committed behavior.

Naturally feelings are often associated with values, but they are simply different things, indeed different categories of things. One may value honesty or truth, but display no perceptible affect in discussing them.

Another distinction should probably be made that is not explicit in the system at the moment. Probably it would be desirable to rechristen the section on product characteristics "Product Characterization" or "Claimed Characteristics," and make clear that this description is *the one provided by the author or publisher.* Thus for a validation of the success claims built into the description, the system user should turn to the evaluation section, or simply face the fact that a large part of the descriptions of style, time needed for use of the materials, etc., which are supplied by the producers are entirely suspect and have no place in a factual description of the materials, except as a factual description of the originators' intentions until they have been verified experimentally.

In short, either build the evaluation back into the description where you will otherwise be faced with repeating a plug, or make clear that you *are* only repeating a plug in that section of the analysis. Many of my earlier criticisms of the long form, communicated to the authors, were on this point and have been incorporated in the modified short form published in the *EPIE Forum,* but there is still an absolutely pervasive sense of confusion about evaluation and description. Take, for example, this description under 2.2 ("General Objectives") "What are the generalized student outcomes that can be expected from the use of these materials?" Obviously, this calls for an evaluation and a crucial one. It *must* be made clear whether this is what the producer *says,* or whether it is, in fact, part of the evaluation tucked back into the rationale sections.

The commitment to the Bloom and Krathwohl classifications is far too pervasive, especially in the "long form." These taxonomies are seriously defective, and much of the critical work since their original publication has documented this. But more seriously, they are also excessively complicated and jargon-ridden. So it seems unfortunate to pull in jargon on top of jargon, or—speaking practically—to require learning these classifications in order to use the Curricula Analysis System. In particular the "Analysis/Synthesis" distinction is really pretty shaky and not particularly important. Of course, no system for analysis can avoid using somebody's taxonomy, but the message is to use the *minimum* taxonomy; i.e., make only those distinctions which are absolutely clear and indisputable *and* important.

In general, then, this analysis system, truly valuable though the idea is, needs a great deal of improvement. It is too committed to methodological or psychological doctrines of excessive dubiety, and above all it is *excessively* complicated, repetitious, and imprecisely described.

EVALUATION
MODELS

The generally-acknowledged purpose of creating models is as an aid to thought. The model itself may range from a full-scale or miniature replica to a completely abstract calculus. The choice of a model will depend in any given circumstance upon many factors—the precise role the model is to play, the state of knowledge in the field and so on.

The building of models of any any kind—but more particularly the analog and theoretical models—has become a near-obsession in the behavioral sciences. No sooner are new ideas promulgated than we tend to sit down and draw diagrams and flow charts that represent our programmatic view of the world. This kind of activity is valuable only if it does not become an end in itself; there must be an effort to test the validity of these exercises.

Most of the models that have been generated in the area of curriculum evaluation have been models **for** the process. Broadly, they may be classed as examples of general systems theory which is based on assumptions of non-linearity and complex interactions among the parts making up the system. All those who have suggested possible models for evaluation activity have acknowledged the complexity of the task and have attempted to allow for cross- and back-checking in their procedures.

Many of the models have been non-specific about the appropriate methodologies that would achieve the kinds of ends that they wish to attain. An early attempt to conceptualize the positions taken by both Cronbach and Scriven is represented by the Taylor-Maguire model which appeared in 1966. This model is typical of several that appeared during 1966 and 1967 and stresses the several emerging aspects of evaluation: the need to be able to identify information for feedback as well as summary purposes; the need to involve informaton about many kinds of variables in the environment as well as the individual pupils; and the need to incorporate value judgements about the worth of goals, processes and products. The Taylor-Maguire model simply attempts to section the evaluative process so that each of these major dimensions may be attended to appropriately.

The Taylor-Maguire model was one representation of the kinds of discussion that had been taking place at the Center for Instructional Research and Curriculum Evaluation at the University of Illinois. It was made increasingly clear that evaluation involved more than the measurement of pupil outcomes and that a need existed to take into account all kinds of antecedent and correlative data. The second attempt at representing the multidimensionality of evaluative ventures is represented by Stake's model, reproduced in his "Countenance" paper. Realizing the need for a more practical guideline for evaluators in the field, Stake suggested sources of variables, desirable checks and a general strategy for evaluation.

An even more practically-oriented model came out of the Evaluation Center at Ohio State University. The Stufflebeam context-input-process-product model (CIPP for short) found a wide and receptive audience and has probably been the most influential of the early crop of models. Stufflebeam wrote about his model in a number of papers, the paper presented here being typical of his viewpoint. A practically-oriented interpretation of the CIPP model is given in the next section (see Ambry, 1969). The huge value of the CIPP model was that it enabled evaluators to develop checklists of questions that needed to be answered as they proceeded with their work. The influence of Stake and of Stufflebeam's co-workers at the Evaluation Center in the development and promulgation of the model is clear. Among these influences must be mentioned the work of Cook (with his expertise in PERT) and of Guba.

It must be stressed that the models that have been chosen here are but a minute fraction of the many, many models that have been produced for use in various evaluation ventures. There have been some very interesting and worthwhile models that have appeared for use in a given project. The omission of any one of these should not be regarded as a value judgement on their worth. It is a most rewarding study to collect examples of models that have been developed and to make comparisons of them. The most remarkable fact is that they are all very much alike conceptually—hence our choice of these models as fairly typical.

A second generation of models began to appear about 1969. This second-generation approach relied more directly upon a systems approach and is represented here by the works of Alkin and Provus. It is especially important to identify the trends which these models take that are different from their predecessors. The summary of the state of evaluation models before this change occurred is nicely presented by Glass's paper.

CHAPTER 12

A THEORETICAL EVALUATION MODEL

Peter A. Taylor
Thomas O. Maguire

Within recent years, the explosive increase in the effort and funds devoted to curriculum development has drawn attention to the necessity for extensive curriculum evaluation. Curriculum evaluation can be viewed as a process of collecting and processing data pertaining to an educational program, on the basis of which decisions can be made about that program. The data are of two kinds: (1) objective descriptions of goals, environments, personnel, methods and content, and immediate and long-range outcomes; and (2) recorded personal judgments of the quality and appropriateness of goals, inputs and outcomes. The data—in both raw and analyzed form—can be used either to delineate and resolve problems in educational programs being developed or to answer absolute and comparative questions about established programs. In many ways, the efficiency of evaluation has been hampered by a lack of clear guiding principles indicating what evaluation is

potentially able to accomplish. What principles there are exist mainly as experientially induced procedures and techniques held by the few who work in the area. Until sufficient evidence has accumulated upon which a theory of evaluation can be based, practical evaluation will be facilitated by the use of a model which sets up the potential steps in the evaluation process. The present paper is an attempt to provide such a model. The uses of the model lie in suggesting variables and relationships to be investigated in the course of evaluation. It may also help the curriculum developer to decide which are, for his purposes, the most pertinent questions to ask. The model also has pedagogical merit both in terms of schematizing the evaluative process and in indicating tasks for which future evaluators should be trained.

In considering the model (Fig. 1) the reader should keep in mind that there is no intention

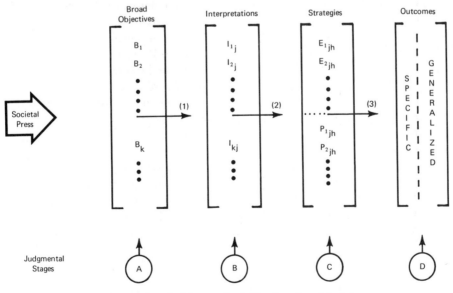

Figure 1. A Theoretical Evaluation Model.

to imply that curriculum developers necessarily act in the consecutive manner suggested by the graphic representation. Regardless of the actual schedule of events in developing a particular curriculum, it is contended that the process can be thought of *as having been developed* in the sequence presented in the diagram. The foregoing does not mean that the model stands or falls only by whether or not it is possible to apply the model *in toto*: one of its merits lies in the fact that the model can be entered and left at those points which the practitioner deems most useful.

Explanation of the Model

To the left of the diagram, what has been termed "Societal Press" refers to those societal and professional pressures that lead to the statement of broad-category objectives which define the relationship between school and society. Amongst these pressures are demands from groups of professionals (e.g., scholars and their interpretations of disciplinary saliences, those responsible for training teachers, teachers themselves) and from societal sources (e.g., legislators, PTA's, news media, taxpayer's associations, malcontents, and cranks). Broad objectives arising from these sources may exist in political and academic pronouncements, lay opinion, voiced generalities, resolutions of organized groups, and regulations at all levels of government. Each broad objective as it is conceived expressed as an element of the *B*-vector in the diagram. Examples of these elements would be: "Our schools should prepare our children for jobs in the unforeseeable future"; "Students should be equipped with the mathematics which enables our country to compete in the 'Space Age'"; "We want to develop a generation which can utilize its leisure time, enforced or otherwise, in a way which contributes to personality integration."

The statements of broad objectives are often insufficiently precise to be of much value for curriculum development since they do not specify behaviors which may be subsequent foci for the development of appropriate classroom procedures. Some effort may be needed to restate these objectives in more operational terminology. The agents responsible for making these restatements function at arrow (1) in the diagram. These agents will be referred to as "Curriculum Planners." Clearly, members of this group may belong to other agencies in the model. For example, some curriculum planners may be professionals from disciplines that are prompting the statement of broad objectives (*B*). They may also be teachers making specific interpretations for their individual classrooms.

The curriculum planners are motivated by the broad objectives and the groups which proposed them. It is their job to interpret the gross statements of *B* into specific descriptions of behaviors that they would anticipate a student to exhibit consequent to exposure to that facet of the educational program to which the objective is oriented. An example of one behavioral interpretation of the broad objective "the student should be able to add" would be "the student demonstrates that he can add correctly sets of four, three-digit numbers, 95 times out of each hundred." For sure, this is a simple example, but it illustrates the point that behavioral objectives have immediate implications for both teaching and measuring that the broad statements do not. More often, one will encounter broad objectives such as: "the student should appreciate good art (music, design . . .)," or, "the student should understand the circumstances leading to the collapse of the League of Nations." (The reader will find Dressel and Mayhew (1954) and Lindvall (1964), useful aids in stating objectives behaviorally.)

As a consequence of the planners' interpretation of the broad objectives, an element of *B* becomes translated into a row vector of the matrix *I* of the diagram. The matrix *I*, of interpretations, therefore consists of behavioral statements corresponding to selected broad objectives from the vector *B*.

The task of the evaluator up to and including *I* would be to obtain data which would enable him to identify gains and losses (additions and deletions to the list of broad objectives) that have occurred between the statement of a broad objective and its translation into behavioral terms. Gains arise from attempts to clarify a vaguely-stated aim, that is, where interpretation leads to a new (not originally intended) objective. Losses could occur due to an inability to restate the broad objectives behaviorally. The evaluator's data may consist of nothing other than statements from the members of the group promoting the broad objective, of the extent to which the behavioral statements do, in fact, convey the essence of their original intention.

A further task for the evaluator is to obtain judgments of the relative worths of each of the broad objectives, i.e., the elements of *B*. The appropriate time at which these data could be gathered is represented in the model by Judgmental Stage A. These value judgments may be opinions given by "social philosophers" and/or may be based upon empirical evidence procured by means of observations of life patterns or by means of such frequency counts as public opinion polls.

The behaviors incorporated in the Interpretation elements would be judged independently (Judgmental Stage B) as to their utility and appropriateness. The concern now is a pragmatic one, in that a behavioral objective is, or is not, included in the I matrix according to whether it is, or is not, seen as satisfying both of the following criteria: (a) that it is a proper concern of the school; and (b) that it is sufficiently important to warrant its inclusion in a school program. At the risk of being redundant, there are two levels of judgment at stage B, viz., the social level and the administrative level, the first involving an accept-reject decision, and the second involving the assignment of priorities. Typical reference persons would include psychologists, philosophers, subject-matter experts, and the evaluators themselves.

Once a set of operationally stated objectives has been obtained, some agency must transform these statements into a form suitable for application to the classroom environment. The agents (arrow (2) on the diagram) who are responsible are the textbook and lesson guide writers, the classroom teachers, producers of audiovisual aids, material programmers, and any others whose role it is to translate behaviorally-stated educational objectives into possible classroom strategies. Because there are several possible alternative ways of turning a particular Interpretation element into a teaching strategy, each I gives rise to a vector in the supermatrix S (strategies) which contains the primary submatrices E (Elicitations) and P (Presentations).

The first of these, E, contains as elements descriptions of activities designed to elicit the behaviors specified. In practice, it is manifested in such items as teachers' manuals, lesson plans, and actual teacher behaviors in the classroom. It specifically excludes the substantive content of behavioral objectives, the information imparted in lessons, library resources, or other research facilities and prescribed texts. The latter constitute the P submatrix.

An example which illustrates the development of the model thus far would be:

Broad objective: To inculcate a knowledge of the rudiments of chemistry.

Some interpretations: To be able to balance elementary chemical equations.

To have a knowledge (and be able to demonstrate that knowledge) of methods of extraction of iron from ore.

To carry out a quantitative chemical analysis of inorganic compounds.

Strategies corresponding to the second of the above interpretations:

A classroom demonstration of the reduction of iron oxide . . .

A filmed presentation illustrating the Bessemer process . . .

Exposure to written material which discusses the open hearth process . . .

The evaluator's concern at this point is with determining (a) the extent to which the Strategy is shaped by I and (b) the effectiveness of the strategy with respect to student outcomes.

The measurement problem in bridging the gap between I and S involves the collection of data on:

a. gains due to additions generated by agents at (2) which go beyond the behaviorallly stated objectives

b. losses due to inability to generate appropriate elicitations for particular Interpretations

c. contamination due to false information, or the use of, or imparting of, inappropriate methodology

At S the activity required of the evaluator is to obtain a set of judgments (Judgmental Stage C) as to the efficiency and adequacy of presentation and elicitation, potential effect on student outcomes, and the correspondence of the Strategies to the Interpretations. The kinds of source personnel needed would include subject-matter experts, learning, educational, and developmental psychologists, and methodological analysts. The evaluator is further responsible for providing feedback information from the classroom situation to those responsible for curriculum development. Such feedback would not, at this point, include test data (i.e., student-generated data). It would include teacher, administrative, and sometimes parental reactions to such things as textbooks and curriculum guides. The purpose of the feedback data is to provide information, on the basis of which the curriculum writers may make adjustments in the strategies and, if necessary, to add to, or delete from the list of behaviors, I.

An important set of determining conditions of the translation from behavioral objective-to-strategies (I to S) phase of the model is the question of feasibility. Briefly, this set of conditions is made up of those administrative considerations which may affect the realization of some of the objectives, such as finance and availability of physical plant and personnel. Much of the data that the evaluator accumulates may need to be considered in the light of these kinds of administrative determinants. Consequently, a duty of the evaluator at this point is to gather information with respect to feasibilty. For the sake of diagrammatic simplicity, the feasibility dimension has not been represented in Figure 1.

At arrow (3) on the diagram, the agent is the student. The student brings to the school situation a network of assimilations and accommodations, as a consequence of which he can connect and manipulate substantive content and he can produce appropriate responses to environmental pressures even though these responses may be mechanical rather than an intellectual commitment. For instance, a student may make responses in an institutional setting that he does not generalize. This raises the necessity for distinguishing at the measurement stage between testing for existence ("can he?") and the testing for more generalized usage ("does he?"). The matrix of outcomes, O, covers these two types of behavior, namely, outcomes on performance specifically oriented toward the school setting, and outcomes (which may, or may not, be derived from the latter) that are generalized. Here, the judgmental process (Judgmental Stage D) involves the assessment of the goodness-of-fit of the observed outcomes to the criterial behaviors listed as objectives in I. In other words, the evaluative task now is one of deciding whether the level of performance which is observed is within acceptable limits. Behaviorally-stated objectives lighten this assessment burden: with reference to a previous example, if an evaluator found that a child could successfully complete the addition task only 80 per cent of the time, he would know immediately that this is outside the "acceptable limit," since this limit had been pre-set at the 95 per cent success level. By making this distinction, the judgmental process of the worth of behavioral outcomes can be aided in that two value levels emerge—value to the formal educative process and value to the life setting.

A digression might be made to point out that, having arrived thus far in the diagram, it may be possible to classify educational objectives in terms of sequential drop-out points on the model. That is, certain pervasive objectives will be traceable from B to O, while others are traceable only to intermediate matrices. The measurement phase connecting S and O once more involves the estimation of gains, losses, and contamination. On the one hand, gains arise due to "over-readiness"—educational promiscuity—and losses result from lack of the same. For example, a student might bring unique experiences to the classroom which give him an advantage in a particular learning setting. On the other hand, contamination results from such things as forgetting and inhibitory prior knowledge. It should be borne in mind that measurement of many outcomes cannot be achieved immediately, for the behaviors involved in those outcomes may not be realized until a considerable time-period is elapsed, i.e., many objectives are, in fact, long-term objectives.

The evaluator also should collect feedback data relating outcomes to strategies (here, use of test data *is* appropriate). In making feedback, data should be presented to the school and to those responsible for revising the material. In addition feedback should be made to the curriculum planner operating at arrow (1), since it is the primary source of student-generated data upon which the planner bases his decisions.

Finally, an attempt should be made to identify side effects. For example: a perfectly worthwhile curriculum in other respects may be so physically exhausting to both student and teacher that it would be unreasonable to adopt it; or, positively: a particular method of presentation may help students with social adjustment. In both these instances, as in others, it is the responsibility of the evaluator to determine the nature of any side effects and their importance in affecting student outcomes.

REFERENCES

Dressel, P. L. and Mayhew, L. B. *General Education.* Washington, D. C.: ACE, 1954.
Lindvall, C. M. *Defining Educational Objectives.* Pittsburgh, Pa.: University of Pittsburgh Press, 1964.

CHAPTER 13

THE COUNTENANCE OF EDUCATIONAL EVALUATION

Robert E. Stake

President Johnson, President Conant, Mrs. Hull (Sara's teacher) and Mr. Tykociner (the man next door) are quite alike in the faith they have in education. But they have quite different ideas of what education is. The value they put on education does not reveal their way of evaluating education.

Educators differ among themselves as to both the essence and worth of an educational program. The wide range of evaluation purposes and methods allows each to keep his own perspective. Few see their own programs "in the round," partly because of a parochial approach to evaluation. To understand better his own teaching and to contribute more to the science of teaching, each educator should examine the full countenance of evaluation.

Educational evaluation has its formal and informal sides. Informal evaluation is recognized by its dependence on casual observation, implicit goals, intuitive norms, and subjective judgment. Perhaps because these are also characteristic of day-to-day, personal styles of living, informal evaluation results in perspectives which are seldom questioned. Careful study reveals informal evaluation of education to be of variable quality—sometimes penetrating and insightful, sometimes superficial and distorted.

Formal evaluation of education is recognized by its dependence on checklists, structured visitation by peers, controlled comparisons, and standardized testing of students. Some of these techniques have long histories of successful use. Unfortunately, when planning an evaluation, few educators consider even these four. The more common notion is to evaluate informally: to ask the opinion of the instructor, to ponder the logic of the program, or to consider the reputation of the advocates. Seldom do we find a search for relevant research reports or for behavioral data pertinent to the ultimate curricular decisions.

Dissatisfaction with the formal approach is not without cause. Few highly-relevant, readable research studies can be found. The professional journals are not disposed to publish evaluation studies. Behavioral data are costly, and often do not provide the answers. Too many accreditation-type visitation teams lack special training or even experience in evaluation. Many checklists are ambiguous; some focus too much attention on the physical attributes of a school. Psychometric tests have been developed primarily to differentiate among students at the same point in training rather than to assess the effect of instruction on acquisition of skill and understanding. Today's educator may rely little on formal evaluation because its answers have seldom been answers to questions he is asking.

Potential Contributions of Formal Evaluation

The educator's disdain of formal evaluation is due also to his sensitivity to criticism—and his is a critical clientele. It is not uncommon for him to draw before him such curtains as "national norm comparisons," "innovation phase," and "academic freedom" to avoid exposure through evaluation. The "politics" of evaluation is an interesting issue in itself, but it is not the issue here. The issue here is the potential contribution to education of formal evaluation. Today, educators fail to perceive what formal evaluation could do for them. They should be imploring measurement specialists to develop a methodology that reflects the fullness, the complexity, and the importance of their programs. They are not.

What one finds when he examines formal evaluation activities in education today is too little effort to spell out antecedent conditions and classroom transactions (a few of which visitation teams do record) and too little effort to couple them with the various outcomes (a few of which are

93

portrayed by conventional test scores). Little attempt has been made to measure the match between what an educator intends to do and what he does do. The traditional concern of educational-measurement specialists for reliability of individual-student scores and predictive validity (thoroughly and competently stated in the American Council on Education's 1950 edition of curricula), attention to individual differences among students should give way to attention to the contingencies among background conditions, classroom activities, and scholastic outcomes.

This paper is not about what should be measured or how to measure. It is background for developing an evaluation plan. What and how are decided later. My orientation here is around educational programs rather than educational products. I presume that the value of a product depends on its program of use. The evaluation of a program includes the evaluation of its materials.

The countenance of educational evaluation appears to be changing. On the pages that follow, I will indicate what the countenance can, and perhaps, should be. My attempt here is to introduce a conceptualization of evaluation oriented to the complex and dynamic nature of education, one which gives proper attention to the diverse purposes and judgments of the practitioner.

Much recent concern about curriculum evaluation is attributable to contemporary large-scale curriculum-innovation activities, but the statements in this paper pertain to traditional and new curricula alike. They pertain, for example, to Title I and Title III projects funded under the Elementary and Secondary Acts of 1966. Statements here are relevant to any curriculum, whether oriented to subject-matter content or to student process, and without regard to whether curriculum is general-purpose, remedial, accelerated, compensatory, or special in any other way.

The purposes and procedures of educational evaluation will vary from instance to instance. What is quite appropriate for one school may be less appropriate for another. Standardized achievement tests here but not there. A great concern for expense here but not over there. How do evaluation purposes and procedures vary? What are the basic characteristics of evaluation activities? They are identified in these pages as the evaluation acts, the data sources, the congruence and contingencies, the standards, and the uses of evaluation. The first distinction to be made will be between description and judgment in evaluation.

The countenance of evaluation beheld by the educator is not the same one beheld by the specialist in evaluation. The specialist sees himself as a "describer," one who describes aptitudes and environments and accomplishments. The teacher and school administrator, on the other hand, expect an evaluator to grade something or someone as to merit. Morever, they expect that he will judge things against external standards, on criteria perhaps little related to the local school's resources and goals.

Neither sees evaluation broadly enough. Both description and judgment are essential—in fact, they are the two basic acts of evaluation. Any individual evaluator may attempt to refrain from judging or from collecting the judgments of others. Any individual evaluator may seek only to bring to light the worth of the program. But their evaluations are incomplete. To be fully understood, the educational program must be fully described and fully judged.

Towards Full Description

The specialist in evaluation seems to be increasing his emphasis on fullness of description. For many years he evaluated primarily by measuring student progress toward academic objectives. These objectives usually were identified with the traditional disciplines, e.g., mathematics, English, and social studies. Achievement tests—standardized or "teacher-made"—were found to be useful in describing the degree to which some curricular objectives are attained by individual students in a particular course. To the early evaluators, and to many others, the countenance of evaluation has been nothing more than the administration and normative interpretation of achievement tests.

In recent years a few evaluators have attempted, in addition, to assess progress of individuals toward certain "interdisciplinary" and "extracurricular" objectives. In their objectives, emphasis has been given to the integration of behavior within an individual; or to the perception of interrelationships among scholastic disciplines or the development of habits, skills, and attitudes which permit the individual to be a craftsman or scholar, in or out of school. For the descriptive evaluation of such outcomes, the Eight Year Study[2] has served as one model. The proposed National Assessment Program may be another—this statement appeared in one interim report:

. . . all committees worked within the following broad definition of 'national assessment.'
1. In order to reflect fairly the aims of education in the U.S., the assessment should consider both traditional and modern curricula, and take into account ALL THE ASPIRATIONS schools have for developing attitudes and motivations as well as knowledge and skills . . . (Caps added).[3]

In his paper, "Evaluation for Course Improvement,"[4] Lee Cronbach urged another step: a most generous inclusion of behavioral-science variables in order to examine the possible causes and effects of quality teaching. He proposed that the main objective for evaluation is to uncover durable relationships—those appropriate for guiding future educational programs. To the traditional description of pupil achievement, we add the description of instruction and the description of relationships between them. Like the instructional researcher, the evaluator—as so defined—seeks generalizations about educational practices. Many curriculum project evaluators are adopting this definition of evaluation.

The Role of Judgment

Description is one thing, judgment is another. Most evaluation specialists have chosen not to judge. But in his recent *Methodology of Evaluation*[5] Michael Scriven has charged evaluators with the responsibility for passing upon the merit of an educational practice. (Note that he has urged the evaluator to do what the educator has expected the evaluator to be doing.) Scriven's position is that there is no evaluation until judgment has been passed, and by his reckoning the evaluator is best qualified to judge.

By being well experienced and by becoming well-informed in the case at hand in matters of research and educational practice the evaluator does become at least partially qualified to judge. But is it wise for him to accept this responsibility? Even now when few evaluators expect to judge, educators are reluctant to initiate a formal evaluation. If evaluators were more frequently identified with the passing of judgment, with the discrimination among poorer and better programs, and with the awarding of support and censure, their access to data would probably diminish. Evaluators collaborate with other social scientists and behavioral research workers. Those who do not want to judge deplore the acceptance of such responsibility by their associates. They believe that in the eyes of many practitioners, social science and behavioral research will become more suspect than it already is.

Many evaluators feel that they are not capable of perceiving, as they think a judge should, the undimensional value of alternative programs. They anticipate a dilemma such as Curriculum I resulting in three skills and ten understandings and Curriculum II resulting in four skills and eight understandings. They are reluctant to judge that gaining one skill is worth losing two understandings. And, whether through timidity, disinterest, or as a rational choice, the evaluator usually supports "local option," a community's privilege to set its own standards and to be its own judge of the worth of its educational system. He expects that what is good for one community will not necessarily be good for another community, and he does not trust himself to discern what is best for a briefly-known community.

Scriven reminds them that there are precious few who can judge complex programs, and fewer still who will. Different decisions must be made— P.S.S.C. or Harvard Physics?—and they should not be made on trivial criteria, e.g., mere precedent, mention in the popular press, salesman personality, administrative convenience, or pedagogical myth. Who should judge? The answer comes easily to Scriven partly because he expects little interaction between treatment and learner, i.e., what works best for one learner will work best for others, at least within broad categories. He also expects that where the local good is at odds with the common good, the local good can be shown to be detrimental to the common good, to the end that the doctrine of local option is invalidated. According to Scriven the evaluator must judge.

Whether or not evaluation specialists will accept Scriven's challenge remains to be seen. In any case, it is likely that judgments will become an increasing part of the evaluation report. Evaluators will seek out and record the opinions of persons of special qualification. These opinions, though subjective, can be very useful and can be gathered objectively, independent of the solicitor's opinions. A responsibility for processing judgments is much more acceptable to the evaluation specialist than one for rendering judgments himself.

Taylor and Maguire[6] have pointed to five groups having important opinions on education: spokesmen for society at large, subject-matter experts, teachers, parents, and the students themselves. Members of these and other groups are judges who should be heard. Superficial polls, letters to the editor, and other incidental judgments are insufficient. An evaluation of a school program should portray the merit and fault perceived by well-identified groups, systematically gathered and processed. Thus, judgment data and description data are both essential to the evaluation of educational programs.

Data Matrices

In order to evaluate, an educator will gather together certain data. The data are likely to be from several sources, gathered in several quite different ways. Whether the immediate purpose is description or judgment, three bodies of information should be tapped. In the evaluation report it can be helpful to distinguish between antecedent, transaction and outcome data.

An antecedent is any condition existing prior to teaching and learning which may relate to outcomes. The status of a student prior to his lesson, e.g., his aptitude, previous experience, interest, and willingness, is a complex antecedent. The programmed-instruction specialist calls some antecedents "entry behaviors." The state accrediting agency emphasizes the investment of community resources. All of these are examples of the antecedents which an evaluator will describe. Transactions are the countless encounters of students with teacher, student with student, author with reader, parent with counselor; the succession of engagements which comprise the process of education. Examples are the presentation of a film, a class discussion, the working of a homework problem, an explanation on the margin of a term paper, and the administration of a test. Smith and Meux studied such transactions in detail and have provided an 18-category classification system.[7] One very visible emphasis on a particular class of transactions was the National Defense Education Act support of audiovisual media.

Transactions are dynamic whereas antecedents and outcomes are relatively static. The boundaries between them are not clear, e.g., during a transaction we can identify certain outcomes which are feedback antecedents for subsequent learning. These boundaries do not need to be distinct. The categories should be used to stimulate rather than to subdivide our data collection.

Traditionally, most attention in formal evaluation has been given to outcomes—outcomes such as the abilities, achievements, attitudes, and aspirations of students resulting from an educational experience. Outcomes, as a body of information, would include measurements of the impact of instruction on teachers, administrators, counselors, and others. Here too would be data on wear and tear of equipment, effects of the learning environment, cost incurred. Outcomes to be considered in evaluation include not only those that are evident, or even existent, as learning sessions end, but include applications, transfer, and relearning effects which may not be available for measurement until long after. The description of the outcomes of driver training, for example, could well include reports of accident-avoidance over a lifetime. In short, outcomes are the consequences of educating—immediate and long-range, cognitive and conative, personal and community-wide.

Antecedents, transactions, and outcomes, the elements of evaluation statements, are shown in Figure 1 to have a place in both description and judgment. To fill in these matrices the evaluator will collect judgments (e.g., of community prejudice, of problem solving styles, and of teacher personality) as well as descriptions. In Figure 1 it is also indicated that judgmental statements are classified either as general standards of quality or as judgments specific to the given program. Descriptive data are classified as intents and observations. The evaluator can organize his data-gathering to conform to the format shown in Figure 1.

The evaluator can prepare a record of what educators intend, of what patrons generally expect, and of what judges value the immediate program to be. The record may treat antecedents, transactions, and outcomes separately within the four classes identified as Intents, Observations, Standards, and Judgments, as in Figure 1. The following is an illustration of 12 data, one of

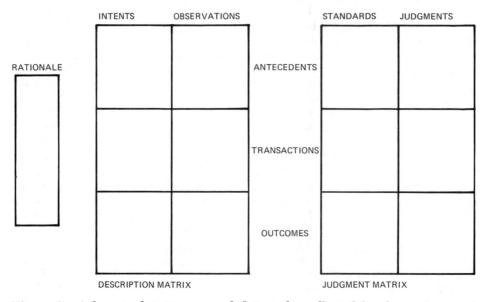

Figure 1. A layout of statements and data to be collected by the evaluator of an educational program.

which could be recorded in each of the 12 cells, starting with an intended antecedent, and moving down each column until an outcome judgment has been indicated.

Knowing that (1) Chapter XI has been assigned and that he intends (2) to lecture on the topic Wednesday, a professor indicates (3) what the students should be able to do by Friday, partly by writing a quiz on the topic. He observes that (4) some students were absent on Wednesday, that (5) he did not quite complete the lecture because of a lengthy discussion and that (6) on the quiz only about 2/3 of the class seemed to understand a certain major concept. In general, he expects (7) some absences but that the work will be made up by quiz-time; he expects (8) his lectures to be clear enough for perhaps 90 percent of a class to follow him without difficulty; and he knows that (9) his colleagues expect only about one student in ten to understand thoroughly each major concept in such lessons as these. By his own judgment (10) the reading assignment was not a sufficient background for his lecture; the students commented that (11) the lecture was provocative; and the graduate assistant who read the quiz papers said that (12) a discouragingly large number of students seemed to confuse one major concept for another.

Evaluation and educators do not expect data to be recorded in such detail, even in the distant future. My purpose here was to give twelve examples of data that could be handled by separate cells in the matrices. Next I would like to consider the description data matrix in detail.

Goals and Intents

For many years instructional technologists, test specialists, and others have pleaded for more explicit statement of educational goals. I consider "goals," "objectives," and "intents" to be synonomous. I use the category title Intents because many educators now equate "goals" and "objectives" with "intended student outcomes." In this paper Intents includes the planned-for environmental conditions, the planned-for demonstrations, the planned-for student behavior. To be included in this three-cell column are effects which are desired, those which are hoped for, those which are anticipated, and even those which are feared. This class of data includes goals and plans that others have, especially the students. (It should be noted that it is not the educator's privilege to rule out the study of a variable by saying, "that is not one of our objectives." The evaluator should include both the variable and the negation.) The resulting collection of Intents is a priority listing of all that may happen.

The fact that many educators now equate "goals" with "intended student outcomes" is to the credit of the behaviorists, particularly the advocates of programmed instruction. They have brought about a small reform in teaching by emphasizing those specific classroom acts and work exercises which contribute to the refinement of student responses. The A.A.A.S. Science Project, for example, has been successful in developing its curriculum around behavioristic goals.[8] Some curriculum-innovation projects, however, have found the emphasis on behavioral outcomes an obstacle to creative teaching.[9] The educational evaluator should not list goals only in terms of anticipated student behavior. To evaluate an educational program, we must examine what teaching, as well as what learning, is intended. (Many antecedent conditions and teaching transactions can be worded behavioristically, if desired.) How intentions are worded is not a criterion for inclusion. Intents can be the global goals of the Educational Policies Commission or the detailed goals of the programmer.[10] Taxonomic, mechanistic, humanistic, even scriptural—any mixture of goal statements are acceptable as part of the evaluation picture.

Many a contemporary evaluator expects trouble when he sets out to record the educator's objectives. Early in the work he urged the educator to declare his objectives so that outcome-testing devices could be built. He finds the educator either reluctant or unable to verbalize objectives. With diligence, if not with pleasure, the evaluator assists with what he presumes to be the educator's job: writing behavioral goals. His presumption is wrong. As Scriven has said, the responsibility for describing curricular objectives is the responsibility of the evaluator. He is the one who is experienced with the language of behaviors, traits, and habits. Just as it is his responsibility to transform the behaviors of a teacher and the responses of a student into data, it is his responsibility to transform the intentions and expectations of an educator into "data." It is necessary for him to continue to ask the educator for statements of intent. He should augment the replies by asking, "Is this another way of saying it?" or "Is this an instance?" It is not wrong for an evaluator to teach a willing educator about behavioral objectives—they may facilitate the work. It is wrong for him to insist that every educator should use them.

Obtaining authentic statements of intent is a new challenge for the evaluator. The methodology remains to be developed. Let us now shift attention to the second column of the data cells.

Observational Choice

Most of the descriptive data cited early in the previous section are classified as Observations. In Figure 1 when he described surroundings and events and the subsequent consequences, the evaluator* is telling of his Observations. Sometimes the evaluator observes these characteristics in a direct and personal way. Sometimes he used instruments. His instruments include inventory schedules, biographical data sheets, interview routines, check lists, opinionnaires, and all kinds of psychometric tests. The experienced evaluator gives special attention to the measurement of student outcomes, but he does not fail to observe the other outcomes, nor the antecedent conditions and instructional transactions.

Many educators fear that the outside evaluator will not be attentive to the characteristics that the school staff has deemed most important. This sometimes does happen, but evaluators often pay too much attention to what they are urged to look at, and too little attention to other facets. In the matter of selection of variables for evaluation, the evaluator must make a subjective decision. Obviously, he must limit the elements to be studied. He cannot look at all of them. The ones he rules out will be those that he assumes would not contribute to an understanding of the educational activity. He should give primary attention to the variables specifically indicated by the educator's objectives, but he must designate additional variables to be observed. He must search for unwanted side effects and incidental gains. The selection of measuring techniques is an obvious responsibility, but the choice of characteristics to be observed is an equally important and unique contribution of the evaluator.

An evaluation is not complete without a statement of the rationale of the program. It needs to be considered separately, as indicated in Figure 1. Every program has its rationale, though often it is only implicit. The rationale indicates the philosophic background and basic purposes of the program. Its importance to evaluation has been indicated by Berlak.[11] The rationale should provide one basis for evaluating Intents. The evaluator asks himself or other judges whether the plan developed by the educator constitutes a logical step in the implementation of the basic purposes. The rationale also is of value in choosing the reference groups, e.g., merchants, mathematicians, and mathematics educators, which later are to pass judgment on various aspects of the program.

A statement of rationale may be difficult to obtain. Many an effective instructor is less than effective at presenting an educational rationale. If pressed, he may only succeed in saying something the listener wanted said. It is important that the rationale be in his language, a language he is the master of. Suggestions by the evaluator may be an obstacle, becoming accepted because they are attractive rather than because they designate the grounds for what the educator is trying to do.

The judgment matrix needs further explanation, but I am postponing that until after a consideration of the bases for processing descriptive data.

Contingency and Congruence

For any one educational program there are two principal ways of processing descriptive evaluation data: finding the contingencies among antecedents, transactions, and outcomes and finding the congruence between Intents and Observations. The processing of judgments follows a different model. The first two main columns of the data matrix in Figure 1 contain the descriptive data. The format for processing these data is represented in Figure 2. The data for a curriculum are congruent if what was intended actually happens. To be fully congruent the intended antecedents, transactions, and outcomes would have to come to pass. (This seldom happens—and often

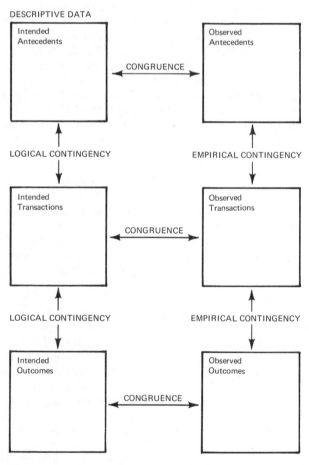

DESCRIPTIVE DATA

Figure 2. A representation of the processing of descriptive data.

---

*Here and elsewhere in this paper, for simplicity of presentation, the educator is referred to as two different persons. The educator will often be his own evaluator or a member of the evaluation team.

should not.) Within one row of the data matrix the evaluator should be able to compare the cells containing Intents and Observations to note the discrepancies, and to describe the amount of congruence for that row. (Congruence of outcomes has been empasized in the evaluation model proposed by Taylor and Maguire.) Congruence does not indicate that outcomes are reliable or valid, but that what was intended did occur.

Just as the Gestaltist found more to the whole than the sum of its parts, the evaluator studying variables from any two of the three cells in a column of the data matrix finds more to describe than the variables themselves. The relationships or contingencies among the variables deserve additional attention. In the sense that evaluation is the search for relationships that permit the improvement of education, the evaluator's task is one of identifying outcomes that are contingent upon particular antecedent conditions and instructional transactions.

Lesson planning and curriculum revision through the years has been built upon faith in certain contingencies. Day to day, the master teacher arranges his presentation and selects his input materials to fit his instructional goals. For him the contingencies, in the main, are logical, intuitive, and supported by a history of satisfactions and endorsements. Even the master teacher and certainly less-experienced teachers need to bring their intuited contingencies under the scrutiny of appropriate juries.

As a first step in evaluation it is important just to record them. A film on floodwaters may be scheduled (intended transaction) to expose students to a background to conservation legislation (intended outcome). Of those who know both subject matter and pedagogy, we ask, "Is there a logical connection between this event and this purpose?" If so, a logical contingency exists between these two Intents. The record should show it.

Whenever Intents are evaluated the contingency criterion is one of logic. To test the logic of an educational contingency the evaluators rely on previous experience, perhaps on research experience, with similar observables. No immediate observation of these variables, however, is necessary to test the strength of the contingencies among Intents.

Evaluation of Observation contingencies depends on empirical evidence. To say, "this arithmetic class progressed rapidly because the teacher was somewhat but not too sophisticated in mathematics" demands empirical data, either from within the evaluation or from the research literature.[12] The usual evaluation of a single program will not alone provide the data necessary for contingency statements. Here too, then, previous experience with similar observables is a basic qualification of the evaluator.

The contingencies and congruencies identified by evaluators are subject to judgment by experts and participants just as more unitary descriptive data are. The importance of non-congruence will vary with different viewpoints. The school superintendent and the school counselor may disagree as to the importance of a cancellation of the scheduled lessons on sex hygiene in the health class. As an example of judging contingencies, the degree to which teacher morale is contingent on the length of the school day may be deemed cause enough to abandon an early morning class by one judge and not another. Perceptions of importance of congruence and contingency deserve the evaluator's careful attention.

Standards and Judgments

There is a general agreement that the goal of education is excellence—but how schools and students should excell, and at what sacrifice, will always be debated. Whether goals are local or national, the measurement of excellence requires explicit rather than implicit standards.

Today's educational programs are not subjected to "standard-oriented" evaluation. This is not to say that schools lack in aspiration or accomplishment. It is to say that standards—benchmarks of performance having widespread reference value—are not in common use. Schools across the nation may use the same evaluation checklist** but the interpretations of the checklisted data are couched in inexplicit, personal terms. Even in an informal way, no school can evaluate the impact of its program without knowledge of what other schools are doing in pursuit of similar objectives. Unfortunately, many educators are loathe to accumulate that knowledge systematically.[13, 14]

There is little knowledge anywhere today of the quality of a student's education. School grades are based on the private criteria and standards of the individual teacher. Most "standardized" tests scores tell where an examinee performing "psychometrically useful" tasks stands with regard to a reference group, rather than the level of competence at which he performs essential scholastic tasks. Although most teachers are competent to teach their subject matter and to spot

---

**One contemporary checklist is *Evaluative Criteria*, a document published by the National Study of Secondary School Evaluation (1960). It is a commendably thorough list of antecedents and possible transactions, organized mostly by subject-matter offerings. Surely it is valuable as a checklist, identifying neglected areas. Its great value may be a catalyst, hastening the maturity of a developing curriculum. However, it can be of only limited value in evaluating, for it guides neither the measurement nor the interpretation of measurement.

learning difficulties, few have the ability to describe a student's command over his intellectual environment. Neither school grades nor standardized test scores nor the candid opinions of teachers are very informative as to the excellence of students.

Even when measurements are effectively interpreted, evaluation is complicated by a multiplicity of standards. Standards vary from student to student, from instructor to instructor, and from reference group to reference group. This is not wrong. In a healthy society, different parties have different standards. Part of the responsibility of evaluation is to make known which standards are held by whom.

It was implied much earlier that it is reasonable to expect change in an educator's Intents over a period of time. This is to say that he will change both his criteria and his standards during instruction. While a curriculum is being developed and disseminated, even the major classes of criteria vary. In their analysis of nationwide assimilation of new educational programs, Clark and Guba[15] identified eight stages of change through which new programs go. For each stage they identified special criteria (each with its own standards) on which the program should be evaluated before it advances to another stage. Each of their criteria deserves elaboration, but here it is merely noted that there are quite different criteria at each successive curriculum-development stage.

Informal evaluation tends to leave criteria unspecified. Formal evaluation is more specific. But it seems the more careful the evaluation, the fewer the criteria; and the more carefully the criteria are specified, the less the concern given to standards of acceptability. It is a great misfortune that the best trained evaluators have been looking at education with a microscope rather than with a panoramic view finder.

There is no clear picture of what any school or any curriculum project is accomplishing today partly because the methodology of processing judgments is inadequate. What little formal evaluation there is, is attentive to too few criteria, overly tolerant of implicit standards, and ignores the advantage of relative comparisons. More needs to be said about relative and absolute standards.

Comparing and Judging

There are two bases of judging the characteristics of a program, (1) with respect to absolute standards as reflected by personal judgments and (2) with respect to relative standards as reflected by characteristics of alternate programs. One can evaluate SMSG mathematics with respect to opinions of what a mathematics curriculum should be or with regard to what other mathematics curricula are. The evaluator's comparisons and judgments are symbolized in Figure 3. The upper left matrix represents the data matrix from Figure 2. At the upper right are sets of standards by which a program can be judged in an absolute sense. There are multiple sets because there may be numerous reference groups or points of view. The several matrices at the lower left represent several alternate programs to which the one being evaluated can be compared.

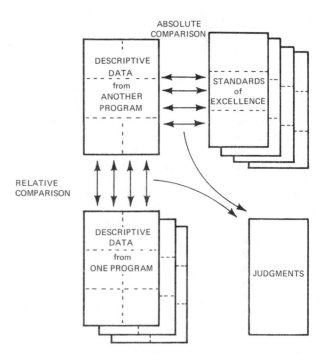

Figure 3. A representation of the process of judging the merit of an educational program.

Each set of absolute standards, if formalized, would indicate acceptable and meritorious levels for antecedents, transactions, and outcomes. So far I have been talking about setting standards, not about judging. Before making a judgment the evaluator determines whether or not each standard is met. Unavailable standards must be estimated. The judging act itself is deciding which set of standards to heed. More precisely, judging is assigning a weight, an importance, to each set of standards. Rational judgment in educational evaluation is a decision as to how much to pay attention to the standards of each reference group (point of view) in deciding whether or not to take some administrative action.***

***Deciding which variables to study and deciding which standards to employ are two essentially subjective commitments in evaluation. Other acts are capable of objective treatment; only these two are beyond the reach of social science methodology.

Relative comparison is accomplished in similar fashion except that the standards are taken from descriptions of other programs. It is hardly a judgmental matter to determine whether one program betters another with regard to a single characteristic, but there are many characteristics and the characteristics are not equally important. The evaluator selects which characteristics to attend to and which reference programs to compare to.

From relative judgment of a program, as well as from absolute judgment we can obtain an overall or composite rating of merit (perhaps with certain qualifying statements), a rating to be used in making an educational decision. From this final act of judgment a recommendation can be composed.

Absolute and Relative Evaluation

As to which kind of evaluation—absolute or relative—to encourage, Scriven and Cronbach have disagreed. Cronbach[4] suggests that generalizations to the local-school situation from curriculum-comparing studies are sufficiently hazardous (even when the studies are massive, well-designed, and properly controlled) to make them poor research investments. Moreover, the difference in purpose of the programs being compared is likely to be sufficiently great to render uninterpretable any outcome other than across-the-board superiority of one of them. Expecting that rarely, Cronbach urges fewer comparisons, more intensive process studies, and more curriculum "case studies" with extensive measurement and thorough description.

Scriven, on the other hand, indicates that what the educator wants to know is whether or not one program is better than another, and that the best way to answer his question is by direct comparison. He points to the difficulty of describing the outcomes of complex learning in explicit terms and with respect to absolute standards, and to the ease of observing relative outcomes from two programs. Whether or not Scriven's prescription is satisfying will probably depend on the client. An educator faced with an adoption decision is more likely to be satisfied, the curriculum innovator and instructional technologist less likely.

One of the major distinctions in evaluation is that which Scriven identifies as formative versus summative evaluation. His use of the terms relates primarily to the stage of development of curricular material. If material is not yet ready for distribution to classroom teachers, then its evaluation is formative; otherwise it is summative. It is probably more useful to distinguish between evaluation oriented to developer-author-publisher criteria and standards and evaluation oriented to consumer-administrator-teacher criteria and standards. The formative-summative distinction could be so defined, and I will use the terms in that way. The faculty committee facing an adoption choice asks, "Which is best? Which will do the job best?" The course developer, following Cronbach's advice, asks, "How can we teach it better?" (Note that neither are now concerned about the individual student differences.) The evaluator looks at different data and invokes different standards to answer these questions.

The evaluator who assumes responsibility for summative evaluation—rather than formative evaluation—accepts the responsibility of informing consumers as to the merit of the program. The judgments of Figure 3 are his target. It is likely that he will attempt to describe the school situations in which the procedures or materials may be used. He may see his task as one of indicating the goodness-of-fit of an available curriculum to an existing school program. He must learn whether or not the intended antecedents, transactions, and outcomes for the curriculum are consistent with the resources, standards, and goals of the school. This may require as much attention to the school as to the new curriculum.

The formative evaluator, on the other hand, is more interested in the contingencies indicated in Figure 2. He will look for covariations within the evaluation study, and across studies, as a basis for guiding the development of present or future programs.

For major evaluation activities it is obvious that an individual evaluator will not have the many competencies required. A team of social scientists is needed for many assignments. It is reasonable to suppose that such teams will include specialists in instructional technology, specialists in psychometric testing and scaling, specialists in research design and analysis, and specialists in dissemination of information. Curricular innovation is sure to have deep and wide-spread effect on our society, and we may include the social anthropologist on some evaluation teams. The economist and philosopher have something to offer. Experts will be needed for the study of values, population surveys, and content-oriented data-reduction techniques.

The educator who has looked disconsolate when scheduled for evaluation will look aghast at the prospect of a team of evaluators invading his school. How can these evaluators observe or describe the natural state of education when their very presence influences that state? His concern is justified. Measurement activity—just the presence of evaluators—does have a reactive effect on education, sometimes beneficial and sometimes not —but in either case contributing to the atypicality of the sessions. There are specialists, however, who anticipate that evaluation will one day be so skilled that it properly will be considered "unobtrusive measurement."[16]

In conclusion I would remind the reader that one of the largest investments being made in U. S. education today is in the development of new programs. School officials cannot yet revise a curriculum on rational grounds, and the needed evaluation is not under way. What is to be gained from the enormous effort of the innovators of the 1960's if in the 1970's there are no evaluation records? Both the new innovator and the new teacher need to know. Folklore is not a sufficient repository. In our data banks we should document the causes and effects, the congruence of intent and accomplishment, and the panorama of judgments of those concerned. Such records should be kept to promote educational action, not disstruct it. The countenance of evaluation should be one of data gathering that leads to decision-making, not to trouble-making.

Educators should be making their own evaluations more deliberate, more formal. Those who will—whether in their classrooms or on national panels—can hope to clarify their responsibility by answering each of the following questions: (1) Is this evaluation to be primarily descriptive, primarily judgmental, or both descriptive and judgmental? (2) Is this evaluation to emphasize the antecedent conditions, the transactions, or the outcomes alone, or a combination of these, or their functional contingencies? (3) Is this evaluation to indicate the congruence between what is intended and what occurs? (4) Is this evaluation to be undertaken within a single program or as a comparison between two or more curricular programs? (5) Is this evaluation intended more to further the development of curricula or to help choose among available curricula? With these questions answered, the restrictive effects or incomplete guidelines and inappropriate countenances are more easily avoided.

Endnotes

1. E. F. Lindquist, ed. *Educational Measurements.* Washington, D. C.: American Council on Education, 1951.

2. Smith, E. R. and Tyler, Ralph W. *Appraising and Recording Student Progress.* New York: Harper & Row, Publishers, 1942.

3. Educational Testing Service. "A Long, Hot Summer of Committee Work on National Assessment of Education." *ETS Developments* Vol. XIII, November, 1965.

4. Cronbach, Lee. "Evaluation for Course Improvement." *Teachers College Record* 64 (1963): 672-683.

5. Scriven, Michael. "The Methodology of Evaluation." *AERA Monograph Series on Curriculum Evaluation* No. 1. Chicago: Rand McNally & Co., 1967, pp. 39-89.

6. Taylor, Peter A. and Maguire, Thomas O. "A Theoretical Evaluation Model." *The Manitoba Journal of Educational Research* 1 (1966): 12-17.

7. Smith, B. Othanel and Meux, M. O. *A Study of the Logic of Teaching.* Urbana, Ill.: Bureau of Educational Research, University of Illinois. No date.

8. Gagne, Robert M. "Elementary Science: A New Scheme of Instruction." *Science* 151: 49-53. No. 3706.

9. Atkin, J. M. "Some Evaluation Problems in a Course Content Improvement Project." *Journal of Research in Science Teaching* 1 (1963): 129-31.

10. Mager, R. F. *Preparing Objectives for Programmed Instruction.* San Francisco: Fearon Publishers, 1962.

11. Berlak, Harold. Comments recorded in *Concepts and Structure in the New Social Science Curricula,* edited by Irving Morrissett, pp. 88-89. Lafayette, Indiana: Social Science Education Consortium, Purdue University, 1966.

12. See Bassham, H. "Teacher Understanding and Pupil Efficiency in Mathematics: A Study of Relationship." *Arithmetic Teacher* 9 (1962): 383-387.

13. Hand, Harold C. "National Assessment Viewed as the Camel's Nose." *Phi Delta Kappan* 47 (1965): 8-12.

14. Tyler, Ralph W. "Assessing the Progress of Education." *Phi Delta Kappan* 47 (1965): 13-16.

15. Clark, David L., and Guba, Egon G. "An Examination of Potential Change Roles in Education." Columbus, Ohio: The Ohio State University, 1965. Multilith.

16. Webb, Eugene J.; Campbell, Donald T.; Schwartz, Richard D.; and Sechrist, Lee. *Unobtrusive Measures: Nonreactive Research in the Social Sciences.* Chicago: Rand McNally & Co., 1966.

	CHAPTER 14
TWO GENERATIONS OF EVALUATION MODELS[1]	**Gene V. Glass**

Introduction

Beginning in the second decade of the twentieth century a small proportion, approximately 4 percent of the money spent on public education throughout the United States was collected through taxes and redistributed by the federal government. Authorized under such legislation as the Smith-Hughes and Smith-Lever Acts, these funds were expended primarily for vocational education and in the rural areas of the country. The character and rate of funds for public education channeled through the federal government changed little from 1920 to 1958. Faced with a new generation of problems and increased public concern for education, Congress has reacted in the last ten years with the National Defense Education Act (1958) and the Elementary and Secondary Education Act of 1965. Federal support for public education has nearly doubled in the last ten years (from 4 to 7 percent on the average for fifty states) and for the first time the thrust of these expenditures is directed toward innovation and changing the nature of education rather than merely extending the services of the schools. It is estimated that almost $8,000,000 will be received under five titles of the Elementary and Secondary Education Act of 1965 by the schools of the state of Nebraska this fiscal year.[2] Although this amount is small when measured against the total expenditure for education, it has had a profound effect on a significant number of schools. In short, the "cake of educational custom has been cracked."

In the midst of frenetic innovative activity in education during the last decade, a significant movement toward the systematic and empirical evaluation of educational programs has been growing. This movement is quite distinct from the accreditation activities and routine school testing programs which have been with us for many years. The evaluation movement has grown out of curriculum research and development activities which were based primarily in universities, e.g., the Eight-Year Study of the 1930's, the Cooperative Study of Evaluation in General Education of the 1950's. In spite of almost fifty years of concern for evaluation, more thought has been given to strategies and models for educational evaluation in the past five years than in the previous forty-five.

Three forces are providing the motivation for the continued interest in developing models for educational evaluation. First, the proportion of funds which reach the public schools through the federal government is apt to increase. It has been predicted that within 25 years 50 percent of the cost of *higher education* will be met by the federal government. The ethical obligation to evaluate (to document and judge) educational programs will be heightened by this restructuring of the distribution of funds. When the entire expense of educating children is born by the local citizenry, feedback on the success of new programs is immediate and is acted upon quickly by those who foot the bill. However, when the cost of a new program is met with the tax dollars of anonymous taxpayers a thousand miles away, abuses and failures of the program may tend to be covered up by the community (whose attitude may be, "So what if things did not work out well, at least we got our share of the money"). Formalized evaluation must now replace the constant monitoring of the school's operations by the local community if the *nation's* stake in public education is to be protected. Whoever wrote the evaluation requirement into Public Law 89-10 was wise indeed.

The second and third forces that are pushing evaluation into the spotlight are the civil rights

1. A paper presented at a meeting of the Nebraska Personnel and Guidance Association in Lincoln, Nebraska, 20 September 1968.
2. *Lincoln Journal*, Tuesday, July 9, 1968, p. 6.

movement and teacher militancy. There is insufficient space to document the case here. However, it can be seen almost daily in the mass media that as minority groups and an aroused teaching profession lock horns with the educational Establishment, each side appeals with increasing frequency to empirical evidence of the outcomes of education to resolve their difficulties. One sociologist, Dan Lortie of the University of Chicago, predicted the advent of a "certified public evaluator" who would serve a function analogous to that of the certified public accountant. His prophetic observation will be born out if action is taken on the following paragraph from the recently published report of the *National Advisory Commission on Civil Disorders*:

To increase the accountability of the public schools, the results of their performance should be made available to the public. Such information is available in some, but not all, cities. We see no reason for withholding useful and highly relevant indices of school (but not individual student) performance and recommend that all school systems adopt a policy of full public disclosure.

The public and bureaucratic clamor for something called "evaluation" caught the academics completely by surprise. Overnight, "evaluation" became a hot issue, and the central question seemed to be, "What is it?"

Two Models for Educational Evaluation

The academics who could first command an audience of educators when writing about evaluation were the men who had been involved in the "curriculum movement" of the last ten years. They had been thinking, speaking, and writing about evaluation of one type for several years prior to 1965. They had come to know evaluation as the handmaiden of curriculum research and development, and their prescription for the evaluation requirement of ESEA was *curriculum evaluation*. The distinguishing characteristics of curriculum evaluation are (a) the statement of the goals of instruction in terms of student performance or behaviors, (b) the analysis of instruction into molecular segments which culminate in student performance, (c) the construction of objective criterion-referenced tests to measure the outcomes on instruction, and (d) the utilization of test data in the restructuring of the curriculum. (See Bruner, 1966; Cronbach, 1963; Carroll, 1965. The work of Ralph W. Tyler has had the strongest influence on those who write about curriculum evaluation. Tyler's most important publications on the subject are Smith & Tylor (1942) and Tyler (1951).)

It quickly became apparent that the type of evaluation called for in PL 89-10 was not just "curriculum evaluation" but something more comprehensive and inclusive. What was called for was not a narrow prescription for improving the "curriculum" (by which was generally meant paper-and-pencil instructional materials), but a model of evaluation that would accommodate activities as diverse as a mobile learning laboratory for children of migrant workers in Washington state, a computerized system of retrieving research information for teachers in Colorado, and legitimate theatre for underprivileged children in New Orleans. The builders of the second generation of evaluation models have chosen with discrimination the best from the first generation "curriculum evaluation" models; but their thinking has not been constricted by the limited purpose which preoccupied those who framed models for evaluating curricula. The architects of these more general evaluation models include Scriven (1967), Stake (1967), and Stufflebeam (1966, 1968). Scriven greatly enriched the conceptual equipment for thinking about evaluation; Stake and Stufflebeam systematized much of the thought of the day into comprehensive models of the evaluation process. These second generation models might be called *educational systems evaluation models*, thus capitalizing on the current connotations of nonspecificity of the word "systems." (The word "system" is used today to refer to an organism, a social institution, a nation, or practically anything else.)

Models for curriculum evaluation are firmly engrained in the educational culture; they have grown out of the educational measurement and the curriculum development movements. They carry along the baggage of objective achievement testing, taxonomies of objectives, the behavioral statement of instructional objectives, etc. The educational system's evaluation models are less widely known, and the names of their components (antecedents-transactions-outcomes; formative and summative evaluation; instrumental and consequential evaluation) have an unfamiliar ring. To introduce the systems evaluation models (and to refresh your memory of the older curriculum evaluation models), these two classes of models will be contrasted in the remainder of this paper with respect to certain distinguishing characteristics.

Program Description

It has too often been assumed in education that mere words—and usually notoriously ambiguous ones—have the power to communicate the essential character of complex programs. Anyone who has even minimal experience with educational innovations knows how loosely titles like "team-teaching," "non-graded organization," and "organic curriculum" are tossed about. More than once a school's switch to "non-grading" has eventuated in little more than replacing names of grades painted on classroom doors with the names of the teachers.

Traditional models for curriculum evaluation have not made the conduct of the program itself the object of direct observation; the complete and detailed description of what constitutes the educational program is a central concern of the systems evaluation models, however. A mere epithet will not serve to describe an educational program. Evaluation requires no less than an exhaustive record of the intended and the actual activities which constituted the program.

An illustration may help clarify this point. My colleagues and I were recently involved in the evaluation of a program of "individualized instruction" in language arts at the elementary-school level. Our evaluation plans called, of course, for the assessment of pupil performance and satisfactions at the end of the program for comparison with conventionally taught classes. However, what is the value of such data if one has only vague knowledge of the activity to which he is attributing different outcomes? What is the value of the data if that which is called "individualized instruction" possesses none of its essential features in the opinion of expert curriculum developers and educational psychologists? These questions prompted us to worry considerably about the real meaning of "individualized instruction" in this instance. Thus we put into the evaluation report a record of the plans and objectives of the people responsible for "individualizing" the language arts instruction. Intended classroom procedures were carefully described. During the program, observers sat in on a sampling of school days to record such things as the number and sizes of subgroups of pupils within a given room, the activities the teacher was engaged in, etc. After the program, an acknowledged expert in individualized instruction and language arts was given all instructional materials and was asked to produce a narrative assessment of the quality of both the classroom organization and the materials. If time and money had been sufficient, we would have required each teacher to keep a daily log book of classroom activities, and then compared the degree of "individualization" in the innovative school with "individualization" in conventional schools.

Innovative programs are prone to vanish without a trace. They seem rarely to survive in human memory; they deserve to be immortalized in evaluation reports. Without a well-kept historical record, this year's innovation may be a repeat of last year's debacle.

The Goals and Roles of Evaluation

Evaluation can play many *roles* in an educational program (it can aid the developers by providing mastery test data, it can determine the staff's expectations for the program by survey research methods, etc.); however, the goal of evaluation must always be to provide an answer to an all-important question: Does the program under observation have greater value than its competitors? Traditional curriculum evaluation models differ from the current generation of evaluation models with respect to the stress laid on playing the roles of evaluation rather than striving to attain its goal. Traditional "curriculum evaluation" models have emphasized playing various roles in the development or operation of a program; in some instances the proponents of these methods have even argued against attempting to achieve the goal of evaluation. In contrast to this traditional viewpoint, the systems evaluation models emphasize the necessity for an evaluation to culminate at some point in an overall judgment of the relative worth of the enterprise. Being of assistance to the program personnel—so that they may better conduct their business—*is a proximate aim of evaluation; the ultimate aim of an evaluation is to decide questions of adoption and support.* Rendering a judgment upon the composite value of an educational program poses a threat to teachers and administrators. Nevertheless, we are obliged to make the judgment, and we cannot safely shirk the obligation.

The distinction between the roles and goals of evaluation is incorporated in Scriven's distinction between *formative* and *summative* evaluation:

Formative evaluation is evaluation at the intermediate stages of a program. The results of formative evaluation are intended to serve as the basis for altering the nature of the program in its formative stages.

Summative evaluation is terminal evaluation concerned with the comparative worth or effectiveness of competing instructional programs. The results of summative evaluation are not intended to serve directly in the revision, improvement or formation of a program; rather they are gathered for use in making decisions about support and adoption.

Any comprehensive evaluation will attend to both formative questions and the overriding summative question.

Comparative vs. Non-Comparative Evaluation

Whether or not two programs should be compared in an evaluation has been an issue on which traditional curriculum evaluation models and the second generation evaluation models have disagreed. Arguments against comparing programs have been put forward most forcefully by Cronbach and by Carroll.

The aim to compare one course with another should not dominate plans for evaluation. . . . Since group comparisons give equivocal results, I believe that a formal study should be designed primarily to determine the post-course performance of a well-described group, with respect to many important objectives and side effects. (Cronbach, 1963)

I would define curriculum evaluation as a process of determining whether a given curriculum attains the ends it seeks, or, rather, of determining which objectives it can attain, under what conditions, and for what kinds of pupils. . . . But ordinarily, curricula do not have precisely identical objectives, and it would generally be improper to compare them, because to do so would be to raise more or less philosophical questions about the comparative worth of their respective objectives. (Carroll, 1965)

In direct response to these arguments, Scriven has written that: "The conclusion seems obligatory that comparative evaluation, whether mediated or fundamental, is the method of choice for evaluation problems." Two specific points which possess some similarities were advanced by Cronbach and Carroll in elaborations of their arguments: Carroll maintained that it does not do any good to compare curriculum A with curriculum B, because one cannot generalize from this comparison to comparisons of A with other rival curricula. Cronbach wrote:

At best, an experiment never does more than compare the present version of one course with the present version of another. A major effort to bring the losing contender nearer to perfection would be very likely to reverse the verdict of the experiment.

Both Carroll and Cronbach are finding fault with the comparative experimental method because it cannot achieve the impossible. If the comparative experiment in evaluation is open to criticism because comparing curricula A and B does not tell us how A would compare with some unknown and unspecified curriculum C (as Carroll maintains), then it is equally at fault for also not giving us any information about whether a curriculum might be produced in the future which will surpass any existing today. Also, it is perfectly obvious that a comparative evaluation performed today compares only the present versions of two or more curricula.

Cronbach's statement that "a major effort" at upgrading the level of the poorer of two curricula would likely cause it to surpass its competitor in excellence is probably true. However, what effect would a similar "major effort" have on the curriculum which was initially superior? Unless some point of diminishing returns has been met in the development of the curriculum which first proved superior, "major efforts" on *both* curricula will likely leave the order of excellence unchanged on subsequent comparative evaluations.

Carroll claimed that curricula do not ordinarily have identical objectives and that to compare

them raises philosophical problems about the comparative worth of different objectives. The *choice* between two competing curricula with greatly different objectives cannot help but raise philosophical questions, or ethical questions, or at least questions of the relative worth of certain values held by a society. Anyone who must make decisions affecting the adoption of curricula or innovative activities for a school is faced with resolving just these questions. I doubt that such questions can be adequately resolved and a rational decision made unless empirical data are gathered which show how well a curriculum attains its own objectives, the objectives of competing curricula, and certain cross-curricular objectives.

Many choices between competing curricula will inevitably involves philosophical questions—or better, questions of *value*. It is not the duty of the evaluator to answer these questions by himself; but he has a vital role to play in cooperation with the curriculum specialist, the educational psychologist, the philosopher, and the administrator in clarifying the questions and bringing empirical data to bear on them.

One of Cronbach's major criticisms of the comparative method of evaluation was that it contributed little to understanding the curriculum:

In an experiment where treatments differ in a dozen respects, no understanding is gained from the fact that the experiment shows a numerical advantage in favor of the new course. No one knows which of the ingredients is responsible for the advantage.

Scriven (1967, p. 65) has answered Cronbach on this point:

. . . understanding is not our *only* goal in evaluation. We are also interested in questions of support, encouragement, adoption, reward, refinement, etc. And these extremely important questions can be given a useful though in some cases not a complete answer by the mere discovery of superiority.

As I see it, Cronbach and Scriven are not so much at odds on this point as they are speaking at cross purposes. Scriven is clearly correct: problems of adoption of a curriculum, deciding between competing curricula, etc., require a comparative evaluation. But Cronbach's remark seems to be addressed more to the developer of a curriculum than to the selector of one. The curriculum developer will probably find data which pinpoint the failures and successes in his materials far more valuable than data from a comparison of his materials with those of a competitor. If given the news that his curriculum has just won last place in a comparative experiment with his chief competitor, the typical curriculum developer would probably choose one of two reactions: (1) he would maintain that the experiment was invalid, biased, and unfair, or (2) he would argue that his curriculum was not compared with its competitor on the "proper," "important" objectives. In either case, he will not find such data useful in subsequent developmental work. Such data may even have the ill effect of causing the curriculum developer to alter the objectives of his materials and begin to prize certain objectives because he can attain them better and not for their intrinsic worth.

The message here is that the curriculum developer wants to know *how* and *why* his materials function as they do and that he will not make good use of comparative data. However, comparative evaluation at some level is necessary. The anarchist who opposes all comparisons of curricula in favor of determining which objectives are met by which students and why, has forgotten that an implicit comparison is present in establishing the objectives of any curriculum. No one is foolish enough to establish the objective for a curriculum in typing of "typing 10 words per minute with no more than 5 mistakes" because existing curricula are already superior to this. At some point in the evaluation of a curriculum these implicit comparisons must be revealed and subjected to a test.

The Elements of Evaluation

The elements of evaluation are the basic data—the phenomena to which the evaluator attends. Traditional curriculum evaluation models and the newer evaluation models differ in their emphasis on which data are worth gathering.

Tylerian curriculum evaluation gives almost exclusive priority to pupil *behaviors*. Objectives must be stated in behavioral terms, and test data on performance of the desired behaviors is all that deserves the evaluator's attention. The curriculum evaluators take pride in their assertion that they are evaluating the *ends* of instruction and not the *means* toward those ends. Whether or not this claim can be justified cannot occupy us now, unfortunately.

In contrast to the narrow perspective of the curriculum evaluation models, the systems evaluation models are fiercely ecumenical about what data should be gathered. Stake (1967) classified the data of evaluation into three broad classes, which I have broken down further in two instances to indicate something of their nature:

A. Antecedents—all conditions existing prior to instruction which may be related to outcomes

   1. Resources—human, financial, etc.
   2. Entry behaviors and biographical data
   3. Objectives

B. Transactions—the succession of activities comprising the instructional program
C. Outcomes—the results of the program
   1. Immediate vs. long-range
   2. Primary, secondary, and tertiary
   3. Behavior vs. non-behavioral
   4. Curricular vs. cross-curricular

A typical innovative program might involve observation of each of the following:

Antecedents—
   1. Pupil entry behavior and biographical data.
   2. Biographical and other data on the project personnel.
   3. Pupil and staff expectations.
   4. Parents expectations and wishes.
   5. Description of the instructional environment.
   6. Description of the instructional materials.
   7. Record of financial resources.
   8. The intended schedule and activities of the program.
   9. Comparative data on the pupils and teachers of non-innovative classrooms.

Transactions—
   1. Actual schedule of activities.
   2. Time sampling studies of how typical classroom hours are spent.
   3. The running record of the classroom (disturbances, significant deviations from intended activities, absences of staff and pupils, etc.).

Outcomes—
   1. Pupil performance and satisfactions both immediate and long-range.
   2. Staff satisfactions and complaints both immediate and long-range.
   3. Parents satisfactions and complaints.
   4. Pupil performance on cross-curricular objectives.
   5. Staff mobility.
   6. Financial costs.
   7. Side effects of the program on non-participating pupils and staff.

Anything that could conceivably be related to the success of the program becomes data for the evaluation. Guided by the systems evaluation models, the evaluator's responsiveness to the dozens of critical ingredients of a successful program is limited only by time and money, and not by his narrow perspective of which data are worth gathering.

Description and Judgment

Scriven (1967) emphasized the central role that judgment must play in evaluation. Stake (1967,

p. 525) incorporated "judgment" as one of the two fundamental activities of evaluation:

The countenance of evaluation beheld by the educator is not the same one beheld by the specialist in evaluation. The specialist sees himself as a "describer," one who describes aptitudes and environments and accomplishments. The teacher and school administrator, on the other hand, expect an evaluator to grade something or someone as to merit. Moreover, they expect that he will judge things against external standards, on criteria perhaps little related to the local school's resources and goals.

Neither sees evaluation broadly enough. *Both* description and judgment are essential—in fact, they are the two basic acts of evaluation. Any individual evaluator may attempt to refrain from judging or from collecting the judgments of others. Any individual evaluator may seek only to bring to light the worth of the program. But their evaluations are incomplete. To be fully understood, the educational program must be fully described and fully judged.

Traditional thinking on educational evaluation held that judgments are subjective, and hence are not fitting material from which to build an evaluation. Judgments are undeniably subjective, but they can be gathered and reported with objectivity. Moreover, the subjectivity of value judgments makes them nonetheless important as determiners of the success of a program. It is totally beside the point to observe that a principal's judgment is subjective, when that principal's judgment that a program has worthless objectives causes him to undercut the program by withdrawing his support. Indeed, *judgments, attitudes, and satisfactions are subjective. However, they can account for the success or failure of a program and they can be objectively measured; hence, they deserve the evaluator's attention.*

There is another sense in which judgments are an important part of evaluation. The mere description of an educational program, no matter how detailed, is not in itself an evaluation. The knowledge that a room temperature is now 150° Fahrenheit is devoid of any evaluative meaning. If I am taking a steam bath in that room, it is *good*; if I am watching television, it is *bad*.

Scriven (1967, p. 40) defined evaluation as follows:

Evaluation is itself a methodological activity which is essentially similar whether we are trying to evaluate coffee machines or teaching machines, plans for a house or plans for a curriculum. The activity consists simply in gathering and combining of performance data with a weighted set of goal scales to yield either comparative or numerical ratings, and in the justification of (a) the data-gathering instruments, (b) the weightings, and (c) the selection of goals.

Frequently, the criteria and standards of performance with which data are compared and the manner in which such data are weighted in combinations to yield global value judgments are poorly understood by both the evaluators and those who make these judgments. (Some progress is being made, however, toward the psychometric description of peoples' judgment policies. See Maguire, 1966, for example.) Although the process may not be well understood, the end product of the process can be reliably measured and objectively recorded. If one has confidence in the rationality of the experts from whom he gathers such value judgments, the expert opinion can serve for the time-being in place of the more mechanistic and less well-understood rational decision making process. To avoid giving the impression that the collection of value judgments is a casual undertaking befitting the "subjectivity" of the raw material, I hasten to add that the most sophisticated techniques of survey research, interviewing, questionnaire construction, attitude and opinion assessment, and psychometric data analysis are required to overcome the considerable hazards of values assessment.

Conclusion

The picture painted here of the educational systems evaluation models differs substantially from what has traditionally passed for evaluation in education. Evaluation has never been so broadly conceived as it has been by such men as Scriven, Stake, Stufflebeam, and a few others. This new conception of educational evaluation sees evaluation as a facilitating force in the creation of the program, as well as evaluation as the arbiter of ultimate worth or value; it includes *all* of the elements, both central and peripheral to the program as worthy of attention, not just behavioral objectives and pupil performance; it incorporates a broad spectrum of social science technology (survey methods, testing, experimental design, attitude measurement, rating scales, check lists, observation schedules, interviewing, etc.) rather than the exclusive use of paper-and-pencil tests of subject-matter mastery; it includes judgment as a fundamental activity of evaluation, not just the description of procedures and outcomes; it acknowledges a comparative question inherent in any attempt to improve the practice of education, and it refuses to let the question go unanswered.

Current writers on educational evaluation are urging us to undertake far more ambitious and costly evaluations than we have in the past. During the early stages of a program one dollar in ten would have to be spent to produce a comprehensive evaluation; such expense for evaluating one's efforts is common in the automobile and drug industries but seems astonishing in the education industry where an infinitesimal fraction of the cost of the enterprise is designated for evaluation.[3] We shall probably never attain the impossible dream of a *complete* evaluation; however, our efforts can be improved by considering the ideal.

3. It is estimated that drug firms in the United States will spend $500,000,000 on research and development in 1968. Yet the single largest industry in the country, the education industry, will spend substantially less than $100,000,000 on research and development activities this year through the U.S. Office of Education, public schools, foundations, and universities.

REFERENCES

Bruner, Jerome S. *Toward a Theory of Instruction.* Cambridge: Harvard University Press, 1966.

Carroll, John B. "School learning over the long haul." In *Learning and the Educational Process,* edited by John D. Krumboltz, chapter 10. Chicago: Rand McNally & Co., 1965.

Cronbach, Lee J. "Course Improvement through Evaluation." *Teachers College Record* 64 (1963): 672-683.

Maguire, Thomas O. "Value Components of Teachers, Judgments of Educational Objectives." Doctoral Dissertation. College of Education, University of Illinois, 1967.

Scriven, Michael. The methodology of evaluation, *AERA Monograph Series on Evaluation,* No. 1. Chicago: Rand McNally & Co., 1967. pp. 39-89.

Smith, Eugene R. and Tyler, Ralph W. *Appraising and Recording Student Progress.* New York: Harper & Row, Publishers, 1942.

Stake, Robert E., ed. *AERA Monograph Series on Curriculum Evaluation,* No. 1. Chicago: Rand McNally & Co., 1967.

Stake, Robert E. "The Countenance of Educational Evaluation." *Teachers College Record* 68 (1967): 523-540.

Stufflebeam, Daniel L. Evaluation as enlightenment for decision-making. Columbus: Ohio State University, Evaluation Center (1712 Neil St., Columbus, Ohio), 1968.

Stufflebeam, Daniel L. A depth study of the evaluation requirement. *Theory Into Practice* 5 (1966): 121-133.

Tyler, Ralph W. The functions of measurement in improving instruction. In *Educational Measurement,* edited by E. F. Lindquist. Washington, D. C.: American Council on Education, 1951.

<table>
<tr><td>CHAPTER 15</td><td></td></tr>
<tr><td>Marvin C. Alkin</td><td>TOWARDS AN EVALUATION MODEL:
A SYSTEMS APPROACH</td></tr>
</table>

CHAPTER 15

Marvin C. Alkin

TOWARDS AN EVALUATION MODEL: A SYSTEMS APPROACH

Evaluation is the process of first identifying and then quantifying, or measuring, the relationships between student inputs and educational outputs and determining the combination of mediating factors which maximizes the educational outputs, given a constant financial input and controlling for the effects of external systems. Evaluation is a complex activity that involves the identification of many factors that contribute to educational outputs.

In our definition of evaluation, "student inputs" refers to the nature and characteristics of the students entering the program to be evaluated. By "educational outputs" we mean two things: (1) cognitive and non-cognitive changes which take place in students after they are exposed to the instructional program. These changes are assumed to be attributable to the program. And, (2) the impact of the program upon systems external to it (home, community, other programs, etc.). "Financial inputs" refers to the financial resources made available for carrying on the program. "Mediating factors" are the descriptive characteristics (e.g., personnel, school organization and programs, and instructional design) of the way in which financial inputs are utilized within the program in combination with the student inputs. And, finally, by "external systems" we mean the framework of social, political, legal, economic, and other systems outside of the school, formal or informal, which encompass the program, have impact upon it, and are, in turn, modified by the outputs of the program.

It should be specifically noted that in the discussion of mediating variables, we act under the assumption that they are the only set of variables which are manipulatable. For the sake of this model we will assume that: (1) external systems are not immediately altered by the outputs of the system; and (2) that the school decision-makers have no control over which ex-

ternal systems are allowed to impinge upon the school. If we were to maintain that feedback immediately changes the system, this would imply a highly dynamic model rather than the static model considered here. The second assumption implies that no attempt will be made to change the nature of the student inputs to the system—that is, we do not usually concern ourselves with the consideration of community changes, which might be made, that would alter the nature of the student inputs. We act, too, under the assumption that student inputs are relatively non-manipulatable from without the system. Thus, we concern ourselves with the mediating variables within the system that can be changed, manipulated and altered in order to maximize student outputs. We recognize the weakness in this assumption, and that there are some school-related manipulations that could be instituted which would change the nature of the student input. Instances of this are bussing, changing of school boundaries in order to "juggle" student inputs to specific schools, community educational resources (such as education resource units in disadvantaged areas), and preschool programs (such as Project Headstart). The assumptions of a static model and of non-manipulatable external systems seem necessary at this early stage of the model development.

With our definition of evaluation and some of the limits we are imposing in mind, it seems appropriate to discuss the evaluation model[1] and, in more general terms, the principles of evaluation which follow from the model. However, before doing this, we will first discuss the general nature and function of an evaluation model and, second, the importance of the size of the unit to be evaluated upon the nature of the evaluation. These sections will set the background for the development of the model presented in this paper.

It should be noted that in this paper we are not primarily concerned with the methodological consideration *per se*. We accept the differentiation by Stake (1967) between the theory of evaluation which identifies what is to be observed and judged and the methodology of evaluation which specifies the manner in which these observations and judgments will be made. It is the function of this paper merely to specify, both by figurative and verbal representation (in the form of a model), the nature of what should be observed and judged.

An evaluation model or, for that matter, any model, is a simplistic statement or representation of sets of complex interrelationships. Such a representation is intended to help the modelers in structuring the universe, or that segment of the universe being considered. Of necessity, models must be functions of the frames of reference of their builders. Thus, an evaluation model constructed by one whose background is psychology and the study of tests and measurements will be a quite different model from that constructed by a sociologist looking at evaluation, or of that constructed by a school administrator or an economist. While each model may view the same set of interrelationships, it is inevitable that certain concerns of the model builders will differ. The resultant generation of different perspectives of the problem is beneficial, not only for the model builder who is better able to "get a handle on" his universe, but to others who may be forced for the first time to consider more seriously some of what they previously may have considered to be lesser concerns in their own model.

We cannot claim that the elements of the model presented here are uniquely different from those mentioned by others concerned with evaluation. In fact, most of the variables and kinds of interactions have been mentioned previously by Stake (1967), Scriven (1967), and, we are sure, many others. Moreover, the model is in many ways not significantly different from the total model of evaluation that guides the efforts of the Center for the Study of Evaluation of Instructional Programs at UCLA, as developed by the committee of authors of the proposal for the Center: Chairman M. C. Wittrock and committee members Marvin C. Alkin, John Bormuth, Reginald Jones, James Liesch, and David Wiley (1965). That model maintains that evaluation cannot take place without considering the nature of the instructional parameters in the program being evaluated, without understanding and quantifying the impact of social and administrative contexts that impinge upon the program, and without considering a multiplicity of outcome measures. This author participated in the development of that model, and the statement presented here simply represents his own personal modifications of that model, as well as deviations based on his own frame of reference.

Units of Aggregation

As a final preliminary, it should be noted that the nature of an evaluation depends, in part, upon the size of the unit to be evaluated—and evaluation may involve many basic units of examination. Where the unit of evaluation is relatively small and discrete (e.g., individual students), the nature of the students and of the financial resources made available, as well as many other variables which mediate in the production of outcomes, can be manipulated by the method of selection of groups. In this instance, the task of evaluation becomes the comparison of a single mediating variable to another variable or to several others. Where more complex units are to be evaluated, other factors may be more diffuse and uncontrollable. In these instances, there might be a need for a total systems analysis in which we attempt to apply statistical controls to many of the dimensions being examined, because randomness of selection cannot be guaranteed in the same way as when smaller units are the basis of analysis. Furthermore, in order to fully develop an evaluation model, it is fundamental and, therefore, necessary to understand the nature of interrelationships between variables being controlled. It is obvious, then, that the nature and sophistication of the evaluation model to be developed is dependent, in large part, upon the level of aggregation of the unit for evaluation.

Let us examine several possible levels of aggregation for the units which might be considered in an evaluation. For instance, at the first level, it is possible to examine the performance of an individual student in a given classroom in a given school. This is done quite frequently when we give a nationally-standardized test to students and we indicate the percentile score of the student as compared to national norms. In this situation, we are appraising the performance of the student on the basis of national criterion dimensions. However, this is not evaluation unless there is a comparison measure available, such as a pre-test or a test in which comparable groups are treated differently. In other words, it seems that a clear distinction can and must be made between an appraisal that is simply a statement of the present achievement or status of an individual and an "evaluation" that measures the changes in these individuals or other units while attempting to determine the set of mediating factors which is most directly related to the given changes. The process of evaluation, then, requires a specific identification of the nature of the student units to be evaluated and stricter controls and understanding of the variables which mediate upon those units to produce the educational changes in a range of different kinds of educational outcomes, such as performance, attitudes, and social adjustment. With this specific meaning of the word "evaluation" in mind, let us proceed to examine other aggregated levels of units for evaluation.

At a somewhat more aggregated level, it is possible to evaluate the performance of groups of children. For example, using classrooms as the unit of examination, we might administer a given test in a specific achievement area to students within a school. Then we could proceed to discuss the variation in scores between these units, indicating the range of the scores, the mean, median, interquartile deviation, and other appropriate measures. In this case, while it is true that we are examining the performance of individual students, we are aggregating or combining their performances to represent a larger unit. The evaluation in this instance still conforms to our previously-indicated definition. The student inputs are designated by the series of measures most descriptive of the total classroom as a unit, and the particular set of mediating variables which has been acting upon this class or upon all of the individuals in the class also is indicated by various measures.

In the examination and comparison of several classroom units, if there have been different financial inputs to each of the units, it is necessary to determine the exact nature of the financial input to each of the units. This would be a preliminary step in determining the manner in which these funds have been utilized in initiating environmental changes which mediate upon the student in the production of the educational outcomes. Finally, it is necessary to represent the educational outcomes of each of the classroom units. It would be possible to compute the average of the scores made by students within one classroom and to compare it with the average score of pupils within another classroom or, for that matter, many other classrooms. These comparisons, when considered along with the other factors in the evaluation model, would represent a first-step evaluation of the performance of groups of individuals. In this case, the evaluation would be made between classrooms.

As we have illustrated, there are a number of different kinds of evaluation that might be made. We might wish to evaluate the results on the students of a number of classes using a specific course of study. Or, we might wish to evaluate—in a *specific* aggregate sense of the words "instructional program"—units which are broader than classroom units. Furthermore, we might wish to

consider all of the curricular elements of the instructional program of the school, (mathematics, English, social studies, etc.), as subsets of the total instructional program, namely, the total field of academic experiences of an individual school. In this sense, we would evaluate the instructional program of the school on a number of output dimensions by using the total aggregated score of all students within the school and statistical measures descriptive of that data.

In an instance where the unit for evaluation is a total school, it would be necessary to examine specific school factors which might have a relationship to the outputs—that is, it would be necessary to ascertain to what extent relevant community characteristics differ between the schools. There are other questions which might be asked: Does each school provide the same amount of financial resources to be utilized in purchasing the important elements within the school system? How much is spent on teachers? On instructional services? What are the unique social characteristics on the school, etc.?

With these somewhat tangential thoughts as a reference point, we will consider more directly the model being presented.

Towards an Evaluation Model

In evaluating instructional programs, the complexities of the interrelationships are so great that we feel that the development of a theoretical model demands a systems approach. For this model, we will consider the school (individual school or school district) as our unit of examination.

There are two categories of input to the school: student and financial.[2] Moreover, there are a group of mediating variables within the school. Some of these variables are "costly" and require the utilization of financial inputs; others are relatively cost-free. Finally, there are a number of external social, political, and economic systems impinging upon the school. These factors taken together produce a number of outputs. Some of these are student outputs (such as changes in attitudes, skills, etc., of students); others are incidental or non-student outputs (such as program-caused or program-related changes in external systems). In succeeding paragraphs, we will consider each of these elements individually. For ease of communication, we will hereafter refer to the school as "the system." The system and its external systems will be called the "macro-system."

One final note must be added: We recognize that there are great overlaps between individual elements of the macro-system. However, to avoid confusion in the discussion of the model, we will think of the elements as being reasonably discrete. Thus, for example, certain aspects of the description of the student inputs are, to a great extent, a reflection of external social systems. They will, however, be considered in one category alone. (See Figure 1, below for a simplified diagram of the conceptual model.)

Student Inputs

We will consider the student input as a description or measure of the student being introduced into the system or, in the case of a larger unit of instructional program, as an aggregated, statistical description of the students being introduced into the system. In the ideal world, when students enter the system, they are given a complete battery of all the traditional kinds of achievement, intelligence, and personality tests, as well as questionnaires and other documentary data describing their homes, status in the community, family background, family memberships in other social systems, and the like. Unfortunately, the ideal world does not exist. We must, therefore, develop a series of proxy measures of student inputs. Very frequently, intelligence scores are available for entering students; there is usually, also, some small amount of family data available

in the cumulative record folder. Occasionally, achievement tests given in the preceding year or two have been transferred and are available as a measure of the achievement starting-point of the students in the system. A considerable amount of additional desired data must, in consequence, either be collected in the school or more often be inferred from other, more accessible measures. As a result, we often look at the community and the characteristics of the community as an indication of the kind of student input that is being introduced into the system. For example, from the works of McClelland (1953) and others, we know that certain family characteristics bear a strong relationship to achievement motivation in children. And, while we would undoubtedly prefer individual achievement-motivation-test scores for each student entering the system, when such information is unavailable, certain implications can, nonetheless, be drawn from certain data items descriptive of family characteristics.

Financial Inputs

There is a second class of inputs to the system—financial inputs. If we think of a district as a system, then not only do students enter the system, but finances are provided from local, state,

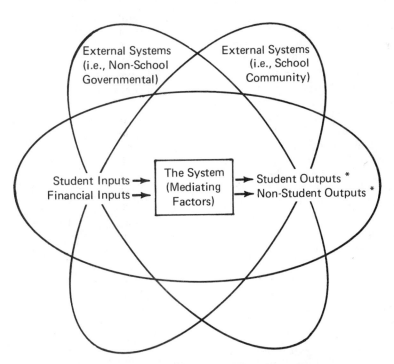

*As student and non-student outputs enter the macro-system, they alter to some extent the nature of the external systems and thus by extension the inputs in succeeding stages.

Figure 1. The Macro-System of an Evaluation Model.

and federal sources and are, in part, a means of implementing different sets of mediating factors within the system. Perhaps it is relevant to determine the portion of the total resources, derived from each of the governmental levels. Perhaps, also, it is important to designate the specific authorizations from federal funds or special state programs in order to be aware "of the strings attached" and consequent implications for resource utilization within the system.

If we were concerned with evaluating a part of the system, such as the mathematics program or the guidance program, it would be necessary to determine the nature and amount of the financial input to that portion of the system. Unfortunately, present accounting practices in all states provide data only on functions of expenditures rather than on programs of expenditures—i.e., data are available on a number of factors such as the amount spent for administration, maintenance, operation, instruction, and fixed charges, but these data are not available on a program basis. What is needed, therefore, is a budgeting system that will allow ready aggregation and disaggregation of funds to provide specific and total cost data on individual instructional programs. In short, we need a system of program budgeting.

External Systems

The school is placed within the framework of numerous social systems (external social contexts). For example, in the case of the individual school some of the contexts are: the community, the district, the nature of the district organization, other governmental systems such as the city, the county, the patterns of community organizations and of community participation. Each of these external systems, by the nature of the differentiated functions it serves, places sets of demands and restrictions both upon the educational system (school) and upon the individuals within the system. Each of these systems serves specific integrative, adaptive, goal-attaining, and pattern-maintaining functions in the macro-system. Consequently, it is necessary to identify and quantify these external systems characteristics and relationships which are relevant in terms of the contribution they make towards producing the educational outputs of the system.

In actuality, the external systems interact with the educational system. While each of them may be conceived as having their own inputs, particular sets of mediating variables, and outputs, they are, in turn, external systems to the educational system and *vice versa*. Thus, each system external to education may, in effect, be considered as both a source of inputs and a receiver of outputs. In this model, we are concerned specifically with only two of the inputs to education, financial and student, and will consider the "inputs" from other external systems as control variables. The outputs of the system to external systems are considered as non-student outputs.

Mediating Factors

A fourth group of elements of the evaluation model is what we call the mediating factors. The financial input to a system can be utilized in a great number of ways. We could decrease the student-to-teacher ratio, establish standards which insure the hiring of teachers with specified characteristics, develop different administrative arrangements within the school, provide more library books, provide more textbooks, introduce different curricula, use different instructional procedures, or provide additional supplies.

Thus the variables that we call "mediating" are highly manipulatable—that is, they are subject to change or manipulation by educational decision-makers at all levels. We have no definitive evidence, however, as to which combination of mediating variables is most effective in achieving the objectives of the school (i.e., in producing desired educational outputs).

At this point, it is only fair to indicate that we do not mean to imply that all mediating factors which have impact on educational outputs are related to financial input. Indeed, some mediating factors are "free." For example, the cost of implementing certain alterations in the school environment or in the attitudes of teachers may be relatively cost-free. Frequently, the instructional procedure used by the teacher in the classroom (the substitution of one procedure for another) has little or no additional cost attached to it. However, some changes in the system are extremely costly (such as some of the administrative or organizational arrangements and many instructional procedures which are technologically based). As a consequence, the potential output achieved by the change must be examined in terms of the costs involved.

It is a relatively easy position to maintain that more money should be provided for teacher salaries and that in this way, in all likelihood, the educational program will be improved. There is evidence that a relationship exists between higher teacher salaries and educational quality. The real question, however, is to what extent a given dollar input, if utilized in an alternate manner, would increase the nature of the educational outputs. This is a cost-effectiveness question and is, after all, one of the elements at the heart of evaluation or, at the very least, one of the reasons why we evaluate.

We have noted that the selection of different sets of mediating factors may lead to the maximization of educational outputs in a system. There is, though, another point to be made: not only are there different sets of mediating variables most applicable for producing given educational outputs, but, significantly, these sets of mediating variables may produce quite different levels of change in the educational outputs in different systems or for different student input groups. James Coleman observed this point in a study for the Civil Rights Commission entitled *Equality of Educational Opportunity*. He noted that the "inference might then be made that improving the school of a minority pupil may increase his achievement more than would improving the school of a white child increase his. Similarly, the average minority pupil's achievement may suffer more in a school of low quality than might the average white pupil's." He concluded that "this indicates that it is for the most disadvantaged children that improvements in school quality will make the most difference in achievement." (Coleman, 1966). Appropriate mediating factors, therefore, are a function not only of the desired educational outputs, but of the nature of the student inputs and of the given system as well.

As mentioned at the beginning of this paper, the mediating variables, as we have defined them, are assumed to be the only set of variables which can be manipulated. (See page 110.) This is a simplifying assumption, in part, because it allows us to deal with a static instead of a more complex dynamic model. Also, it should be noted that the bias implied by this assumption follows from the basic intent of the model we are seeking to construct—that is, a decision-making model or, more specifically, a model designed to aid school administrators in their day-to-day operations.

Student Outputs

Another set of elements of the evaluation model is the student outputs. Changes take place in students from the time they enter the system to the time they leave, and many of these changes are produced by the nature of the mediating factors within the system. Here, again, there is a problem, for the outputs of a school or of a district cannot simply be measured by the scores of students on academic achievement tests.[3] What are the noncognitive aspects of output? How has the behavior of students changed? What is the relationship between the activities that take place in a district or a school and the eventual success of students in their vocational or future educational endeavors? How does the student's educational experience aid him in dealing with political problems and activities as well as cultural

affairs? To what extent does the social situation present in the school, as well as what is learned in classes, affect the student? These are only some of the unanswered questions related to the identification of educational outputs, and, of course, they can be solved only through further research and investigation.

While there are two prime inputs into the system (student and financial), we will consider that there are no direct, financial outputs except as a portion of the student outputs—there are no financial outputs except as we are willing to place financial value on certain behavioral changes or except as student outputs yield financial or economic returns, either individual or societal.[4]

Non-Student Outputs

The final set of elements of the model is the non-student outputs. The two groups of outcome measures (student and non-student) may be thought of as feedback loops in which each modifies, to some extent, the nature of future inputs to the system. The changes in students, for example, have social, political, and economic implications—that is, the very nature of the external systems is altered by changes in student outputs. There are, however, other outputs of the school—the impact of educational decisions made as a part of the "mediating factors" has repercussions in the external systems. Frequently, these outputs are only tangentially related to individual students or to student outputs. For example, the nature of many of the decisions as to the proper utilization of resources may produce innumerable educational outputs not directly student-related. That is, decisions which influence the number and salaries of teachers, as well as the number and salaries of classified personnel, could, in many ways, modify the nature of some external systems, especially if these employees were to reside in the district. To what extent do teachers paid at different salary levels have the economic ability to forego other earnings and instead participate in community activities and organizations? And, how is the nature of these external systems modified by the educational decision that determined the particular combination of mediating factors which allowed greater salaries for the teachers? Also, how does the type and quality of teachers selected affect the changing nature of the community? Other examples might be the impact upon the economy of the community brought about by the selection of mediating factors which include large capital investment or a large amount of supplies and materials locally purchased. How do the educational decisions related to whether school transportation will be provided, or the hours of school, or the scheduling of student time, in terms not only of regular session classes but with respect to recreational and summer use of school facilities, have implications for parental employment patterns or avocational participation? And, to what extent does the school, as a merchant of facts, knowledge, and ideas, influence community attitudes on political, social, and cultural issues? Finally, although the list could be extended greatly, how does the impact of selection of mediating factors upon the social patterns within the school relate to breaking down or reinforcing patterns within the systems external to the school?

Conclusion

We recognize that it is not possible to isolate every conceivable element of the total system and to determine its value or its individual, contributory relationship to the educational outputs of the system. Nevertheless, it is requisite in any evaluation scheme to identify and control for as many of the factors as possible thought to be significant. It is true that in discussing each of the sections of this paper, we have asked many questions and, undoubtedly, could have asked countless more; but few answers have been given. This is in keeping with the general intent of the paper. We are primarily attempting to set forth the skeleton of a model that will guide our thinking and research in the years to come, and will probably become vastly expanded in the process. In this case, we are describing what we choose to call a systems approach to evaluation, which has considered within it the full range of systemic problems including those related to input utilization.

FOOTNOTES

1. More specifically, this is a mathematical model which will be used in evaluating instructional programs.
2. Economists would classify inputs to the system in a somewhat different manner: In addition to the above mentioned inputs, they would include teacher resources (including time) and student time.

This kind of classification implies a concern for total manpower utilization. On the other hand, while we are concerned with such things as student time, we are taking as a prime consideration the decisional requirements of individual educational administrators at the local level. Thus, the model discussed is more an education-decision model than a total manpower model.
3. We would readily admit, however, and to the chagrin of many reluctant school administrators, that at least this measure would be a feasible starting point.
4. There is evidence that this is a reasonable approach. See: Becker (1962), Miller (1962), and Schultz (1961).

REFERENCES

Becker, G. S. "Investment in Human Capital: A Theoretical Analysis." *Journal of Political Economy* 70 (1962): 9-49. Part 2.

Coleman, J. S., et al. *Equality of Educational Opportunity*. Washington, D. C.: U.S. Dept. of Health, Education and Welfare, Office of Education, FS 5-238:38001, 1966, 22.

McClelland, D. C., et al. *The Achievement Motive*. New York: Appleton-Century Crofts, 1953.

Miller, H. P. "Income and higher education: Does education pay off?" In *Economics of Higher Education*, edited by S. J. Mushkin, pp. 129-146. Washington, D. C.: U.S. Dept. of Health, Education and Welfare, Office of Education, OE50027, 1962.

Schultz, T. W. "Investment in Human Capital." *American Economic Review* 51 (1961): 1-16.

Scriven, M., Tyler, R. W., Gagné, R. M. "The Methodology of Evaluation." In *Perspectives of Curriculum Evaluation*. pp. 39-83. Chicago: Rand McNally & Co., 1967.

Stake, R. E. "An emerging theory of evaluation—borrowings from many methodologies." Paper presented at the annual meeting of the American Educational Research Association, New York, February 23, 1967.

Wittrock, M. C.; Alkin, M. C.; Bormuth, J. R.; Jones, R. L.; Liesch, J. R.; and Wiley, D. E. The Center for the Study of Evaluation of Instructional Programs. Unpublished proposal, November 15, 1965, submitted to the U.S. Commissioner of Education under the provision of Public Law 531, The Center for the Study of Evaluation of Instructional Programs, University of California, Los Angeles.

	CHAPTER 16
THE DISCREPANCY EVALUATION MODEL	**Malcolm M. Provus**

The Discrepancy Evaluation Model described in this report is the result of an attempt to apply evaluation and management theory to the evaluation of programs in city school systems.

There is surprisingly little theory on which to base meaningful evaluation practice. The references which have been most relevant to the work reported in this model are listed in the bibliography at the end of this volume.

Daniel Stufflebeam and Egon Guba have published a number of private papers which make substantial contributions to the understanding of institutional change and growth and provide a theoretical frame of reference for the assessment of change. However, despite the name of an education publication at Ohio State University, *Theory Into Practice*, there appears to be very little linkage between program evaluation going on in public schools today and the kind of theory under discussion by a few university theorists.

Assumptions

1. Many educational programs, especially federally-funded programs, are installed in public school systems without adequate planning.

2. Given this fact, evaluation should be a process for program development and stabilization, as well as a means of assessment. To accomplish this purpose, evaluation must provide information which decision makers can use to improve, stabilize, and assess programs.

3. Two decision-making audiences exist for program evaluation information. Those responsible for making decisions to improve and stabilize specific programs are the first and primary audience. This audience is composed of all strata of program staff—from paraprofessionals up through the top program administrator. Those responsible for making decisions to retain or terminate various educational programs, that is, decisions relative to the allocation of resources, are the ultimate audience for evaluation information. This audience is at the policy-making level of an entire school system.

4. The involvement of program staff in the process of evaluation fosters commitment to program improvement and a more analytical approach to the program which results in desired changes in staff behavior.

5. Evaluation and decision making are separate, yet complementary, functions. Therefore, program evaluators must maintain their independence of program staff and at the same time assume a nondirective role.

The Stages of Evaluation

Evaluation at its simplest level may be seen as the comparison of performance against a standard. When evaluation is viewed as a process for program development, stabilization, and assessment, as is the case in the Discrepancy Evaluation Model, there are five such relevant comparisons. For convenience, the comparison of each level of performance with an appropriate standard designates an evaluation stage. These relationships are shown in Figure 1.

At all stages, some indicator of performance is obtained which is compared with a standard which serves as the criterion of performance.

At Stage I, a description of the program's design is obtained as "performance" information. This performance is compared with the "Design Criteria" postulated as a standard. Discrepancy between performance and standard is reported to those responsible for the management of the program. At Stage II the standard for comparison is the program design arrived at in Stage I. Program performance information consists of observations from the field regarding the program's installation. Discrepancy information may be used

Stage	Performance	Standard
I	Program Design Input Dimension Process Dimension Output Dimension	Design Criteria
II	Program Operation	Program Design Input Dimension Process Dimension
III	Program Interim Products	Program Design Process Dimension Output Dimension
IV	Program Terminal Products	Program Design Output Dimension
V	Program Cost	Cost of Other Programs with Same Product

Figure 1. Evaluation Stages.

by the program manager to redefine the program or change installation procedures. At Stage III the standard is that part of the program design which describes the relationship between program processes and interim products. Discrepancy information is used either to redefine process and relationship of process to interim product or to better control the process being used in the field. At Stage IV the standard is that part of the program design which refers to terminal objectives. Program performance information consists of criterion measures used to estimate the terminal effects of the project. At this point in time, if decision makers have more than one project with similar outcomes available to them for analysis, they may elect to do a cost-benefit analysis to determine program efficiency. The "Design Criteria" constitutes a basic assumption on which all other criteria for standards are based. The "Design Criteria" has been defined so as to contain three basic elements, each of which may subsume many variables. These basic elements of any program (as described in a vast "systems" literature) are Input, Process, and Output.

If an evaluation staff is to have the support of the program staff it seeks to evaluate, it must provide visible assistance to the staff of that organization effecting change. Such assistance must be in a form acceptable to program staff. The only assurance of such acceptability is that program purposes be defined by the program staff and the methods of change be determined by them as well. There must be maximum involvement of program staff in every step of the evaluation process. Further, it follows that there must be continual rapport between program staff and evaluation staff, fostered at the initiative of the evaluation staff and resulting in a continuous communication of affect as well as publicly acceptable verbalizations. The relationships to which an evaluation unit submits itself are binding and

pervasive; however, it does not follow that evaluation therefore operates at the discretion of the administrator of the program unit. Evaluation is the handmaiden of program development and quiet counselor to administrators—but it operates in accordance with its own rules and on an authority independent of the program unit.

An organizational paradigm which makes these intricate and demanding relationships understandable is that of an action system which contains a feedback loop. The processing of input is at the discretion of the program unit. The definition of output and the shaping of input are at the discretion of the parent organization. The management of the feedback loop is in the hands of evaluation staff. The feedback consists of discrepancy between performance and standard. There can be no evaluation without discrepancy information. There can be no discrepancy without a standard; therefore, the first task of any evaluation is to obtain program standards.

A feedback loop of discrepancy information based on standards derived from the program staff will necessarily be of interest to a program staff which has been given responsibility for the success of its program.

The evaluation of any school program, which is already staffed and underway, goes through four major developmental stages of comparison—each of which may deal with input, process, and output.

This process of comparison over stages takes the form of the flow chart in Figure 2.

In the chart S = standard, P = program performance, C = compare, D = discrepancy information, and A = change in program performance or standards. Stage V represents a cost-benefit option available to the evaluator only after the first four stages have been negotiated. Notice that the use of discrepancy information always leads to a decision to either (1) go on to the next stage, (2) recycle the stage after there has been a change in the program's standards or operations, (3) recycle to the first stage, or (4) terminate the project. From the program manager's point of view, discrepancy information permits him to pinpoint a shortcoming in the program for one of two purposes: to change the operation of the program, or to change the speci-

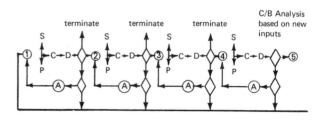

Figure 2

fications under which the program operates. A superintendent of schools or board of education will be as concerned with the rate of movement of a project through its evaluation stages as with discrepancy information at any given stage. Generally, the longer it takes to get to stages two, three, and four, the greater the cost if the project fails. The faster a project moves into advanced stages, generally the less the risk of its failure.

Various kinds of performance and standards and the implementation of comparisons will be discussed in greater detail under each stage.

Stage I

At Stage I, the performance to be assessed is the program design. Experience suggests, however, that with ESEA Title I programs there are usually at least three designs of the program in existence: one is the funding proposal, another is that held by program administrators, and at least one other exists in the minds of program practitioners. The question is raised, then, as to which program design to assess. This question is settled under the model by rejecting inadequate designs and by generating a new dynamic baseline design by means of a group interview with the program staff. This interview takes place at the design meeting.

If the program staff is not too large, all members may be invited to attend the meeting. If it is quite large, a sample of each job type may be selected. The entire group may be divided into smaller groups on the basis of staff level to avoid status conflicts that would inhibit discussion. Or, the groups may contain representatives from all levels. The evaluator structures the meeting to fit the individual program. Whatever the case, all design meetings have these two common ingredients: *all* levels of program staff are represented, and the larger group is broken down into smaller groups to facilitate discussion.

The purpose of the design meeting is to obtain information which will ultimately become the program design. Prior to the meeting a set of very specific questions is drawn up by the evaluator of the program to elicit this information. These questions are derived from the "Program Design Criteria" shown in Figure 3.

The "Design Criteria" includes a comprehensive list of program elements. An educational program is viewed as a dynamic input-output system with specifications for inputs, process, and output being necessary and sufficient for program design.

By examining Figure 3, it can be seen that every program must specify the variables it seeks

Inputs	Process	Outputs

I. Variables—the things the program is attempting to change
 	
A. Student Variables
B. Staff Variables
C. Other Variables
	Variables—those activities which change inputs into desired outputs
	
	A. Student Activities
	B. Staff Activities
	
	  1. Functions and Duties
	  2. Communication
	
	    a. Intra-staff
	    b. With Others
		Variables—the changes that have come about
		
		A. Student Variables
		B. Staff Variables
		C. Other Variables

II. Preconditions—the things that are prerequisite to program operation yet remain constant throughout the program Student Conditions Staff Qualifications Administrative Support Media Facilities Time		Preconditions—same throughout the program
III. Criteria must be specified for each input variable and precondition above. The criteria specified for student variables and preconditions constitute the selection criteria of the program.	Criteria must be specified for each of the process variables.	Criteria are specified on the variables to define the goals of the program. The participant is released from the program if he achieves the goal of the program or if he violates a precondition.

Figure 3. Design Criteria.

to change. These variables will have limits or values set on them to specify the entering levels of students under inputs and another set of values to specify the goals of the program under outputs. For each pair of change variables (that is, for each input-output pair) there is a process to transform the value of the input dimension to the desired value of the output dimension. In defining the process it is necessary to find conditions sufficient to effect this change.

In addition to the change variables, there are preconditions for each program. These designate the resources prerequisite for, but unchanged by, program operation in terms of students, staff, administrative support, facilities, media, and time. As in the case of the variables a limit or level is set on each precondition. The combination of the student preconditions and the student variables constitutes the selection criteria of the program. The goals of the program, however, are defined only in terms of the variables. Thus, a student may be released from the program either when he achieves the goal(s), which would constitute a successful completion, or without achieving the goal but by violating a precondition such as the completion of a specific grade level, which would constitute an unsuccessful completion.

Aside from the purpose of gathering information to satisfy design criteria, the program design meeting serves another important function—that of consensus building. Through the process of give and take that occurs in a discussion group, program staff come to some agreement about their purposes and procedures. In the course of reaching consensus, strong opinions are promulgated and contested, forcing the discussants to think more analytically and carefully about their program and fostering a commitment to the program. The consensus which is generated constitutes the authority for use of the program design as a standard in Stage II.

Once a design has been derived from program staff, activity is channeled toward making the Stage I comparison. The program design (performance) is assessed for comprehensiveness and internal consistency against the "Design Criteria" (standard). The vehicle for conducting the Stage I comparison is a panel meeting.

The panel is composed of those persons who are most involved in and knowledgeable about the program: the program administrator, the program evaluator, a consultant who is an expert in the area of the program content, the Coordinator of Evaluation, and a resource person from the Office of Research who has a background in program design. The panel is the mechanism used to preserve the judgmental function of evaluation and at the same time to reduce the possibility

of error by using expert opinion in the formulation of those judgments.

In assessing the adequacy of a program design, there are two basic questions relative to the criterion of comprehensiveness: (1) "Is there specific and complete information for each element of the program design?" (2) "Is the information in useable form?" That is, "Is there an adequate criterion for each of the variables and preconditions?" The answers to these questions will depend on the adjudged face validity of the program design relative to the "Design Criteria." In the case of a disagreement among panel members, the evaluator is responsible for final judgment.

The consultant, on the other hand, has the final authority in determining the internal consistency of a program design. Questions of internal consistency will revolve around the relationships between the various elements in the design. For example, "Are student activities sufficient to change the variables from their input state to the defined output state?" "Is sufficient time allotted to program activities to be able to achieve program goals?" and "Are staff qualifications sufficient to enable the staff to perform their functions and duties?" In short, internal consistency has to do with the soundness of the design in relating theory to practice. A complete list of questions to be asked in determining the internal consistency of the design is included as Figure 4.

		Yes	No
1.	Staff qualifications are sufficient for performing staff functions and duties.	____	____
2.	Staff duties are clearly related to staff functions.	____	____
3.	The administrative support is sufficient for program operation.	____	____
4.	Media are related to and sufficient for student activities.	____	____
5.	Facilities are adequate for program operation.	____	____
6.	The time allotted for program operation is sufficient to accomplish program goals.	____	____
7.	At least one of the student variables is a selection criterion.	____	____
8.	Student activities are related to student goals.	____	____
9.	Staff activities are related to student goals.	____	____
10.	A process is defined that is sufficient to change each input variable into the output variable.	____	____
11.	Communication activities within the program and between the program staff and others are sufficient to support operation.	____	____

Figure 4. Checklist for Internal Consistency.

In addition to assessing the program design on the criteria of comprehensiveness and internal consistency at Stage I, the panel also investigates the external consistency of the program. This involves a study of the compatibility of the program with other programs operative in the entire school system. It is essential that programs in conflict with each other be identified. In the absence of explicitly defined system values, the opinions of major staff—both members of the given program and those who have a more comprehensive view of the system, such as the principal—are solicited. Although judgments arrived at in this manner are indeed gross, it is important to have information about possible value conflicts as to the use of student or staff time, facilities, and media. Problems relating to compatibility are difficult to solve since they often require the ranking of values for the entire system. If any such obstacle to program success is present, it is important to identify it at the beginning.

The evaluator conducts field interviews using Basic Interview Questions for Program Compatibility shown in Figure 5. He presents the findings of these interviews at the panel meeting for review, and is the ultimate authority in making judgments relative to compatibility.

In summary, the purpose of evaluation at Stage I is to derive a design of the program and to assess that design according to its comprehensiveness and internal consistency. In addition, the compatibility of the program within the school system is determined. The standard for making Stage I judgments is the "Design Criteria." The

first design of a program is likely to lack specificity and internal consistency, but Stage I procedures provide a mechanism for making it ever more refined and sound.

Stage II

At Stage II the design, which was the performance at Stage I, becomes the standard against which to judge the program operation. In making the comparison between program operation (performance) and program design (standard), the evaluator proceeds item by item through the program design, considering each item for a congruence test. All statements in the program design are subject to a comparison with what is going on in the field. However, the evaluator bases his decision of which variables to test at a given time on considerations of convenience and knowledge he has gained from the panel meeting as to the possible inoperability of certain design elements. This selectivity is introduced because of the limited resources available to the evaluator. A tradeoff at any given time is effected between those aspects of the program easiest to investigate and those most likely to evaporate. Eventually the evaluator will submit all elements of the design to a congruence test.

The congruence test is facilitated through a series of observations—some of which may require indirect measurement. All of the usual problems of measurement may pertain here and standard references and techniques are used by the evaluation staff. However, the wise evaluator limits his first round of congruence testing to easily understood referents which have high credibility for the program manager. In practice, it has been found that a congruence test of "input" elements can and should generally precede a test of "process" elements. After discrepancy information on "input" has been formalized and feedback given to the program manager, a new cycle of "process" congruence testing can be initiated. This latter test is characterized by verification of the *existence* of process elements. It is *not* concerned with verifying whether the relationship between input and output due to process does in fact exist. Such a study of causation is dealt with in Stage III.

After each series of congruence tests, the evaluator provides the program manager with the information obtained. If there are discrepancies, the program manager has only two options: he can either modify the design of the program or modify the program operation. We can thus see how the program manager, on the basis of information provided, proceeds to equalize program operation and design.

---

1. Is sufficient time available for student participation in the program?
   What activity does the student give up in order to participate in the program?
   Does this reallocation of student time result in sacrifice to other objectives of the school program?
   Does it have an effect on the operation and/or goal attainment of this program?

2. Is sufficient time available for participation by the program staff and cooperating personnel?
   What activities do staff or cooperating non-program personnel sacrifice in order to participate in the program?
   Does this reallocation of their time result in a sacrifice to other objectives of the school program? How does it affect this program?

3. Are facilities and media now available to the program? If not, why are they absent?
   Is allocation of facilities and/or media to this program resulting in sacrifice of other objectives of the school program?
   Is this program affected by the manner in which facilities and media are allocated?

4. Are the gains for students anticipated by this program equal to, less than, or greater than possible sacrifices in other educational objectives of the school program?

Figure 5. Basic Interview Questions for Program Compatibility.

The question as to the criteria to be used or how much discrepancy is to be considered as inevitable has not yet been resolved under the model. In the absence of a criterion, the procedure used is a group judgment of the same type obtained in Stage I. The panel meeting is called by the evaluator when a first set of elements of the program design has been subjected to a congruence test. Again the consultant brings his theoretical expertise to bear on the subject, and the evaluator draws on his knowledge of the program design. In addition, where indirect measures have been used the psychometrician is responsible for the construction of instruments, and comments on the validity and reliability of findings. The questions to be answered by the panel are: (1) "Is the information on each program element complete?" (2) "Is it reliable and valid?" (3) "Are the discrepancies uncovered ones which will significantly diminish the program's chances for success?" The evaluator is the ultimate authority in answering the first question, the psychometrician the second, and the consultant the third.

Through Stage II work the congruence between the program design and operation is continually increased. Such an increase in congruence is what is meant in this model by program improvement. When the panel decides the program is sufficiently stable, a decision is made to move to Stage III.

Stages III and IV

At Stage III, the first cause and effect comparison is made. The relationship tested is between the variable to be changed (from input to output) and the process or treatment used to effect this change. This relationship, as predicted in the design, is the "standard." The relationship found to obtain empirically is the "performance." Another way of stating this is, does "P" change "I" into "O"? This question is asked in two sequential stages: at the microlevel of specific program process activities producing specific enabling outcomes (Stage III) and at the macrolevel of the entire program or gross treatment producing the anticipated outcomes of the total program (Stage IV). Stage IV adheres to the traditional use of experimental and quasi-experimental designs and is discussed only briefly here.

The purpose of Stage III evaluation is to provide program staff with an estimate of the effect of the process elements (or treatment variables) on the output elements (or dependent variables) as a function of time. In order to accomplish this goal, continuous measurements must be taken both of treatment variables and dependent variables.

These assessments result in graphs, which taken together provide a useful description of the process effects on the dependent variables. In order to assess interaction effects, these graphs may be kept for each class and each school in which the program is installed. In addition, a graph should be kept on total program population. The frequency of the measurements will vary from program to program and will generally be determined by the program staff's assessment of the minimum unit of time it takes to produce a measurable change in the dependent variable. If the dependent variable is achievement in a math text, this unit of time might conceivably be defined as a week's work. If the dependent variable is change in attitude, a measurement might be taken every few months.

In Stage III the initial effects of partial treatment are assessed, further adjustments in treatment are made based on an analysis of interim product data, and greater understanding is achieved of the relationship between treatment outcomes and the conditions of the experiment. At Stage III, the evaluation staff should collect data describing the extent to which student behavior is changing as predicted. Most of this activity is microscopic in nature. Such evaluation depends heavily on the production and use of highly specific instruments that provide empirically determined answers to cause and effect questions. As a consequence of this stage of evaluation, the program staff learns whether or not its intermediate program payloads are being realized on target dates, and if not, why not.

Consider the following example:

A program is installed to improve reading achievement. The primary treatment is an individual tutorial program in which the teacher works with one student at a time while the other students are engaged in various individual assignments. Suppose, for example, as often happens, a pretest and posttest are administered. The results indicate that the students in this program improve their reading ability no more than similar students in previous years who were not involved in the program. A traditional report would indicate no differences, and program staff would be uninformed as to reasons for the failure. Now consider what could occur under a system of continuous assessment of treatment and dependent variables.

Figures 6 and 7 represent some rather exaggerated but nevertheless possible examples of what the line might have looked like if continuous assessment had been used.

Each time period represents a measurement.

Given these two plots, it would be possible at point C, or at least D, to inform program staff that the amount of time spent in individual in-

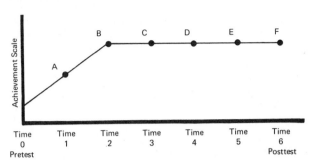

Figure 6. Achievement Plot—Restricted Growth.

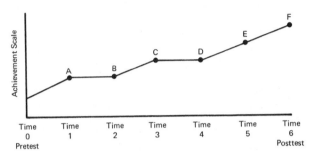

Figure 7. Achievement Plot—Gradual Growth.

struction has fallen off and no growth in reading is in evidence. Program staff could step in at this point and either change the design of the program or investigate the existence of new variables to be operationally controlled or stabilized.

Finally, at Stage IV the evaluator may cast an experimental design which answers the question: "Has the program achieved its major objectives?"

Stage IV calls for the kind of designs we have long employed in educational research and have more recently employed in error in evaluation. "Employed in error," not because the quasi-experimental designs of the type described by Stanley and Campbell do not belong in an evaluation strategy, but because they have consistently been used in the wrong stage of a program's development.

There are conditions prerequisite to the use of experimental design in a school setting, and one of the purposes of the early stages of an evaluation is to secure these conditions—just as the early stages of program development form the base on which later program growth may be realized.

In Stage IV, many of the relationships between treatment conditions and effects discovered in Stage III can be properly expressed as independent variables in the experimental design stage. The administrative control secured over the new program in Stages II and III ensures treatment stability. Problems of experimental design, sampling, and instrumentation are more likely to be solved because of increased staff knowledge of factors interacting with treatment.

Stage V

Having completed evaluations at each stage of the program's development, it is possible to conduct a cost-benefit analysis of the entire program and to compare the results of that analysis (performance) with similar cost analyses of other educational programs designed to achieve similar results (standard). The objective of such comparisons is to determine the most effective allocation of resources. The key to achieving a functional cost-benefit analysis is the extent to which inputs and outputs can be given measurable costs and benefits. If objectives and elements of the design criteria of various programs are given similar quantifiable classifications initially, comparison of cost-benefit analyses is useful.

Cost-benefit analysis normally depends on the establishment of a curve which is a function of benefits relative to costs. Such a curve permits one to relate increments of benefit to cost. The development of such curves goes beyond this model.

It is early in the development of cost-benefit analysis in the public sector to be specific about the procedures to be employed. In fact, at this time, information is simply not available for comparisons across programs. However, cost-benefit analysis is the ultimate rational step in the process of program development and assessment put forth in the Discrepancy Model. In anticipation of its eventual use, the cost-benefit analysis is posited as Stage V.

The Dynamics of Evaluation

Although for purposes of explication the stages of evaluation have been presented above as if they were self-contained and sequential, the real nature of evaluation work is dynamic, with much overlapping and interplay between the stages. This is so because evaluation not only stimulates program development but also must be conducted in light of program change. What occurs, therefore, is evaluation, program change, and reevaluation, allowing sufficient time between evaluations for program change to take place.

In actual practice it turns out that an evaluation requires frequent recycling through those stages which are prior to the stage under negotiation at any point in time. Successive reappraisal of program operations and the program design from which program operations are derived is generally a consequence of the decisions made by program staff on the basis of discrepancy information reported at Stages II, III, and IV. If a decision is made to reformulate program design rather than to revise program performance, there are immediate implications for the renegotiation of all subsequent evaluation stages. Hence, the soundness of judgment of program decision makers and the support they derive from their organizational milieu are of prime importance to evaluators.

This is particularly true of evaluation activity in Stages I and II where major program changes can be expected to occur. When a program is first defined, the design is generally neither comprehensive nor internally consistent. The panel meeting is then held and problem areas in the design are identified. It is sometimes possible at a panel meeting to resolve difficulties or to fill in gaps from information provided by the program administrator. If so, some changes in the design can be incorporated but a large number of questions remain to be recorded and brought to the attention of the entire program staff at a later date.

Vague and inconsistent as the first design is, there are usually some elements which are specific and complete enough to provide a standard for Stage II congruence testing. After statements in the design have been compared to program operation, the program administrator is supplied with the discrepancy information. (Experiment has shown that at this early stage in program development, discrepancies almost always exist.) He then has two alternatives: to change the design of the program or, as is more usually the case, to adjust program operation through communication of program intent to the practitioners in the field. Whichever the case, some change occurs which, after the time lag for implementation, must then be evaluated.

At this point a second design meeting is often held to obtain needed additional information, to refine existing statements which are not specific, or to restore internal consistency after changes have been made in one section of the design as a result of previous evaluation activity. For example, if the panel meeting made a change in the statement of goals, process would then have to be adjusted to make it consistent with goals.

The second design is usually far more developed than the first. However, if, in the opinion of the evaluator, problems still exist, a second panel meeting may be called. As changes in design occur, more Stage I work is done, program operation is amended, and the process repeats itself until the decision is made (in a Stage II panel meeting) that the program is sufficiently stable to measure initial outputs. Even while Stage III work is being undertaken program operation is being monitored to maintain its accord with program design. Thus, it is necessary to emphasize that not only is the movement through stages not sequential, it is also not linear. The stages of evaluation activity may more accurately be said to occur concurrently and can be represented as shown in Figure 8.

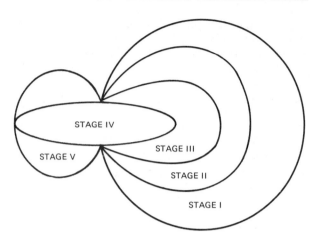

Figure 8. Inter-Stage Relationships.

Stage I activity is represented by the largest circle; Stage II then occurs within the context of Stage I work; Stage III work is accompanied by the monitoring of Stages I and II; Stage IV is accompanied by the monitoring of Stages I, II and III; and Stage V work utilizes the findings of Stage IV work for the specific program while overlapping onto the Stage IV work of other program evaluations.

Thus, we see that the process of evaluation is organic and dynamic and grows not only out of previous evaluation findings but out of program change as well. It is a long and complex process, but when the benefits of a stable program can be assessed and then compared to the benefits of other such programs with the aim of determining the most efficient means of reaching an educational goal, the preliminary travail should prove to be worthwhile. The real payload of this elaborate approach is the increased probability of improved programs.

At a more practical operational level, evaluation activity, which is by its nature continuous, is divided into manageable segments called cycles. The cycle begins with a plan which includes a group of questions immediately relevant to the demands of the evaluation of a particular program and sets out the procedures to be used in answering those questions. After a cycle of evaluation has been conducted which includes the entirety of Stage I, any additional cycles will include questions pertaining to more than one stage. At the completion of a cycle, a cycle report is discussed with the program administrator. This verifies the requirement that evaluation provide information for decision making.

Information for Decision Makers

As stated in the assumptions, those responsible for making decisions about one or more programs are the first and primary audience for evaluation information. The types of feedback given may be characterized as formal or informal.

After each cycle of evaluation activity, members of the program staff are provided with formal feedback in the form of a cycle report. The report contains information about the problems in program design or operation which require adjustments. The evaluation function is not seen as providing a solution or alternate solutions to the problems, but rather as presenting problems based on discrepancy information. The evaluation model represents a method for dealing with these problems.

The cycle report is always given to and discussed with the program administrator, who has the courtesy of a preview of each written report before it is issued. Since it is assumed that all strata of program staff have some decision-making powers, the criterion used in further distributing reports is whether a given group or level of staff can make decisions to affect program change on the basis of given information. Thus, if the findings concern only teacher activities, the report is distributed to teachers, but not to paraprofessionals. In addition, reports are distributed to adults in the system, regardless of whether they are members of the program staff, who have contributed to evaluation findings.

Feedback of the informal type is provided to program staff by the evaluator who interacts almost continuously with both administrative and field personnel. The degree of interaction is determined both by the size and scope of the field to be covered and by the number of scheduled activities. Program activities such as in-service training meetings and group planning sessions, as well as scheduled evaluation activities, provide opportunities for informal contacts. The evaluator seizes every opportuniy for communicating recent evaluation findings. The timeliness of feedback is important. Thus, it is provided as promptly after each set of evaluation activities as is consistent with care and accuracy of data handling and may be presented in oral form while written reports are in preparation.

The crucial factor in a program's ultimate chances for success is the receptivity of the program administrator to evaluation information. The first evaluation efforts with a program may produce a vague design and serious discrepancies between design and operation. However, given the program manager's cooperation and sufficient time, these problems can be solved. On the other hand, another program may have a much superior first design and fewer discrepancies between design and operation. In either case, if the program manager is not receptive to information provided, the program will not mature to the point where a product evaluation is tenable.

The program administrator's ability to utilize evaluation information is a second aspect of the program's chances for success. It may be that the administrator is not sufficiently analytical to devise solutions to problems identified in findings or that he is simply overwhelmed by them. Or, it may be that the source of the problem is simply beyond the administrator's control and is a problem of the system. This is the case with insufficient budget allocations or variation in program implementation due to conditions in the schools.

The ultimate audience for evaluation information is at the policy-making level of an entire school system. Although providing information to this audience may appear to violate the relationship established with the first audience, the fact remains that policy makers need evaluation information in order to make *rational* decisions to retain or terminate programs and to allocate resources among them.

As a great deal of time is required to implement all of the evaluation stages described here, policy makers of the school system will ask for information relevant to a program's chances for success prior to the completion of the evaluation. They will want indications of risk before the program product has been measured and a cost-benefit analysis performed. The provision by the evaluation staff of such information may irreparably damage cooperative staff relations painstakingly built by the evaluation staff. However, the decision to jeopardize evaluation staff work must be at the discretion of the chief school administrator.

Generally, information on program risk *is* requested by policy makers. This information is provided to the policy makers by the evaluation staff through use of the Program Interim Assessment Profile shown in Figure 9. This profile provides information as to the program administrator's amenability to program improvement and receptivity to discrepancy information. This amenability to improvement is measured by the number of changes in the program relative to the number of evaluation reports he has received.

The Program Interim Assessment Profile is based on seven criteria of program adequacy. Three of these criteria — "Comprehensiveness," "Compatibility," and "Internal Consistency" — relate to the adequacy of program design and have already been discussed at length under Stage I of the Model. "Program Implementation" is a summarization of all Stage II discrepancy information, and "Relation of Process to Outcomes" is a summarization of all Stage III discrepancy information. The last two criteria are not based on evaluation staff work. "Program Effectiveness" information deals with the adequacy or importance of program outputs in terms of the changing goals and values of a school system, and "Program Efficiency" asks whether the purposes of the program are of sufficient value to warrant the use of resources identified under the design of program as necessary to achieve program outputs.

An interim assessment of program is achieved by substituting information needed to satisfy Program Interim Assessment Criteria called for in factors 1 to 6 into a risk of failure index equation shown at the bottom of Figure 9. The profile provided in Column "C" and the information or lack of information in Column "A," as well as the response to factor 7, are considered by the decision maker in forming a judgment as to whether a program should be continued or terminated.

The formula calls for a comparison of program performance with the number of times information has been reported for each factor in the profile (C-B). Factor 6, program efficiency, calls for some kind of determination of cost relative to the value of service being rendered. Some index number of value of service ("S") is used such that where "S" is equal to "C" (cost) then benefits are of appropriate value. If "C" exceeds "S" then a negative term is added to the equation. The risk of failure index should not be interpreted too literally. The formula is merely a convenient way of comparing and reviewing pertinent information relative to each program in a system.

One other important aspect of providing information to decision makers is communication. All audiences entitled to evaluation information are relatively unfamiliar with the terms and concepts of evaluation work of this type. Although evaluation activity such as design meetings and informal contacts provides a kind of in-service training for staff, the effort must be made to communicate with program staff at their present level of understanding and sophistication. It is incumbent on the evaluation staff to do this successfully. Evaluation findings must, therefore, be presented as concisely and clearly as possible—concisely to ensure that they are read and clearly to ensure that they are understood. Although the time-consuming task of searching for the right word for the right place may be a source of frustration to the evaluation unit, it is imperative. Evaluation findings not read and not understood are not used. Technical information is generally reported in state and federal annual reports.

Staffing for Evaluation

Evaluation of the type described above requires the following categories of staff:

Age of program _____
Age of evaluation _____
Number of previous cycle reports _____

Factors	Information Available from Evaluator* (A)	Number of Previous Mentions in Cycle Report** (B)	Criteria Level of Performance*** (C)		
			Low	Median	High
1. Comprehensiveness					
2. Internal Consistency					
3. Program Compatibility					
4. Program Implementation					
5. Relation of Process to Outcomes					
6. Program Effectiveness (Adequacy)					
7. Program Efficiency					

*Compute (C-B) values only if a "yes" appears in this column.
**$0 = 0, 1 = 1, 2 = 2, 3 = 3, 4 = 4$.
***Low = 0, Median = 1, High = 2.
Risk of failure equation: $(C_1 - B_1) + (C_2 + B_2) + (C_3 + B_3) + (C_4 - B_4) + (C_5 - B_5) + (S - C) + [(C_7 - B_7)(3)] =$ signed value = index of risk.
(Negative = High Risk)
(Positive = Low Risk)

Figure 9. Program Interim Assessment Profile.

1. Administrator (capable of maintaining high quality in research activities)
2. Evaluator
3. Editor
4. Secretary
5. Data handler
6. Consultants in subject areas of programs being evaluated
7. Consultants in instrument development and research design
8. Data processing specialists

In the list above, the staff mentioned in numbers 1 through 5 are regular members of the evaluation unit. The consultants and the data processing specialists are necessary adjuncts to, but not part of, the evaluation unit.

Thus, it can be seen that the evaluators are non-technicians who have access to specialists or experts as they are needed. The person responsible for the quality control of the evaluation activity acts as a liaison between evaluators and consultants.

In Pittsburgh, evaluators come from a wide variety of disciplines: anthropology, economics, education, English, mathematics, psychology, sociology, and even the ministry. Almost all have graduate degrees. Since no one person possesses all the skills needed to conduct this type of evaluation work, the two most important factors in considering applicants are flexibility and the ability to do analytical or critical thinking. It is felt that flexibility will permit the evaluator to adapt to the varied demands of the job and that his ability to do analytical thinking will be an asset in understanding and implementing the model. In-service training is provided throughout the year as the staff needs it.*

The job of the evaluator is varied, but may be described as containing the following functions: planning, quantifying behavior, data collection and analysis, report writing, and small group leadership.

Under the planning function, the evaluator is administratively responsible for the evaluation activities conducted with respect to his assigned program or programs. The fewer the programs he is responsible for, the more work gets done in each and the possibility of frequent feedback is increased. From experience in Pittsburgh it has been found that an evaluator can efficiently handle only one or two programs at a time.

The evaluator plans and executes each cycle of evaluation activity for his program(s). It is helpful, in this respect, if he knows something about problem analysis and has command of various management techniques such as flow charting, block diagramming, and PERT.

As a quantifier of behavior, the evaluator should be able to design simple instruments such as questionnaires, interview schedules, observation schedules, scales, and checklists. Once instruments have been devised, the evaluator must not only employ accepted techniques in collecting the data but must also conform to the conventions established for entrance to and work in schools. The evaluator should be conversant with, though not necessarily an expert in, methods of data handling and analysis.

The evaluator needs to understand group process and techniques of group leadership. He must also be able to relate to program administrators and field personnel for exchange of information and interpretation of findings. The relationship with the program administrator is crucial to the acceptance and use of evaluation information.

Under the reporting function the evaluator must be able to write reports in standard research format and terminology (for federal requirements) and to write reports in lay language and format (for the two local audiences). Although he may have the assistance of an editor in the latter task, it is primarily the responsibility of the evaluator to assess the level of understanding of his program staff.

Finally, the evaluation unit works as a team. Not only does the evaluator have the administrative responsibility for the evaluation activities in his program(s), he also assists other evaluators in conducting design meetings, data collection, and other activities. The evaluation unit meets at least once a week to conduct routine business, to critique each other's work, for in-service training, or to bring the collective wisdom of the group to bear on particular problems. A spirit of openness and candor obtains as the group shares learning experiences and work problems.

*A compilation of evaluation training documents is available from the Office of Research, Pittsburgh Board of Education.

CHAPTER 17

Gordon Welty

EVALUATION AND PLANNING IN EDUCATION: A COMMUNITY CONCERN*

The noted education editor of the *New York Times*, Fred Hechinger, recently characterized the American educational community as being "like a parent who, though unsure of the validity of his own values, knows that he is expected to transmit them to his children." He then raises a critical question: Given this crisis of confidence, "Who can determine what is relevant—what obsolete?"[1]

Some educationists would give the appearance that they have an answer to Hechinger's question. For example, Dr. Herbert Striner, Dean of the College of Continuing Education at American University in Washington, D. C. was recently quoted as saying "We're responsible for quality," when asked about university-community relations regarding an educational program.

Dean Striner asks rhetorically "Who in the community gets involved?" and answers that he'll be "damned" if he'll allow the community, which he characterizes as consisting of "numbers runners, dope pushers and Mafia," to be involved in providing direction.[2] Such attitudes as the Dean's, we submit, are in part responsible not only for the San Francisco State's and Columbia's of the late Sixties, but also for the general malaise of American education. Authoritarian responses to Hechinger's question, prevalent as they may be in the educational community, are doomed.

In some good part, the direction, planning, and evaluation of the educational system must be democratized, which is to say, turned over to the community.[3] The traditional, authoritarian approach to educational planning and evaluation has clearly failed. In the past, program proposals were prepared by the "Madison Avenue approach": a team of experienced proposal writers isolated themselves in a motel room and spent a weekend writing out the future of a hundred thousand children.

Project evaluation has been no less remiss: the traditional approach has the evaluator acquire a copy of the proposal. He supposes that this is the program design, and trundles off to see if this is happening. In general, of course, this *isn't* what is happening. The program proposal is properly a *funding* proposal, not a program blueprint. The evaluator is well advised to look elsewhere for that blueprint.

Have we thus set the evaluator an impossible task? If he can turn neither to authority nor to program proposals, how can he study a program at all? Instead of considering the demands of a pluralistic society, perhaps he should consider his ulcers and throw up his hands in despair.

Yet there is an alternative to despair. In earlier work, the possibility of combining the demands upon a program made by diverse interest groups was established. A basically social psychological change model enabled conflicts to surface and consensus to be established, while providing the evaluator with a timely statement of the program design.[4] We will discuss how such a model can be employed in the planning and evaluation of educational programs. This model, when applied to educational evaluation, has two stages.

*I would like to thank Dr. Sanford Temkin for helpful comments and criticism on this essay; of course he is not responsible for any errors remaining.

1. Fred Hechinger, "The 1970's: Education for What?" *New York Times,* January 12, 1970.
2. Quoted in the American University campus newspaper *Eagle,* December 19, 1969, p. 6.
3. For thoughtful discussions of the theoretical and philosophical issues involved, cf. Richard La Brecque "Social Planning and the Imperium Humanum" *Educational Theory* 19 (1969): esp. pp. 369-371; and M. L. Kafoglis "Equality of Opportunity in Decision Making," *American Journal of Economics and Sociology* 29 (1970): 1-16.
4. Cf. M. J. Duda, "The Pittsburgh Evaluation Program," *Big City Title I Evaluation Conference* (Pittsburgh, 1967); G. A. Welty, "Evaluation of Public School Programs," presented at The Learning Research and Development Center, Pittsburgh, November 18, 1968; and M. Provus, *The Discrepancy Evaluation Model* (Pittsburgh, 1969).

The first requirement of the evaluation effort is a program design or blueprint. Out of the congerie of conceptions of what an educational program should be, one unique blueprint must emerge. To achieve this it is necessary to assemble representatives of the interest groups, teachers, community members, even students (!), and ask them to express themselves about their conception of the program. It is possible to assemble the members of this group in one spot, and use heterogeneous or homogeneous grouping to facilitate communication. It is possible, depending on the size of the group, to assemble the whole group or perhaps samples of the group. Then the evaluator asks them a series of very specific questions about the program. In essence he asks them "What should the program be trying to do here?" and when they tell him, the evaluator writes it down. This is the rudimentary program design.

The first time around, the design is obviously going to be vague and ambiguous. The members of the group will probably employ the usual clichés. However, the meeting with the group is repeated as soon as a first draft of the design can be prepared and distributed.

By the second or third time around, more precision is attained. Thus it is implicit in our discussion here that the evaluation work will be an ongoing endeavor. We see that we can assemble information for the preparation of a program design by questioning members of the several interest groups.

A second function of the meeting, independent of that information gathering just discussed, is the function of consensus building. We want one and only one program design. Thus teacher, community members and students must view the project in a unified fashion. But what is meant by consensus with regards to the program, it may be asked. For the purposes at hand, consensus is the establishment of a working agreement, and can be defined as the minimization of variance of rank-ordered objectives. If we have three items, representing three objectives, with the items listed as rows, and possible ranks as columns, we have a square matrix with the response of members of the group entered in the cells as x's and o's for two hypothetical members.

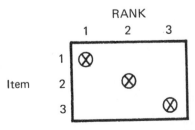

Here variance in ranking is minimal. This is consensus. A working agreement has been achieved.

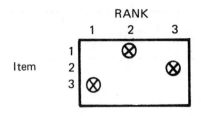

Here too we have consensus.

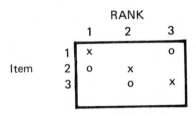

Here we have dissensus. These arrays have proved convenient ways of discovering values to which the members subscribe. Of course, we are using strictly behavioral definitions: in this context "consensus" does not refer to a theoretical or transcendental entity.[5] As the members of the group interact at the meetings, conflicts of interest and other problems arise and can be resolved or accommodated by the well-known methods of group dynamics. As these problems about the program are resolved, consensus is achieved.

We have examined two functions of the meetings of the interest groups: to provide data for the design and to generate consensus on that design. These functions are concurrently filled. Now we have a program design which meets our initial requirements of avoiding both authoritarianism and grantsmanship.

The question immediately arises: Is this design a *good* design? Evaluation is comparison of actuality with a standard, with negative reports facilitating program improvement. Thus we want first of all to improve the program design.

The criticism of a design is two-fold. On the one hand, we must answer the question, "Is this design reasonable in its objectives?" Here the philosophy and the theory germane to the particular program is pertinent, and a disinterested expert in the field is required to pass judgment.

On the other hand, we examine the program design structurally. Unlike the method for examining the theory, where we use an expert to analyze the design, structurally we must compare

5. We would like to acknowledge the value of criticism by the late Professor Edward Suchman for this section. Cf. also my monograph, *The Logic of Evaluation* (Educational Resources Institute, 1969) pp. 4-7, for further discussion.

it with a set of generalized design criteria. The schema of such criteria is given below.

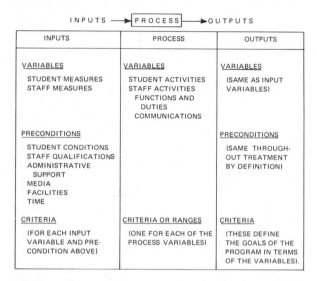

Design Criteria.

These criteria delineate the logical and systematic structure of *any* educational program.

We can conceive a program as consisting of inputs which go through some process and give us outputs. First we will consider inputs. To characterize inputs we have three elements; first, we have *variables*, which might consist of student performance measures, staff measures, indeed anything which is to *vary* as a result of the program. We also have *preconditions* which further describe students, staff, and other necessities or overhead items. These do not vary through the program. Thus the difference between precondition and variable is that the variable can be changed by the program, while the precondition cannot. For instance, educational attainment could well be a variable for an educational program, while membership in a minority group could be a precondition.[6]

The third category we see under inputs is *criteria*. The criteria specify ranges or values of our preconditions and variables. Specifically, the criteria on student measures and student conditions represent the selection criteria of the program. For instance, an educational program design might specify that the student must have graduated from an elementary school to be eligible for admission to a high school program. This means that as a student variable we would have educational attainment. Here the selection criterion would specify that attainment is at least completion of the eighth grade.

Under process we again find variables. These would include student activities such as home-

work, problem solving, tests, etc. Also we find staff activities which will correspond to the student activities. Then if the student activity is "taking a test," the staff activity will be "administering a test." When we turn to criteria we must find sufficient conditions for transforming the input variables from their initial value into the terminal, or exit value of the output variables.[7]

In the case of output variables, we find the same aspects of behavior as we found under input variables. This is a logical necessity. If a student measure such as educational attainment was what we wanted to change upon the student's entry to the program, then we must measure this when he leaves the program. Preconditions, of course, remain the same.

For output variables, the *criteria* specify the goals of the program in terms of the variable. For instance, a goal could be specified by the criterion that educational attainment be a high school diploma. It is of course possible that educational attainment is not brought to the level of a high school diploma. Performance may remain at virtually the same point the whole way through the program. At the end of the program, success has not been achieved in this case.

The design for an educational program will be systematically compared to the design criteria, and gaps (such as the absence of criteria) noted. This comparison complements the expert opinion on the design. Both of these functions enable us to rectify the program design we have. When this is done, when the information is gathered and consensus about the design is generated, when the implicit theory is criticized and the structure is compatible with the design criteria, then all of this data is given back to the program staff and the group of informants as a Stage I report. This provides the basis for a recycling, where the program staff and the group of informants sit down and decide how the program could be improved. The Stage I activities begin anew with another meeting for redefinition of the program. This concludes the discussion of Stage I.

At the same time this Stage I activity is going on, the evaluator is looking around in the field to see what is actually going on there. Part of this is compatibility testing. The evaluator must pinpoint conflicts in facilities, use of media and so forth. Of particular importance are conflicts of space, and human resources. The other part of the fieldwork in Stage II is the congruence testing part of evaluation. It does no good to have

6. The reader should consult Oskar Morgenstern, *Prolegomena to a Theory of Organization* (Santa Monica, 1951), p. 24ff.

7. Morgenstern op. cit. p. 24, refers to this requirement as the necessity of "competences."

the best of blueprints, if the staff are doing what they please out in the field.

Congruence testing is the comparison of some observed aspect of the program with the program design. Thus we have the rather elementary situation of the one independent sample research design.[8] We derive the norm or hypothetical distribution from the standard,[9] and the observed distribution reflects what is happening in the field. The evaluator proceeds item by item through the program design considering each variable for a congruence test. His decision on which variables to test is based on (a) consideration of researchability, and (b) the possibility of significant discrepancies being uncovered. These criteria are introduced because of the limited resources for empirical research, such as time and personnel, available to the evaluator.

A tradeoff is effected between those aspects of the program easiest to look at, and those aspects most important or most likely to be amiss.[10]

We are thus trying to find problems in the program. As anyone who has undertaken evaluation research knows, it does no good to find insignificant differences across treatment levels if the lack of effects cannot be attributed to some specific failure in the program. The only decision rule for an aggregate statement of "no effects" is a cutback in program resources throughout the relevant range. On the other hand, a specific statement of "no effects due to a malfunction of component x" is the basis for program change and improvement. When the evaluator has completed his study of discrepancies between program operation and design, he reports the findings to the program manager.[11] This decision-maker can either make changes in the program operation, or else take the discrepancy information back to the next meeting of teachers, community members, students, etc., and change the program design. By this means, we see how the rationally managed program proceeds to equalize program operation and design. We also see how the educational system becomes responsive and responsible to the wider community. In Stage I the program blueprint is ever refined, and in Stage II congruence between the standard and operation is ever increased. There is a constant interplay between the two.

Thus we have a plan for the evaluation of educational projects which is based on a social-psychological model to establish consensus, and a structural paradigm to establish form. On this basis the planning and evaluation of educational programs can proceed along more democratic lines.

We recall John Dewey's judgment: "If conditions do not permit renewal to take place continuously it will take place explosively." Current social unrest reflects the wisdom of his comment. If the educational profession recognizes program planning and evaluation as truly a community concern, then no longer will it be subject to Dewey's further stricture "Too often the man who should be criticizing institutions expends his energy in criticizing those who would reform."[12]

8. Thus the arguments to the effect that research designs are inherently inapplicable in evaluation studies are misplaced. Cf. G. A. Welty, *The Logic of Evaluation*, Section III.

9. Alternately, we can follow G. E. P. Box and N. Draper. *Evolutionary Operation*. New York: 1969, pp. 70-72 and refer to the "current best-known conditions" as establishing the base point.

10. For an alternative procedure here, Box and Draper op. cit. pp. 18-20; 147-149, propose the mechanism of an "evolutionary operation committee."

11. Thus we are explicitly concerned with program evaluation for program change and improvement. The model underlying this discussion is formalized in Gordon Welty and Alfred Beradino "Structural Models and Dynamic Organizational Research: A Possibility Theorem," presented to the Eastern Psychological Association (April 2, 1970) Atlantic City, New Jersey.

12. John Dewey, *Human Nature and Conduct*. New York, 1930. pp. 167-168.

APPLICATION
OF THE NEW
APPROACHES
TO EVALUATION

No matter how hard one tries, there is simply no way in which the demands of every practically-oriented evaluator can be met in an anthology such as this is. The demands of each situation are virtually unique and have to be met with the ingenuity and expertise of the evaluator on-the-job. There are methodologies which are simple to impose and there are some which cannot reasonably be employed without access to sophisticated computing devices. There are techniques which have been used but which have appeared as illustrations in only the most remote places.

The most general proscription one can give for applying a model of evaluation is to search for methods that might realize it in a new and exciting way. There are many techniques that have been used in branches of the various behavioral sciences which are useful and have a high payoff—scaling techniques, Q-sorts, the Semantic Differential and multidimensional scaling are but a few. But there is no question that these techniques require a level of sophisticated supervision that is frequently not available in the front line where the data have to be gathered. The following selections are intended to raise questions that might help evaluators make decisions about the nature and purpose of the data they collect as well as to provide illustrations of the application of evaluation at a very general level.

CHAPTER 18

EVALUATION FOR ENVIRONMENTAL EDUCATION

Edward J. Ambry

Development of Evaluation Instrument

The plan for self-evaluation was developed by the above committee at a series of meetings held between October, 1967 and March, 1968. The first edition was presented as a working paper to persons attending the National Conference on Environmental Education, Skylands Manor, Ringwood, New Jersey, on May 19-22, 1968. Conferees, working in small groups with members of the original committee became members of an expanded National Committee for the development of this instrument. Individuals and small groups discussed, made suggestions, and recommended changes for the final draft. The above Committee, during 1968-69, made revisions and produced this document. The original instrument is available from ERIC Document Reproduction Service, The National Cash Register Company, 4936 Fairmount Avenue, Bethesda, Maryland, 20014. The ERIC number is ED 024 503.

This instrument is based on a "systems analysis" approach and draws heavily upon suggestions made in a paper prepared by Daniel L. Stufflebeam, Ohio State University, entitled: "The Use and Abuse of Evaluation in Title III," delivered at the National Seminar on Innovation, sponsored by the Kettering Foundation and the U.S. Office of Education in July, 1967.

A series of questions has been formulated which will help a project director and his staff to evaluate their efforts at various stages of the project operation.

The Following Definitions Are Basic in the Design:

Context

(Objectives)—These are the goals (broad and specific) that were set for the project on the basis of the determination of needs.

Input

(Resources)—These are the ingredients of the project that make it work, including money, time, facilities, natural resources, materials, equipment and personnel.

Process

(Program)—This is the operational plan or procedure that is used, utilizing the "input," and describes the primary activities of the project.

Persons using this instrument will find it necessary to read an entire page before answering the questions. Those questions with the same numerical heading; i.e., 1 — follow to the right across the page, from the C-*context* column through the I-*input* and P-*process* columns to the O-*outcomes* column. When there is more than one related question in any of these columns, then each of these questions is designed by a letter; i.e., 1(a). All of the questions listed below a standard are intended to afford some measure of that standard.

Scoring the Evaluation Items

The self-rating score is based on a 0-10 scale. The project director and staff should consider the standard, and after answering the questions, should determine the extent to which the project is meeting the standards.

A score of 0-3 indicates that the standard is not being met, or being met to an insignificant degree.

A score of 4-6 indicates that the standard is being satisfied approximately half the time, or in about half of the instances.

A score of 7-10 indicates that the standard is being achieved or is being satisfied most of the time.

Evaluation of the complete operation of a Title III project should afford the director and staff a better opportunity to assess decisions made, as well as future decisions. This should favorably influence the degree of success achieved in reaching stated or modified goals for the project.

Glossary

The following list has been designed as a guide in the use of the evaluation instrument. Any terms, not listed below, which present a doubt to the reader, are to be defined as found in any Dictionary of Common English Usage, or the Dictionary of Education.

COMMUNITY RESOURCES—Those adjunct to curriculum found within the local community-(ies).

FACILITY—A site established to serve a particular project or program.

GOALS AND OBJECTIVES—The end toward which all effort is made:
  a. Goals are not necessarily measurable.
  b. Objectives are always measurable.

"IN-KIND"—Of similar nature.

LEA—Local education agency or local school district.

PROGRAM—Activities planned (or unplanned) within a project.

PROJECT—Planned and definitely formulated undertaking.

USE AREA—Physical setting utilized for teaching purposes.

Categories for Evaluation for Environmental Education

A. Planning & Design

1. Origination of the Idea
2. Pre-planning
3. Identification of Needs
4. Philosophy
5. Community Involvement
6. Outside Involvement
7. Resource Identification
8. Design Production
9. Financing
10. Priorities

B. Content

1. Goals & Objectives
2. Curriculum
3. Faculty & Staff Activities
4. Student Involvement
5. In-Service Preparation
6. Resource Utilization
7. Material & Equipment Utilization

C. Operation

1. Organizational Pattern
2. Personnel
3. Facilities
4. Materials & Equipment
5. Budget
6. Student Participation
7. Scheduling
8. Dissemination
9. Record Maintenance

D. Productivity

1. Fiscal Policies
2. Personnel Evaluation
3. (a-1) Personnel Growths & Attitudes Project Personnel
   (a-2) Personnel Growths & Attitudes LEA Personnel
   (b-1) Project Personnel Growth—Skills
   (b-2) LEA Personnel Growth—Skills
   (c-1) Success in Role—Project Personnel
   (c-2) Success in Role—LEA Personnel
4. (a) Student Changes in Attitudes
   (b) Student Changes in Knowledges
5. Project Effectiveness
6. Effect in School District
7. Project and Community Long-Term Effects

Statistical Summary for Evaluation for Environmental Education

Project Title: _____   USOE # _____

Address: _____   Phone _____

ZIP # _____

Director's Name: _____

Total population of area served:

Population characteristics of area served:

Inner-City	%
Urban	%
Rural	%

Service coverage in square miles:

Economic characteristics of area served:

Agricultural	%
Industrial	%
Business	%
Other	%

Number of School Districts (LEA's) being served:

Total student population of school districts (LEA's) being served:

Student characteristics of school districts (LEA's) being served:

Inner-City	%
Urban	%
Suburban	%
Rural	%
Public	%
Non-Public	%

Current expenses for education per student (ADE) in school districts (LEA's) being served: approximately $_____

Total project budget (except capital outlay) divided by number of pupils served: $_____

Number of students being served by project (yearly)

Characteristics of students being served by project:

Inner-City	%
Urban	%
Suburban	%
Rural	%
Public	%
Non-Public	%

Number of students still in need of service:

Characteristics of students still in need of service:

Inner-City	%
Urban	%
Suburban	%
Rural	%
Public	%
Non-Public	%

Summary

Are similar programs in operation within area served?

Do existing programs in area conflict in any way?

What curriculum or special education area are covered in project? (List)

Are field experiences (out of school) presently part of the school program? (Describe)

In what ways does the community to be served have particular need for the project? (Explain)

Why is this project of special potential value for the community to be served? (Describe)

A-1 STANDARD: Origination of the Idea

Sources of ideas for initiating innovative projects should be identified and assessed for feasibility and potential educational advantages.

Self-rating Score _____

C	I	P	O
a. Were new ideas for prospective programs encouraged? __Yes __No __Neither If yes, by whom?	a. Were new ideas actually presented by various staff members? __Never __Occasionally __Often	a. Who presented the idea which became the basis for this proposal? (Give position or title of person or name of group)	a. Was the originator of the idea further involved in developing it into an acceptable proposal in the LEA? __Yes __No If no, why?
		b. What factors gave the original stimulus to this proposal? (Be specific)	b. How readily was the proposal accepted by the decision-maker in the LEA? __Readily __With Hesitation __After Much Deliberation __Without Enthusiasm
		c. How long was this proposal considered before it was actually presented to the assessing agent in the LEA?	c. Who made the final determination on the feasibility of the proposal in the LEA? (Give position or title of person or name of group)
			d. Was the availability of Federal funds a major factor in the acceptance of this proposal in the LEA? __Yes __No

A-2 STANDARD: Pre-Planning

Acceptable ideas should be reviewed by knowledgeable persons in order to develop and expand them into an educationally sound proposal.

Self-rating Score _____

C	I	P	O
a. Were procedures established to allow for a knowledgeable review and expansion of the original idea? __Yes __No	a. Were acceptable new ideas actually reviewed to formulate them into an educationally sound proposal? __Yes __No	a. Who performed this review? (Give position or title of person or name of group)	a. (1) Did this review result in modifications to the original proposal? __Yes __No a. (2) If so, to what degree? (Give brief explanation)

A-3 STANDARD: Identification of Needs

In order to facilitate the planning for projects involving behavioral changes in people as well as increasing their knowledge and skills, the needs of the people to be served should be identified.

Self-rating Score _____

C	I	P	O

a. Were the needs of these groups considered? (Check those that apply)
 	
 __Yes __No __N/A
 Community
 School
   District
 Children
 Teachers
 Parents
 Other
   (Specify)
	a. (1) Were the needs of these groups actually applied in planning?
	
	 __Yes __No __N/A
	 Community
	 School
	   District
	 Children
	 Teachers
	 Parents
	 Other
	   (Specify)
		a. (1) How did you attempt to meet these needs in general terms utilizing primary involvement? (i.e., Plan for types of experiences— Explain)	a. (1) What modifications were made to the original proposal in order to fulfill these needs?

	a. (2) What were the needs?	a. (2) What criteria did you use for selecting specific needs? (Give brief explanation)	a. (2) What new needs did you identify in designing the proposal? (Specify)

b. Were the following types of needs considered?
 	
 __Yes __No __N/A
 Curricular
 Economic
 Social
 Emotional
 Other
   (Specify)
	b. Were the following types of needs actually applied in planning?
	
	 __Yes __No __N/A
	 Curricular
	 Economic
	 Social
	 Emotional
	 Other
	   (Specify)		

A-4 STANDARD: Philosophy

The philosophy of the proposal should reflect the recognized needs and the educational philosophy of the school district.

Self-rating Score _____

C	I	P	O
a. Were the previously established needs considered in determining the proposal's general philosophy? __Yes __No __No needs established	a. Does the proposal's philosophy reflect the established needs? __Fully __Partially __Not at all	a. List the needs which are relected in the philosophy.	a. State your proposal's general philosophy.
b. Was the educational philosophy of the school district considered in planning this proposal? __Yes __No	b. Does the proposal's philosophy reflect the school district's educational philosophy? __Fully __Partially __Not at all	b. What process was utilized in relating an approach to building the proposal's philosophy to the school district's philosophy?	

A-5 STANDARD: Community Involvement

The broadest possible cross-section of community representation is desirable for initial and continual planning of the proposal.

Self-rating Score _____

C	**I**	**P**	**O**
a. Were various community based groups considered for involvement in the initial planning? (Check all that apply)	a. Were they actually involved in the initial planning? (Check all that apply and indicate % of involvement)	a. How were these various groups involved in the initial planning?	a. (1) What positive contributions were made by these groups in the initial planning?

C — __Yes __No __N/A

Lay Groups
In-Community
  Consultants
Non-Public
  School Pers.
Local Industry
Public School
  Pers.
Other

I — __Yes __No __N/A __%

Lay Groups
In-Community
  Consultants
Non-Public
  School Pers.
Local Industry
Public School
  Pers.
Other

O — a. (2) Which group made meaningful contributions in the initial planning? (Check all that apply)

Lay Groups ___
In-Community
  Consultants ___
Non-Public
  School Pers. ___
Local Industry ___
Public School
  Pers. ___
Other ___

C	**I**	**P**	**O**
b. Were various community based groups considered for involvement in the continual planning? (Check all that apply)	b. Were they actually involved in the continual planning? (Check all that apply and indicate % of involvement)	b. How are these various groups involved in the continual planning?	b. (1) What positive contributions were made by these groups in the continual planning?

C — __Yes __No __N/A

Lay Groups
In-Community
  Consultants
Non-Public
  School Pers.
Local Industry
Public School
  Pers.

Other

I — __Yes __No __N/A __%

Lay Groups
In-Community
  Consultants
Non-Public
  School Pers.
Local Industry
Public School
  Pers.

Other

O — b. (2) Which group made meaningful contributions in the continual planning? (Check all that apply)

Lay Groups ___
In-Community
  Consultants ___
Non-Public
  School Pers. ___
Local Industry ___
Public School
  Pers. ___
Other ___

A-6 STANDARD: Outside Involvement

All pertinent and up-to-date knowledge available from sources outside the community should be considered in planning the proposal.

Self-rating score _____

C	I	P	O
a. Were various outside specialists consulted in initial planning of the proposal? (Check all that apply)	a. Were outside specialists actually involved in the initial planning of the proposal? (Check all that apply and indicate % of involvement)	a. How were the services of these outside specialists utilized in the initial planning of the proposal?	a. What specific contributions to the initial planning resulted through the use of outside specialists? (Specify specialists)
___Yes ___No ___N/A Other Project Directors State Dept. of Ed. Personnel Outside Consultants Labor & Indus. Reps. College & Univ. Pers. Published Research Govt. Agencies Other	___Yes ___No ___N/A ___% Other Project Directors State Dept. of Ed. Personnel Outside Consultants Labor & Indus. Reps. College & Univ. Pers. Published Research Govt. Agencies Other		
b. Are various outside specialists consulted in the continual planning of the proposal? (Check all that apply)	b. Are outside specialists actually involved in the continual planning of the proposal? (Check all that apply and indicate % of involvement)	b. How are the services of these outside specialists utilized in the continual planning of the proposal?	b. What specific contributions to the continual planning resulted through the use of outside specialists? (Specify specialists)
___Yes ___No ___N/A Other Project Directors State Dept. of Ed. Personnel Outside Consultants Labor & Indus. Reps. College & Univ. Pers. Published Research Govt. Agencies Other	___Yes ___No ___N/A ___% Other Project Directors State Dept. of Ed. Personnel Outside Consultants Labor & Indus. Reps. College & Univ. Pers. Published Research Govt. Agencies Other		

A-7 STANDARD: Resource Identification

To determine the limitations, capabilities and potential of the program, all currently available and anticipated resources should be identified and classified.

Self-rating score _____

C	I	P	O
a. Was the importance of resource identification considered in planning the proposal? (Check all that apply)	a. Were available resources identified according to some criteria relative to the proposal?	a. (1) How did proposal planning utilize available and anticipated resources?	a. How did the final proposal reflect an understanding of program limitations, in the light of available and anticipated re-

A-7 STANDARD: Resource Identification [Continued]

Self-rating Score _____

C	I	P	O
__Yes __No __N/A Personnel: Specialists Consultants Other Site: Natural Buildings Other Information: Library Other	__Yes __No	a. (2) What limitations were set on proposal planning by a lack of resources?	sources, capabilities and potential?

A-8 STANDARD: Design Production

The appropriate proposal design can be developed best by blending all of the previously gathered information and material into a workable plan for meeting the general philosophy of the proposal.

Self-rating Score _____

C	I	P	O
a. Was the design developed in keeping with the general philosophy and needs as previously established? __Yes __No	a. How functional was the design? __Highly functional __Functional __Partially functional __Not functional (Please describe why)	a. (1) To what extent does the design reflect the general philosophy of the proposal? 80 to 100% __ 50 to 80% __ 30 to 50% __ less than 30% __ not at all __	a. (1) Was the proposal design sufficient for achieving the philosophy of the proposal?
		a. (2) How does the design reflect the general philosophy of the proposal?	a. (2) List any obvious shortcomings or overemphasis in the design relative to general philosophy.

A-9 STANDARD: Financing

The financial feasibility of the proposal can be determined only after a preliminary budget has been prepared, which shows all anticipated expenditures and identifies all potential sources of funds.

Self-rating Score _____

C	I	P	O
a. Was the necessity of having a complete preliminary budget prior to making final dispositions and assignment of priorities realized? __Yes __No	a. Was a preliminary budget prepared? __Yes __No Did it show all anticipated sources of funds? __Yes __No Did it provide a complete overview of anticipated expenditures? __Yes __No	a. Attach a copy of the preliminary budget. (Give a brief explanation of any unusual items)	a. (1) What revisions were required in the preliminary budget as the proposal became operational? (Attach a copy of the final budget) a. (2) Briefly explain any changes of 20% or more.

A-10 STANDARD: Priorities

The implementation of an effective proposal and the efficient use of finances requires that priorities be determined and assigned in the planning stages of the proposal.

Self-rating Score _____

C	I	P	O
a. Was consideration given to the establishment of proposal priorities based on: __Yes __No __N/A Financial Structure Educational Needs Material Needs Physical Needs Other Needs	a. (1) Were actual priorities established in view of: __Yes __No __N/A Financial Structure Educational Needs Material Needs Physical Needs Other Needs	a. (1) How were priorities determined?	a. (1) Were these priorities compatible in terms of the actual proposal? __Yes __No __None assigned
	a. (2) List the priorities below:	a. (2) Who made the final determination on priorities? (Give title or position or identify group)	a. (2) What changes would you (or did you) make in your listing of priorities as a result of project operation to date?
			a. (3) On what basis were the priorities changed?

B-1 STANDARD: Goals and Objectives

The project should establish goals and objectives which are consistent with the broad philosophy and objectives of the local agency(ies), and they should be stated in measurable terms.

Self-rating Score _____

C	I	P	O
a. Have goals and objectives for the project been established and stated in measurable terms? __Yes __No	a. Are specific objectives formulated for each facet of the project? __Yes __No	a. Is there a plan for the systematic review and revision of objectives? __Yes __No	a. Is data available to support claims of movement toward objectives? __Yes __No
b. Are the objectives consistent with the philosophy of the LEA? __Yes __No	b. (1) If yes, are specific objectives formulated, consistent with specific objectives of each curriculum area? __Yes __No	b. (1) If yes, is there a plan for the systematic review and revision of these objectives? __Yes __No	b. (1) Did the LEA philosophy affect the formation of the project philosophy? __Yes __No
Are the goals drawn from the philosophy of the LEA? __Yes __No	b. (2) If no, what is the basis of the project philosophy in the formulation of specific objectives?	b. (2) If no, can the inconsistencies between objectives be compensated for, to allow the project to operate? __Yes __No	b. (2) Did the project philosophy affect the LEA philosophy? __Yes __No

B-2 STANDARD: Curriculum

Realistic goals and objectives representing a complement or supplement to those already established by the participating local education agency(ies) should be developed for the project.

Self-rating Score _____

C	I	P	O
a. Was the existing school curriculum material reviewed in developing project curriculum? ___Yes ___No	a. (1) If yes, does new material reinforce established curriculum, or does it expand curriculum into additional areas? ___reinforce ___expand ___replace ___other	a. Is there provision or plan for the gradual introduction of the innovative changes of this project into the curriculum? ___Yes ___No	a. (1) Were the innovative changes incorporated into existing curriculum? ___Yes ___No To what extent? (State as a percentage) ___%
	a. (2) If no, what was the basis for the project curriculum?		a. (2) Did the incorporated innovations result in: ___reinforcement? ___extension? ___replacement? ___other?

B-3 STANDARD: Faculty and Staff Activities

The faculty and staff roles for performing their curricular tasks should be clearly defined.

Self-rating Score _____

C	I	P	O
a. Has staff been selected on the basis of curricular needs? ___Yes ___No	a. Are staff assignments and responsibilities clearly defined within educational program areas? ___Yes ___No	a. Is there a systematic plan for assessing staff effectiveness in terms of curricular needs? ___Yes ___No	a. Is the staff effective in terms of curricular needs? ___Yes ___No
b. (1) Is there versatility in staff capabilities regarding project curriculum? ___Yes ___No	b. Are staff members restricted in terms of subject material they can teach, or are their project capabilities versatile? ___restricted ___versatile	b. Is there a plan for using individual abilities of staff for the benefit of the project? ___Yes ___No	b. Is the use of the staff effective in terms of curricular needs? ___Yes ___No
b. (2) Is there flexibility in staff approach re: project activities? ___Yes ___No			
			c. How were the objectives defined? ___subjectively ___objectively ___formally ___other

B-4 STANDARD: Students

A plan for student involvement in the planning and the execution of the project should be established.

Self-rating Score _____

C	I	P	O
a. Was provision made for student planning of total project activities? ___Yes ___No	a. (1) Are students involved in planning the project's activities? ___Yes ___No a. (2) If no, stop here and go on to Standard B-5.	a. How are they involved? (Percentage of project planned by students) Content ___% Student role ___% Pre-activity plan ___% Post-activity plan ___% Evaluation plan ___% Leader role ___% _____ ___% Other (name)	a. (1) Does actual project activity show positive evidence of planning? ___Yes ___No a. (2) Is there a change from the amount of previous student planning activity? ___Yes ___No ___less activity ___more activity ___no change a. (3) Is there a greater amount of student involvement in the project now than when the project started? ___Yes ___No a. (4) What effect has this student involvement had on student activity in the continued planning of the project? ___increase ___decrease ___no change the rest of the school curriculum? ___increase ___decrease ___no change

B-5 STANDARD: In-Service Preparation [Continued]

A program of in-service preparation for classroom teachers providing for acquisition of new understandings, perceptions, skills and techniques required in the project should be developed and established.

Self-rating Score _____

C	I	P	O
a. (1) Has an in-service program been developed? ___Yes ___No	a. (1) Is in-service training an established and continuing facet of the project? ___Yes ___No	a. (1) How is the in-service training implemented? (Check all that apply)	a. (1) Is the in-service training program effective in terms of the total project? ___Yes ___No

B-5 STANDARD: In-Service Preparation [Continued]   Self-rating Score _____

C	I	P	O
a. (2) If yes, check those areas that are applicable:	*Type of Program:* (Check all that apply)	Class of students with teachers ___ Lecture ___ Demonstration ___ Skill practice using children ___ Method practice using children ___ Teacher alone ___ Seminars ___ Other (specify) ___	a. (2) Were teacher skills and learning developed in the in-service program utilized in project activities?
Skills ___ Methods (list) _____ _____ _____	College credit ___ Salary credit ___ Voluntary ___ Required ___ Free time ___ School time ___		___Yes ___No
Research ___ Concepts ___ Content (list) _____ _____	Stipend ___ No stipend ___ Summer ___ Special course by outside agency ___ Other (specify) ___		a. (3) If yes, how? (Check all that apply) Leadership in activities ___ Communication with staff ___ Improved technique ___
Teaching aids or materials ___ Personal growth and understanding ___ Other _____ _____	a. (2) Expenses borne by: Project ___ LEA(s) ___ Teachers ___ Other (specify) ___	a. (2) The in-service training is led by? (Check all that apply) Project staff ___ Consultant ___ School personnel ___ Other (specify) ___	Improved teacher effectiveness with students ___ with other teachers ___ Assists project staff ___ Develops own materials ___ Other (specify) ___
a. (3) If no, go on to Standard *B-6*	b. Was a validated instrument developed to measure teacher behavioral change? ___Yes ___No		

B-6 STANDARD: Resource Utilization

Resources for carrying out the project should be continually inventoried and their utilization evaluated on a continuing pattern.   Self-rating Score _____

C	I	P	O
a. Were the following kinds of resources inventoried for use in the project? ___Yes ___No	a. (1) Are concurrent records kept on all resource use? ___Yes ___No	a. (1) Are resource inventories and evaluations available for: Program planning ___ Teacher use ___ Student use ___ Public use ___ (Other)	a. (1) Were resource inventories effectively used? ___Yes ___No By whom? Teachers ___ Students ___ Project Staff ___ Evaluators ___ Specialists ___ Other (specify) ___
Personnel: Specialists Consultants Other Site: Natural Buildings Other Information:			

B-6 STANDARD: Resource Utilization [Continued]   Self-rating Score _____

C	I	P	O
Library Other (Specify below)	a. (2) Were additional resources needed and secured? ___Yes ___No	a. (2) How is the information disseminated?	a. (2) Were resource evaluations effectively used? ___Yes ___No

P:
Resource guides (teachers) ___
Library ___
Publications ___
Speaking engagements ___
Correspondence ___
Audio-Visual Media ___
Other (specify) ___

O:
By whom?
Teachers ___
Students ___
Project Staff ___
Evaluators ___
Specialists ___
Other (specify) ___

a. (3) Is there a plan for the evaluation of resources?

___Yes ___No

B-7 STANDARD: Materials and Equipment

Materials and equipment needed for carrying out the project should be continually inventoried and their utilization evaluated on a continuing pattern.   Self-rating Score _____

C	I	P	O
a. Were the following kinds of materials and equipment inventoried for use in the project?	a. (1) Are concurrent records kept on all materials and equipment? ___Yes ___No	a. (1) Are materials and equipment inventories and evaluations available for:	a. Were materials and inventories and evaluations effectively used? ___Yes ___No

C:
Please check   Yes No
Transportation ___ ___
Science ___ ___
Field math ___ ___
Camping ___ ___
Other (specify)
___ ___
___ ___
___ ___

P:
Program planning ___
Teacher use ___
Student use ___
Public use ___
Other (specify) ___

O:
By whom?
Teachers ___
Students ___
Project staff ___
Evaluators ___
Specialists ___
Others (specify) ___

a. (2) Is there a plan for the evaluation of materials and equipment?

___Yes ___No

a. (2) How is this information disseminated?

Materials and Equipment Guides (Teachers) ___
Library ___
Publications ___
Others (specify) ___

a. (3) Is there a preventive maintenance program set up for equipment?

___Yes ___No

a. (4) Were all purchased materials and equipment found to be appropriate?

B-7 STANDARD: Materials and Equipment [Continued]   Self-rating Score _____

C	I	P	O •
	__Yes __No Per Cent of appro- priateness: __%		

C-1 STANDARD: Organizational Pattern

An organizational pattern with clear-cut lines of responsibility is
essential to an efficiently operating project.   Self-rating Score _____

C	I	P	O

a. (1) Did the original proposal provide for a plan of structural organization for the project?
 	
    __Yes __No
	a. Was the organizational plan implemented?
	
	    __Yes __No
		a. (1) Describe how the organizational plan was implemented.	a. Was the original organizational plan effective?
			
			    __Yes __No

a. (2) If no, was an organizational plan developed later? __Yes __No Date of project inception Date organizational plan was developed		a. (2) What criteria were employed in developing the original organizational plan?	

b. Was either the original organizational plan or the one developed after the project began, modified?
 	
    __Yes __No
	b. (1) What were the forces or conditions that made modification advisable?	b. What criteria were employed for modifying the organizational plan?	b. Was the modified organizational plan effective?
			
			    __Yes __No
			
			(Attach a copy of your organizational chart)

	b. (2) Who modified the organizational plan? Project director __ Project staff __ School Administrator __ H.E.W. Dept. __ Other		

C-2 STANDARD: Personnel

A. All personnel involved in the project should be assigned clearly defined
responsibilities.   Self-rating Score _____

C	I	P	O

a. Did your project proposal, as funded and/or amended, contain clearly defined arears of responsibility?
 	
    __Yes __No
	a. (1) If no, when were project responsibilities and personnel coordinated to their proper positions?	a. Is there constant assessment of personnel in terms of areas of responsibility?
		
		    __Yes __No
			a. Are all project responsibilities being met?
			
			    __Yes __No

C-2 STANDARD: Personnel [continued]   Self-rating Score _____

C	I	P	O

	___planning phase
	___early operational
	    phase
	___late operational
	    phase
	___not at all
			b. If no, why not?

a. (2) If yes, was it nec-
        essary to modify
        the areas of re-
        sponsibility to per-
        sonnel?

*B. Project personnel should be chosen and appointed on the basis of their
    individual capabilities for fulfilling specific staff positions.*   Self-rating Score _____

C	I	P	O
a. Were personnel chosen on the basis of individual capabilities for specific staff positions? ___Yes ___No	a. (1) If yes, on what basis were capabilities assessed? ___Testing ___Professional back- ground ___Ability ___Previous experience ___Interest ___Recommendation ___Other (explain) a. (2) If no, explain.	a. Is there continual assessment of individual capabilities for assigned positions? ___Yes ___No	a. Do program personnel capably fulfill assigned positions? ___Yes ___No

*C. Personnel should be thoroughly familiar with their individual responsibilities
    and their relationships to the overall project.*   Self-rating Score _____

C	I	P	O
a. Are personnel thoroughly familiar with their individual responsibilities in the overall program? ___Yes ___No	a. (1) Does an organizational table exist? ___Yes ___No	a. (1) Are personnel being assessed periodically in terms of an awareness of their jobs in relation to the overall project? ___Yes ___No	a. Does the project reflect the familiarity of personnel with their individual responsibilities in relation to the overall project? ___Yes ___No
	a. (2) How are personnel informed of job descriptions? Posted scheme of organizational positions ___ Staff Meetings ___ Staff Manual ___ Other (explain) ___	a. (2) If yes, By whom? How frequently? By what means?	

C-3 STANDARD: Facilities

*Sufficient, adequate and appropriate facilities and/or use area for the proper
and efficient operation of the program should be provided and maintained
in such a manner as to be available and useable at all times while the
project is in operation.*   Self-rating Score _____

C	I	P	O
a. (1) Were suitable basic facilities and/or use	a. (1) Was it necessary to renovate and adapt	a. (1) Was the selection of facilities and/or	a. (1) Did the basic facilities and/or use

C-3 STANDARD: Facilities [Continued]   Self-rating Score _____

C	I	P	O
area to fit the needs of the project immediately available?	the facilities and/or use area to the project program?	use area arrived at by cooperative agreement of the project's planners?	area effectively provide for the program's objectives?
__Yes __No	__Yes __No	__Yes __No	__Yes __No

a. (2) When?

__During the planning
   stage?
__At the beginning of
   the project's operation?
__During the first six
   months of the project operation?
__During the first year?
__Later? (Specify
   when)

a. (2) Was the program adapted to meet the facilities and/or use area?

     __Yes __No

a. (2) If no, who was responsible for the selection of facilities and/or use area?
   (Give title or position)

a. (2) If no, did it reflect on original planning?

     __Yes __No

a. (3) Were new facilities and/or use areas provided to meet the program?

     __Yes __No

a. (3) Were the facilities and/or use area established on a year-round permanent basis?

     __Yes __No

a. (3) Were any major changes required in the project's facilities and/or use area?

     __Yes __No

a. (4) If no, were the facilities and/or use area rented or leased on a temporary basis, to be used as required?

     __Yes __No

a. (4) If yes, what changes were required and why?

a. (5) Were program facilities and/or use area established for resident, day use, or both types of programs?

__resident   __both
__day

b. Was it necessary or advisable to secure facilities and/or use area outside the boundaries of the LEA?

   __Yes __No

b. If yes, was the selection of "distant" facilities and/or use area based on providing better programs at a lower per unit cost?

     __Yes __No

If yes, was the selection of distant facilities and/or use area based on:

__Providing a better
   program at a lower
   per unit cost?

__A temporary expedient?

b. What processes were employed to select the facilities and/or use area outside the boundaries of the LEA?

b. Were the "distant" facilities and/or use area adequate for the program of the project?

     __Yes __No

C-3 STANDARD: Facilities [continued]   Self-rating Score _____

C	I	P	O
	__No facility and/or use area available within the boundary of the LEA? __Other (explain)		

C-4 STANDARD: Materials and Equipment

Appropriate materials and equipment for the proper and efficient operation of the project should be provided and maintained in such a manner as to be available in sufficient quantity and useable condition at all times while the project is in operation.   Self-rating Score _____

C	I	P	O
a. Was provision made to have adequate materials and supplies? __Yes __No	a. (1) Did the budget provide for necessary materials and supplies? __Yes __No	a. (1) Were supplies and/or equipment obtained or purchased through regular school purchase channels? Supplies __Yes __No Equipment __Yes __No	a. (1) Was the purchase procedure used a satisfactory one? For supplies __Yes __No For equipment __Yes __No
	a. (2) Were supplementary funds required to provide materials and equipment? __Yes __No If yes, explain:	a. (2) If not, how were they obtained?	a. (2) Was acquisition through methods other than purchasing satisfactory? Explain:
		a. (3) What problems were presented if supplies and/or equipment were purchased through school purchase channels? (List)	
		a. (4) How were these problems resolved?	
b. Was provision made for maintaining equipment? __Yes __No	b. (1) Were funds available for equipment maintenance? __Yes __No	b. What problems were presented in maintaining equipment? (List)	b. Were you satisfied with maintenance procedures and results? __Yes __No If no, explain why not.
	b. (2) Who was responsible for maintenance of equipment?		

C-5 STANDARD: Budget

A. *A clearly defined budget should be prepared, utilizing acceptable accounting which takes into consideration all areas of income and expenditure.*   Self-rating Score _____

C	I	P	O
a. Did the project proposal contain a clearly	a. (1) Was the original budget approved	a. (1) Was the budget workable?	a. (1) Did you achieve the project objec-

C-5 STANDARD: Budget [continued]   Self-rating Score _____

| C | I | P | O |

defined budget?

__Yes __No

and put into operation?

__Yes __No

__Yes __No

tives within the original or revised budget?

__Yes __No

a. (2) If no, how was it modified?

__% increase
__% decrease

a. (2) Was the revised budget workable?

__Yes __No

a. (2) If no, did you modify the program to achieve the project objectives?

__Yes __No

a. (3) Were additional funds, other than federal funds, provided?

__Yes __No

By whom? (Identify)

a. (3) Was the USOE financial accounting system (OE 22017) adopted?

__Yes __No

a. (3) If no, were additional funds, facilities, or services obtained from other sources?

__Yes __No

By whom? (Identify)

a. (4) What % of the total budget was provided from non-federal funds?

__%

a. (4) If not, what variables presented themselves which resulted in modifications?
(List)

B. The budget should be managed in accord with all rules and regulations of the school district.   Self-rating Score _____

a. (1) Are clear budget records kept (district and project)?

Project   __Yes __No
District   __Yes __No

a. (1) Are the project's budget records kept accurately and up-to-date?

__Yes __No

a. (1) Was record-keeping achieved without undue friction?

__Yes __No

a. (1) Did control of fund accounts and expenditures reflect sound project budget planning?

__Yes __No

a. (2) Are the project's budget records maintained by an LEA fiscal officer?

__Yes __No

a. (2) If no, how did you (or will you) rectify this?
(Explain)

a. (2) List reasons why the project's budget records were not kept current.

a. (2) If no, what changes were required?
(List)

a. (3) Are the project's budget records maintained by a special project fiscal officer?

__Yes __No

b. Was an audit planned for the project?

__Yes __No

b. (1) Were funds provided for auditing the project's financial records?

__Yes __No

b. Was an audit made?

__Yes __No

b. (1) Did an audit indicate a need for project budget revision?

__Yes __No

C-5 STANDARD: Budget [Continued]

Self-rating Score _____

C	I	P	O
	b. (2) If funds were not provided, how did you finance an audit? (Explain)		b. (2) If yes, list those revisions.

C-6 STANDARD: Student Participation

Where program learning content dictates student participation in the physical operation of the facilities, such participation should be set with specific duties and responsibilities assigned for each student.

Self-rating Score _____

C	I	P	O
a. Did the project proposal contain a detailed plan describing specific duties and responsibilities assigned to students? __Yes __No	a. (1) Was the plan implemented? __Yes __No	a. (1) Was the original plan workable? __Yes __No	a. (1) In the original or modified plan, did the student willingly participate in the assigned duties? __Yes __No
	a. (2) Was the original plan modified? __Yes __No	a. (2) Was the modified plan workable? __Yes __No	a. (2) List duties and responsibilities assigned to students.
		a. (3) If no, to either a. (1) or a. (2), list factors which caused the plan to be unworkable.	a. (3) Was an adult leader involved in assigning the duties and following them through to completion? __Yes __No
			a. (4) How well was this plan implemented into the program? __very well __moderately well __not well

C-7 STANDARD: Scheduling

An efficient method of scheduling staff and students for facilities and equipment should be employed in order to obtain maximum effective utilization of these resources.

Self-rating Score _____

C	I	P	O
a. Did the project proposal contain an efficient method for scheduling project personnel and students, for use of available facilities and equipment? __Yes __No	a. (1) Was the original method for scheduling implemented? __Yes __No	a. (1) Is scheduling for use of facilities and equipment completed well in advance? __Yes __No	a. (1) By employing the original schedule, was maximum utilization of staff, student, and facility resources achieved? __Yes __No

C-7 STANDARD: Scheduling [Continued]

Self-rating Score _____

C	I	P	O
	a. (2) Was the original method for scheduling modified? __Yes __No	a. (2) How far in advance is the scheduling completed? 3 to 6 weeks __ 4 months __ Other __	a. (2) By employing a modified schedule was maximum utilization of student, staff and facility resources achieved? __Yes __No
		a. (2) Did scheduling involve sharing facilities? __Yes __No	a. (3) Was sharing of facilities satisfactory? __Yes __No
		a. (4) If yes, did serious scheduling problems result? __Yes __No	a. (4) Were these problems satisfactorily resolved? __Yes __No
		a. (5) What was the major cause of the scheduling problem? Time __ Competition from other groups __ Transportation __	a. (5) Who resolved scheduling problems? Superintendent __ Principal __ Project Director __ Other __
			a. (6) What criteria did you employ to assure the utilization of these resources? (List or attach data)

C-8 STANDARD: Dissemination

A. Pertinent data and information compiled as a result of the project should be properly cataloged, interpreted in a meaningful manner, and distributed to interested and concerned parties.

Self-rating Score _____

C	I	P	O
a. (1) Was a system established for cataloging, interpreting and distributing information developed in the project? __Yes __No	a. Who implemented the system? (Give title or position)	a. (1) Was the original system workable? __Yes __No	a. (1) Did the __ original, __ modified, system enable you to meet the objectives for dissemination of information? __Yes __No
a. (2) Was the system: __In operation at the inception of the project? __During first 6 months of operation? __After 6 months of operation?		a. (2) If modification occurred, list factors which caused the system to be modified.	a. (2) What are the criteria for judging that dissemination of information was successful? (List or attach data)

C-8 STANDARD: Dissemination [continued]   Self-rating Score _____

C	I	P	O
		a. (3) Was the modified system workable? ___Yes ___No	
b. If a dissemination plan was not established, check here. ___	b. Who decided that dissemination should not be implemented? (Give title or position)	b. What factors prevented implementation?	b. What have been the effects of not having a dissemination system implemented?

B. Any materials prepared for dissemination should be aimed at the level of the proposed recipients.

Self-rating Score _____

C	I	P	O
a. In the preparation of materials for dissemination, was the audience level kept in mind? ___Yes ___No	a. Who determined the audience level? Project director ___ Project staff ___ Other ___	a. How was the audience level determined? (List criteria below)	a. Were the desired interpretations by the audience realized? ___Yes ___No (List criteria below)

If no, go directly to Section C.

C. Dissemination of information should not be limited to one or two methods, but should rather include various methods and techniques for reaching the respective audience.

Self-rating Score _____

C	I	P	O
a. Was a plan incorporating a variety of methods for dissemination prepared? ___Yes ___No	a. List the methods used for dissemination.	a. (1) Were the original methods adequate and workable? ___Yes ___No	a. (1) Were the project's objectives for dissemination of materials achieved? ___Yes ___No
		a. (2) What factors affected the operation of the original plan? (List)	a. (2) What is the basis for this judgment? (Attach supporting data or list criteria)
		a. (3) Were any changes made? (List)	a. (3) What factors prevented success? (List)
		b. (1) Was a revised method of dissemination developed? ___Yes ___No	b. (1) Was the revised plan successful? ___Yes ___No
		b. (2) Was the revised method of dissemination workable? ___Yes ___No	If no, what factors prevented success? (List below)

C-9 STANDARD: Records Maintenance

An efficient system for maintaining any and all records must be devised in order to insure a clear and complete record of all activities and functions, and provide continuity despite possible staff changes.

Self-rating Score _____

C	I	P	O
a. (1) Was an efficient system for carrying	a. (1) Were the records kept up-to-date?	a. (1) Was the system put into practice?	a. (1) Did a complete record of all activi-

C-9 STANDARD: Records Maintenance [Continued]

C	I	P	O
out the above planned? __Yes __No	__Yes __No	__Yes __No	ties and functions throughout the project afford continuity to the project? __Yes __No
a. (2) If no, was a system planned later? __Yes __No	a. (2) Was the responsibility for keeping records delegated to: Office personnel __ Professional personnel __ Director __ Other (explain) __	a. (2) If no, list reasons why the system was not implemented.	a. (2) List the major areas in which records were kept.
a. (3) If yes, Immediately __ Short time __ 6 months or more __			a. (3) Who has benefitted most from these records? Project personnel __ LEA personnel __ Funding agency __ Other (explain) __

D-1 STANDARD: Fiscal Policies

The effectiveness of fiscal policies must be continuously evaluated, with subsequent adjustments of policy to meet the fiscal needs of the program as they are influenced by changes in the financial structure, and changes in sources and availability of funds.

C	I	P	O
a. Were fiscal policies developed in the project plan? __Yes __No	a. (1) Was flexibility in fiscal policy provided for? __Yes __No	a. (1) Were fiscal policies modified during the project? __Yes __No	a. (1) Were desirable fiscal policy changes made? __Yes __No
	a. (2) If no, indicate reason:	a. (2) What factors influenced fiscal policy change? a. (3) Was modification within LEA fiscal policy impossible or not feasible? __Yes __No	a. (2) Did said changes produce desired results?
b. Will local districts be capable of assuming the cost of the project?	b. What personnel were involved in fiscal policy modification? (Give title or position)	b. (1) Are fiscal policy changes planned for cessation of federal funding?	
			b. (1) What is present local per capita support? What would the per capita cost be if local

D-1 STANDARD: Fiscal Policies [continued]   Self-rating Score _____

C	I	P	O
			support took over the project? If local support is not possible or insufficient, what other sources of support have been planned or guaranteed? What % of program can be supported by these sources?
		b. (2) Are fiscal policy changes planned for reduction in federal funding prior to the scheduled phase out? __Yes __No If yes, describe.	b. (2) If reduction in funding occurs can the project be maintained? What part of program would have to be eliminated? Would local funding take over?

D-2 STANDARD: Personnel Evaluation

Program productivity in terms of personnel growth, behavioral changes and success in their respective roles must be continuously observed and correlated with other aspects of the program in order to interpret program effectiveness.   Self-rating Score _____

C	I	P	O
a. Was evaluation of program productivity in terms of personnel growth planned? __Yes __No	a. (1) Was a personnel evaluation developed for project staff? __Yes __No	a. (1) Was such an evaluation plan utilized? __Yes __No	a. (1) Did personnel show growth during the project activity? __Yes __No
	a. (2) What procedures for evaluation of personnel were utilized? __Check list __Interview __Standardized Instrument __Observation __Staff sessions __Other (Attach detailed description of evaluation procedures)	a. (2) Was base line data collected? __Yes __No	a. (2) If no, what remedial steps were taken? (Attach documents to support response.)
	a. (3) Were personnel involved in selecting or developing procedures? __Yes __No	a. (3) Was data collected at the conclusion of the report period? __Yes __No	

D-2 STANDARD: Personnel Evaluation [Continued]　　　　　　　Self-rating Score _____

C	I	P	O
	a. (4) Who was responsible for final decisions on staff? (Give title or position)		

D-3 (a-1) STANDARD: Personnel Growths and Attitudes—Project Personnel

Project personnel should demonstrate an acceptability to a change in attitudes.　　Self-rating Score _____

C	I	P	O
a. Were attitude changes anticipated in the operation of the project? __Yes __No	a. Who selected the attitudes for project personnel? (Give title or position)	a. (1) Were desired attitudes presented to the project personnel through: __Discussion __Administrative policy __Others	a. (1) Did project personnel willingly accept or develop desired attitudes? __Yes __No
		a. (2) Was there an evaluation of the change in attitudes of the project personnel? __Yes __No	a. (2) If yes, what was the result of this evaluation?
		a. (3) Was there feedback relating to change in attitudes? __Yes __No	a. (3) If yes, in what form was this feedback gained? __Discussion __Written evaluation __Other

D-3 (a-2) STANDARD: Personnel Growths and Attitudes—Local Education Agency(ies)

LEA personnel should demonstrate an acceptability to a change in attitudes.　　Self-rating Score _____

C	I	P	O
a. Were attitude changes anticipated in the operation of the project? __Yes __No	a. Who selected the attitudes for LEA personnel? (Give title or position)	a. (1) Were desired attitudes presented to the LEA through: __Discussion __Administrative policy __Other	a. (1) Did LEA personnel willingly accept or develop desired attitudes? __Yes __No
		a. (2) Was there an evaluation of the change in attitudes of the LEA personnel? __Yes __No	a. (2) If yes, what was the result of this evaluation? (Explain briefly)
		a. (3) Was there feedback relating to change in attitudes?	a. (3) If yes, in what form was this feedback gained?

D-3 (a-2) STANDARD: Personnel Growths and Attitudes—Local Education Agency(ies) [Continued]

Self-rating Score _____

C	I	P	O
		__Yes __No	__Discussion
			__Written evaluation
		(Attach details concerning gathering of feedback)	__Other

b. Were desired attitudes communicated to the LEA personnel?

__Yes __No

b. What attitudes were assimilated by LEA personnel?

D-3 (b-1) STANDARD: Personnel Growth—Skills (Project Personnel)

Project personnel should demonstrate effectiveness in the utilization of an increased number of teaching skills in the appropriate educating environment.

Self-rating Score _____

C	I	P	O
a. Do project personnel use out-of-class references and direct experiences more frequently as a basis for learning? __Yes __No	a. Are project personnel trained to utilize the outdoors for direct learning experiences for children? __Yes __No	a. (1) Are opportunities provided for direct experiences in the curriculum? __Yes __No	a. (1) Do project personnel use concrete examples of the natural environment to introduce abstract concepts or generalizations? __Yes __No __N/A
		a. (2) List some of the educational environments utilized, and degree of involvement by project personnel.	a. (2) Do project personnel plan outdoor experiences for their classes? __Yes __No __N/A
			a. (3) Do project personnel assign direct environmental study as opposed to vicarious study (e.g., text reading)? __Yes __No __N/A
			a. (4) Others
b. Do project personnel share the decision-making process with their students? __Yes __No	b. Are project personnel trained and encouraged to share the decision-making process? __Yes __No	b. (1) Are student decisions encouraged and supported by the project administration? __Yes __No	b. (1) Do project personnel encourage students to make pre-experience decisions concerning their own learning experiences? __Yes __No __N/A
		b. (2) List some areas of student responsibility in decision-making.	b. (2) Do project personnel encourage students to make decisions concerning their actual experiences? __Yes __No __N/A

D-3 (b-1) STANDARD: Personnel Growth—Skills (Project Personnel) [continued]

Self-rating Score _____

C	I	P	O
		b. (3) Degree of involvement: —Great deal —Some involvement —Little involvement	b. (3) Do project personnel encourage self-evaluation of learning experiences, after the experiences have been encountered? —Yes —No —N/A
c. Do project personnel adopt improved techniques for encouraging learning? —Yes —No	c. Is innovation by project personnel encouraged? —Yes —No	c. How is innovation by personnel encouraged or nurtured? —Recognition —Salary increase —Released time to develop or test proposed techniques —Other	c. (1) Do project personnel use the skills learned in the outdoor environment in the classroom as well? —Yes —No —N/A
			c. (2) Do project personnel use audio-visual aids appropriate for environmental education more effectively? —Yes —No —N/A
			c. (3) Do project personnel use techniques which require maximum student involvement in the classroom, such as: —Discovery —Problem-solving —Small groups —Independent study —Yes —No —N/A If yes, check appropriate item.
			c. (4) Others
d. Do project personnel gain a better insight concerning the student-teacher relationships? —Yes —No	d. Are status and recognition provided for teachers developing this skill? —Yes —No	d. Is special training in human relations, such as sensitivity training or some equivalent, provided or encouraged for the project personnel? —Yes —No	d. (1) Do project personnel become more aware of the individual needs of children? —Yes —No —N/A
			d. (2) Do project personnel become more aware of

D-3 (b-1) STANDARD: Personnel Growth—Skills (Project Personnel) [Continued]

Self-rating Score _____

C	I	P	O
			children's relationship to their classmates? __Yes __No __N/A
			d. (3) Do project personnel make gains in their own knowledge of the teaching-learning process? __Yes __No __N/A
			d. (4) Are project personnel more perceptive of the real values held by children or adults? __Yes __No __N/A
			d. (5) Do project personnel increase in their ability to communicate with children? __Yes __No __N/A
			d. (6) Do project personnel increase in their ability to listen to children? __Yes __No __N/A
			d. (7) Others

D-3 (b-2) STANDARD: Personnel Growth—Skills (LEA Personnel)

LEA personnel should demonstrate effectiveness in the utilization of an increased number of teaching skills in the appropriate educating environment.

Self-rating Score _____

C	I	P	O
a. Do LEA personnel use out-of-class references and direct experiences more frequently as a basis for learning? __Yes __No	a. Are LEA personnel trained to utilize the outdoors for direct learning experience for children? __Yes __No	a. Are opportunities provided for direct experiences in the curriculum? __Yes __No	a. (1) Do LEA personnel illustrate abstract learning concepts in the classroom with concrete examples from the natural environment? __Yes __No __N/A
			a. (2) Do LEA personnel use concrete examples of the natural environment to introduce abstract concepts or generalizations? __Yes __No __N/A
			a. (3) Do LEA personnel plan outdoor experiences for their classes? __Yes __No __N/A

D-3 (b-2) STANDARD: Personnel Growth—Skills (LEA Personnel) [continued]

Self-rating Score _____

C	I	P	O
			a. (4) Do LEA personnel assign direct environmental study as opposed to vicarious study (e.g., text reading)? __Yes __No __N/A
			a. (5) Others
b. Do LEA personnel learn to share the decision-making process with their students? __Yes __No	b. Are LEA personnel trained and encouraged to share the decision-making process? __Yes __No	b. (1) Are student decisions encouraged and supported by the LEA administration? __Yes __No	b. (1) Do LEA personnel encourage students to make pre-experience decisions concerning their own learning experiences? __Yes __No __N/A
		b. (2) List some areas of student responsibility in decision-making.	b. (2) Do LEA personnel encourage students to make decisions concerning their actual learning experiences? __Yes __No __N/A
		b. (3) Degree of involvement: __Great deal __Some involvement __Little involvement	b. (3) Do LEA personnel encourage self-evaluation of learning experiences, after the experiences have been encountered? __Yes __No __N/A
			b. (4) Others
c. Do LEA personnel adopt improved techniques for encouraging learning? __Yes __No	c. Is innovation by LEA personnel encouraged? __Yes __No	c. How is innovation by personnel encouraged or nurtured? __Recognition __Salary increase __Released time to develop or test proposed techniques __Other	c. (1) Do LEA personnel use the skills learned in the outdoor environment in the classrooms as well? __Yes __No __N/A
			c. (2) Do LEA personnel use audio-visual aids appropriate for environmental education more effectively? __Yes __No __N/A
			c. (3) Do LEA personnel use techniques which require maximum student involvement in the classroom such as: __Discovery __Problem-solving

D-3 (b-2) STANDARD: Personnel Growth—Skills (LEA Personnel) [continued]

Self-rating Score _____

C	I	P	O
			__Small groups __Independent study __Yes __No __N/A If yes, check appropriate item. c. (4) Others
d. Do LEA personnel gain a better insight concerning the student-teacher and student-student relationships? __Yes __No	d. Are status and recognition provided for LEA personnel developing this skill? __Yes __No	d. Is special training in human relations, such as sensitivity training or some equivalent provided or encouraged in LEA(s)? __Yes __No	d. (1) Do LEA personnel become more aware of the individual needs of students? __Yes __No __N/A
			d. (2) Do LEA personnel become aware of student's relationship to their classmates? __Yes __No __N/A
			d. (3) Do LEA personnel make gains in their own knowledge of the teaching-learning process? __Yes __No __N/A
			d. (4) Are LEA personnel more perceptive of the real values held by children or adults? __Yes __No __N/A
			d. (5) Do LEA personnel increase in their ability to communicate with students? __Yes __No __N/A
			d. (6) Do LEA personnel increase in their ability to listen to students? __Yes __No __N/A
			d. (7) Others

D-3 (c-1) STANDARD: Success in Role—Project Personnel

Project personnel should become increasingly aware of the roles they play in an environmental education program.

Self-rating Score _____

C	I	P	O
a. Are project personnel informed about the variety of roles, i.e.,	a. Is a plan provided to assess the changing role of project per-	a. What method(s) are used for creating an awareness of role?	a. (1) Are project personnel able to adjust to the variety of roles?

D-3 (c-1) STANDARD: Success in Role—Project Personnel [Continued]   Self-rating Score _____

C	I	P	O
teachers, public relations officer, guidance, subject specialist, required of them? __Yes __No	sonnel on a continuing basis? __Yes __No	__Staff meetings __Memos __Periodic reports __Project staff evaluation __Other	__Yes __No __N/A a. (2) What evidence is there that success was achieved?

D-3 (c-2) STANDARD: Success in Role—LEA Personnel

LEA personnel should become increasingly aware of the roles they play in an environmental education program.

Self-rating Score _____

C	I	P	O
a. Are LEA personnel informed about the variety of roles, i.e., teacher, public relations officer, guidance, subject specialist, required of them? __Yes __No	a. Is a plan provided to assess the changing role of LEA personnel on a continuing basis? __Yes __No	a. What method(s) are used for creating an awareness of role? __Staff meetings __Memos __Periodic reports __Project staff evaluation __Other	a. (1) Are LEA personnel able to adjust to the variety of roles? __Yes __No __N/A a. (2) What evidence is there that success was achieved?

D-4 (a) STANDARD: Student Changes in Attitudes

An effective program should show evidence of change and growth in attitudes through modifications in observable behavior.

Self-rating Score _____

C	I	P	O
a. Is student attitudinal change an important objective of the project? __Yes __No	a. Do the project personnel and LEA personnel give high priority to the selection of attitudes? __Yes __No	a. Are desired attitudes presented to the student through: __Discussion __Learning situations __Social interaction __Other	a. Did students develop desired attitudes? __Yes __No
b. For example, did the project select the following behavioral view of a desirable attitudinal change? "Students gain in ability to communicate with their teachers." __Yes __No	b. If yes, who were involved in attempting to influence behavior expressive of this attitude? __Project staff __LEA staff __Other	b. What activities were employed to evoke these modified behaviors?	b. (1) Answer questions or react to discussion? __Yes __No __N/A b. (2) Ask questions voluntarily? __Yes __No __N/A b. (3) Suggest alternative procedures? __Yes __No __N/A b. (4) Converse with adult leaders? __Yes __No __N/A

D-4 (a) STANDARD: Student Changes in Attitudes [continued]

Self-rating Score _____

C	**I**	**P**	**O**

c. Describe method of evaluation. (Attach any instruments used. Include summary of data.)

b. (5) Confide in adult leaders?

___Yes ___No ___N/A

b. (6) Others?

Include supporting evidence for statements made above.

c. Did the project select the following behavioral view of a desirable attitudinal change?

"Students have permanently changed behaviors with their classmates indicating an increased liking or 'understanding' of them."

___Yes ___No

c. Who were involved in attempting to influence behavior expressive of this attitude?

___Project staff
___LEA staff
___Other

c. What activities were employed to evoke this attitude?

c. (1) Did the evaluation indicate that:

The students associate with a larger percentage of their classmates?

___Yes ___No ___N/A

c. (2) An increased number of stars or central clustering found on a Pre-Post Sociogram?

___Yes ___No ___N/A

c. (3) Classroom behavior shows an increased acceptance of "fringe" students?

___Yes ___No ___N/A

c. (4) New or peripheral students become more "absorbed" rapidly?

___Yes ___No ___N/A

c. (5) Students like school better?

___Yes ___No ___N/A

c. (6) Others?

d. For example, did the project select the following behavioral view of a desirable attitudinal change?

"Students demonstrate an increase in their concern for the welfare of others."

___Yes ___No

d. Who were involved in attempting to influence behavior expressive of this attitude?

___Project staff
___LEA staff
___Other

d. What activities were employed to evoke these modified behaviors?

d. (1) Were students:

Sympathetic with behavior of others?

___Yes ___No ___N/A

d. (2) Sympathetic with physical needs of others?

___Yes ___No ___N/A

D-4 (a) STANDARD: Student Changes in Attitudes [continued]

Self-rating Score _____

C	I	P	O
			d. (3) Sympathetic with social behavior related to religious requirements of others? __Yes __No __N/A
			d. (4) Willing to reduce the number of stereotypic notions of their peers with respect to ethnic, nationality, and socio-economic grouping? __Yes __No __N/A
			d. (5) Others?
e. Were other attitudinal goals selected? __Yes __No If yes, please evaluate in a similar fashion.	e. If yes, please respond as in d. above.	e. If yes, please respond as in d. above.	e. If yes, please develop behavioral statements as in d. above.
g. Do students broaden or expand their resource use ethic? __Yes __No	g. Do teachers and administrators accord these attitudes high priority? __Yes __No	g. Are outdoor and indoor experiences utilized? __Yes __No	g. (1) Do students show concern for the preservation or maintenance of organisms in their environment? __Yes __No __N/A
			g. (3) Do students express a concern for the conservation and management of natural resources? __Yes __No __N/A
			g. (3) Do students express an abhorence of waste and demonstrate this in classroom or other school group visitation? __Yes __No __N/A
			g. (4) Is actual waste of classroom materials decreased? __Yes __No __N/A
			g. (5) Is greater interest shown by students in life processes or organisms and their food chains through projects,

D-4 (a) STANDARD: Student Changes in Attitudes [continued]

Self-rating Score _____

C	**I**	**P**	**O**

writings, art or music
expression, etc.?

__Yes __No __N/A

g. (6) Others?

h. Do students develop
attitudes or feelings
which will influence
their use of leisure
time or influence their
leisure time activities?

__Yes __No

h. Do teachers and ad-
ministrators accord
these attitudes high
priority?

__Yes __No

h. Are outdoor and in-
door experiences
utilized?

__Yes __No

h. (1) Do students express a
desire to be out-of-
doors?

__Yes __No __N/A

h. (2) Do students desire
physical as well as
intellectual types of
leisure time activities?

__Yes __No __N/A

h. (3) Do students indulge in
socially oriented activi-
ties?

__Yes __No __N/A

h. (4) Do students develop
leisure time activities
in the outdoors?

__Yes __No __N/A

h. (5) Do students demon-
strate greater interest
in studying ecology?

__Yes __No __N/A

h. (6) Others?

i. Do students share ex-
periences with an ap-
parently desirable
group of persons
whose values may be
other than their own?

__Yes __No

i. Do teachers and ad-
ministrators accord
these attitudes high
priority?

__Yes __No

i. Are outdoor and in-
door experiences
utilized?

__Yes __No

i. (1) Do students share experiences outside their
immediate peer groups?

__Yes __No __N/A

i. (2) Are students' peer
group lines crossed to
form activity groups,
play groups, etc.?

__Yes __No __N/A

i. (3) Do students show increased respect to
minority groups?

__Yes __No __N/A

i. (4) Do students show increased receptivity to
ideas and values of

D-4 (a) STANDARD: Student Changes in Attitudes [continued]

Self-rating Score _____

C	I	P	O
			groups other than their own? __Yes __No __N/A
			i. (5) Do students show greater empathy towards others' feelings? __Yes __No __N/A
			i. (6) Others?
j. Do students undergo a series of novel experiences (novel with respect to their background)? __Yes __No	j. Do teachers and administrators accord these attitudes high priority? __Yes __No	j. Are outdoor and indoor experiences utilized? __Yes __No	j. (1) Is student's attention increased during experience? __Yes __No __N/A
			j. (2) Do students actively wish to participate in experience? __Yes __No __N/A
			j. (3) Do students show excitement with the interaction during the experience? __Yes __No __N/A
			j. (4) Do students orally express newness at discovery? __Yes __No __N/A
			j. (5) Do students make references to experience as a common source of reference? __Yes __No __N/A
			j. (6) Do students' experiences lead to further research study? __Yes __No __N/A
			j. (7) Do students make statements comparing, contrasting and evaluating this experience with other past experiences? __Yes __No __N/A
			j. (8) Others?

D-4 (a) STANDARD: Student Changes in Attitudes [continued]

Self-rating Score _____

C	I	P	O
k. Were other broad behavioral goals selected? __Yes __No If so, please evaluate in a similar fashion.	k. Do teachers and administrators accord these attitudes high priority? __Yes __No	k. Are outdoor and indoor experiences utilized? __Yes __No	k. If yes, please develop behavioral statements, as in "j".

D-4 (b) STANDARD: Student Changes in Knowledges

Activities and experiences provided by the project will increase knowledge related to environmental education.

Self-rating Score _____

C	I	P	O
a. Is evidence sought to determine increases in students' knowledge at the level of imitating, duplicating, recognizing, identifying, remembering, recalling and classifying? __Yes __No	a. Are activities and learning situations provided in the project designed to produce specific responses to accomplish this level of learning and knowledge? __Yes __No	a. Indicate the type of activities used, and the methods involved.	a. (1) Are students able to identify at least 10 species of birds, animals, trees, ferns (or items appropriate to any project program)? __Yes __No __N/A a. (2) List other categories pertinent to your project program. a. (3) Do students display competency in describing or representing relationships of objects or concepts encountered in environmental education, such as: types of rock, land use capability classes, biotic succession, etc.? __Yes __No __N/A a. (4) List other relationships germane to your project program. a. (5) How are student competencies appropriate for your project program determined?
b. Is evidence sought to determine whether students gain an understanding of concepts and processes by comparing, relat-	b. Are activities and experiences provided to allow students to attain a learning level which will produce concept formation and	b. Describe the activities, experiences and methods used.	b. (1) Do students display a knowledge of basic concepts related to the maintenance or modification of their environment or other en-

D-4 (b) STANDARD: Student Changes in Knowledges [continued]   Self-rating Score _____

C   **I**   **P**   **O**

C:

ing, discriminating, reformulating, estimating, interpreting, making critical judgments, and drawing inferences?

___Yes ___No

I:

an understanding of processes?

___Yes ___No

O:

vironments? (For example: food chain, biotic community, water pollution, food supply sources, community resources, etc.)

___Yes ___No ___N/A

P:

b. Describe procedures for evaluation. (Attach for each objective)

O:

b. (2) List concepts pertinent to your project program.

b. (3) Are students able to explain several processes related to outdoor learning situations (i.e., soil formation, photosynthesis, seasonal changes, area deterioration, ecological succession, etc.)?

___Yes ___No ___N/A

b. (4) List processes pertinent to your project program.

b. (5) What criteria are employed to test students' competence in providing satisfactory explanations for concepts or processes listed above?

C:

c. Is evidence sought to determine whether students discover, create, reorganize, formulate new hypotheses, gain new insights, test generalizations by deduction, develop new generalizations by inference or induction, and, in general, can operate on a level of understanding which displays original and productive thinking?

___Yes ___No

I:

c. Are activities and experiences provided which encourage a high level of understanding and accumulation of knowledge resulting in creative decision-making?

___Yes ___No

P:

c. Describe the activities, experiences and methods used.

O:

c. (1) Can students deal with abstract concepts and explain them to others?

___Yes ___No ___N/A

c. (2) List some abstract concepts germane to your project program.

c. (3) What criteria are employed to test students' competency in dealing with concepts in c. (2) above?

c. (4) Can students state hypotheses and organize procedures or activities to test the hypotheses?

___Yes ___No ___N/A

c. (5) What criteria are employed to test students' competencies in c. (4)?

D-4 (b) STANDARD: Student Changes in Knowledges [continued]

Self-rating Score _____

C	I	P	O
			c. (4) Can students state hypotheses and organize procedures or activities to test the hypotheses? __Yes __No __N/A
			c. (5) What criteria are employed to test students' competencies in c. (4)?

D-5 STANDARD: Project Effectiveness

The effectiveness of a project can only be determined as an outgrowth of a continual process of evaluation involving all phases of the project from conception through completion, this evaluation must provide for continuous feedback and re-evaluation of every step as related to every other step, with sufficient flexibility of structure to allow for changes and modifications of the program as needed to accomplish the accepted goals and objectives of the project more effectively.

Self-rating Score _____

C	I	P	O
a. Was provision made for continual evaluation? __Yes __No	a. Was an on-going procedure for evaluation designed? __Yes __No	a. (1) Was the procedure modified in use? __Yes __No	a. Did the evaluation provide sufficient data on project effectiveness to serve as a basis for decision-making? __Yes __No
__Originally __During course of project	__Check list __Formal Instrument __Observation __Other	a. (2) Was the procedure for evaluation implemented? __Yes __No	
b. Was provision made for continuous feedback? __Yes __No	b. What form did feedback assume? __Written __Oral __Both	b. Which method was more effective? __Written __Oral __Both	b. In which ways did feedback effect change? __Project __State __Local __National __Other
c. Was there sufficient flexibility in structure for evaluation? __Yes __No	c. How was flexibility provided for? __Administrative decision __Staff decision __Other (explain)	c. Was sufficient flexibility provided by: Administrative decision? __Yes __No Staff decision? __Yes __No Other? __Yes __No	c. What changes were arrived at administratively? Through the staff? Other?

D-6 STANDARD: Effect in Local Education Agency(ies)

The relationships between the project and its sponsoring and/or cooperating LEA(s) and its subsequent long-term effects in the LEA(s) must be assessed in order to determine general project effectiveness.

Self-rating Score _____

C	I	P	O
a. Was the project conceived jointly by the sponsoring and cooperating LEA(s)? __Yes __No	a. Was sufficient time provided for planning? __Yes __No	a. (1) Is the project following the design? __Yes __No a. (2) Has cooperation continued successfully? __Yes __No	a. Is the project meeting the objectives as originally conceived? __Yes __No
b. Were policies initially established to govern the relationship of the sponsoring LEA(s) and/or cooperating LEA(s)? __Yes __No	b. (1) Were these policies designed jointly? __Yes __No b. (2) Were these policies agreed upon jointly? __Yes __No	b. (1) Are these policies adhered to? __Yes __No b. (2) How are the policies enforced?	b. How have the policies helped in the carrying out of the project?
c. Were provisions made to evaluate and modify, where necessary, relationships and policies? __Yes __No	c. Was an instrument designed for this evaluation? __Yes __No	c. (1) Was the instrument used? __Yes __No	c. (1) Were relationships and policies effective? __Yes __No
		c. (1) Were modifications indicated? __Yes __No	c. (2) Did the modification improve the relationship? __Yes __No __N/A

D-6 STANDARD: Effect in Local Education Agency(ies) [continued]

Self-rating Score _____

C	I	P	O
d. Has the provision for local adoption of the effective programs been established? __Yes __No		d. Is the project evaluation being presented in a usable form for the local decision-making body? __Yes __No	d. Has the local education agency indicated a willingness to adopt effective programs? __Yes __No __By board action __Present financial commitment __Increasing support __Definite plan for future commitment If the answer to the above question is no, how will effective programs be continued? __Other grants __Private funds __Program discontinued

D-7 STANDARD: Project and Community and Long-Term Effects

Long-term effects of the project upon the community should be noted to attain an overall view of the effectiveness of the project.

Self-rating Score _____

C   I   *   P   O

What long-range effects of the project have been noted such as:

__Conservation legislation
__Resource use behavior
 if public
__Increased concern for
 maintenance and pres-
 ervation of public and
 private property.

CHAPTER 19	
C. M. Lindvall	**THE TASK OF EVALUATION IN CURRICULUM DEVELOPMENT PROJECTS: A RATIONALE AND CASE STUDY**[1]

A problem of major concern to many educators is that of how the effectiveness of new curricula and other innovations can best be determined.[2] The purpose of this paper is to describe a basic rationale for such evaluation procedures and to discuss certain steps associated with this rationale, as these have evolved as part of a large-scale curriculum development project.

The Curriculum Continuity Demonstration

The Curriculum Continuity Demonstration (CCD), a joint project of the Pittsburgh Schools and the University of Pittsburgh,[3] has had as its goal the development and demonstration of an educational program which will be so co-ordinated from grade to grade as to constitute a true continuum for the student as he progresses from kindergarten to college. As a result of the CCD work, over twenty secondary level courses and an essentially complete elementary curriculum are now being given a careful trial in selected Pittsburgh schools. A key aspect of this program has been an attempt to provide a continuing evaluation of the materials and courses produced.

The Initial Evaluation Program

The initial steps in evaluating CCD courses were employed with a limited number of high-school courses, the first ones to be given an actual trial in the classroom. These steps involved the use of some rather conventional instruments and procedures and had some obvious limitations, but also provided much worthwhile information in the early stages of the course development work. Although these steps were largely superseded as the evaluation program progressed, they are described here to provide necessary background for the rationale and procedures that eventually evolved.

1. Use of standardized tests.—Students in each of these classes were given a carefully selected standardized test as an end-of-course exam. One reason for this step was the feeling that some of the evidence concerning pupil achievement should be obtained through the use of an instrument that was largely independent of the judgments of the project staff. The use of these tests also made provision, in the norm group for the test, for a type of comparison group. In addition, by examining pupil performance on subscores and on individual items, it was possible to determine certain strengths and weaknesses produced by a course. This was of particular value at a stage when a course was being studied for purposes of revision.

2. Use of locally developed tests.—In view of the recognized limitations in the validity of the standardized tests for use with these new and unique courses, the original evaluation plans of the CCD also involved the construction of local tests. Typically, these tests were developed by the teacher of the course working with selected members of the curriculum development committee. Results from these tests were also used in analyzing strengths and weaknesses of the new courses.

3. Use of "comparison" or "control" groups.—The original evaluation plan also called for comparing achievement of pupils in CCD classes with that of pupils in "conventional" classes. One simple aspect of this involved an examination of the performance of the CCD pupils with respect to the norms on the standardized tests. In some cases it also involved a more direct comparison of the test scores, both on published and locally developed tests, of pupils in the experimental class with scores of pupils taking the same course in a non-CCD class. Here the rather predictable results occurred in that CCD pupils scored significantly higher on the specially developed tests while the comparison pupils scored significantly higher on the published tests. That is, the courses were designed to achieve different immediate goals and the pupils in each group performed at a higher level on the test which covered the goals of their particular course.

4. Use of expert observers.—The final aspect of the evaluation effort involved the selection of qualified persons to provide subjective assessments of the various courses. From one to three persons were selected to examine each course. Each person studied the course outline and related materials, visited the class to see it in action, and interviewed teachers and pupils. Each expert or team of experts then prepared a written report discussing the strong and weak points of the course and making suggestions for changes in content or procedure. Suggestions obtained in this way have proved to be of great value to the project.

It will be recognized that in employing the above steps the evaluation staff of the CCD was using some rather typical procedures. While these steps provided worthwhile information, a reassessment of the evaluation program at the end of the first two years of the project convinced the staff that new directions were indicated. This reassessment started with some rather elementary thinking concerning what is involved in the evaluation of any type of educational innovation. This led to the development of a simple and basic rationale which, in turn, provided the basis for revised evaluation efforts. The following sections describe the results of this re-thinking.

A Rationale for Planning an Evaluation Program

Any evaluation effort is an attempt to provide answers to some question or questions. Unfortunately, in too many such efforts data are obtained and presented and comparisons made before the questions to be answered are clearly specified. From a re-examination of our CCD evaluation program and from contacts with persons attempting similar assessments in other projects, the staff became convinced that the starting point for new plans had to be a consideration of the basic question involved in any evaluation effort.

The Evaluator's Question

Phrased in general terms, which would permit its application to a variety of types of innovations and situations, the comprehensive question to which an evaluator would ultimately be seeking an answer can be posed as follows:

THE QUESTION: Does *this innovation*, in the *situation* with which we are concerned, do *what is desired better* than *alternatives?*

In any specific case the evaluator might well be concerned with only a part of this question. He might, for example, be seeking an answer to the question, "Does this innovation do what is desired?" That is, can a given teaching procedure produce certain results? In such situations the broad question, including the concern for comparisons with possible alternatives, may ultimately be of concern, but before this step is appropriate good answers must be obtained concerning smaller parts of the total question.

The implications of the evaluator's question can probably best be seen if it is analyzed in terms of the follownig component parts:

(1) Does *this innovation*—
(2) in the *situation* with which we are concerned—
(3) do *what* is desired—
(4) *better*—
(5) than *alternatives?*

The following sections examine each of these parts.

(1) Does *this innovation*—A first focus of attention must be on determining exactly what it is that is being evaluated. Just what does the innovation include? This may be a particular problem in situations where new instructional materials are being tried out and where the use of them requires major changes in method of presentation. If these accompanying changes in method are not included in a description of the innovation, any results may be erroneously ascribed solely to the new materials. Another illustration of this problem is found in many recent assessments of programmed instruction where, in ascribing either positive or negative results to programmed instruction per se, the evaluator overlooks the fact that the program may deal with somewhat different content, or differ from the comparison materials in many ways in addition to the fact that it is programmed.

(2) in the *situation*—All too frequently, efforts in evaluation tend to ignore the limitations placed on the generalizations that can be made from a study by the restricted nature of the tryout situation. In the development of an innovation, it is frequently essential that the first trial be carried out in a very limited situation. The person developing a teaching-machine program typically conducts his first trial of a sequence of frames with only one student. In the CCD work the first tryout of any course was with one class. The essential point is that, whether the trial being assessed is this type of preliminary effort or a later one involving broad-scale sampling, the evaluator should describe the situation quite clearly and not tempt readers to draw implications for situations that are quite different.

(3) do *what is desired*—Both parts (3) and (4) in our breakdown of the evaluator's question deal

with aspects of the criterion used. The first of these, considered here under "what is desired," may be thought of as centering on the time at which criterion data are to be gathered. Frequently, or even typically, we concern ourselves with immediate criteria. We specify the abilities a pupil should have when he has completed a course and then use an end-of-course examination to assess these. This may be the ideal type of criterion in some cases. However, with many innovations, the real changes they are designed to produce are expected to manifest themselves at a much later time. A new high-school math curriculum may have as its main purpose the better preparation of pupils to do the type of thinking required in college math. If an innovation is primarily intended to produce more ultimate changes of this type, then the evaluator should attempt to obtain information on these more ultimate criteria. Still another alternative is the use of intervening criteria. For example, in assessing a new curriculum it may be important to obtain data concerning teacher performance and pupil behavior while the new materials are being used in the classroom. For one thing, such evidence may serve as an important basis for any needed revisions. Determining the time when it is most meaningful to obtain criterion data is a key step in spelling out what an innovation is expected to produce.

(4) *better*—The second aspect of the question of the criterion to be employed concerns the type of data to be used. Probably the most common type of data is the level of achievement attained. However, it must be recognized that the real purpose of many innovations is to enable pupils to attain a standard level of achievement in a more efficient manner. In this case the real criterion may be the time needed to reach this level. Other innovations may have as their goal that of making the teacher's task somewhat simpler. If this is so, it is essential that the criterion involve some assessment of change in what the teacher must do. Too frequently, evaluation efforts are centered on measures of achievement, when the real purpose of the innovation is something quite different.

(5) than *alternatives*—As suggested previously, an evaluator may not be concerned with comparing an innovation with alternatives. This may be true because no true alternatives are available. In our CCD effort, it was decided that it was meaningless to compare the achievement of pupils in most of the new courses with that of pupils in "conventional" classes because, although the courses had the same names, the real objectives of instruction were quite different. In other cases, the true concern of the innovator may be to concentrate on the improvement of

his innovation. For example, many persons doing basic work with programmed instruction feel that so much remains to be done in investigating the most effective procedures for programming that it is entirely premature to compare this method of instruction with more standard procedures.

When it is decided that meaningful comparative studies can be made, the evaluator is faced with the need for a careful identification of the alternatives so that the data obtained can be interpreted in terms of exactly what it is that is being compared. He must also take into consideration the various possible sources of error that must be of concern in any experimental or quasi-experimental design.[4]

The Revised CCD Evaluation Program

The re-examination of the evaluation program of the CCD in the light of the rationale described in the preceding section served to make obvious some of the weaknesses associated with the steps that had been followed. As a result it was decided that, for the immediate future, evaluation efforts would be most fruitful if they were centered on only a part of the evaluator's total question, that of "Does this innovation do what is desired?" Phrased in terms specific to our project, the question was, "Does each CCD course as taught in the demonstration schools produce end-of-course pupil achievement in line with specified objectives?" We wished to be able to say something quite specific about the type and extent of pupil achievement produced by a given course. As has been suggested, this decision was based partly on the realization that there were no true alternatives against which the CCD courses could be compared. It was also a result of the feeling that the innovations, the new courses, needed further definition and further refinement. It was felt that a concentration on the above question would contribute to meeting both of these needs.

In line with the centering of attention on this question, the first step in the new evaluation effort involved a more careful and detailed specification of the objectives of each of the CCD courses. Although the original development of each course had included considerable attention to the defining of objectives in behavioral terms,[5] it was felt that such lists of objectives did not involve sufficient detail or specificity. To develop the needed lists of objectives, a small committee of two or three members was assigned to each course. Each such list was to be so comprehensive that it could be said that the person who could exhibit all of the abilities listed would have command of all that the course was intended to teach. Also, each objective was to be so specific that there could be no disagreement between competent persons as to how a student would exhibit the ability involved. The resulting lists of objectives run from about ten to forty typewritten pages. These lists not only serve now as a basis for the development of evaluation instruments, but also serve as supplements to course outlines in providing a more specific definition of a course.

The second step in the revised evaluation effort was to develop new tests and evaluation devices. Each small committee assigned to this task was instructed to produce a device that would assess a representative sample of the objectives for a course. The resulting devices involved objective-type tests, essay questions, and certain project-type assignments.

The obvious next step was to administer these tests to the students and to analyze the results. For the most part, these devices were used as end-of-course examinations. The results obtained were, in each case, given a detailed analysis by the person teaching the course. This analysis included a determination of the percentage of students passing each item as well as information on discriminating capacity. A major purpose of the analysis was to alert the teacher and the project staff to certain strengths and weaknesses of each course.

The final, formal step in the revised evaluation program was to make use of the information yielded by the foregoing steps. The reports prepared from the analysis of test results were used as a basis for course revision and changes in teaching tactics as well as for the development of improved evaluation devices.

Conclusion

Certainly these evaluation steps that were developed for the CCD should not be considered as a final answer as to what steps will be most effective in the assessment of a curriculum innovation. These were found to be useful for the present needs of the CCD program. Other programs will probably require different steps. However, it is suggested that the rationale presented here, or some modification of it which can serve to center attention on the exact question being asked, should be useful in guiding the thinking of persons responsible for any of a number of types of evaluation efforts. Such efforts, together with efforts to attack most educational problems, can best be undertaken, not by jumping to employ whatever devices, techniques, and procedures seem to be in vogue, but by a careful and painstaking analysis of the task involved.

NOTES

1. A paper presented at the annual meeting of the American Educational Research Association in Chicago, Illinois, February 10-13, 1965. The Curriculum Continuity Demonstration, one phase of which served as a basis for this paper, has, during its first five years, been partially supported by a grant from the Fund for the Advancement of Education.
2. See Lee J. Cronbach, "Course Improvement Through Evaluation," *Teachers College Record,* LXIV (May, 1963):672-83; and Robert Glaser, "Instructional Technology and the Measurement of Learning Outcomes," *American Psychologist,* August, 1963.
3. See C. M. Lindvall, "The Importance of Specific Objectives in Curriculum Development," in C. M. Lindvall, ed., *Defining Educational Objectives* (Pittsburgh: University of Pittsburgh Press, 1964).
4. See Donald T. Campbell and Julian C. Stanley, "Experimental and Quasi-Experimental Designs for Research on Teaching," in N. L. Gage, ed., *Handbook of Research on Teaching* (Chicago: Rand McNally & Co., 1963).
5. *Ibid.*

CHAPTER 20

Richard R. Schutz

EXPERIMENTATION RELATING TO FORMATIVE EVALUATION[1]

I am going to restrict my remarks to one-half of the title of the symposium. I'll be talking about development strategies and instructional improvement and will not attempt to deal with research or theory refinement. Research and theory go together like development and improvement. The distinction is primarily in terms of the outcomes generated. Research produces refined knowledge; development produces usable products. Research seeks the answer to the question "How now?" Development seeks the answer to the question "How to?"

I make these distinctions because they pertain directly to my topic: Experimentation relating to formative evaluation. Scriven, you will recall, introduced the term "formative evaluation" to describe the evaluation of educational programs that are still in some stage of development. Formative evaluation contrasts with summative evaluation, the evaluation of finally developed educational programs. The product of formative evaluation activities is expected to be an improved instructional program, while the product of summative evaluation is normally a set of descriptive statements about a single program or about the relative merits of two or more programs. An extensive methodology is associated with summative evaluation, since researchers have had extensive experience in comparing two or more existing programs. Formative evaluation, however, is a different matter.

At present, formative evaluation methods have much the same status as the invisible needle and thread used by the tailors in the "Emperor's New Clothes." For a variety of social, political, and economic reasons, educational researchers have derived satisfaction in viewing their efforts as contributing to educational improvement. But the inescapable fact is that reliable ways of effecting educational improvement have yet to be iden-

tified either by researchers, manufacturers, or school personnel.

J. M. Stephens, in his highly provocative little book *The Process of Schooling*, summarizes the summaries of experiments on instruction over the last fifty years. This is a disturbing treatise which I highly recommend. Stephens comments upon "the remarkable constancy of educational results in the face of widely differing deliberate approaches." He goes on to state bluntly, "Every so often we adopt new approaches or new methodologies and place our reliance on new panaceas. At the very least we seem to chorus new slogans. Yet the academic growth within the classroom continues at about the same rate, stubbornly refusing to cooperate with the bright new dicta emanating from the conference room." A spectacularly elegant NSD.

Stephens' prescription is to relax and enjoy the powerful and pervasive educational forces which apparently work well apart from any deliberate direction. Get a few adults, put them in contact with kids for as much time as possible, and count on spontaneous factors to take care of everything else.

I find this line of reasoning a very threatening but compelling argument—*things being what they are*. The aim of development, however, is to insure that things do *not* remain as they are. Development seeks to produce materials and methods called *products* which can be used to produce a specified outcome. That the desired outcome *can* be produced is always a matter of faith while the development is in progress.

Educational development is at present in a state of conceptual deprivation. All of the terms available for describing instruction have reference to instructional operation systems—keeping school—

1. Presented at the Annual Meeting of the American Educational Research Association, Chicago, Illinois, February, 1968.

rather than to instructional development. For example, grade and subject matter dimensions and pupil characteristics are useful in defining school operations. To indicate that someone is producing a high school American history program, for example, appears to communicate a good deal. However, the information relates almost exclusively to use of the instruction in the schools. It indicates very little about the instruction per se and indicates nothing about the operations involved in producing the instructional materials and procedures.

The principle dimension traditionally manipulated in instructional development has been subject matter content—a la the new math, science, and social studies "curriculum development" projects. Formative evaluation efforts have been highly content oriented. Measurement results have been used as a basis for making decisions dealing with the sequencing of substantive concepts and for modifying the instructional verbiage associated with a given concept. When the measurement results are not easily interpreted, one of two events takes place. (1) The proposed outcomes of the instruction are modified, or (2) the goals are redefined in more general or abstract terms to facilitate agreement about the interpretations of the measurement efforts. But substitutions in instructional goals should not be confused with improved attainment of these goals. Nor is it defensible to retreat behind a mystique of complicated and intangible criteria.

If one takes a product-oriented approach, the criteria for gauging instructional improvement become straightforward and the application of formative evaluation procedures more meaningful. Remember that we have defined a product as consisting of the materials and accompanying procedures to accomplish specified instructional outcomes. In this setting we are concerned with three criteria dimensions: Reliability; Utility; and Cost.

We must be concerned first with the *reliability* of the product in accomplishing the objective. How well does it work? Here we are considering such things as dependability of the outcome, generalizability or exportability to a variety of locales, and with replicability. Until an effect can be produced with an acceptable degree of dependability, there is really nothing for a potential user to evaluate. Thus reliability of effect is an important criterion.

A second set of criteria involves *utility*. How useful is the result? Here we can distinguish between social utility, which involves an outcome that is useful at present, and instructional utility which involves an outcome that provides a base for future educational attainment. To be useful, a given outcome must have clearly demonstrable social and/or educational utility.

When we are able to produce an instructional effect with a given degree of dependability and it is judged to be worth producing, then we must necessarily be concerned about *cost*. Here we are talking about either the time or the money required to produce a given result. Any other form of cost can be transformed into one of these two dimensions.

It's only when one is able to produce useful outcomes with a reasonable degree of reliability that it makes any sense to talk about cost benefit analysis. But with reliability, utility, and cost targeted you can very reasonably talk about both cost efficiency and cost effectiveness. Cost efficiency involves the ratio of reliability to cost; cost effectiveness involves the ratio of both reliability and utility to cost.

Education has yet to cope adequately with the first set of criteria—reliability of effect. We simply lack the wherewithal at present to dependably accomplish the attainment of the educational outcomes for which the schools have assumed responsibility. At present we can at best plan strategies which have some likelihood of leading to the improvement desired. Several general alternative strategies can be formulated which themselves will provide the basis for a grand experiment. I shall limit my considerations to the experimentation possible within a single such general strategy.

The strategy is derived by analogy from engineering; underscore analogy. Analogy is the weakest form of argument, but the relationship at present between educational and engineering development is analogous at best.

The foundation of the strategy is planned iteration—a set of sequenced and coordinated activities which through careful management cumulate to effect the improvement desired. That's fine. But, what do we iterate? Or, what should we iterate? Well, we have to start with what we've got. Here we can identify several manipulable dimensions of instruction. For example:

The *instructional media*—at present this is typically the teacher or printed matter, although a wide spectrum of auditory and visual presentation mechanisms are possible.

The *pacing mode*—at present instruction is group paced, although various degrees of differentiation toward individual pacing can be identified.

The *monitoring contingency*—at present the attainment of instructional outcomes is norm-referenced, if contingent at all. That is, one lesson typically follows another, irrespective of whether all learners have attained the outcomes the lesson was designed to produce.

The final example of possible dimensions is the *monitoring agent.* At present, this is the teacher. The teacher is responsible for insuring that the instruction is sequenced, coordinated with other activities. But the pupil himself could make a contribution in the area as could other pupils, parents, computers, etc.

Describing current school practices using the four dimensions of (1) Instructional Media; (2) Pacing Mode; (3) Monitoring Contingency; and (4) Monitoring Agent, formal public education at the present time can be characterized as print mediated, group paced, managed against relative norms, and teacher-based. There is good reason to believe that instruction which is multiple mediated, individually paced, managed against objectives, and computer-based would be much more effective. My hunch is that it will be at least a decade before such a system is operationally feasible. But this hinges on the referents for the term feasible. From a researcher's point of view, any phenomenon which can be conceptualized and potentially manipulated is regarded as feasible. If the development does not occur easily, the researcher honestly believes that the persons responsible for translating his efforts into usable instructional products and operating the instructional program have hopelessly fouled-up the concepts. The developer, on the other hand, finds himself in an awkward "Mr. In-between" role. He views the researcher's ideas as perpetually incomplete and inadequate as a development guide. At the same time, he necessarily views current school operations as obsolete since his efforts are directed toward improving it. School personnel, for their part, forever find the present work of both the researcher and the developer unrelated to immediate everyday problems. Each is accurate. Moreover, this is not an undesirable state of affairs, so long as it is recognized; it provides the basis for an efficient division of professional labor.

How is this educational improvement to be effected? I should like to suggest two concurrent and compatible tactical approaches. Each recognizes the present print-mediated, group paced, weakly managed, and teacher-based instructional system. One approach involves a series of straightforward trial-revision cycles to sharpen up the accomplishment of given instructional outcomes, working within the boundaries of the present instructional system. An analogy is provided by the modifications in the Volkswagen annually to improve its performance in specified ways. The second approach involves a major manipulation of a system dimension *per se* which produces a new *generation* of the product. Following through on the automobile analogy, this might be an electric car.

Each of these two approaches involves a convergent iterative methodology. Let me mention the sequence we find useful at the Southwest Regional Laboratory in pursuing the first approach It involves first the preparation of *instructional specifications.* This is a set of sequenced statements of desired instructional outcomes accompanied by specifications of requisite entry behavior, learner activities, specific conditions under which practice must be given to assure that appropriate behavior does and does not occur, and specifications for testing if the outcome is attained.

Component preparation and tryout involves the initial production and tryout of component methods and materials which relate to various aspects of the instructional specifications. These tryouts involve "mock-ups" designed to reflect the critical features of the aspect of instruction about which further information is needed before it can be considered a reliable prototype component.

Product preparation and tryout involves combining and extending the prototype components into instruction suitable for classroom use. The objective is to produce methods and materials which are attractive to pupils, manageable by teachers, at as low a cost and requiring as little instructional time as possible. The product tryout is conducted by regular school personnel under standard school conditions.

Each of these stages involves a continuous sequence of trial-revision iterations to successively eliminate the defects in the product and to increase its effectiveness. The sequenced instructional objectives provide the criterion against which base-rate performance data can be generated. This provides an assurance that the changes introduced cumulate in improvement and avoids expensive unevaluated modifications which fail to improve overall performance.

The principles of scientific experimentation—for example those discussed by Campbell and Stanley under the rubrics internal and external validity—are highly relevant at each stage of the cycle. But, development is concerned with the management of variance rather than the analysis of variance. The comparisons of interest involve variations and refinements introduced sequentially over time rather than concurrently at a single time. Note that I'm not talking here of a time-series design in the Campbell-Stanley sense. Treatments A_1, A_2, etc., are compared sequentially in toto as each treatment is successively reviewed, refined, and recycled on fresh samples. Treatment A_2 always incorporates "the best" of A_1; A_3 the best of A_2; and so forth. If a given iteration yields worse rather than better results, one goes back to the pre-condition and reformulates the modification to be made. Our experience to date has been that this iterative approach does pay off.

So much for the first approach, effecting *cycles* of improvement. In effecting *generations* of improvement one is seeking to introduce a modification in at least one system dimension with the objective of concomitantly increasing effectiveness along other dimensions. This involves complex development work that is completely removed from the refinement cycles within a present generation.

Consider the instructional monitoring dimensions. The Southwest Regional Laboratory, in conjunction with System Development Corporation, is currently engaged in the development of a computer-based instructional management system. Here the immediate concern is *not* with all instructional functions, but simply in developing workable procedures to provide the teacher with frequent information concerning the progress of each student with respect to the instructional outcomes of interest to the teacher together with suggestions for activities which are consistent with the student's performance.

Thus in contrast to computer-assisted instruction system, we are seeking a technologically less sophisticated but more feasible computer-managed instruction system. The computer technology problems are being solved using the same iterative strategy outlined above. However, rather than pupil performance, the criteria involve teacher management performance. Although live classes are being used in developing the system, there is no expectation that pupil performance will be improved at this point. However, when the system is functioning adequately, the greater monitoring capability it will provide is expected to improve performance sufficiently to introduce a new generation of instructional effectiveness. Analogous programmatic efforts in media and pacing are also being conducted by the Laboratory.

In sum, educational development appears to be as vast and promising an enterprise as nuclear or space development. Just as engineering enterprises find it necessary to use all existing relevant knowledge plus, so does educational development. With this effort the concept of formative evaluation will be clothed with a technology of instructional product development. This is at once a challenging and threatening enterprise for those who become involved in it. The "produce or perish" imperative associated with educational development is an even tougher task master than the "publish or perish" imparative of academia and the "profit or perish" imperative of business. However, it is an imperative which the education profession can ill afford to ignore, considering the tenor of the times. The frontier is there, with lots of wide open territory to be pioneered. If you are bright and brave, blast into it.

CHAPTER 21

Hulda Grobman

THE PLACE OF EVALUATION
IN A CURRICULUM STUDY

I should like to review some of the facets of evaluation as they have been reflected in the evaluation activities of the Biological Sciences Curriculum Study (BSCS) over the last five years. While many aspects of such an evaluation are standard to research on curriculum, others raise new problems which may be common to other curriculum project evaluation activities.

The BSCS was set up for the purpose of improving biology education. It was not set up for the purpose of evaluation. In the BSCS, the participants are primarily high school biology teachers and college research biologists. These are discipline people, and it is their project. As the evaluation helps them implement their program, fine. But evaluation must remain a service function, and only as it remains that can it continue. Evaluation is not an end in itself, and there are times when evaluation aims must be set aside, since they interfere with the major project objectives. (For example, it might be relevant to the evaluation to obtain I.Q. scores for test teachers or to request teacher salary information, but both of these might antagonize some of the cooperating teachers and so jeopardize the over-all study aims.)

What Does Evaluation Include?

Some people feel that evaluation is synonymous with quantification. That is, if you cannot measure it, it does not exist. Certainly quantification is desirable, and quite often possible. However, simply because one cannot quantify certain aspects of a curriculum does not mean that the evaluation is not a good one or that the curriculum is not doing what we hope it will do. Some day we may be able to measure some areas that now defy quantification, but we still can do a good evaluation job even if we cannot show statistical tables relevant to all project goals.

Of course, evaluation includes written tests. And these may be multiple-choice tests, essay tests, tab tests, individual one-to-one testing and follow-up testing at a later date. But in the BSCS it also includes observation of students; it includes teacher, student, parent and administrator interviews; reports by teachers and reviews by specialists. At some future point, it may include case studies and interaction studies.

One very useful evaluation tool was the teacher weekly "feedback" reports, using a separate sheet for comments on each chapter of text and each laboratory exercise. (In this way, teacher feedback could be filed by chapter or exercise, and the persons revising the materials could study several dozen comments on the text section or the lab exercise before starting their writing.) Naturally, working with feedback requires careful interpretation. For example, if teachers report that the tests are completely inadequate, it is important to know why they reach this view. Does the teacher object because the test items are ambiguous or mis-keyed? Or is the teacher looking for a direct-recall type of question when the authors are deliberately trying to test for ability to apply learnings to completely new situations? When a teacher reports that a laboratory exercise is not effective, it is important to know whether he has a laboratory in which the exercise could work; that is, are electricity, running water and gas outlets available?

Teacher feedback reports also provided a link of communication with teachers. And it is very important to read all of these promptly. The writers do not have a monopoly on good ideas and it is not only possible, but also probable that teachers will come up with useful ideas the writers never thought of. Furthermore, the feedback gives an idea of teacher pacing of the course, whether the teacher is actually using all the materials and using them in the requested sequence.

For example, one year, through teacher reports, the BSCS learned that a few teachers spent the entire first semester teaching one month's work, despite suggested schedules to the contrary; without some type of log such as could be obtained from the feedback report, semester test scores for students in such classes would be subject to serious misinterpretation. Often trouble spots can be cleared up before the teacher has further difficulty. Also, the teachers will know whether you read the feedback, since, despite instructions to the contrary, teachers ask questions in the feedback and if they do not get answers, they know you are ignoring the feedback.

The teacher reactions should not be underestimated. Unless the teachers find the material usable, the project cannot be successful in the long run. It may be a matter of lack of teacher preparation or insight rather than the fault of the new curriculum. Nevertheless, the situation must be corrected if the curriculum project is to find long-term success in actually improving curriculum in the schools.

BSCS staff and writers visit all BSCS test classrooms at some time during the year. This gives a kind of information difficult to obtain on written reports; it gives a perspective in which to place the teacher report, and also may provide information concerning the way in which BSCS is presented. It may be that the teacher is really teaching the old curriculum, using the new experimental book to do this. It may be that other factors supposedly built into the experimental situations are not, in fact, present in the situation, despite earlier written assurances that they would be. Visits to the classroom are really the only way the evaluator can be sure the situation required by the experimental design actually exists. This does not mean that the evaluator himself must visit classrooms. But someone fully cognizant of the implications of the experimental curriculum and the evaluation should.

Who Should Do the Evaluation?

Evaluation in a curriculum study could be something quite apart from the study; that is, it could be carried out by an independent evaluator. Or evaluation can be built into the study as one of the functions of the study. The problem of who should do the evaluation is related to the function of the evaluation. During the time the materials are in formative stages, the evaluation serves to tell the writers how successful their materials are and where changes are indicated. Later, evaluation serves to describe the new materials to others, and to compare them to other materials.

Having an independent evaluation would have the theoretical merit of lack of bias. However, during the years in which the curriculum is being prepared and the writers are dependent on it for direct feedback, the disadvantages would seem to outweigh the advantages. For the evaluation to be an effective part of the curriculum-building process, it is important that there be feedback to the writers in terms of the writers' objectives rather than of external criteria. Thus, there must be assurance that the instruments used in the evaluation reflect the objectives of the writers. This does not mean that there is no purpose served in using existing tests, whether or not these reflect the objectives. To give an existing test, say of writing skill, which reflects the objectives of the writers would have merit. To give a test in traditional biology materials, which does not reflect the intentions of the BSCS writers, would *not* give a reflection of the adequacy of the curriculum. But it could be useful in describing the differences in learnings of control and experimental students.

In its initial years, the BSCS had an external evaluation through a testing agency, and found that it was not possible for a third party to adequately appreciate and reflect the aims and objectives of the writers, while these are still in developmental stages. Thus, in the summer of 1961, a BSCS Evaluation Committee was set up of the persons in supervisory positions responsible for preparing the new materials. This Committee supervises the evaluation, and its subcommittee builds the evaluation instruments. This process accomplishes two things. First, it insures that the writers are satisfied with the criterion measures being used. In other words, the writers are put in a position where they either say, "Yes, this is the kind of learning skill or understanding we are concerned with. We will be satisfied if the students are able to answer this question." Or they must suggest alternatives. And, second, the process of constructing evaluation instruments helps the writers define their own objectives more precisely. While it is well and good to say that before starting to write curriculum materials the authors should have a list of aims and objectives, in actual practice this is extremely difficult and often leads to long and unprofitable semantic arguments or to generalized lists not useful for working purposes. On the other hand, the review of test items and preparation of new items is a good way of clearly pinpointing the objectives. Furthermore, from time to time, in writing test items the BSCS writers found that there were questions they wanted to ask but could not, because the curriculum materials did not cover them. Thus, the process of writing tests not only clarified aims but occasionally pinpointed shortcomings in the materials.

This does not mean that outside agencies cannot help. The BSCS has consistently called on psychometricians to advise and assist in its evaluation, and will continue to use them. But it does mean that the BSCS found need for closer integration of evaluation with curriculum building than was practical with an outside independent agency doing the evaluating. Evaluation then became an intradependent rather than an independent function.

One may ask, "Is an evaluation really an honest evaluation unless it is done by an independent source?" To assume that it is not, would be to question the validity and honesty of the majority of education research studies and the integrity of scientists in scientific endeavors.

When the new curriculum materials are in their final form would seem to be a useful time for an external evaluator to step in for some phases of evaluation. Certainly there should be an impartial look by outsiders at the new product, with the outside evaluator constructing instruments which reflect his own objectives. But these objectives should be very carefully defined. They may or may not be the same as the objectives of the curriculum study. They may stress aspects that were not stressed in the curriculum study, or they may attempt to measure aspects the curriculum study failed to measure. But the frame of reference and the value system for such an evaluation must be fully described. There have been all too many outside evaluators reporting that an experimental curriculum is or is not good because students do well or do not do well on a test that predates the curriculum and is unrelated to the objectives of the curriculum. If the curriculum really needs drastic change in biology, certainly the old test suitable for measuring learnings prior to the curriculum study cannot conceivably measure the new objectives. At the same time, it should be recognized that use of such older tests reflecting very different objectives may adversely affect the classroom teaching of the new curricula, since it may give teachers and students expectations which are traditional rather than new.

Thus, while the materials are in their formative stages, a curriculum study must have evaluation activities in order to feed back to the study information on whether the materials are teachable, what is effective and what is not effective and whether the curriculum is achieving its goals. This is information that is vital and can only be gotten by the study itself, since it is study personnel who know what is needed. After the materials are generally released, it would seem to me that two types of evaluation are indicated. First, the continuing need of the study to find out how and when the materials work, what are the weaknesses and what is reasonable expectation. And second, an external evaluation as a type of audit of the study evaluation and also to look at aspects not important to the curriculum builders, or not measured by them. Further, there is a need for an external comparison among new curricula where several exist. But the external evaluation is outside the jurisdiction of the curriculum study. Certainly others should take a critical look at one or more curricula in terms of sequence, combined effect, actual outcomes. Who does this and how are not the prerogatives of the curriculum project.

The Objectives of the New Curriculum

In planning an evaluation program, it is important to know what the new course is trying to do. One might ask the writers for a list of objectives. But it is difficult for people to verbalize about concrete objectives. It may not be until the course is actually written and the writers begin to write test items that they are able to focus more clearly on the verbalization of the objectives. And to compile a list of objectives simply to have a list is not going to help in getting on with the job.

If the evaluator is able to get such a list of objectives from the writers, it is a useful tool. But failure to get a list does not mean that the evaluation cannot progress. The objectives may be an emergent thing. And even if you start with a list, it will require modification. The BSCS now has a set of clearly defined objectives. These were not on hand before the writing conferences; rather, they emerged from speeches, from prepared statements circulated among the writers and the BSCS staff, from the introductory material in the books and from teacher materials. It was a matter of clarifying and pinpointing as time went on. The writers could look at test items and say, "This is what I mean." Or "This is not what I mean," even when they could not list aims in advance.

One of the problems of lists of objectives prepared in advance of the work is that they may not represent the real objectives. For example, today the battle cry among educators is "creativity." Everyone wants students to be creative. Or at least everyone says he wants students to be creative. But do we really want them to be creative? And if they are creative, do we reward or punish them? Creativity can be a nuisance. It delays classes. We do not get through the planned lesson. Do we really want students to ask, "Why?" "How do you know?" and "How can you prove it?" Do we want them to go off on ideas of their own? This is creativity, and it makes for a lot of trouble in the classroom.

It is easy to write the word "creativity" down on a list of aims, but unless the curriculum builders and the teachers really want creativity and are willing to put up with it when they get it, a measure of creativity as an outcome will not be relevant. Even if the writers really want to develop inquiring minds, do the tests they write reflect this? And do the experimental teachers also have this aim? For example, in a BSCS class when one youngster questioned the keyed answer on a teacher-made quiz, he was told, "Your answer is wrong because that isn't what the book says." The BSCS curriculum is intended to stress creativity, encouraging the student to bring his experience to bear on new situations; but this unfortunate teacher stressed an opposite process. Thus, when the evaluator comes in later to look for the development of creative thinking, the students will probably implement the type of behavior they have been rewarded for previously; that is, conformity. When the evaluator does not find the desired results, where does the fault lie? He needs enough information about the teaching process in this experimental school to be able to interpret his data adequately.

Selection of Test Sample and Sample Attrition

In selection of test sample, the aims of the materials must be considered. The BSCS attempted to prepare materials for the average tenth-grade student in the average school. Ideally one might say that to test materials, we need an accurate cross-section of America's schools, teachers and students. But there are many reasons why this is impractical and even undesirable. Whi'e various types of school situations were included in its experimental samples, the BSCS made no attempt to use a representative sample of schools and students in America.

While theoretically it might be well to try to accurately reflect the geographic distribution of school population in the United States, this was considered impractical. During several test years, the BSCS asked all test teachers to meet weekly to prepare feedback for the BSCS. We found that group feedback often varied from individual feedback or elaborated on different points. Thus it was a valuable adjunct to the evaluation. These weekly sessions were also valuable as an in-service training device, since teachers could help each other on difficulties, they furnished needed support for the individuals in the experimental situations and also teachers could share respon·i-bility for obtaining and preparing lab materials. For example, one teacher might take responsibility for collecting pond cultures, another for ordering a chemical available only in bulk and

sharing it with other teachers, etc. To utilize Test Center organizations meant that teachers had to be located in geographic clusters and so the sparsely populated areas of the country were under-represented. This did not seem to be a serious drawback, since there were enough of each kind of teaching situation to enable examination of use of materials in this environment. For example, there were a number of rural, urban and suburban schools; schools in most regions of the country; public and private sectarian and non-sectarian schools; laboratory schools, large and small schools; schools with excellent laboratory facilities and those where labs were almost non-existent; schools with large classes and those with small classes; and teachers with excellent preparation and those with little biology background.

Also, if one is to use volunteers, it should be recognized that it is generally the more able, more alert teacher who will volunteer. This, too, prevents getting an accurate cross section of the teaching population. On the other hand, the BSCS was not preparing a biology course to be used by a home economics teacher or a football coach. While the BSCS recognizes that all biology teachers do not have optimal preparation, we were concerned with whether the materials can be taught by most biology teachers. The BSCS was not concerned with the question of whether its materials can be taught by non-biology teachers. In a curriculum project, a decision must be made as to whether the goal will be materials for the lowest common denominator of teaching situations or whether a reasonable requisite in teacher competence and school situation should be set and the course materials based on this assumption. The latter was the choice made by the BSCS.

For testing purposes, the BSCS considered it necessary to have the same teacher throughout the year for two reasons. First, change of teacher introduces an additional variable. And, second, since the curriculum was new, and it was felt that without proper orientation it probably could not be presented to students in the intended fashion; test teachers were given a six-day pre-school orientation. If there were a change of experimental teachers during the year, the new teacher would not have had this orientation. (Some may say this orientation biases the results. However, it should be kept in mind that most teachers have been specifically oriented over many years for the conventional courses they have been teaching. Thus, why is it unfair to give an even briefer orientation to the new course? Further, not only is very new subject matter included in the experimental course—subject matter not generally included in the collegiate preparation of these teachers—but also the method of implementation to the course materials is considered by the BSCS to be at least as important as the written student materials. Unless teachers understand this, how can they teach the course successfully?)

The BSCS materials constitute a one-year course, and the BSCS was interested in the impact on students of the full course. Thus, only students in the course all year were considered in the statistical studies of achievement. (To identify students in the course all year, the BSCS uses the rosters of a beginning-of-the-year general ability test and an end-of-the-year achievement test.) The BSCS was not investigating the impact of the course on students who transferred in late or who transferred from BSCS Biology to traditional courses. While these are valid questions for some researcher, the task the BSCS set for itself was to build a one-year curriculum. And so evaluation was based on a full-year curriculum. Thus, we needed schools that had a relatively stable student body. To choose a school with more than fifty per cent student turnover in the year would not only deplete the study population but create learning situations far different from that for which the materials were designed, since the BSCS course consists of units which are cumulative rather than independent of each other. To include schools in a one-industry area, where cancellations of a single defense contract might result in wholesale exodus of workers and their families would also be shortsighted.

While certainly "large samples" of teachers and students are not necessary, what is an adequate sample? The answer, of course, depends on the questions to be answered. But also in setting up the research design for several BSCS classroom studies, we have found that despite care in initial selection, the sample attrition may be as high as a quarter of the teachers, not through any error in selecting sample or lack of desire of teachers and principals to cooperate, but through other factors. Some years the attrition has been far less, but we cannot depend on this and we have been unable to accurately estimate in advance what the attrition will be. Teachers transfer; they move during the year; they get sick; they have babies. One BSCS test year, many units of the U.S. Army Reserve were called up, and we lost teachers. Each winter there are a number of broken limbs; and husbands of biology teachers are transferred and the wife must go along.

If one is testing outside the geographical area with which one is intimately familiar, it is extremely difficult to determine the extent to which a school meets the research design criteria. For example, one may get commitments in advance that at least eighty per cent of the students will be at a particular grade level; or that teachers have had or will have a specific kind of preparation; or that only one teacher is involved; or that the teacher will have a minimum of three sections in that course at that grade level. But the actual teaching situation after school starts may not reflect this. In planning to test the BSCS Special Materials for lower ability students, principals and teachers signed an agreement that students assigned to the class for low-ability students would be tested in the spring and that no student above the fiftieth percentile on an ability test would be assigned to that class without specific justification. Many schools honored this commitment fully; others did not. There was no way of telling which schools failed to honor their commitments until after the start of school when the BSCS itself administered an ability test, and then it was too late to change the test sample. A hypothesis being tested was that the BSCS Special Materials were suitable for use in classes relatively homogeneous for general ability. One could test the effect in heterogeneous classes, but this was not the purpose of the BSCS study. The failure of schools to comply with prior commitments was not a matter of carelessness on the part of the BSCS, or lack of specificity in instructions to the schools. This simply happens in a free school system where the evaluator does not run the school; he must accept things as they are. In later studies, the BSCS can refuse to accept those schools which did not live up to past commitments; but nothing can be done to remedy the loss for the test year. And unless the sample is large enough to stand such attrition, the entire evaluation for the year can be jeopardized.

The problem of evaluating a full year curriculum is complicated by the practice in many high schools of scrambling classes at mid-year. This has happened even in schools where the BSCS had only one section of a new curriculum, radically different from what was taught in all other sections of the biology course at this grade level. In some schools, only five or six students of the original thirty-five were assigned to the same section (and curriculum) the second semester. While this problem would not occur in the elementary grades, it can be a serious one in the large junior and senior high schools. Why did the BSCS not ask the schools for continuity in class assignments? First, one must anticipate the situation, which we did not the first time it occurred. We expected, and I think not unreasonably, that if there is a one-year experimental sequence that is described as radically different from anything taught at that grade level before, the class would be kept relatively intact for the year. But in later years, with schools warned about this, the results will not necessarily be different. Schools are complicated administrative organizations and school personnel changes and commitments may be forgotten.

The BSCS had to select the experimental teachers in the spring in order to give them pre-school training and also to have the beginning-of-the-year test in the schools by the first of September. But there is considerable last minute teacher turnover from April to September. Teachers are transferred; there may be programming difficulties requiring shifts of teachers; the last minute a teacher in a related subject may drop out and the experimental teacher may be assigned to that other subject. And so new, untrained teachers appear. Thus, violating the research design.

The BSCS even encountered problems related to Spanish-speaking Cuban students. One year, we learned rather indirectly that there were Cuban students with no English scheduled into BSCS experimental classes; this meant that, without our knowledge, we might have been testing BSCS Biology with students who did not have mastery of the English language. Granted this may be a worthwhile research study, but it is not a suitable study during the feasibility period of the BSCS and it was not the intent of the BSCS to study this. And the school system which had assured us of its eagerness to cooperate, which had made promises in order to be accepted in the program, had not even advised us of this situation.

In a study which uses schools within a limited distance from its headquarters, there may be considerable familiarity with the schools and school systems, and it might be easier to anticipate these kinds of problems and avoid them. However, using a larger geographic area for experimental teachers, the sample should certainly be large enough to take some of this type of attrition into account.

It is certainly helpful for a new curriculum if the experimental teachers have interns during the year, since this is a way of introducing new teachers to the new curriculum and preparing them to teach it. However, particularly when an intern arrives in the middle of the school year, this can create an extremely difficult situation. Some interns have never seen nor heard of the BSCS materials before they arrive at the high school; they do not have time to read the first semester's materials which the students have already covered, and so they are thrust into a teaching situation which is completely strange. Certainly experimental teachers should be encouraged to have interns, but there should be a close liaison with the college sending interns, so that before leaving the college they are familiar with the materials and rationale, and read at least as much of the materials as the students have already covered. This may seem to be an elementary observation; however, there are high

schools that have used BSCS Biology for four years where interns from the local colleges continue to come to the internship post without ever having seen the BSCS books and having had little or nothing in their collegiate preparation to prepare them for teaching BSCS Biology.

Selection of a Control Group

The BSCS is funded primarily through the National Science Foundation. As a recipient of public funds, it has the responsibility to make full information concerning its activities widely available. Further, through such public information programs it is possible to enlist the aid of more persons in preparing the new curricular materials. And, by keeping persons interested in biological education informed, when the materials finally were ready for general release, they found a more sympathetic audience than would have been the case had there not been the advance information. However, the more successful the curriculum venture in this regard, the more problems of contamination of the control group.

For example, in the BSCS 1960-61 and 1961-62 evaluation, visitors to schools in which there was only one BSCS teacher reported seeing materials related to BSCS experiments in non-BSCS classrooms. The other biology teachers had seen an interesting experiment in the one BSCS class, mimeographed it and used it in conventional classrooms. Because of this experience, in 1962-63, it was decided to draw control classes only from those schools where no classroom sets of BSCS Biology had been sold, and often from cities where no classroom sets of books had been sold. Despite such a careful check, when questioned on an end-of-school year questionnaire, over one-quarter of the control group teachers reported that they were using "some BSCS materials" in the classroom, and so it was necessary to drop them because of contamination.

Granted an uncontaminated control group, the problems do not disappear. What instruments can be used to measure achievement of control and experimental students? In biology, the goals of the new materials are so radically different from those of the existing curricula that existing tests are not pertinent, and the measure suitable for the new curricula are not relevant for the conventional classes. Thus, the findings using such instruments are a foregone conclusion. Each group will do best on the test related to its curriculum. The BSCS administered a conventional and BSCS test to control and experimental groups, and naturally the control group did better on the conventional test and the experimental group did better on the experimental test. (Possibly the experimental group did too well on the conventional test. Perhaps students could not have done this well unless the BSCS experimental teachers had taught considerable non-BSCS materials, since as many as one-third of the items in the conventional test—and these were factual items—could not have been answered on the basis of information included in the BSCS materials.) To administer a test only on those materials or subjects which conventional and experimental courses have in common again distorts the perspective of the course and of student achievement.

There may be new courses—such as the BSCS tenth-grade biology course for the lower ability students—which do not replace or parallel any existing course. These are simply new materials taught to students who heretofore would not have taken a regular biology course. No tests exist, and no parallel courses exist to provide a basis of comparison. Here, no attempt is being made by the BSCS to set up a regular control group. Students are being tested before, during and after the course, and their progress will be described. Data are available on some of the instruments on classes of average students to give a view of what average performance is. But no meaningful comparison of learnings with a control group is possible. This type of situation is discussed by Lee J. Cronbach (1963).

Even where a control group is feasible, the problems of matching on significant variables raises problems sufficiently great as to make comparisons precarious. Since BSCS includes more than materials in a set of books but also a method of teaching, it is unlikely that one teacher can teach an experimental and control group without contamination. Further, the chore of preparing two different courses instead of one and of setting up different laboratories for each class precludes using the same teacher in both control and experimental groups. And we find contamination in the same school. If we avoid the same teacher and the same school for matching teacher, what should we match for? Until the materials have been tested in the schools, no one knows what the significant variables are. Where materials are being developed and evaluated simultaneously, there is not time for extensive testing to determine variables before making a comparison. And if we wait until we have all the information on this, the degree of possible contamination has increased. For example, in BSCS, we have identified six variables which account for seventy-five per cent of the variance in BSCS student achievement on BSCS tests (Grobman).* We have not yet been able to account for the remainder of the variance. Possibly we will be able to identify other factors as time goes on. But in the meantime, possibly one-fifth to one-fourth of the biology teachers in the United

States have attended some type of preparation to teach BSCS Biology. Thousands of speeches have been given about the BSCS and articles on the BSCS have appeared not only in science teaching journals, but in biology journals and virtually every education journal of large circulation. The BSCS NEWSLETTER has had a peak circulation of 35,000. (There is an estimated total of 35,000 biology teachers in the United States.) How could an uncontaminated control be found now or in future years? And to compare BSCS teachers with teachers using some BSCS techniques or materials is not a real comparison of BSCS with what happened before BSCS. And how would one distinguish between those BSCS teachers not fully implementing the course and those non-BSCS teachers using "some" BSCS materials.

Possibly the more functional method of selecting a control would be to select teachers a year in advance of the testing of the new materials, and to thoroughly test students of these teachers for one year while conventional materials are being taught. And then to use these same teachers the following year with the experimental materials. Granted classes change in composition from year to year, certainly this change is less than the differences that exist between schools, and it would eliminate the teacher variable. The possibility of contamination would not exist. And the Hawthorne Effect, if any, would be the same for both years.

The Hawthorne Effect

The question has been raised on a number of occasions as to whether the outcomes indicated by evaluation in the curriculum studies have simply been the result of the Hawthorne Effect rather than of a better curriculum; that is, the result of an extra effort by teachers simply because they participated in an experiment. I have several reactions here which may be pertinent. First, in school systems today there is so much experimentation going on, that there may be a negative Hawthorne Effect to an experimental project. One principal, whose school was using BSCS Biology, reported that he was glad he had BSCS this year because his parents expected him to have an experiment going every year and he was running low on ideas; quite understandably, the teachers in this school might look with a somewhat jaundiced eye on the idea of experimentation. Furthermore, not all the teachers who "volunteered" for BSCS were actually volunteers. In one county, the word came down from the central office that every biology teacher in the county

*Hulda Grobman, Student Performance in New High School Biology Program. *Science*, 143, 3603, 265-266.

was to volunteer for the BSCS work, and everyone did; again, one might expect something less than a positive attitude toward the new curriculum materials among these "volunteers."

On the other hand, certainly the BSCS teachers as a group were extremely enthusiastic about the BSCS, and virtually all teachers asked to participate for a second or third year during the experimental period. This apparently amounted to a personal commitment to the materials which they were helping to develop. It was clear that teachers—most of them for the first time—felt their ideas were being sought after honestly and respected. This BSCS procedure of involving many people in curriculum building has been recommended for many years in modern curriculum books. But most of the biology teachers who worked with the BSCS had never developed their own classroom materials, or had a hand in developing them. These teachers had generally used standard texts and, granted they supplemented these from other sources, their courses were pretty much regimented by the standard presentation common to the biology textbooks that had been generally available. Is the positive attitude resulting from this honest participation in the BSCS program and seeing his own recommendations implemented in a new curriculum a Hawthorne Effect on the teacher or is it something else?

What Kind of Outcome Should One Expect from an Evaluation?

First, it is important to recognize that the tests built by the evaluators and writers may not seem applicable or appropriate to the teachers. Teachers are used to a very direct test of recall and direct application, where answers to questions are to be found unmistakenly in the book. Questions which go into the higher cognitive levels may appear to the teachers to be unfair or not relevant. The BSCS had many complaints about the tests from new teachers the first and second year. When the same or similar test questions were asked in later years, these teachers felt that the tests had improved; probably the teachers were simply getting more used to this type of testing. This negative reaction to BSCS tests was not limited to high school teachers. One college reviewer of BSCS tests commented that the tests were not fair since "the answers to the items cannot be found in the book."

How large must a difference on testing be to be educationally significant? Many of the writers of the BSCS materials were convinced that the BSCS materials were outstanding and were having a tremendous impact. They could only conclude that the testing procedures were simply not adequate because the differences between control and experimental groups were a matter of some four points or one standard deviation on a forty-item test. These writers felt that the BSCS courses were so revolutionary that the difference should be of far greater magnitude. These critics may have lost sight of several things. First, a forty-item test is a relatively short test and only samples the total biology knowledge and skills of the student. In scientific experiments, they accept statistically significant differences as meaningful, but they do not use the same standard in considering biology education but have no other finite standard to substitute. And they overlook the fact that there are many forces besides the BSCS course impinging on the student, and the longer he remains in the school system, the more impact these other forces will have had on him.

A student who reaches biology at the age of 15 has been going to schools for nine or ten previous years. He has had fifteen years of other environmental experiences, many of which are in direct conflict with those in biology. Concurrently with the biology course, he will be having experiences which conflict with what he is learning in biology. Then, he will be faced with college entrance exams and with standardized tests administered by the school system which may represent the dead hand of the past. For example, in one school system using BSCS Biology, a conventional standardized test was used at the end of the year because school officials insisted on having a standardized test and there was none available from the BSCS since the course was experimental and therefore were no norms of the BSCS exams. This was done despite the fact that what the traditional test measured was not related to what the BSCS was trying to teach. In another class, the teacher was concerned with teaching her class inquiry and skepticism. She thought students should not accept data without substantiating evidence. She found that some of her best students were having difficulty with the English teacher who expected all of her statements to be taken at face value, without argument. Thus, the student learns to question in biology but not outside of biology.

Furthermore, one should recognize that people do not change quickly. Change is a slow process and even though some change may be building up, there may be a time lag before the overt manifestations of these changes are observable. It may take considerable input of the idea of inquiry and questioning before the student is able to manifest behavior reflecting this. This does not mean that the student is not changing, or that the materials are not effective. Rather there is a time lag during which there is an accumulation of new expectations, before changes are manifested in behavior. For example, during the early years of the BSCS, we found that test questions which involved the higher cognitive levels were more often answered correctly towards the end of the year than at the beginning of the year. This was not a matter of the student having more information related to the test questions, but possibly reflected his being able to handle that type of test question more adequately after he had further experience with this type of mental process.

If the evaluator is concerned with follow-up testing to see the long range impact of BSCS Biology, his findings will be drastically affected by the influence of a multitude of stimuli. Possibly the best follow-up study of an experimental course would include students who had had a nucleus of courses with similar objectives, in a school where these objectives were consistently rewarded. For example, if the BSCS student had a course in SMSG Math, CHEM Study, PSSC and other experimental materials concerned with developing a sense of inquiry in English and social studies, the type of outcome reflected in follow-up studies might be quite different than when the student has had only one course concerned with developing a questioning attitude out of a four-year high school program of traditional and dogmatic nature. Until the broader type of study is done, evaluation of the new curricula will be incomplete, since no one subject area or single year course can be adequately evaluated in isolation from the rest of the school curriculum.

References

Cronbach, L. J. "Course Improvement Through Evaluation," *Teachers College Record* 64 (1963): 676-677.

Grobman, Hulda. Student performance in new high school biology program. *Science*. 143: 265-266. #3603.

CRUCIAL PSYCHOLOGICAL ISSUES IN THE OBJECTIVES, ORGANIZATION AND EVALUATION OF CURRICULUM REFORM MOVEMENTS[1]

David P. Ausubel

The Biological Sciences Curriculum Study may be taken as typical in approach and objectives to many of the flourishing curriculum reform movements that have arisen in the past fifteen years, particularly those in the natural sciences. Its principal objective is to re-establish the close contact and congruence of high school biology with current conceptual and methodological developments in biological science, while still maintaining, and even increasing, its congruence with current psychological and pedagogic ideas about the learning-teaching process as they apply to tenth-grade students (Schwab, 1963). According to Schwab, the content of high school biology, during the heyday of Progressive Education, "was no longer mainly determined by the state of knowledge in the scientific field," because of its excessive preoccupation with such matters as intellectual readiness, the learnability of material, and individual differences among learners. The BSCS approach, however, has veered precisely toward the opposite extreme in trying to correct this unsatisfactory state of affairs: its three texts[2] are reasonably congruent with the content and methods of modern biology, but, except for the Green Version, are psychologically and pedagogically unsound for the majority of tenth-graders.

Actually, of course, there is no *inherent* incompatibility between subject matter soundness, on the one hand, and pedagogic effectiveness, on the other. It is no more necessary to produce pedagogically inappropriate instructional materials in an attempt to make them reflective of the current state of knowledge in a given discipline, than it is necessary to present discredited concepts or inaccurate facts in order to make the subject matter more learnable. In practice, however, as the Yellow and Blue BSCS versions demonstrate, preoccupation with the recency of subject-matter content, and with the completeness of conceptual, methodological, and historical cover-age, can easily lead to the neglect of such basic pedagogic considerations as the educational appropriateness of course approach and objectives, the adequacy of the pupils' existing academic background for learning the content of the course, and the psychological tenability of the chosen ways of presenting, organizing, and sequencing materials. The inevitable outcome, under these circumstances, is the production of instructional materials that are admirably thorough, accurate, and up-to-date, but so ineffectively presented and organized, and so impossibly sophisticated for their intended audience, as to be intrinsically unlearnable on a long-term basis.

Although the BSCS does not state explicitly its specific dissatisfactions with conventional high school biology textbooks, these dissatisfactions can be readily inferred from the content of its numerous publications: (a) Conventional texts abound in outmoded ideas and incorrect information, and ignore important contemporary developments in the biological sciences. (b) They are written at a largely descriptive level, and contain relatively few explanatory concepts; too much stress is placed on structural detail, useless terminological distinctions, and classification, thereby placing a premium on rote memory. (c) Their approach is too naturalistic, and insufficiently experimental, quantitative, and analytical. (d) They tend to focus excessively on the organ and tissue levels of biological organization, whereas recent biological progress has been greatest at the molecular (biophysical and biochemical),

1. Paper presented at Conference on Vocational-Technical Education at the University of Illinois, sponsored by the American Vocational Association, May 18, 1966.

2. The three BSCS texts referred to in this paper are the Yellow Version (*Biological Science: An Inquiry Into Life.* New York: Harcourt, Brace, and World, 1963); the Blue Version (*Biological Science: Molecules to Man.* Boston: Houghton Mifflin, 1963); and the Green Version (*High School Biology.* Chicago: Rand McNally, 1963).

cellular, population, and community levels. (e) They are written at too low a level of sophistication and contain a profusion of elementary and self-evident generalizations. (f) Insufficient emphasis is placed on biology as a form of inquiry, as an experimental science, and as an ever-changing, open-ended discipline. (g) The biological ideas they contain are not presented in terms of their historical development, and are not related to the social and technological contexts from which they arise. (h) They lack organizing and unifying themes, present a mass of disconnected facts, and fail to integrate related concepts and different levels of biological organization. (i) They place excessive emphasis on the application of biology to such areas as medicine, public health, agriculture, and conservation, and insufficient emphasis on basic biological principles as ends in themselves.

Specification of Objectives in Behavioral Terms

For many years now, evaluation specialists have been exhorting curriculum workers, "State your objectives in behavioral terms, so that their realization can be subjected more easily to objective evaluation." As Atkin (1963) points out, however, such exhortation often does more harm than good. In the first place, relatively trivial but readily definable goals may be accorded more attention by both psychologists and subject-matter specialists than goals that are intrinsically more important but resistive to precise behavioral definition. Second, few curriculum specialists are trained to define goals in behavioral language. Most important, however, is the fact that behavioral terminology more often obscures than clarifies educational goals. The taxonomy of educational objectives (Bloom, 1956; Krathwohl, Bloom, & Masia, 1964), for example, categorizes educational goals in great behavioral detail. But since such terms as "memory," "application," "understanding," "transfer," "meaning," "cognitive," and "affective" have very different meanings for psychologists and educators of different theoretical persuasion, classification of curriculum objectives along such lines merely results in considerable pseudo-agreement among psychologists and curriculum workers, without ever defining what the actual objectives in question are. Everyone is happy because of the fine degree of "scientific" precision achieved in defining goals, even down to two decimal places; but nobody seems to care whether this achievement is psychologically or educationally meaningful.

"Basic" versus "Applied" Science Approach

The strong emphasis in the Yellow and Blue BSCS versions on "basic science" principles, and their relative lack of concern with applications to familiar or practical problems, is in accord with current fashionable trends in science education. Current curriculum projects have tended to overemphasize the "basic sciences" (because of their great generalizing power and relative timelessness), and unwarrantedly to denigrate the role and importance of applied science in general education. If the aim of the science curriculum is to acquaint the student with the goals and limitations of the scientific enterprise, and to help him understand, as an end in itself, the conceptual meaning of the current phenomenological world that confronts him, it cannot afford to overlook the applied sciences. They constitute a significant aspect of modern man's phenomenological and intellectual environment, and hence an important component of general education. Knowledge about such subjects as medicine, agronomy, and engineering should be taught *not* to make professional physicians, agronomists and engineers out of all students, or to help them solve *everyday* problems in these areas, but to make them more literate and intellectually sophisticated about the current world in which they live.

The time-bound and particular properties of knowledge in the applied sciences has also been exaggerated. Such knowledge involves more than technological applications of basic science generalizations to current practical problems. Although less generalizable than the basic sciences, they are also disciplines *in their own right*, with distinctive and relatively enduring bodies of theory and methodology that cannot simply be derived or extrapolated from the basic sciences to which they are related. It is simply not true that only basic science knowledge can be related to and organized around general principles. Each of the applied biological sciences (e.g., medicine, agronomy) possesses an *independent* body of general principles underlying the detailed knowledge in its field, in addition to being related in a still more general way to basic principles in biology.

Applied sciences also present us with many strategic advantages in teaching and curriculum development. We can capitalize on the student's existing interest in and familiarity with applied problems in science to provide an intellectual and motivational bridge for learning the content of the basic sciences. Previously acquired knowledge in the applied sciences, both incidental and systematic, can serve as the basis for rendering basic science concepts and propositions both potentially meaningful to the learner and less threatening to him. There is also good reason for believing that applied sciences are intrinsically more learnable than basic sciences to the elementary-school child, because of the particularized and intuitive nature of his cognitive processes and their dependence on the "here and now" properties of concrete-empirical experience. For example, before the tenth-grader ever enters the biology class, he has a vast fund of information about immunization, chemotherapy, the symptoms of infection, heredity, etc. Finally, knowledge in the applied sciences probably is retained longer than knowledge in the basic sciences because of the greater frequency of their subsequent use (by virtue of more frequent applicability to intellectual experience in adult life).

Overemphasis of Analytical, Quantitative and Experimental Aspects of Science

One of the characteristic features of the curriculum reform movement is an overcorrection of the unnecessarily low level of sophistication at which many high school subjects have been and still are taught. In the sciences this tendency is marked by a virtual repudiation of the descriptive, naturalistic, and applied approach and an overemphasis of the analytical, experimental, and quantitative aspects of science. In introductory high school biology, for example, much of the new content consists of highly sophisticated biochemical content that presupposes advanced knowledge of chemistry on the part of students who have no background whatsoever in this subject. The implied rationale of this policy is Bruner's untenable assertion that any concept can be taught to any person irrespective of his cognitve maturity or level of subject-matter sophistication.

By any reasonable pedagogic criterion, introductory high school biology should continue to remain predominantly naturalistic and descriptive in approach rather than analytical and experimental. This does not imply emphasis on descriptive information or on disconnected facts unrelated to theory, but on *explanatory* concepts that are stated in relatively gross and descriptive language, instead of in the more technical, quantitative, and sophisicated terminology of biochemistry and biophysics. In short, high school biology should concentrate on those broad biological ideas that constitute part of *general* education—physiology, evolution, development, inheritance, uniformities and diversity in life, ecology, and man's place in nature—rather than on a detailed and technical analysis of the physical and chemical basis of biological phenomena or of the morphology and function of intracellular microstructures. This is particularly true for the substantial number of students who will receive no further instruction in biology. As a matter of fact, there is still much significant but as yet unexploited *conceptual* content in introductory biology than can be treated in much more sophisticated terms

at a descriptive level, without having to resort to the depth of biochemical and cellular detail given in the Yellow and Blue BSCS versions.

Contrary to the strong and explicitly stated bias of the Blue and Yellow versions, there is still much room in introductory biology for the naturalistic approach. It is much more important for the *beginning* student in science to learn how to observe events in nature systematically and precisely, and how to formulate and test hypotheses on the basis of independent sets of naturally occurring antecedents and consequences, than to learn how to manipulate an experimental variable and control other relevent variables, by design, in a laboratory situation. The former approach not only takes precedence in the student's intellectual development, and is more consonant with his experiential background, but also has more transfer value for problem solving in future "real-life" contexts. To dogmatically equate scientific method with the experimental-analytical approach also excludes, rather summarily from the domain of science, such fields in biology as ecology, paleontology, and evolution, and such other disciplines as geology, astronomy, anthropology, and sociology.

Retention of the naturalistic and descriptive emphasis, and of some applied content, in introductory high school biology is thus consistent with the fact that tenth-grade biology is the terminal course in science for many students. It is also more consistent than is the analytical-experimental approach with the tenth-grader's existing background of experience, his interests, his intellectual readiness, and his relative degree of sophistication in science. This proposed emphasis is also in no way inappropriate for those students who will subsequently take high school physics and chemistry, as well as more advanced biology courses. These latter students would be much better prepared, after taking such an introductory course, for a second course in biology, in the twelfth grade or in college, that takes a more quantitative and experimental-analytical approach, introduces more esoteric topics, and considers the biochemical and biophysical aspects of biological knowledge. By this time, they would also have the necessary mathematical sophistication and greater experience with experimental methodology.

Level of Sophistication

In the Yellow and Blue BSCS versions, it appears as if little effort was made to discriminate between basic and highly sophisticated content—between what is appropriate and essential for an introductory high school course and what could be more profitably reserved for more advanced courses. These versions include topics, detail, and level of sophistication that vary in appropriateness from the tenth grade to graduate school.[3] Only the Green Version gives the impression of being at an appropriate level of sophistication for a beginning course. And since the unsophisticated student cannot be expected to distinguish between more and less important material, he either throws up his hands in despair, learns nothing thoroughly in the effort to learn everything, or relies on rote memorization and "cramming" to get through examinations.

The Blue Version, especially, appears sufficiently sophisticated and challenging to constitute an introductory college course for students who *already* had an introductory biology course in high school as well as courses in chemistry and physics. It is true, of course, that subjects once thought too difficult for high school students (e.g., analytical geometry, and calculus) *can* be taught successfully to *bright* high school students with good quantitative ability. But in the latter instances, students are adequately prepared for these advanced subjects by virtue of taking the necessary preliminary, and sequentially antecedent courses in mathematics. The Blue Version, on the other hand, presents biological material of college-level difficulty and sophistication to students who do not have the necessary background in chemistry, physics, and elementary biology for learning it meaningfully. It should also be remembered that college-level mathematics is not considered appropriate for *all* high school students, but only for those brighter students with better-than-average aptitude in mathematics, who are college bound and intend to major in such fields as mathematics, science, engineering, and architecture.

An introductory high school course in any discipline should concentrate more on establishing a general ideational framework than in putting a great deal of flesh on the skeleton. Generally speaking, only the framework is retained anyway after a considerable retention interval; and if more time is spent on overlearning the framework, plus a minimum of detail, than in superficially learning a large mass of oversophisticated and poorly understood material, both more of the important ideas are retained in the case of students taking the subject terminally, and a better foundation is laid for students who intend to take more advanced courses later.

Oversophisticated detail is not only unnecessary and inappropriate for a beginning course, but also hinders learning and generates unfavorable attitudes toward the subject. The student "can't see the forest for the trees." The main conceptual themes get lost or become unidentifiable in a welter of detail. Both the average student, and the student not particularly interested in science,

would tend to feel overwhelmed by the vast quantity and complexity of detail, terminology, methodology, and historical material in the Blue and Yellow versions. And a student who feels overwhelmed by a subject tends to develop an aversion toward it, and to resort to rote memorization for examination purposes.

It is not necessary for a beginning student to be given so much sequential historical detail about the development of biological ideas, related experimental evidence from original sources, and pedantic information about *all* of the various misconceptions and twistings and turnings taken by these ideas before they evolve into their currently accepted form. As a result, the ideas themselves—which are really the important things to be learned—tend to be obscured and rendered less salient. This practice also places an unnecessary and unwarranted burden on learning and memory effort—effort that could be more profitably expended on learning the ideas themselves and the more significant aspects of their historical development.

To give students the flavor of biology as an evolving empirical science with a complex and often circuitous history, it would suffice to cite several *examples*. It is unnecessary to give the detailed ideational and experimental history of *every* biological concept and controversy. Unsophisticated students also tend to be confused by raw experimental data, and by the actual chronological and experimental history underlying the emergence of a biological law or theory—especially when long quotations are given from original sources that use archaic language, refer to obscure controversies, and report findings and inferences in an unfamiliar and discursive manner. It is sufficient (as the Green Version does) to review the historical background of biological concepts in a schematic, telescoped, simplified, and reconstructed fashion, deleting most of the detail, and disregarding the actual chronological order of the antecedent ideas and their related experiments.

In an introductory course, simplification of content—*without* teaching wrong ideas that have to be unlearned later—is always justifiable and indicated. This can be accomplished by simply presenting more general and less complete versions of much of the same material that can be presented subsequently in greater depth and at high levels of sophistication. Although the Green Ver-

3. Much of the inappropriately high level of sophistication of the BSCS textbooks is undoubtedly a deliberate overreaction to the outdated content, paucity of explanatory ideas, the completely descriptive approach, and the kindergarten writing style and level of difficulty characterizing most textbooks in introductory high school biology.

sion probably lacks sufficient detail, it is less damaging, in my opinion, to present inadequate historical detail and experimental evidence than to obscure the major concepts by providing excessive historical and experimental data. This book unquestionably stimulates the student to delve deeper on his own. In any case, the missing detail can always be furnished by the teacher or from other sources.

It is possible to present ideas relatively simply—yet correctly—by deleting a great deal of the dispensable terminological, methodological, and historical detail, as well as many of the intermediate steps in argumentation; by telescoping or condensing material; by eliminating tangential "asides" and less important qualifications; by limiting the scope of coverage; by omitting formulas, equations, and structural diagrams of comp'ex molecules that are actually meaningless to unsophisticated students; by keeping the level of discourse general and simple; by writing lucidly, using terms precisely and consistently, and giving concise and familiar examples; by using schematically simplified models and diagrams; and by bearing in mind that a satiation point exists for any student. An atypically high level of sophistication may sometimes be employed simply to *illustrate* the complexity of a given topic; but in these instances students should be explicitly instructed not to master the details.

Collaboration of Subject Matter, Learning Theory, and Measurement Specialists

A basic premise of all curriculum reform projects is that only a person with subject-matter competence[4] in a given discipline should prepare curriculum materials in that discipline. Only such a person is sufficiently sophisticated (a) to identify unifying and integrative concepts with broad generalizability and explanatory power in the field; (b) to perceive the interrelationships between different ideas and topics so as to organize, sequence, and integrate them optimally; (c) to comprehend the process of inquiry and the relationship of theory to data in the discipline, in order to select appropriate laboratory exercises and to integrate process and content aspects of the curriculum program; and (d) to understand the subject-matter content well enough either to prepare textual materials lucidly himself, or to judge whether others have done so.

To be pedagogically effective, such curriculum materials also have to conform to established principles in the psychology of classroom learning, and must include evaluative devices that conform to established principles of evaluation and measurement. Obviously, it is difficult for any one person to possess all three competencies. But a *pure* educational psychologist or measurement specialist cannot collaborate with a subject-matter specialist in producing curriculum materials and measuring instruments—apart from communicating to him *general* principles of learning theory and measurement.

This type of help, however, is inadequate for the *actual* collaborative task that needs to be done. In the actual operation of producing curriculum and evaluative materials that are sound on both subject-matter and learning theory-measurement grounds, the educational psychologist and measurement specialist can collaborate effectively with their colleagues in subject-matter fields, *only* if they themselves are sufficiently sophisticated in the subject matter to participate actively in the production of the curriculum materials from the *very start*. Only in this way can they ensure that the *detailed* content and structure of the material conform to established principles of learning and measurement theory. One possible solution to this problem of producing sound instructional materials is to train a new type of curriculum worker: either a subject-matter specialist who is sophisticated (but not expert) in learning theory or measurement to collaborate with learning theory and measurement specialists; or a learning theory or measurement specialist who is sophisticated (but not expert) in some subject-matter field to collaborate with subject-matter specialists.

Single-Unit versus Integrated Curriculum Approach

Generally speaking, it is not pedagogically tenable to produce science curriculum materials apart from an integrated plan encompassing each of the separate scientific disciplines at successively higher levels of difficulty from elementary school through college. A collection of supplementary grade-appropriate units in various scientific disciplines, even when used in conjunction with existing curriculum materials, presents many difficulties: (a) It does not further the construction of a sequentially organized curriculum in any particular discipline at any grade level that is logically coherent and systematic in its component topics. (b) Students fail to develop a conception of each scientific discipline as a sequentially organized, logically integrated, and coherently interrelated body of knowledge. (c) For a given discipline to be organized for optimal learning on a longitudinal basis, one must plan in advance for the articulation of the various levels of dif-

---

4. In actual practice three different kinds of persons provide different kinds of subject-matter as well as pedagogic competence in projects such as the BSCS: a professional biologist, a specialist in the teaching of biology, and a classroom biology teacher.

ficulty so that some topics are considered at progressively higher levels of sophistication, whereas other topics are introduced *de novo* when specified levels of sophisication are reached.

This kind of large-scale, integrated curriculum planning requires no greater "certainty in the minds of the specialists on exactly how science materials should be scheduled to guarantee learnings" than does the production of small unintegrated units of material. The *same* principles are involved but on a much more massive scale. One starts with the same tentative outline based on logical interrelationships between the component aspects of a discipline, as modified by pertinent developmental and learning theory considerations; prepares tentative units; and revises these units on the basis of try-out experience or alters their grade-placement level. If this is done by a team, say twenty times larger than the one ordinarily envisaged, it can prepare an integrated science curriculum in the same length of time that it takes an average-sized team to prepare an unintegrated series of units. Admittedly, this involves many more administrative problems; but if one adheres to the principle of immediate try-out of component units, there should not necessarily be any problem of "rigidity." The deficiencies in the existing large-scale, integrated projects stem more from (a) untenable theoretical ideas about teaching and learning (e.g., overemphasis on the importance of discovery in learning; overemphasis on the "basic science," experimental-analytic approach); (b) uncoordinated team effort, resulting in the production of textbooks consisting of unintegrated units, and no pervasive organizing ideas that are organically related to the textual material (e.g., Blue and Yellow BSCS versions); (c) failure to try out the materials empirically until the *entire series* is completed; and (d) lack of *active* collaboration, on a day-to-day basis, of learning-theory and measurement specialists (who are also sophisticated in the subject matter) in the actual preparation of curriculum and measurement materials.

Early Try-Out of Materials

An essential aspect of the preparation of instructional materials that is, unfortunately, ignored much too frequently by many curriculum reform projects is the matter of early and continuous try-out, both with individual pupils and in classrooms. Only in this way is it possible to ascertain their appropriateness and effectiveness, and to modify the original logically-developed outline in terms of empirically relevant information regarding learnability, lucidity, difficulty level, sequence, organization, practicality, and attitudes of pupils, teachers, and administrators. All

too often huge sums of money are invested in preparing an integrated series of curriculum materials without making any provision for try-out and evaluation until the finished product is published.

Difficulties in Evaluating the New Curricula

As Brownell (1965) points out, curriculum evaluation is more difficult than it often appears on the surface. This, in large part, is a function of the fact that standardized achievement tests both cover various traditional subject-matter units deliberately ignored by the new curricula, as well as fail to measure knowledge of the more modern concepts which the latter emphasize. Further, many curriculum projects either make no provisions whatsoever for evaluation, or fail to provide for an adequate control group and to eliminate the Hawthorne Effect. The weight of the evidence indicates that on the basis of achievement test results the new curriculums in mathematics and science are approximately as effective as existing curriculums. If this were our ultimate criterion of effectiveness, these findings would be quite disappointing. Much more important, however, are results on delayed tests of retention and performance in more advanced, sequentially related courses. Unfortunately, however, such data are not available.

Evaluation of Learnability and Measurement of Achievement

The principal shortcoming of scores on conventional achievement tests, in my opinion, is that they measure *immediate* retention of understanding and ability to apply knowledge (e.g., quarterly and final tests), instead of (a) delayed retention, and (b) performance in sequentially related, more advanced courses. Ability to make satisfactory scores on immediate retention tests of understanding and application is not proof that the material is adequately learnable, lucid, properly programmed, etc., because any reasonably bright pupil can do enough cramming before an announced test to make a satisfactory score on a test of immediate retention, even if the materials are generally unsound by *any* criterion, in fact, this *has* been the case for the last 2500 years of formal education.

When the learnability of curriculum materials is assessed by conventional tests of achievement, these latter tests often give spurious and misleading impressions of genuine learnability. This is apparently the case when the Yellow and Blue BSCS versions are evaluated by means of the conventional achievement tests. Achievement test data show that the three BSCS versions are approximately as "learnable" as conventional textbooks. It was demonstrated, for example, that students using the BSCS texts score somewhat higher than students using conventional texts, on a final *Comprehensive BSCS Test,* and somewhat lower on a final *Cooperative Biology Test* (Wallace, 1963). In the first place, it is questionable how well such final tests *really* measure the learnability of subject-matter content. Most adequately motivated students can "learn," for examination purposes, large quantities of overly sophisticated and poorly presented materials that they do not really understand; unfortunately, however, in such circumstances, little evidence of retention is present even a few days later. Second, one of the main objectives of any new, elaborately prepared curriculum program is presumably to exceed by far, rather than merely to approximate the level of academic achievement attained in conventionally taught courses.

The didactic use of substantive and programmatic devices to strengthen cognitive structure and thus to increase the functional retention of background knowledge (available for future learning and problem solving) focuses attention on the need to develop more valid measures of the organizational strength and availability of such knowledge. The "transfer retention" test (Ausubel & Fitzgerald, 1962) constitutes a new approach to the problem of measuring functional retention. It attempts to do this by measuring the extent to which retained knowledge of subject-matter is sufficiently stable and well organized to be available as a foundation for learning new, sequentially related material that could not be efficiently learned in the absence of such availability. At the same time, of course, it also provides a measure of knowledge available for problem solving, because if retained knowledge is available for new sequential learning, it is reasonable to assume that it is also available for problem solving.

Conventional retention measures, covering previously studied material at the end of a given course of instruction, are not truly reflective of the later availability of this material for new learning and problem solving purposes. Because a short retention interval cannot adequately test the organizational strength and viability of newly acquired knowledge, and because of the contaminating influence of rote memory in poorly constructed retention tests, such conventional measures of retention are often misleading. They fail to distinguish adequately between the individual who merely understands and retains material well enough to answer rote and meaningful questions restricted to the substance of this material, and

the individual whose understanding and retention are sufficient to serve as a springboard for learning new, sequentially related material. Both individuals may frequently make identical scores on immediate tests of retention.

Problem solving items, on the other hand, are less influenced by rote memory, and also directly test ability to use and apply retained knowledge. But since successful problem solving also depends on many traits (e.g., venturesomeness, flexibility, perseverence, problem sensitivity) that are unrelated to the functional availability of knowledge, success or failure on such items is as much a reflection of the influence of these latter traits as of the availability of usable knowledge. Hence, it can be reasonably argued that the most valid way of testing the organizational strength and viability of knowledge is not to test retention per se or to use problem solving items, but to test retention in the context of sequential learning, i.e., in situations where ability to learn new material presupposes the availability of the old.

The transfer retention test may be administered in addition to or independently of the conventional retention test. When used for routine course examinations, the test procedure requires that students study an unfamiliar new learning passage that is sequentially related to and pre-supposes knowledge of the previously studied material on which they are being examined. "Their scores on a test of this *new* material are transfer retention scores" and measure the functional availability of the previously learned material for new learning.

REFERENCES

ATKIN, J. M. Some evaluation problems in a course content improvement project. *Journal of Research in Science Teaching,* 1963, *1,* 129-132.

AUSUBEL, D., and FITZGERALD, D. Organizer, general background, and antecedent learning variables in sequential verbal learning. *Journal of Educational Psychology,* 1962, *53,* 243-249.

BLOOM, B. S. (Ed.) *Taxonomy of educational objectives; the classification of educational goals, by a committee of college and university examiners.* New York: McKay, 1956.

BROWNELL, W. A. The evaluation of learning under different systems of instruction. *Educational Psychologist,* 1965, *3,* 5-7.

KRATHWOHL, D. R., BLOOM, B. S., and MASIA, B. B. *Taxonomy of educational objectives: the classification of educational goals. Handbook II: Affective domain.* New York: McKay, 1964.

SCHWAB, J. J. (Sup.) *Biology teachers' handbook.* New York: Wiley, 1963.

WALLACE, W. W. The BSCS 1961-62 evaluation program—a statistical report. *BSCS Newsletter,* 1963, *19,* 22-24.

CHAPTER 23	
Alan B. Knox	**CONTINUOUS PROGRAM EVALUATION***

Contribution of Evaluation to Program Improvement

Victor Balancesheet had arrived at his office an hour early this morning. For the past six months since he was appointed as director of the continuing education division, he had found that the hour before school starts is a good time for planning. Victor Balancesheet was not one to be carried along on the tide without plan or direction.

During the previous year, the superintendent of the Franklin school district had asked Victor if he were interested in becoming the half-time director of continuing education. The state legislature had appropriated funds with which local districts could hire directors of adult and continuing education. Victor was the high school business education teacher, and he had expressed an interest in continuing education from the first day that he taught at Franklin four years ago. His wife insisted that part of his commitment resulted from his father's experience as a university dean of extension. There was, however, no doubt about Victor's dedication to life-long learning. His enthusiastic teaching had made his evening classes on business very popular with adults. And, he had been instrumental in the organization of a citizens advisory committee to the continuing education program. One of the other teachers had commented at the time that he had probably picked up the idea in one of his courses at the university where he was working on an administrator's certificate. Even now, the ideas that he wanted to try resulted in his spending more time as director than he spent on his half-time position as the business teacher.

Victor privately characterized the course offerings that he had inherited as a hodgepodge. Most of them were either federally reimbursed vocational courses or hobby courses. On the average, about half of those who registered at the beginning of each term had dropped out by the end.

Victor believed strongly that substantial program improvement was needed. That was his major concern this morning. What approach could he use that would be most likely to result in program improvement? He had mentioned his concern about program improvement, to the superintendent several weeks before, with the result that he had agreed to present a plan for improvement during the following year. The problem was in getting a handle on it. He had thought of evaluation, but the approaches that had been covered in his graduate course on tests and measurements did not seem very relevant. They were aimed at testing students to decide on grades. Few of the continuing education courses gave grades, and having grades for continuing education courses did not seem to be a move in the right direction.

"There must be a more useful approach to program improvement," mused Victor Balancesheet, "there must be a way."

The quandary of the fictional Victor Balancesheet has been shared by many directors of programs of continuing education for adults. Just testing adult students *does not* seem to be a satisfactory way to improve programs, and yet some procedure is needed to produce evidence upon which to base judgments about program effectiveness. The literature of adult and continuing education abounds with admonitions about the desirability of evaluation. The test and measurement books describe procedures for the collection and analysis of data. What has been substantially missing, has been a more general framework, an approach to establishing connections between the goals of evaluation, the functioning of the continuing education programs, and the technical procedures for data collection and analysis. This chapter on continuous program evaluation is an attempt to present

*Chapter 18 for *Public School Continuing Education.*

and illustrate the major elements of an approach to program improvement, such as an ambitious young man like Victor Balancesheet would probably have developed before long.

The purpose of program evaluation is program improvement. The previous chapters of this book indicate how complex a task it is for a director such as Victor Balancesheet to plan and implement an effective continuing education program for adults. If he is to provide leadership within the division regarding program improvement, there must be provision for systematic feedback of information related to program effectiveness to policy makers, administrators, teachers, and learners so that they can make sound judgments regarding program effectiveness. Continuous program evaluation is the process by which evidence regarding program effectiveness is systematically collected, analyzed, and used to improve programs of continuing adult education. The purpose of this chapter is to suggest ways in which the director might strengthen program evaluation procedures.

Purposes of Evaluation

Before suggesting an approach that a director such as Victor Balancesheet might take to the program evaluation process, it might be helpful to be more specific about the purposes of the program evaluation process. The general purpose of evaluation is to improve the educational program by facilitating judgments about its effectiveness based on evidence. The specific purposes of program evaluation are:

1. To make more explicit the rationale for the educational program as a basis for deciding which aspects of the educational program are most important to evaluate regarding effectiveness and what specific types of data to collect.
2. To collect evidence or data upon which to base the judgments regarding effectiveness.
3. To analyze the data and draw conclusions.
4. To make judgments or decisions which are based at least in part on the data.
5. To implement the decisions so as to improve the educational program.

Symptoms of Inadequate Evaluation

If Balancesheet's program was small and stable, then program evaluation could occur informally as he, school board members, his teachers, and even the adult learners discuss the program and make decisions about its improvement. Under these conditions, Balancesheet should be able to recognize emerging difficulties and make adjustments as the program proceeds. However, if his pro-

gram was large, growing, and diversified, then more systematic feedback procedures would be required. There are a variety of symptoms that might indicate to Balancesheet or any director, that evaluation procedures may be inadequate. Although any one symptom may result from other causes, the occurrence of several symptoms together should be recognized by the director as evidence that there are major discrepancies between goals, resources, and procedures that are not being accommodated. Some typical symptoms are as follows:

1. Slow increase in the number of adults enrolled, compared with similar programs.
2. Difficulty in attracting adults from a specified target population.
3. High drop-out rate associated with an incompatibility between learning style and teaching style.
4. Low rate of learner persistence from year to year.
5. Limited learner directedness regarding planning, conducting, and assessing of his own educational efforts.
6. High incidence of complaints by learners or teachers regarding a discrepancy between goals, resources, procedures, and learner backgrounds.
7. Unwillingness of the most qualified teachers to accept teaching positions in the division or to continue for another term.
8. Slow improvement of beginning teachers in the division.
9. Difficulty in placing those participants who successfully complete a course of study in the division, in jobs or further education.
10. Frequent complaints from employers regarding the obsolescence of the knowledge and skills that their employees have obtained from courses in the division, or the inability of the employees to apply what they have learned.
11. Few sequences of courses.
12. Lack of articulation between courses that are presumably part of sequences.
13. High incidence of friction in relationships with the preparatory education programs of the institution.
14. Lack of support from policy makers regarding budget requests and proposals for new programs.

If a director assesses the functioning of his division and discovers that several of these symptoms exist, he should review in detail the current procedures for program evaluation to identify points at which they should be improved.

In practice, the range of activities upon which program evaluation procedures might focus, extends far beyond available time or money. Therefore, one of the most crucial decisions by the director deals with the appropriate extent of evaluation activity within the division, so that the investment of resources for evaluation is sufficient to maximize the other investments, but *does not* exceed the anticipated benefits. The director should expect to get his money's worth from evaluation.

An Approach to Evaluation

Too often, continuing education evaluation consists of course examinations or learner satisfaction forms or a review of enrollment and income. By contrast, the theme of this chapter is that a more comprehensive approach to the evaluation process must be taken if substantial program improvement is to result. The proposed approach to evaluation which is presented in the remainder of this chapter, is divided into the following five sections: 1. Important ideas about evaluation; 2. Program evalation data; 3. Related agency functions; 4. Methods of collecting and analyzing data, and 5. Using evaluation results. In each section, the basic steps or ideas are concisely stated, followed by a brief explanation or example.

Important Ideas About Evaluation

The extensive literature on educational evaluation contains many ideas and principles that can be helpful to adult educators. Many are contained in the selected list of references presented at the conclusion of this chapter. The following brief list of important ideas about evaluation were selected because of their special importance and relevance to adult education program improvement.

1. *Evidence*—Why bother about formalized evaluation procedures? *People associated with a program will make judgments about effectiveness even without formal evaluation procedures. The function of systematic and continuous program evaluation procedures should be to provide more adequate evidence and to improve the soundness of the judgments.* The learner will decide whether he is receiving enough benefit from a course to warrant 'his continued investment of time and money. The teacher will decide to try some new instructional methods and to discontinue others. The administrator will decide to rehire some teachers and not others. The school board member will decide whether to vote additional district funds for a proposed expansion of an adult education program. As each of these people associated with a program makes these and other judgments about program effectiveness, he does so on the basis of the evidence which is most familiar to him. If the evidence is adequate for

making sound judgments which are then used for program improvement, then existing evaluation procedures are probably sufficient. However, if this is not the case, then the director should assess the existing evaluation procedures to identify the major points at which they should be improved so that more adequate evidence and sounder judgments will result. Examples of points at which evaluation procedures might be improved include the use of self-administered diagnostic tests, anonymous end-of-course student opinionnaires, periodic clientele analysis, summary of the charcteristics of those who drop out and their reasons for dropping out, a follow-up study of former participants regarding their application of what they learned, and a cost-effectiveness study comparing lecture and discussion methods regarding cost, achievement, application, and motivation.

2. *Benefits*—How extensive should the evaluation procedures be? *The extent of the evaluation procedures should depend on the importance of making sounder judgments. There should be a balance between costs of evaluation and the benefits received.* If evaluation procedures are too limited, the anticipated results from the large investments by learner, teacher, and school may not be realized. In this case, a modest increase in evaluation should produce a substantial program improvement. For instance, in a division that uses few formal testing, counseling, or feedback procedures, the introduction of end-of-course opinionnaires for both learners and teachers can inexpensively identify many suggestions for program improvement. However, extensive evaluation procedures aimed at a minor problem may not be worth the effort. The important question is, how important is it to be able to make sounder judgments regarding program effectiveness? If the judgments towards which evaluation efforts are aimed are inconsequential or if satisfactory judgments can be made with less evidence, then a reduction in the extent of evaluation procedures is justified. But, if faulty judgments are being made on important issues related to program effectiveness, then more extensive evaluation efforts are warranted.

3. *Frequency*—How often should evaluation data be collected? *The frequency with which evaluation data should be collected depends upon the aspect of the program that is being assessed and the anticipated use of the results.* Some information, such as learner achievement related to course objectives, should be collected periodically during each course. Information, such as learner expectations or a summary of the dropout rate for each course, can be collected once each term. Some information, such as a clientele analysis that compares the characteristics of participants with the adult population that the division is attempting

to serve, might be collected every five years. One purpose of the more frequently collected data is to identify *when* to collect more detailed information about selected aspects of the program. For instance, a high dropout rate due to learner dissatisfaction, might lead to an evaluation study of registration and counseling procedures.

4. *Feedback*—Who should receive the results of evaluation? *One major function of evaluation should be continuing internal feedback to enable adjustments in the ongoing program.* A major shortcoming of informal evaluation procedures is that evidence of program effectiveness tends not to reach those who could use it. Even though their primary purpose is to facilitate pass-fail decisions, end-of-course examinations in preparatory education tend not to be used as much as they might for program improvement to the benefit of learners in subsequent terms. An example of evaluation for feedback includes periodic brief anonymous tests to provide the learner with evidence of achievement as a basis for adjusting study plans. Summaries each term of participant characteristics to assist both program planning and program promotion might be provided as well as summaries of learner opinionnaires which may assist in the planning and revision of future courses.

5. *Commitment*—To what extent should those who are affected by evaluation participate in the process? *Those who are affected by the evaluation and who must use the results if improvements are to occur, should participate in the evaluation process so that the likelihood of their using the results will be increased.* This idea differentiates evaluation from research. In social and behavioral science research, one objective is to minimize the extent to which those who are being studied influence decisions that might bias the findings. However, as Corey stressed in his book on *Action Research* (5), when a primary purpose is program improvement, reduced validity and generalizability may be the price that is paid for a greater commitment to use of the findings. For example, teachers who decide that a study of teaching style is needed and then help to develop the procedures, are more likely to read the report and use some of the findings to modify their teaching than would be the case when a similar study is conducted exclusively by an outside consultant.

6. *Objectivity*—Then how can greater objectivity be achieved? *The outside evaluation specialist can help to increase the objectivity and validity of evaluation procedures.* There is a tendency for persons who evaluate their own program to rationalize somewhat. Long standing conditions, such as budget level or personnel, tend to be accepted as unchangeable whereas they may constitute the major leverage for program improvement. Also,

personal involvement in a program may make candid appraisal difficult. Greater objectivity can be achieved by the assistance of an outside evaluation specialist who may be associated with another part of the institution, or with a nearby university. The outside evaluation specialist can help to offset this subjectivity. He can also provide technical assistance regarding procedures of data collection and analysis.

7. *Objectives*—How can a clearer statement of objectives be obtained? *The evaluation specialist should assist those who plan the educational program in making more clear and explicit their intents and objectives as the major basis for judging effectiveness.* There are several bases for judging the effectiveness of an educational program, but the major basis should be the extent to which the objectives were achieved. The development of detailed evaluation procedures requires greater clarity and precision in the statement of objectives than do many other aspects of program planning and teaching. For example, the selection of questions for an achievement test, opinionnaire, or follow-up study requires that a decision be made about how the learners are expected to change as a result of the course. In some instances, at least half of the effort of the evaluation specialist is devoted to clarification of program objectives. The resulting statement of objectives contributes not only to evaluation but also to other aspects of program development such as selection of materials and instructional personnel. It is important to recognize, however, that many programs have benefits aside from the stated objectives.

8. *Standards*—How can standards of comparison be obtained? *The evaluation specialist should also assist in identifying appropriate standards of comparison, both the relative performance of similar programs and absolute standards of excellence.* The evaluation specialist should have a familiarity with relevant evaluation studies that will enable him to bring an outside perspective to the development of an evaluation plan. It is in part through the comparison of a program evaluation report with evaluation reports for similar programs and with standards of excellence such as standardized test norms or standards of job performance, that the stated objectives of the program are assessed.

9. *Relevance*—On what basis should the data to be collected, be chosen? *Data should be collected and analyzed which is highly relevant to the intents and objectives.* This is the question of validity that is so central in writings on educational measurement. Is the teacher testing for what he is teaching? When the focus is shifted from evaluation of learners to program evaluation, somewhat different types of information should be collected. The decisions regarding which infor-

mation to collect and its subsequent interpretation depends on the rationale for the program. The rationale should include a brief review of the past history of the program being evaluated, its current demands and constraints, and expectations regarding future developments. The statement of intents should include the anticipated outcomes such as learning gain or application of what was learned by the learner in a subsequent job setting. In addition, the statement of intents should describe the anticipated inputs of learners, teachers, materials and other resources, along with the anticipated transactions between these inputs that are expected to produce the outcomes. Similarly, some information should be collected regarding the actual inputs, transactions, and outcomes of the educational program.

10. *Values*—Should evaluation be limited to empirical data? *The process of making judgments should include in addition to data—appropriate values, consensus, and continuing commitment.* The collection and analysis of data is a crucial ingredient in the evaluation process. However, in addition, those who are engaged in the process should be concerned with two other ingredients. One is values. People hold differing convictions regarding desirability. Some people may place emphasis on critical judgment as a priority outcome; while others may stress skillful performance. The second ingredient is consensus and continuing commitment. The success of an educational program depends on the continuing contribution by various persons. The process of making judgments regarding effectiveness should include provision for achieving consensus and a commitment to use the findings to improve the educational program.

Program Evaluation Data

Each continuing education program has broad goals, one of which is the long term benefits that participation brings to the learner. For the purpose of evaluation, however, it is necessary to focus on specific educational objectives, the achievement of which will substantially assist the learner to move towards the long term goals. In addition to specific educational objectives, there are often other program outcomes in the form of benefits to the community or sponsoring institution. Community benefits may include a reduction in the numbers of people on welfare or who are unemployed, and an increase in productivity or greater survival of small businesses. Institutional benefits include greater plant utilization, increased citizen support for preparatory education, and increased teacher familiarity with adult life settings within which preparatory education students will later have to function. Part of the purpose of program evaluation is to collect

data regarding the extent to which the intended program *outcomes* and other unanticipated benefits are achieved. In addition to outcomes, educational program development includes attention to intended *inputs* and transactions. Intended inputs include the characteristics of learners, teachers, materials, and other needed resources. Intended *transactions* include the activities in which learners and teachers engage together and with instructional materials that are intended to transform the inputs into the intended outcomes. In the total process of evaluation of an effective continuing education program, data are collected regarding the actual or observed *inputs, transactions,* and *outcomes.* Because it is never possible to collect data on all of the variables related to a functioning program, evaluation efforts must be selective. One basis for deciding on which variables to collect data, is the *rationale* of the program including its history, current demands and constraints, and expectations regarding future developments. These four aspects of the program from which to collect data (*rationale, inputs, transactions,* and *outcomes*) provide a framework which the director can use in assessing current evaluation procedures and in developing more satisfactory procedures for continuous program evaluation. Listed below are the four aspects of the program from which to collect data, along with examples of the specific data that might be collected.

1. *Rationale*—The rationale within which a continuing education program is developed and evaluated, typically has three parts, its history, the current demands and constraints, and expectations regarding future developments. If the program to be evaluated is entirely new, it would be helpful just to note what led to the establishment of the program. Otherwise, a brief program history might record the number of years that it had been operating, trends in size and emphasis, and major influences that helped or hindered. Current demands and constraints, such as legal mandates and budget limits, may eminate from the national or community setting of the division, or from the sponsoring institution. Community influences include the level of supply and demand of the competence that the program would develop, the competitive position of the program for resources, the relation to the program of preparatory education, and relevant social, economic, and political trends. Institutional influences include the locus of decision making between the division and the remainder of the school system, and the competitive position of the program for resources. Expectations regarding future developments may relate to the program itself or to related activities. An example of a program expectation is that the program is a demonstration project

in preparation for the development of many similar programs, in comparison with a single course that is to be offered once each year as long as demand warrants. An example of an expectation regarding related activities, is that many other continuing education agencies are developing similar courses on a topic that has had a relatively stable demand, in comparison with a course in response to an emerging demand for which the division has unique resources.

If the evaluator has a familiarity with the program rationale, he will be better able to decide on the scale on which the evaluation of the program should be occurring, and on the aspects of the program which should receive primary attention. For example, a greater investment in evaluation would be warranted when the program is a demonstration project on a new topic of growing importance, than when the program has been offered satisfactorily for years. Also, an understanding of situational demands and constraints may explain limited results that might otherwise be attributed to the performance of learners and teachers. Examples include inadequate published instructional materials, or severe budgetary restrictions.

2. *Inputs*—This type of program data includes descriptions of both the intended inputs that are planned and the observed inputs that are actually achieved. Part of the evaluation process is a comparison of the description of the intended inputs with a description of the observed inputs to ascertain the extent to which they are congruent. A finding of incongruence would indicate an adjustment in either or both. Four major inputs are learners, teachers, materials, and administrators. Illustrative data regarding learners includes the number, and their characteristics such as estimated learning ability, competence related to objectives that the learner has at the outset of the program, educational level, age, occupation and community size. Illustrative data regarding mentors (persons who participate in the teaching-learning transaction such as teachers, counselors and writers) includes the number, and their characteristics such as educational level, subject matter competence, experience teaching adults, and teaching style. Illustrative data regarding materials, equipment and facilities includes their availability both in general and to individual learners, and the procedures that are used for acquiring or developing them. Illustrative data regarding administrators and support staff includes the number, and their characteristics such as their previous experience and their relationship with the program development process. In the evaluation process, inputs should be compared with both the standards of excellence and similar programs. The resulting analysis can indicate which portion

of the outcomes is attributable to the input of resources and which portion is attributable to what is done with them.

3. *Transaction*—The teaching-learning transaction includes the activities that produce changes in the learner's knowledge, skills, and attitudes that achieve the educational objectives. Some activities are shared by the teacher and learner, and for some, the teacher or the learner works alone reading or writing or working with equipment. Each teaching-learning transaction occurs within one of four settings, individual, temporary group, organizational, and community. The *individual* setting includes correspondence study and E.T.V. courses. The *temporary group* setting includes the typical evening class in which adults without previous contact assemble for the class each week and at the end of the course go their separate ways. The *organizational* setting includes in-service training for work groups in which the prior and subsequent working relationships between the learners have a major influence on the program. The *community* setting emphasizes working relationships between different organizations and segments of a neighborhood or community. Within each of these four settings, the balance of responsibility for planning and directing the learning experience may rest with the mentor, or with the learner, or at some intermediate point of shared responsibility. In combination, these two dimensions of setting and locus of responsibility provide a basis for the classification of types of teaching-learning transactions. One type of program data that should be provided regarding the teaching-learning transaction is a classification regarding setting and balance of responsibility. For programs that include two or more settings, such as a combined correspondence study and evening class, information should be included regarding the amount of time devoted to each segment. Additional information should be collected regarding learner activity, teacher activity and outside support. Illustrative data regarding learner activity includes amount of time spent in each type of activity in a group and hours spent in each type of activity by himself. Illustrative data regarding teacher activity includes amount of time spent giving information, obtaining information, and guiding learner search. Illustrative data regarding outside support includes contributions by institutional support staff such as a librarian, and extent of encouragement by persons in the learner's reference groups, such as an employer or a spouse. In many continuing education programs, the major ways to improve an educational program relate to the teaching-learning transaction. Therefore, a major purpose of program evaluation is to identify aspects of this transaction that can be improved.

4. *Outcomes*—The purpose of a continuing education program is to produce the intended outcomes. These outcomes or objectives are typically stated in several stages of impact, which serve as the criteria for assessing effectiveness. The more immediate stage describes direct changes in the learner's knowledge, skills, and attitudes. Ways of assessing this type of change include achievement level on a test, gain in competence from beginning to end of program, performance in a simulated situation, and application in life through change in practices. The more remote stage of outcome is stated as a benefit to the community. As an objective it may relate to specific institutions such as employers, families, or organizations, or it may be more generalized and refer to productivity, economic growth, cultural level, or social participation. This set of variables from individual educational achievement, through application, and benefit to specific institutions, and generalized benefit to the community constitutes a type of continuum. At the more specific individual end, the emphasis is on the benefits to the individual and it is somewhat easier to collect valid data. At the more generalized end, the emphasis may be on the benefits to the individual but it is more difficult to collect valid data. This is due in part to influences other than the educational program, such as opportunities related to neighborhood, ethnic background, or personality. Of special usefulness is performance in a simulated situation such as a driver training car or a computer based decision making game. This type of simulation allows the learner to show how he would perform in a real life situation without the distractions of outside influences such as a supervisor who might not allow the learner to try a new practice. One aspect of the evaluation process is to ascertain the extent of congruence between the intended outcomes and the observed outcomes, that is, to discover the extent to which the objectives have been achieved.

In stating the intents of an educational program, the primary test for adequacy is logical contingency. Does it seem reasonable that with the intended inputs the intended transactions could produce the intended outcomes? The primary test in comparing the intended with the observed is congruence. Did they do what they planned? The primary test for the relationships between the observed inputs, transactions, and outcomes is empirical contingency. To what extent did the inputs contribute to the transactions, and the transactions to the outcomes? These six aspects of program evaluation can be compared with two outside standards in the process of making specific judgments regarding effectiveness. One standard is descriptive data from other programs. This yields conclusions such as, the per-

formance in the program being evaluated was better than half of the similar programs for which evaluation reports are available. Another standard is general hallmarks of excellence, such as the statement that at least ninety percent of the eligible voters should vote in each election. The relationship between these aspects of the program evaluation process is presented schematically in Figure 1.

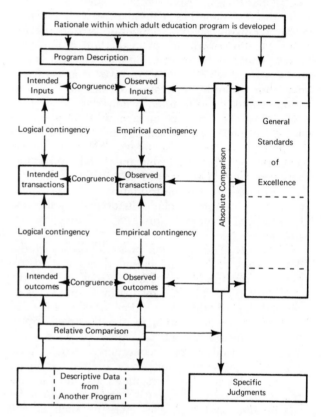

Figure 1. Program Evaluation Process*

*Adapted from Stake, Robert E., "The Countenance of Educational Evaluation," *Teachers College Record* 68:523-540, April, 1967.

Related Agency Functions

Depending upon the aspect of the program that is the focus of evaluation efforts, it is typically necessary to include within the evaluation procedures, the collection of data that extend beyond variables that are directly related to the teaching-learning transaction. Examples of these related agency functions are program interpretation, staffing, policy, facilities, and finance. To be sure, each of these are reflected in intended inputs and outcomes. The results of staffing efforts provide the input of teachers and the results of policy formulation influence the selection of objectives. However, if the purpose of program evaluation is program improvement then it will sometimes be necessary to include in the evaluation plan not only the results of these related agency functions, but also the procedures by which they are accomplished. Thus, if the focus of evaluation is a failure to reach and teach a larger proportion of blue collar workers, part of the evaluations plan may be an analysis of the procedures for program interpretation and recruitment of learners, as well as a description of the intended learners compared with those who actually attend. This analysis may compare the program that is being evaluated with others that have reached a higher proportion of blue collar workers, regarding the extent of recruitment activities that utilize face to face communication in informal friendship groups compared with mass media like newspapers and television. If the focus of evaluation is inadequate facilities and equipment, part of the evaluation plan may be an analysis of the procedures for arranging for outside facilities when needed facilities and equipment are not available within the sponsoring institution.

Methods of Collecting and Analyzing Data

The process of data collection and analysis is a crucial aspect of program evaluation, and is in some respects the most technical. A detailed guide to the development of valid and reliable tests, questionnaires, and interview schedules, and to the statistical analysis of the resulting data is beyond the scope of the present chapter. Guidance for data collection is provided by references in the list at the conclusion of this chapter, especially those by Bloom (2), Bryn (3), Krathwohl (8), Mager (10), Thorndike (14), and Webb (15). Guidance for data analysis can be provided by standard texts on statistics and research methods in the social and behavioral sciences such as Hays (7). The purpose of this section of the present chapter is to identify some of the major activities in the collection and analysis of program evaluation data, and to suggest relationships between these activities. The activities that are described briefly below are: deciding on types of data, selecting sources of data, using methods of collecting data, and chosing data analysis procedures to facilitate arriving at conclusions.

1. *Deciding on Types of Data*—In the evaluation of a specific continuing education program, the types of data that should be collected depend very much upon the purposes and anticipated use of the results. Those who develop an evaluation plan have many types of potential data from which to select. The most familiar types of data result from the use of verbal paper and pencil multiple choice tests to assess level of knowledge, attitude, and skill. Categories of knowledge objectives along with illustrative test ques-

tions are provided by Bloom (2) and comparable materials regarding attitudes are provided by Krathwohl (8). A comparable taxonomy has been developed recently for skills by Simpson (12), and there are numerous brief skill tests that have been developed for use in the appraisal of employee aptitudes. Attitude scales and opinion poll questions yield additional types of data regarding attitudes. In addition to the verbal paper and pencil tests, there are non-verbal tests that are used for assessing ability and achievement in fields such as mathematics, art, music, and use of equipment. The data may focus on the content of the topic being studied, or on the process of doing something with the content, such as understanding of relationships or using critical judgment. This type of data may be collected at the beginning and at the end of an educational program to assess progress. In some instances it may be satisfactory to find out afterwards from the learner or from someone close to him, such as a supervisor, his opinion of how much was learned. A more convincing but less accessible type of data is based on the ability of the learner to perform either in an actual or a simulated situation. This type of data would typically result from the report and/or the observation of the learner, regarding how well he was able to apply what he learned. Examples include computer programs written following a programming course, skill in play following bridge lessons, reduction in erosion following a soil conservation course, and estate plans prepared following an estate planning course. In some respects, the simulated situation such as the Link Trainer for pilot training or the computer based decision making game for the preparation of administrators, provides a more satisfactory basis for assessing the extent to which the course has prepared the learner to apply what he has learned. This is because it eliminates the interference of the actual situation, such as a supervisor who blocks the efforts of the learner to apply ideas gained from a course.

2. *Selecting Sources of Data*—Data should be collected from the most valid sources that are feasible, given the purposes of a specific evaluation plan. Pre- and post-testing of learners provides a more valid indication of learning gain than the opinions of administrators regarding learner progress, but for some purposes, administrator opinions may be satisfactory. Observations of teaching style and consensus by class members are equivalent sources of data, each of which may be preferable in a specific instance. Both participant observers and outside observers can record information about the teaching-learning transaction. In addition to learners, teachers, administrators, and observers, records provide an important source of data. The records may be

agency records such as student registration forms or lists of methods that were used to inform the community about available courses, or community records such as voting figures by precinct, or categories of people on welfare or unemployed. The important point is to attempt to collect data from the appropriate source, which depends upon the type of data to be collected and the purposes for which the data are to be collected.

3. *Using Methods for Collecting Data*—The most familiar method of collecting evaluation data in preparatory education is the test that is administered under controlled conditions in the classroom. In addition, there are several other major methods of collecting data for continuing education program evaluation. One typical method is the questionnaire or opinionaire, which may be signed or anonymous. The signed questionnaire may be necessary when it must be combined with other information for each learner or teacher. If the frank expression of possibly unpopular views is important, the anonymous opinionnaire may be preferable. An intermediate procedure, when it is desirable to combine information that is collected from the same participants on several occasions, is to ask each person to assign a familiar number (such as telephone, social security, license, or house) to the first questionnaire that is completed, and to make a record of the number that was selected so that it can be assigned to the subsequent questionnaires. The following two items illustrate the types of questions that can be included in brief end-of-session opinionnaire forms. Other items might collect data on how time was spent, especially useful ideas that were gained, and suggested program improvements. The tabulations from a session can be compared by the teacher with similar tabulations, and a substantially less positive reaction can be a cue for a more detailed appraisal. For brief evaluation interviews, an interview schedule can be prepared that contains the sequence of questions

to be asked, and spaces for the interviewer to record the responses. A similar schedule can be prepared for observers. Another method of collecting evaluation data is consulting public records or accessible private records, such as registration forms, that may have been prepared for other purposes but which contain valuable data that can be appropriately used for evaluation purposes. Examples of registration form items include occupational type, educational level, age, and experience and interests related to the program topic. Detailed suggestions for the use of unobtrusive measures are provided by Webb (15). Again, both desirability and feasibility are criteria in deciding which methods are most appropriate, given the types and sources of data to be collected.

4. *Choosing Data Analysis Procedures*—The purpose for analyzing the evaluation data that are collected, is to be able to draw conclusions from the evidence that can provide a major basis for making judgments regarding program effectiveness and improvement. The elegance of the data analysis procedures that should be used largely depends upon the precision of the conclusions to be drawn. A basic analysis procedure is coding, in which someone may read all of the responses to a question and prepare a list of all of the different types of responses that occur. The resulting inductive classification categories can be used to code the original responses for data processing purposes. A similar but more elaborate procedure is content analysis in which a transcript, tape recording, or video tape recording is analyzed regarding the occurrence of predetermined ideas or themes. A standard procedure for presenting coded data or the responses to test or questionnaire questions, is the frequency distribution in which the number of persons in each category is noted. It is sometimes helpful to also compute the percentage of persons in each category. The same applies to cross tabulations in which a table is prepared that may for instance present the number of persons in each of four age categories who had achieved each of four levels of preparatory education. An illustration of such a table containing both frequency distributions and percentages, is presented in Figure 2. When tests or attitude scales are used, it is sometimes necessary to use item analysis and other procedures to increase the reliability and validity of the set of items. In some instances it is important to obtain a more precise understanding of the extent to which distributions of data differ significantly from what would be expected by chance in a larger population. When the data is in table form, significance tests can be used such as Chi Square. When the difference between two distributions is to be tested, a parametric procedure such as

---

1. How important was this subject and discussion topic for you? (Check one)

       Most important ....1( )
       Very important ....2( )
       Some importance ....3( )
       Little importance ....4( )
       No importance ....5( )

2. Did the presentations have clear and to the point explanations? (Check one)

       Exceptional ....1( )
       Very good ....2( )
       Good ....3( )
       Fair ....4( )
       Poor ....5( )

analysis of variance or a non-parametric procedure such as Mann-Whitney U can be used. Parametric procedures are appropriate when the distribution is similar to the normal bell shaped curve, with most persons in the middle of the range and fewer persons at the extremes. Many more elaborate statistical procedures are available for use when warranted, such as the correlation coefficient, which indicates the extent to which a high degree of one variable, such as intelligence, is associated with a second variable, such as achievement. The important point regarding all of these data analysis procedures is that the purpose is to place the data in a form that will enable the most valid conclusions to be drawn.

Age	Years of Formal Education								Total No.
	-9		9-11		12		13+		
	No.	%	No.	%	No.	%	No.	%	
-25	(2)	20	(4)	20	(8)	16	(3)	12	(20)
25-34	(4)	40	(6)	30	(25)	50	(15)	60	(50)
35-44	(2)	20	(6)	30	(10)	20	(4)	16	(22)
45+	(2)	20	(4)	20	(7)	14	(3)	12	(16)
TOTAL	(10)	100%	(20)	100%	(50)	100%	(25)	100%	(108)

Figure 2. Number and percentage of continuing education participants in four age categories within four educational levels.

Using the Results

The basic criteria for the effectiveness of a plan for continuous program evaluation is the extent to which the results are used. There are several ways in which a director can assist in increasing the likelihood that the results of program evaluation will be used for program improvement.

1. *Validity*—The best assurance that evaluation findings will be used is evaluation procedures that are well planned and implemented to produce valid results.

2. *Communication* — The results of evaluation efforts should be communicated to those who can use them, in a form that they can readily understand. Included are learner, teacher, administrator, and policy maker.

3. *Commitment*—Those who would use the results of evaluation should be sufficiently involved in the evaluation process, so that not only are the results valid, but also through involvement they develop a commitment based on understanding. Special efforts may be required to use evaluation findings to justify programs to policy makers such as institutional administrators and boards, legislators, and state education department personnel.

4. *Timing*—The evaluation results should reach those who can use them, during a time period in which their use is feasible. The ideal time is often just before a decision is to be made. Earlier, the results have sometimes not become relevant, and later they are sometimes obsolete.

5. *Implications*—The major implications of the findings should be included in both the evaluation report and the discussion of it.

6. *Time*—Ways should be found to allocate time for the study and utilization of evaluation findings. This time allocation should be reflected in planning for both program development and staff schedules.

7. *Assistance*—Technical assistance should be available for both additional analysis and interpretation of findings.

Summary and Application

The application of the foregoing ideas about continuous program evaluation by a director such as Victor Balancesheet might proceed in the following way. Imagine that Victor decided to prepare an evaluation plan for just one course, and to discuss this plan with the superintendent and several others, before proceeding to prepare a plan for a more extensive evaluation of courses in the division. He wanted his preliminary effort to go well because he recognized that the improvement of program evaluation procedures is one of the major ways in which he can help to increase program effectiveness. He felt that it was especially important to develop a feasible evaluation plan and to encourage the use of results to improve the selected course. The course that he selected was one on business law that showed declining initial enrollments in recent years and a high dropout rate. Following is an outline that Victor Balancesheet might have prepared for his course evaluation plan.

I. *Background regarding the anticipated contribution of evaluation to program improvement*

  A. *Primary purpose of evaluation for this course*
To provide evidence upon which to base sound judgments regarding the effectiveness of the course and the reason for the high dropout rate.

  B. *Symptoms that indicated that the existing procedures were inadequate*

    1. An apparent decline in initial enrollments in recent years, although accurate enrollment records had not been maintained. Enrollments in other business courses were increasing.

    2. A higher dropout rate than for most other courses.

3. Little information from the teacher, present or former participants, or from employers regarding course effectiveness.

II. *The approach to the evaluation plan*

  A. *Ideas about evaluation to keep in mind*

    1. *Evidence*—Especially if the conclusions indicate that the course should be substantially changed or dropped, or that the current instructor should not be rehired, then the evidence upon which the decision is based should be convincing to those affected.

    2. *Benefits*—The cost in time and money should be justified by the anticipated benefits of the program evaluation.

    3. *Frequency*—Existing evaluation data for the course are sparse. The results of moderate evaluation procedures should indicate which data to collect each term, which data to collect in a more detailed study in a year or two, and which data does not appear relevant.

    4. *Feedback*—The evaluation plan should provide for feedback of appropriate information to learners, teacher, and to the administrator.

    5. *Commitment*—The way in which the evaluation procedures are conducted should encourage the instructor to use the results constructively to improve the course, if possible. This suggests that he should become involved in the planning and conducting of the evaluation procedures as soon as possible.

    6. *Objectivity*—It might be helpful to have someone skilled in program evaluation, but outside the division, assist in conducting the evaluation.

    7. *Objectives*—An early step should be the preparation of a clear set of objectives that describe what the learners should know, feel, and be able to do at the the conclusion of the course if it is successful. These objectives will provide a basis for assessing effectiveness.

    8. *Standards*—It would be useful to obtain descriptions of similar courses in similar institutions and communities, with an indication of enrollment trends, dropout rates, and major outcomes.

    9. *Relevance*—Care should be taken to collect data that is relevant to what the teacher is attempting to accomplish and to the course objectives.

    10. *Values*—In arriving at conclusions, value judgments should be identified, and an effort should be made to achieve consensus on the conclusions and next steps by those who are affected.

  B. *Types of evaluation data to be collected*

    1. *Rationale regarding the setting of the course*—The course has been offered in the division about once a year for about twenty years. It has usually been taught by the person who also teaches it in the day time for the preparatory education students. The participants have been young adults entering the business field. Outside governmental funds reimburse the division for part of the costs. Employers in the community have indicated that such a course is useful to their personnel development efforts and should continue to be in the future.

    2. *Inputs*—The most readily specified input is the teacher who has taught the course during the past two years since he started teaching. There is little information on hand about the characteristics of the learners, or of the instructional materials.

    3. *Transaction* — The instructional setting consists of a two-hour class session once a week for twelve weeks, plus homework. It would seem useful to find out how teacher and learners spend their time related to the program.

    4. *Outcomes*—There appear to be no statements of intended outcomes, beyond the broad course purpose of teaching principles of business law. It is assumed that teacher and learners could identify the objectives that are implicit in the current course. One intended outcome seems to be to assist employers in personnel development.

  C. *Functions of the division that may relate to course effectiveness*—It would appear that the functions that might be related to course effectiveness are publicizing courses, working relationships between the division and employers, and procedures for staff selection and supervision.

  D. *Probable methods of data collection and analysis*

    1. *Types of data*—Primarily factual information about personal characteristics and course procedures, opinions regarding course objectiveness and effectiveness, and test results regarding learner achievement.

    2. *Sources of data*—At this stage, the data would be collected primarily from teacher, current participants, and former participants (separated by those who completed the course and those who dropped out).

3. *Methods of collecting data*—An informal interview with the teacher and an anonymous opinionnaire for participants.
4. *Data analysis procedures* — The forms would be tabulated separately for the teacher and the three categories of participants.

E. *Using the results*—The following procedures will be employed to increase the likelihood that the findings will be used.
  1. *Validity*—Working closely with both the teacher and the outside evaluation specialist should increase the validity of the findings.
  2. *Communication* — Make sure that the teacher is involved or informed at each step of the process.
  3. *Commitment*—Endeavor to establish and maintain the constructive interest of the teacher in the process.
  4. *Timing*—Plan to complete the project so that the results can contribute to planning for next year.
  5. *Implication*—Include implications for action in the report.
  6. *Time*—Recognize the extra time that the teacher and participants will be spending on the evaluation process.
  7. *Assistance*—Make provision for the needed technical assistance for designing evaluation procedures and data processing.

The foregoing outline of an evaluation plan would provide a starting point for Victor's conversation with the superintendent. It is likely that after conversations with the superintendent, the teacher of the business law course, and an outside evaluation specialist, the plan would be modified substantially. Information gained in the early stages of the process would contribute to detailed planning of later stages. If all goes well with the course evaluation, Victor would probably explore with his teachers the points at which more widespread evaluation procedures would be most useful. In this way, over several years, it would be possible to set up procedures for continuous program evaluation that would contribute to the achievement of increasingly effective programs of continuing education for adults.

And isn't that what we're all striving for? By the way, what procedures are you using for continuous program evaluation?

REFERENCES

Following are fifteen of the most useful references for further study, which deal with aspects of program evaluation.

1. American Educational Research Association: *Perspectives of Curriculum Evaluation*, AERA Monograph Series on Curriculum Evaluation, No. 1. Chicago: Rand McNally & Co., 1967. 102 pp. (A collection of excellent papers on aspects of program evaluation.)
2. Bloom, Benjamin S. et al. *Taxonomy of Educational Objectives*: *Handbook 1*: *Cognitive Domain*. New York: David McKay Co., Inc., 1955. (A rationale, with examples, for stating specific educational objectives regarding knowledge, along with illustrative evaluation questions.)
3. Byrn, Darcie et al. *Evaluation in Extension,* prepared by U.S. Federal Extension Service, Division of Extension Research and Training, Topeka, Kansas: H. M. Ives, 1959. 107 pp. (A practical handbook containing illustrations and examples related to adult education.)
4. Cook, Desmond L. *An Introduction to Pert.* Columbus, Ohio: Bureau of Educational Research and Service, 1964. 15 pp. (A rationale for developing a plan for continuous evaluation of a complex educational program.)
5. Corey, Stephen M. *Action Research to Improve School Practices.* New York: Bureau of Publications, Teachers College, Columbia University, 1953. 161 pp. (One of the most comprehensive statements on the use of research procedures for the purpose of evaluation and program improvement.)
6. Knox, Alan B. "Adult Education Agency Clientele Analysis," Chapter IX In *Review of Educational Research* 35 (1965): 231-239. (A review of studies that have compared the characteristics of adult education participants with the general adult population.)
7. Hays, William L. *Statistics for Psychologists.* New York: Holt, Rinehart, & Winston, Inc., 1965. (An excellent standard text on statistics.)
8. Krathwohl, Daivd R. et al. *Taxonomy of Educational Objectives*: *Handbook II*: *Affective Domain.* New York: David McKay Co., Inc., 1964. (A rationale, with examples, for stating specific educational objectives regarding attitudes, along with illustrative evaluation questions.)
9. Lee, Doris M. "Teaching and Evaluation," *Evaluation as Feedback and Guide,* 1967 Yearbook, Association for Supervision and Curriculum Development, 1967. Chapter 4, pp. 72-100. (Papers on program evaluation, oriented towards the schools.)
10. Mager, R. F. *Preparing Objectives for Programmed Instruction.* San Francisco: Fearon Publishers, 1962. (A guide to preparing detailed objectives to parallel learning activities.)
11. Miller, Harry and McGuire, Christine. *Evaluating Liberal Adult Education.* Boston: Center for the Study of Liberal Education for Adults, 1961. 184 pp. (A rationale and illustrative evaluation approaches for four adult education areas: community participation, political affairs, the arts, ethical issues.)
12. Simpson, Elizabeth J. "The Classification of Educational Objectives, Psychomotor Domain," *Illinois Teacher of Home Economics* 10: 110-144; Winter 1966-67. (The final report on an ex-

ploratory study that includes a tentative classification system for psychomoter skills.)

13. Stake, Robert E. "The Countenance of Educational Evaluation," *Teachers College Record* 68 (1967): 523-540. (A comprehensive rationale for program evaluation.)

14. Thorndike, Robert L., and Hagen, Elizabeth. *Measurement and Evaluation in Psychology and Evaluation.* New York: John Wiley & Sons, Inc., 1961. 602 pp. (A standard text on the development of evaluation instruments.)

15. Webb, Eugene J. et al. *Unobtrusive Measures.* Chicago: Rand McNally & Co., 1966. (Descriptions of ways to collect data that do not influence the behavior of the people being studied.)

CHAPTER 24

EVALUATING THE COST-EFFECTIVENESS OF INSTRUCTIONAL PROGRAMS

Marvin C. Alkin

Cost-Benefit Versus Cost-Effectiveness Evaluation

What is cost-benefit and analysis? What are some of the difficulties encountered in applying the technique to the kind of decision situation which concerns most educators at the individual school or district level? Finally, what kind of evaluation technique might be used instead of cost-benefit analysis for evaluating educational systems?

Techniques such as cost-benefit analysis are designed primarily as aids in making prescriptive decision statements. Consequently, those interested in using such procedures are concerned with providing data about real world situations that will allow decision-makers to act. In this kind of analysis, therefore, we attempt to find the value of alternative courses of action not only in terms of the outcome dimensions or outputs of the treatment but also in terms of the financial costs that are associated with each alternative. Most educators, it seems, have much less difficulty accepting benefits or outcome measures as an indication of value than they do in accepting costs. Despite the educators' disdain for them, costs are also of considerable importance. The only time an individual can safely disregard cost is when he finds himself in the happy situation of having unlimited resources—not only in terms of material goods and services but also in terms of time and energy. To be in a situation in which costs can be disregarded is certainly not the reality of today.

The idea of cost-benefit analysis is deceptively simple. It requires only that we identify the costs and benefits associated with our alternatives. Once we ascertain the costs and benefits of alternatives, we can easily select the alternative that yields the largest benefits for a given cost, or we can select the alternative which will yield the least cost for a given level of benefits. The often-stated idea that cost-benefit analysis attempts to maximize gains or benefits while minimizing costs is not true; however, if it were true, the task would be impossible. It is analogous to asking a geographer to find the deepest lake at the highest elevation. No matter which lake he selected, there would always be a slightly shallower lake at a slightly higher elevation; eventually, he might find himself beside a drop of water on the summit of Mount Everest. However, if we restate this task by limiting either the depth of the lake or the elevation, then the problem can be solved. The same logic applies to cost-benefit analysis. It is impossible to choose a policy which simultaneously maximizes benefits and minimizes costs. There is no such policy. If we compare policies A and B, we might find that occasionally A yields greater benefit yet costs less than B. In this case we might say that A dominates B. A, however, does not minimize cost while maximizing benefits. Maximum benefits are infinitely large, and minimum cost is zero. If we seek a policy which has this outcome, we obviously shall not find it.

In order to use cost-benefit analysis in a fruitful way, we must be able to specify all costs and benefits—our decision criteria. In addition, we must specify those which are variable and those costs or benefits which are limited or constrained. At the very least, limits must be set on the variability which will be allowed to each (costs and benefits) and on the acceptable trade-offs between gains on one dimension and losses on another.

Cost-benefit is primarily an economic analysis. In other words, the method of cost-benefit analysis is a tool of the economist developed primarily to examine economic entities. *One of the main requirements of cost-benefit analysis is that both input and output measures be specified in the same units, namely dollars.* This concept is important if one is to make judgments about specific programs. Thus, in the private sector of the economy, a specific business firm might decide to increase its capitalization in order to expand one of its programs which has a favorable cost-benefit ratio; that is, it is likely to yield a monetary profit.

Applications of cost-benefit analysis in the public sector of the economy primarily have been made in the areas of water resource development and national defense. In each instance the technique demands a specification of the multiple outcome dimensions in terms of dollar benefits. As a result, while the major direct benefit of the construction of a hydroelectric project might be the dollar value of the electrical energy which has been produced, there are indirect benefits—such as relief from losses of home, property, farm crops, etc.—from potential flooding. Somewhat more intangible benefits, such as the physical and mental well-being of individuals relieved of the fear of floods, are also assigned dollar values (McKean, 1958).

Traditional applications of cost-benefit analyses in education have been primarily at very large levels of educational aggregation, e.g., states, regions, nations. This situation is easily understandable, for it is primarily at such levels that data are more readily available on dollar values of educational outcomes. Thus, Becker (1962) focused his attention on the social gain from college education as measured by its effects on national productivity and concluded, among other things, that "private rates of return on college education exceed those on business capital" (Becker, 1962). In another study (Hansen, 1963), the internal money rates of return were calculated for successive stages of education where returns were estimated from cross-section data of the incomes of individuals classified by age and education. Finally, in 1966, Hirsch and Marcus examined the costs and benefits of universal junior college education as compared to alternative uses of the same financial resources for summer programs in secondary schools.

What is evident in the limited number of examples above is that, in each case, the outcome dimensions have been transformed into dollar benefits utilizing traditional economic indices. But, because school district boundaries are very often not coterminous with other governmental entities, economic indices are not available at the level of individual schools or school districts. Yet, even if economic indices were available, cost-benefit analysis might still prove appropriate by virtue of the mobility of student populations in school districts, complicated by other difficulties related to identifying long-range economic benefits for educational units as small as individual schools. Moreover, cost-benefit analysis may not address itself to the most relevant question for the kind of unit about which we are concerned. In short, we are concerned not so much with the economic consequences of certain investment decisions in education as with evaluating the system components in terms of the objective dimensions defined.

Unlike cost-benefit analysis, which poses no direct challenge to the general decision-making machinery of the political system, we wish to examine a real-world decision situation in which not all outcomes are definable in economic terms.

In summary, when cost-effectiveness is referred to in the context of this paper, it should bring to mind a model that will enable us to consider relevant elements of educational systems at school or district levels of aggregation in order to (a) compare educational outcomes of different units, (b) assess impact of alternative levels of financial input, and (c) select alternative approaches to the achievement of specified educational outcomes.

Components of a Cost-Effectiveness Model

What are the components of a model that allows the decision-maker to evaluate education through a cost-effectiveness evaluation? First, it is necessary to define what we mean by a model.

To put it briefly, a model is simply an attempt at classifying the major elements of an entity or a phenomenon with regard to their functions and interrelationships in order to observe more easily how the elements function within the entity, how they enable the entity to operate, and how they act upon one another. In this way, we can also determine the consequences of modifying the elements. Most models reflect the bias and interests of their developers. This one is no exception; our prime interest is a consideration of administrative and financial variables in education, specifically where a single school or a school district is the unit of analysis. To be sure, an evaluation model, or for that matter any model, is a simplistic statement or representation of sets of complex interrelationships; but such a representation is intended only to help the model builder to structure the universe which concerns him.

What elements comprise our model of evaluation? "Student inputs" are an aspect of our evaluation model. The term refers to the nature and characteristics of the students entering the program to be evaluated. "Educational outputs" are another aspect of the model. By "educational outputs" we mean two things: (a) cognitive and non-cognitive changes which take place in students after they are exposed to the instructional program and (b) the impact of the program upon systems external to it (home, community, other programs, etc.). A third component of the evaluation model is "financial inputs," which refer to the financial resources made available for carrying on the program. "Manipulatable characteristics," a fourth element of the model, are the descriptive characteristics (e.g., personnel, school organization and programs, and instructional program) of the way in which financial inputs are utilized within the program in combination with with the student inputs. Finally, our evaluation model must consider "external systems," an aspect which is the framework of social, political, legal, economic, and other systems outside the school, formal or informal, which encompass the program, have impact upon it, and are, in turn, modified by the outputs of the program.

In the discussion of manipulatable characteristics, we act under the assumption that they are the only administratively manipulatable set of variables. For the sake of this model, we will assume that (a) external systems are not immediately altered by the outputs of the system and (b) that the school decision-makers have no control over which external systems are allowed to impinge upon the school. If we were to maintain that feedback immediately changes the system, this would imply a dynamic model rather than the static model considered here. The second assumption implies that no attempt will be made to change the nature of the student inputs to the system; that is, we do not usually concern ourselves with the consideration of possible changes in the community that would alter the nature of the student inputs. We act, too, under the assumption that student inputs are relatively non-manipulatable from outside the system. Thus, we concern ourselves with the manipulatable variables within the system that can be manipulated and altered to maximize student outputs. We recognize that there is a weakness in this assumption and that there are some school-related manipulations that could be instituted which would change the nature of the student input. Instances of this are bussing, changing of school boundaries in order to "juggle" student inputs to specific schools, community educational resources (such as education resource units in disadvantaged areas), and pre-school programs (such as Project Headstart). The assumptions of a static model and of nonmanipulatable external systems seem necessary at this early stage of the model development.

With our definition of evaluation and some of the limits we are imposing in mind, it is now possible to discuss the evaluation model.

Student Inputs

We will consider the student input as a description or measure of the student being introduced into the system or, in the case of a larger unit of instructional program, as an aggregated, statistical description of the students being introduced into the system. (See Figure 1.) In the ideal world, when students enter the system, they are given a complete battery of all the traditional kinds of achievement, intelligence, and personality tests, as well as questionnaires and other documentary data describing their homes, status in the community, family background, family memberships in other social systems, and the like. Unfortunately, the ideal world does not exist. We must, therefore, develop a series of proxy measures of student inputs. Very frequently, intelligence scores are available for entering students; also, there is usually a small amount of

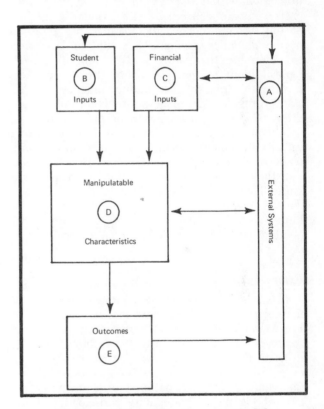

Figure 1. Cost-Effectiveness Model.

family data available in the cumultive record folder. Occasionally, achievement tests given in the preceding year or two have been transferred and are available as a measure of the achievement starting-point of the students in the system. A considerable amount of additionally desired data must, consequently, either be collected in the school or, more often, inferred from other more accessible measures. As a result, we often look at the community and the characteristics of the community as an indication of the kind of student input that is being introduced into the system.

Financial Inputs

There is a second class of inputs to the system—financial inputs. If we think of a district as a system, then not only do students enter the system, but finances are provided from local, state, and federal sources and are, in part, a means of implementing different sets of mediating factors within the system. Perhaps it is relevant to determine the portion of the total resources derived from each of the governmental levels. Perhaps it is also important to designate the specific authorizations from federal funds or special state programs to be aware of the "strings attached" and consequent implications for resource utilization within the system.

If we were concerned with evaluating a part of the system, such as the mathematics program or the guidance program, it would be necessary to determine the nature and amount of the financial input to that portion of the system. Unfortunately, present accounting practices in all states provide data only on functions of expenditures rather than on programs of expenditures; i.e., data are available on a number of factors such as the amount spent for administration, maintenance, operation, instruction, and fixed charges; but these data are not available on a program basis. Thus, the desire to include financial input data in evaluation studies would require special budget review or new accounting procedures, depending upon the level of aggregation under consideration.

External Systems

The school is placed within the framework of numerous social systems (external social contexts). For example, in the case of the individual school some of the contexts are the community, the district, the nature of the district organization, other governmental systems such as the city and the county, and the patterns of community organizations and of community participation. Each of these external systems, by the nature of the differentiated functions it serves, places sets of demands and restrictions both upon the educational system (school) and upon the individuals within the system. Each of these systems serves specific integrative, adaptive, goal-attaining, and pattern-maintaining functions in the macro-system. Consequently, it is necessary to identify and quantify these external systems' characteristics and relationships which are relevant in terms of the contribution they make towards producing the educational outputs of the system.

In actuality, the external systems interact with the educational system. While each of them may be conceived of as having its own inputs, particular sets of mediating variables, and outputs, each is, in turn, an external system to the educational system and *vice versa*. Thus, each system external to education may be considered as both a source of inputs and a receiver of outputs.

Manipulatable Characteristics

A fourth group of elements of the evaluation model is termed manipulatable characteristics. The financial input to a system can be utilized in a great number of ways. We can decrease the student-to-teacher ratio, establish standards which insure the hiring of teachers with specified characteristics, develop different administrative arrangements within the school, provide more library books, provide more textbooks, introduce different curricula, use different instructional procedures, or provide additional supplies. Thus, these manipulatable characteristics are subject to change or manipulation by educational decision-makers at all levels. We have no definitive evidence, however, indicating which combination of these characteristics is most effective in achieving the objectives of the school, i.e., in producing desired educational outputs.

At this point, it is only fair to indicate that we do not mean to imply that all these characteristics which have impact on educational outputs are related to financial input. For example, the cost of implementing certain alterations in the school environment or in the attitudes of teachers may be relatively cost free. Frequently, the instructional procedure used by the teacher in the classroom (the substitution of one procedure for another) has little or no additional cost attached to it. However, some changes in the system such as some of the administrative or organizational arrangements and many instructional procedures which are technologically based are extremely costly. Consequently, the potential output achieved by the change must be examined in terms of the costs involved.

To maintain that more money should be provided for teacher salaries and that in this way, in all likelihood, the educational program will be improved is an easily defensible position. There is evidence that a relationship exists between higher teacher salaries and educational quality. The real question, however, is to what extent a given dollar input, if utilized in an alternate manner, would increase certain educational outputs. This is a cost-effectiveness question and is, after all, one of the elements at the heart of evaluation or, at the very least, one of the reasons why we evaluate.

We have noted that the selection of different sets of mediating factors may lead to the maximization of educational outputs in a system. There is, though, another point to be made: not only are there different sets of manipulatable characteristics applicable for producing given educational outputs; but, significantly, these sets of variables may produce quite different levels of change in the educational outputs in different systems or for different student input groups. James Coleman observed this point in a study for the Civil Rights Commission entitled *Equality of Educational Opportunity*. He noted that the "inference might then be made that improving the school of a minority pupil may increase his achievement more than would improving the school of a white child increase his." Similarly, the average minority pupil's achievement may suffer more in a school of low quality than might the average white pupil's. He concluded that "this indicates that it is for the most disadvantaged children that improvements in school quality will make the most difference in achievement" (Coleman, 1966). Appropriate manipulatable characteristics, therefore, are functions not only of the desired educational outputs but of the nature of the student inputs and of the given system as well.

As mentioned earlier, we believe these characteristics to be the only set of variables that can be manipulated. This belief is a simplifying assumption, in part, because it allows us to deal with a static, instead of a more complex dynamic model. Also, the bias implied by this assumption follows from the basic intent of the model we are seeking to construct, that is, a decision-making model or, more specifically, a model designed to aid in evaluating schools and the operations of schools.

Outcomes

The first set of outcomes of concern to us in the model is student outcomes which are affected by changes that take place in students from the time they enter the system to the time they leave it. Many of these changes are produced by the nature of the costly manipulatable factors within the system. Here, again, there is a problem, for the outcomes of a school or of a district cannot be measured solely by the scores of students on academic achievement tests.[1] What are the non-cognitive aspects of outcome or output? How has the behavior of students changed? What is the relationship between the activities that take place in a district or a school and the eventual success of students in their vocational or future educational endeavors? How does the student's educational experience aid him in dealing with political problems and activities and with cultural affairs? To what extent does the school's social situation, as well as what is learned in classes, affect the student? These are only some of the

unanswered questions related to the identification of educational outcomes; and, of course, they can be solved only through further research and investigation.

While there are two prime inputs into the system (student and non-student or financial), we will consider that there are no financial outcomes except as we are willing to place financial value on certain behavioral changes or except as student outcomes yield financial or economic returns, either individual or social.[2]

The second set of outcomes in the model is the non-student outputs. The two groups of outcome measures (student and non-student) may be thought of as feedback loops in which each modifies, to some extent, the nature of future inputs to the system. The changes in students, for example, have social, political, and economic implications; that is, the very nature of the external systems is altered by changes in student outputs. There are, however, other outcomes of the school: the impact of educational decisions made as a part of the "manipulatable characteristics" has repercussions in the external systems. Frequently, these outputs are only tangentially related to individual students or to student outputs. For example, the nature of many of the decisions about the proper utilization of resources may produce innumerable educational outcomes not directly student-related. In brief, decisions which influence the number and salaries of teachers, as well as the number and salaries of classified personnel, could, in many ways, modify the nature of some external systems, especially if these employees were to reside in the district. To what extent do teachers paid at different salary levels have the economic ability to forego other earnings and instead participate in community activities and organizations? Furthermore, how is the nature of these external systems modified by the educational decision that determined the particular combination of manipulatable characteristics which allowed greater salaries for the teachers? Also, how do the type and quality of teachers selected affect the changing nature of the community? Another example might be the impact upon the economy of the community brought about by the selection of manipulatable characteristics which include large capital invest-

1. We would readily admit, however, to the chagrin of many reluctant school administrators, that this measure at least would be a feasible starting point.

2. There is evidence that this is a reasonable approach. See Becker; also Miller, "Income and Higher Education: Does Education Pay Off?" (Ed.) S. J. Mushkin, *Economics of Higher Education* (Washington, D. C.: U.S. Department of Health, Education, and Welfare, Office of Education, 1962); and Schultz, "Investment in Human Capital," *American Economic Review* 51 (March, 1961): 1-16.

ment or a large amount of supplies and materials locally purchased. How do the educational decisions related to whether school transportation will be provided or the hours of school or the scheduling of student time, in terms not only of regular session classes but with respect to recreational and summer use of school facilities, have implications for parental employment patterns or avocational participation? And, to what extent does the school, as a merchant of facts, knowledge, and ideas, influence community attitudes on political, social, and cultural issues? Finally, although the list could be extended greatly, how does the impact of the selection of manipulatable characteristics upon the social patterns within the school relate to breaking down or reinforcing patterns within the systems external to the school?

We realize that it is not possible to isolate every conceivable element of the total system and to determine its value or its individual, contributory relationship to the educational outputs of the system. Nevertheless, it is requisite in any evaluation scheme to identify and control as many as possible of the factors thought to be significant; for the more we can isolate these factors, the more accurate our analysis can be.

Our next step must be an analysis of how our model might be used in different kinds of evaluation situations.

Potential Applications of the Cost-Effectiveness Model

As we have already noted, traditional cost-benefit approaches do not provide the necessary data or meet the educational needs to which we have addressed ourselves. In this section, therefore, the cost-effectiveness analysis model we propose is clarified, and its uses in different evaluation situations are described. For purposes of this paper, "program" pertains to a package which encompasses all the agency's efforts to achieve a particular objective or set of allied objectives. In educational terms, programs are defined as secondary education, junior college education, etc. However, it is difficult to assemble and describe a package which would encompass all the efforts to achieve a sub-objective like teaching elementary school children to read; that is, it would be extremely difficult to consider the cost elements and program elements of all aspects of the total school program related to the reading achievement of children.

Thus, "program alternatives" are differing possible approaches towards achieving the same or similar objectives. In education, public schools and private schools might be program alternatives; if different schools are assumed to be working towards the same objectives, in whole

or in part, then the total programs of these schools also may be considered as program alternatives. Different schools have different program alternatives. Consequently, one might evaluate the success of different program alternatives in achieving the specified objectives of the programs. Since there is varying quality in student inputs to programs, one would, of course, expect that the outputs would vary; and in order to evaluate the program alternatives, one must somehow be able to control for differences in student input and external systems.

This notion of alternative programs can be extended. If programs are similar in their uncontrollable characteristics (student inputs and external systems) but different in the levels of financial input, they may be thought of as alternative programs for achieving the same or similar objectives. By taking the "black box" approach to the problem, one could evaluate the cost-effectiveness of alternative programs where alternative programs are defined as differences in financial inputs to the system, without regard for the manner in which these inputs are utilized.

Consider this evaluation in terms of the model described in Figure 1, where variable set A refers to the external system, variable set B refers to the student inputs, variable set C refers to the financial inputs, variable set D refers to the costly manipulatable characteristics, and variable set E refers to the outcomes. Using this simple diagram and the variable sets as numbered, note that alternative instructional programs (school financial resources) can be evaluated in terms of cost-effectiveness, using variable sets A and B as controls with variable set C financial inputs as the predictor variable set, and variable set E as the criterion (see Figure 2). A question emerges from the model: When student inputs and external systems are held constant statistically, what is the outcome change (on each of a number of dimensions) associated with a dollar increase in financial input?

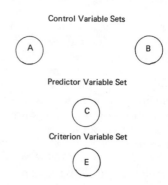

Figure 2. Evaluating cost-effectiveness of alternative instructional programs—school financial resources.

A second kind of cost-effectiveness evaluation might be concerned with the assessment of specific instructional programs. In this case, we would study specific total institutional programs of schools on the basis of their performance on the outcome dimensions after we have accounted for the effects of specific uncontrollable characteristics of their own system. Thus, if one merely wanted to evaluate schools as institutions, in terms of what kind of job they are doing relative to the resources (human and fiscal) available to them, the model discussed above could be invoked to perform a cost-effectiveness analysis. In short, if financial inputs are considered one of the uncontrollable variables in the system and are, therefore, contained in the model, the degree to which an individual institution achieved success on the outcome dimensions at the level we would predict is a measure of the cost-effectiveness of the institution's total program. For example, institution 1 with student inputs (S_1), external systems characteristics (E_1), and financial inputs (F_1), might be predicted as achieving various criterion dimensions at stipulated levels, $C_{1,\,1}, C_{2,\,1}, C_{3,\,1} \ldots C_{i,\,1}$. When the institution matches or exceeds these predictions in terms of outcomes or consequences assumed to be favorable, or at least not deleterious, the institution is being run efficiently, relative to each of the specified outcome dimensions.

Thus, the second type of cost-effectiveness study that might be done is of a particular school. The evaluation of an individual school program would be in terms of the statistically derived expectations for that program in light of its own uncontrollable characteristics (see Figure 3). The cost-effectiveness scores for a school would be determined on the basis of ratios of actual to predicted achievement on each of the criterion dimensions. Therefore, a school whose actual achievement on a criterion measure exceeds its predicted achievement could be said to be cost-effective with respect to the specified criterion dimension.

We may consider the concept of "alternative ways to do a given job" borrowed from PPBS (Planning Programming Budgeting Systems) as a useful means of providing the framework for a third type of cost-effectiveness evaluation. The "given job" notion means that the output to be produced and the program have been predetermined. The question at any phase of the program becomes: Can we alter the production or distribution technique and by doing so (a) improve the timing of the production or delivery (fulfill program objectives in a shorter period of time, thereby consuming less student time), or (b) improve the quantity and quality of the items being produced (educate a greater number of students in the program or achieve a higher level of objectives or fewer undesirable consequences), or (c) modify the unit cost or total cost of the production or delivery (which, in education, would refer to fewer financial input dollars to achieve the same objectives)? "Alternative ways to do a given job" takes the program as given or specified and increases the possibilities for changing the mix of input utilization alternatives, thereby modifying the program. This function seems quite appropriate in terms of the problem at hand, for while the question about alternative educational programs provides some answers in terms of the cost-effectiveness of total educational systems, it fails to render insights into the attributes of the system which make a difference in the production of educational outputs.

There are, of course, vast differences from place to place in the quality of resources available for use as alternatives or options. Where the economist thinks of teachers, materials, etc., as inputs to the system, he refers to quality differences in inputs. In this model, which is geared to the decision-making of the educational administrator, cost factors such as teachers, textbooks, clerks, and aides are viewed as costly manipulable characteristics of the system. Each of them represents a potential means of financial input utilization.

A major responsibility of the state is to make available to local districts input utilization options of high enough quality to insure that the school districts may operate efficiently. States assume this responsibility in a number of ways. In part, the input utilization options are defined by the economy of a state, by alternative employment opportunities, by access to higher education, etc. Also, the state government defines the quality

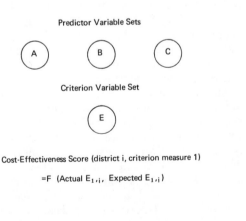

Figure 3. Evaluating the cost-effectiveness of individual school programs.

of the input utilization options by the state-established legal requirements for education and by state procedures for credentialing teachers. Thus, what a financial input will buy in a school district (the purchasing power of a financial input) is determined, in part, by the state government, the geographic region, and even, perhaps, by the nature of the individual community.

We have noted that it is not possible or appropriate to maximize effectiveness while minimizing costs. In terms of the problem posed here, then, it is impossible to consider simultaneously fulfilling program objectives in a shorter period of time, modifying the unit cost of the production of educational outcomes, and providing a higher level of achievement of educational objectives. Several of these must be specified as program constraints with one specifically designated as the purpose of the cost-effectiveness analysis. A consideration of the evaluation of the cost-effectiveness of specific costly manipulatable characteristics of the system (teachers, textbooks, clerks, equipment) has been proposed. This proposal implies a concern for the maximization of outputs which utilize the options for resource allocation within the system, the total financial input and student inputs, including time, constrained within the model. In terms of our model, this process requires the consideration of variable sets A, B, and C as control variables, individual variables D as predictors, and variable set E as criterion measures.

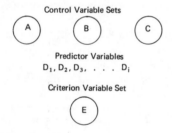

Control Variable Sets

Predictor Variables
$D_1, D_2, D_3, \ldots D_i$

Criterion Variable Set

Figure 4. Evaluating cost-effectiveness of input utilization options.

Another question inevitably arises: When student and financial input characteristics of the external system are held constant statistically, what is the effect of each costly manipulatable characteristic of the system upon increased educational outputs? Such an evaluation requires, in addition to drawing the relationship between the costly manipulatable characteristics and the various outcome dimensions, that one examine the cost functions of the costly manipulatable characteristics.

The procedure, then, is to determine the change in output associated with each incremental unit

change in each of the costly manipulatable characteristics. There are at least three major problems that one might anticipate at this stage of an analysis: (a) there would be difficulty in obtaining accurate cost data related to the manipulatable characteristics; (b) there would be difficulties in dealing with cost-effectiveness estimates in the light of systems interrelationships, and (c) there would be difficulties in generalizing to individual cases (if such generalization were desired).

With respect to the first of these problems, actual data would, of course, be preferable. However, accounting systems do not usually provide this information. In instances where actual data is not possible or feasible, costs might be derived by constructing a cost production function; e.g., in the analysis of a number of cases, data might be derived relating the presence and extent of various manipulatable characteristics to some cost function, such as current expense of education. In this way, a cost curve could be derived describing the production costs related to those characteristics. Such a production function might be derived using historical or longitudinal data, as was done in a study reported by Adelson, Alkin, Carey, and Helmer (1967); or a production function might be produced using cross-sectional data (Katzman, 1967).

There is no simple solution for the second of these problems, systems interrelationships. One might seek to isolate the individual variable from its covariants through appropriate statistical controls. From these statistics on the interrelationships between covariants, one could then determine the expected changes in them that would be associated with an incremental unit change in a given mediating variable. Perhaps systematic use of judgment might be utilized to obtain and isolate the nature of the interrelationships. Then, starting with the statistical data, appropriate cost characteristics could be assigned to elements of the system. Moreover, procedures such as path analysis possibly could be utilized to provide greater insight into the data.

Another possible solution is the use of expert judgment, systematically obtained, e.g., the Delphi Method (Gordon and Helmer, 1964; also Adelson, Alkin, Carey, and Helmer, 1967). It could be quite fruitful to assemble a group of knowledgeable, educational decision-makers representing a variety of backgrounds and interests. They could be allowed to consider the nature of the system interrelationships between variables and from these relationships form some judgment of the cost-effectiveness of each of the available manipulatable characteristics of the system. This Delphi process of summarizing findings—allowing for discussion and presentation of deviant views, feedback to participants, and several additional rounds of the same procedure—might lead to consensus or at least to an understanding of the nature of the dissenting opinions.

The third problem posed is related to the difficulties of generalizing to individual cases. One possible solution to this problem rests with the development of a typology of schools to be used as the moderator variable in the prediction of outcomes in the analysis. There are difficulties related to the use of statistics (such as regression coefficients derived from the analysis of a set of data) in predicting criterion measures (outcomes) for individual cases. The accuracy of a predicted outcome for an individual school, will depend considerably on the type of school as the school varies its costly manipulatable characteristics. To put it simply, one would not expect the same effect from changing the counselor-student ratio at Beverly Hills High School as he would at a small, rural high school. There is certainly a typology of schools that will act as a moderator variable in the prediction of outcomes. The notion of grouping variables being worked on by Klein, Rock, and Evans (1967) at Educational Testing Service might be quite appropriate for use in solving this problem.

Conclusion

In this paper, we drew the distinctions between cost-benefit analysis and cost-effectiveness evaluation. We showed that cost-benefit analysis relies almost exclusively on financial benefits and is, therefore, of limited value in assessing education, where many outcomes cannot be defined economically.

Moreover, we outlined the various components of a model that we believe will enable the decision-maker to perform cost-effectiveness evaluations in education. In the model, we spoke of the need to consider "student inputs"—the characteristics of students entering the system; "educational outputs" — cognitive and non-cognitive changes that occur in students after exposure to an instructional program; "financial inputs"—financial resources available to carry on the program; "external systems"—the social, political, legal,

and economic structure of society; and, lastly, "manipulatable characteristics"—those aspects of the program which are resource-consuming and which are administratively manipulatable.

Finally, we indicated the potential applications of the cost-effectiveness model in different kinds of evaluation situations and how one model is to be used to evaluate the cost-effectiveness of various financial inputs and of individual school programs. In conclusion, we showed that the cost-effectiveness evaluation model could be used to assess the worth of "alternative ways to do a given job."

REFERENCES

Adelson, M.; Alkin, M.; Carey, C.; and Helmer, O. "Planning Education for the Future: Comments on a Pilot Study," *American Behavioral Scientist, 10,* April, 1967, total issue.

Becker, J. S. "Investment in Human Capital: Theoretical Analysis," *Journal of Political Economy,* October, 1962.

Coleman, S. *Equality of educational opportunity.* Washington, D. C.: United States Department of Health, Education, and Welfare, Office of Education, 1966.

Gordon, T. J., and Helmer O. *Report on a long-range forecasting study.* Santa Monica, Calif.: RAND Corporation, 1964.

Hansen, W. L. "Total and Private Rates of Return to Investment in Schooling," *Journal of Political Economy,* April, 1963.

Hirsch, W. Z., and Marcus, M. J. "Some Benefit-cost Considerations of Universal Junior College Education," *National Tax Journal,* June, 1966.

Katzman, M. T. Distribution and production in a big city elementary school system. Ann Arbor, Michigan: University Microfilms, 1967.

Klein, S. P., Rock, D. A., and Evans, F. *Using multiple moderators in the prediction of academic success.* Princeton, N. J.: Educational Testing Service, 1967.

McKean, R. N. *Efficiency in Government Through Systems Analysis.* New York: John Wiley & Sons, Inc., 1958.

Mushkin, S. J., ed. *Economics of Higher Education.* Washington, D. C.: United States Department of Health, Education, and Welfare, Office of Education, 1962.

Schultz, T. Investment in human capital. *American Economic Review,* 51 (1961): 1-16.

CHAPTER 25

Carol H. Weiss

UTILIZATION OF EVALUATION: TOWARD COMPARATIVE STUDY

The problem to which this paper is addressed is the frequent failure of decision-makers to use the conclusions of evaluation research in setting future directions for action programs. I will offer some hypotheses on conditions under which evaluation is or is not utilized, and propose that research be done to test them. In short, this is a proposal for empirical evaluation of evaluation research.

The basic rationale for evaluation is that it provides information for action. Its primary justification is that it contributes to the rationalization of decision-making. Although it can serve such other functions as knowledge-building and theory-testing, unless it gains serious hearing when program decisions are made, it fails in its major purpose.

The record to date appears to be an indifferent one. There are some well-known examples of prompt utilization of evaluation. The New York City Higher Horizons program is one. Evaluation demonstrated the effectiveness of the prototype "Demonstration Guidance Program" in one junior high school, and steps were taken to implement the program in other schools in the system. Unfortunately, in the process, budgets were cut and authority diffused, and the ensuing program never again realized similar success. But this was a problem of inappropriate administration rather than of failure to accept and act on the basic findings.

On the other hand, institutions often do not change their activities in response to evaluation. They explain away the results, sometimes casting aspersions on the evaluator's understanding, the state of his art, and his professional or theoretical biases. Evaluators complain about many things, but their most common complaint is that their findings are ignored.

What accounts for the high rate of non-utilization? I will give some suggestions, which are to be taken as hypotheses for study rather than as an addition to the flood of advice and exhortation to social scientists on how to win more friends and influence more people. The first class of factors leading to non-utilization lies in the organizational systems that are expected to use the evaluation results, and the second class lies in the current state of evaluation practice.

Organizations invariably respond to factors other than the attainment of their formal goals. Even rudimentary knowledge of organizational behavior indicates the salience of the drive for organizational perpetuation, personnel's needs for status and esteem and their attachment to the practice skills in which they have invested a professional lifetime, conservatism and inertia and fear of the unknown consequences of change, sensitivity to the reactions of various publics, costs, prevailing ideological doctrines, political feasibility, and the host of other consideration. Evaluation's evidence of program outcome cannot override all the other contending influences.

What evaluation can do is add its weight to the thrust for change. Few organizations are so monolithically self-satisfied that counterpressures do not exist. Most of them face some discrepancy between the ideal and the actual that generates a search for better ways of operation. (This discrepancy sometimes provided the impetus that led to embarking on evaluation in the first place.) There is at least a potential for utilization. But rather than ignore the forces that tend to subvert the implementation of evaluation results and trust in the good will and rationality of the organization, evaluators might well pay greater attention to the organization-maintenance imperatives that influence decision-making, perhaps even address the covert goals as well as the formal goals of the organization in their research. With better knowledge of the kinds of resistance to be expected, they may be able to devise more effective strategies for defining evaluation issues and for gaining their results a hearing.

A fascinating example of resistance to utilization can be borrowed from military history. In 1940-41 the RAF Bomber Command refused to accept the evidence of aerial photography on the failure of its missions. Photographs indicated that only one of every four aircraft reporting an attack on target had actually gotten within five miles of it. An officer who passed on to this chief an interpretation showing that an attack had missed its mark found it later on his desk with a note scrawled across it in red: "I do not accept this report." The author of the account of these events states, in words that will echo familiarly to social evaluators, "it was very natural that many of those whose work it affected jumped to the comforting conclusion that something must have been wrong with the camera or the photographs or the man who wrote the report."[1]

Fortunately the case had a happy ending, the style of which has implications for our discussion. Professor Lindemann, Churchill's scientific advisor, found the evidence convincing and urgent, and brought it directly to Churchill's attention. "So it was at these topmost levels that the evidence of the photographs was finally faced, and at these levels that the necessary priority was given to developing the new navigational aides . . . which were to change the entire outlook for British night bombing."

Use of evaluation appears to be easiest when implementation implies only moderate alterations in procedure, staff deployment, or costs, or where few interests are threatened. For example, in the Bail Bond project of the Vera Foundation,[2] where only the bail bondsmen stood to lose, use of the evaluation was immediate and dramatic.

On the other hand, application of results can threaten the function of a total organization or an occupational group—such as a detached-worker agency whose program for gangs is found ineffective in reducing delinquency, or psychotherapists, if treated and untreated patients show similar recovery rates. In such cases, even overwhelming demonstration of failure is unlikely to convince the practitioner group or its sponsoring agency to use the findings and go out of business. Use must be made at higher (or lower) levels, by groups that set policy and determine the allocation of resources, or at least hypothetically, by the clients or potential clients themselves.

The other major limitation on use of evaluation results is the current state of evaluation practice. Much evaluation is poor, more is mediocre. Evaluation in action settings is a difficult and demanding enterprise, and calls for a high order of imagination and tenacity as well as research ability. Much has been written in anguished prose about the problems that plague the conduct of evaluation, and just about all of it is true.[3]

The achievement is that good evaluations can be done at all, and yet they are. They use appropriate change criteria and relatively reliable measuring instruments; they use control groups or apply other checks to rule the possibility that observed effects are attributable to non-program factors; their statistical methods and interpretation are sound. If they are not models of exemplary or sophisticated methodology, then they do meet the basic canons of research.

But technical competence by these standards does not imply the absence of methodological problems. Evaluation has special requirements. One of the most serious difficulties in evaluation is the imprecision of the program that is subjected to study. Evaluators usually accept the description of the program given by practitioners as sufficient. They rarely attempt to specify the theoretical premises on which it is based, define the principles that guide its practice, or even monitor its operation so that there is confidence that the program as officially described actually took place—and at a reasonable level of competence. It is possible that the observed effects (or "no effects") to a phantom program, or to one of such marginal caliber that it hardly provides a fair test of the program concept.

The imprecision of program input poses even more basic difficulties. Social action programs are complex undertakings. To quote John Mann:

A positive change in behavior may be found. Assuming that the study itself was carefully designed and executed, this finding may be accurate. But to what is it to be attributed? When the method (program) is carefully examined, it is quickly seen to be an amalgam of components of unknown or partially controlled proportions.[4]

We will return to some of these problems later. Let me turn now to the theme of the paper—a

1. Constance Babington-Smith, *Air Spy*, Ballatine, 1957.

2. National Conference on Bail and Criminal Justice, *Interim Report, May 1964-April 1965*.

3. The catalog includes inadequate academic preparation for research in action agencies; the low status of evaluation in academic circles; program ambiguity and fluidity; practitioner suspicion and resistance; organizational limitations on boundaries for study, access to data, and design requirements; inadequate time for follow-up; inadequacies of money and staffing; controls on publication; etc. Cf. Sidney H. Aronson and Clarence C. Sherwood, "Social Action Research: Some Problems in Researcher, Program Designer, and Practitioner Relationships," May 4, 1966, mimeo; Hyman Rodman and Ralph L. Kolody, "Organizational Strains in the Researcher-Practitioner Relationship," in Gouldner and Miller (eds.), *Applied Sociology*, Free Press, 1965; Carol H. Weiss, "Planning the Evaluation of Action Programs," in Department of HEW, *Learning and Action* (forthcoming); John Mann, *Changing Human Behavior*, Scribner's, 1965, Appendix A.

4. Mann, op. cit., p. 12.

proposal for systematic study of conditions associated with utilization of evaluation results.

The Study of Utilization

There may be value in taking the kinds of impressions discussed here and subjecting them to empirical study. If we can discover here patterns and regularities, if we can get better leads to where, by whom, and under what conditions evaluation results are most likely to be applied, it may become possible to wedge a wider opening.

We can differentiate three major types of use. First is use within the ongoing program, to improve its operation as it goes along. Although this is the type of use that program administrators often expect, it calls for a special kind of short-term, limited-effect, quick-feedback study, and is not always compatible with the evaluation design and schedule that researchers develop. The second use is also at the original site of the program, but occurs at the completion of a total cycle of programming, to decide whether to terminate, modify, or restructure the program, or to continue it and possibly carry it over to other units of the organization. The third use is in outside settings—by agencies operating similar programs, by standard-setting or granting bodies, or by policy-making units at federal, state, or local levels. Such groups make decisions of wider scope, which can affect the initiation or discard of programs throughout a federal, state, or voluntary system. An intermediary "use" can also be recognized—the transmission of evaluation results by linking agents who, persuaded by the evidence, become advocates for its application. State and federal consultants and faculty members of professional schools are examples of such linking intermediaries, whose commitment and influence provide the potential for future utilization. In these days of maximum feasible representation, target group members may be able to play a similar role.

For a study of conditions associated with utilization, one variable must be the direction of results—positive or negative. The implementation of negative results poses issues different in kind as well as degree from the use of positive results.

To eliminate confusion arising from non-use of incompetent, unduly small-scale or fragmentary evaluation (where lack of use can be viewed as a responsible position), it is proposed to limit the study to results of relevant and technically sound evaluations, preferably confirmed by replication or the accumulation of independent evidence.

Types of conditions to be studied include those both outside and inside the evaluator's purview.

A study, or more properly a series of inquiries, might look into such diverse questions as these:

Are new and relatively innovative agencies more responsive to implementing evaluation results than long-established agencies? Is the rigidity of agency doctrine important? What combinations of evaluation results and political or elite pressures are effective? What kinds of threat, and to which levels or staff, generate most resistance? Is utilization affected by the support of top-level administrators for the study—or the evaluator's position or influence in the organizational hierarchy—or the conduct of the evaluation by a university or other outside research organization—or publication of results in books or professional journals? Effects of such factors, and others mentioned earlier in considering organizational behavior, can be studied singly, additively, and in interaction.

I am particularly interested in investigating ways in which evaluation itself is carried out that enhance its utilization. At present, evaluation usually examines conditions before and after the program and comes up with global findings on the extent of change. But rarely can it answer questions about which elements of the program amalgam worked or did not work, and how and why. Yet it is just such information that is vital for institutionalizing a program into routine practice and transferring it to other locations. Without it we are saddled with a load of irrelevant specificities and likely to miss the essential ingredients.

Therefore, utilization might be increased if the evaluation included such elements as these:

(1) the explication of the theoretical premises underlying the program, and direction of the evaluation to analysis of these premises.
(2) specification of the "process model" of the program—the presumed sequence of linkages that lead from program input to outcomes, and the tracking of the processes through which results are supposed to be obtained.
(3) analysis of the effectiveness of components of the program, or alternative approaches, rather than all-or-nothing, go or no-go assessment of the total program.

Evaluation can—and some evaluations have—selected a limited number of program theories or notions and concentrated study on these. They run the gamut from narrow to very broad-range issues. An example of relatively restricted scope can be taken from the evaluation of a program for using young indigenous aides in a community action program. Rather than look at the effectiveness of their total performance, which is a slippery undertaking at best when standards are ambiguous and functions change to fit people, it is possible to look at one premise. This might be the notion that as on-the-job workers, previously unemployed adolescents learn skills more readily than they do as pupils in a work training program. This type of evaluation begins to provide a test for a concept that can be generalized to other places and structures, rather than merely a description of the outcomes of one specific project.

The "process model" diagrams the expected channels of change. For example, a group counseling project is operated for problem girls in an effort to reduce delinquent behavior. By what causal chain is the counseling expected to reach this goal—by changing the girls' self-image? by providing information on other opportunities for self-expression and self-esteem? by motivating them to greater interest in school and vocational achievement? by providing role models for alternative behavior? After the initial stage, what ensuing consequences are expected? The process model makes clear what intermediate effects the evaluation has to look for, and directs attention to the essentials. Tracking the progress of the program input along its putative path allows a test of the theoretical linkages and enables the evaluation to say useful things about the stage where things go awry and adjustment is needed.

Analysis of components of the program and of alternative approaches, can provide information on the effectiveness of specific strategies. The issue for decision is rarely the choice between this program and no program, but the choice among alternative ways of programming.

For utilization, the immediate advantage of these related ways of pursuing evaluation is that they tend to avoid the dead-end of finding the whole program ineffective (or even effective) without any indication of why or what alternative courses of action are likely to be better. Moreover, evaluation findings are more apt to be comparable and additive, and contribute to the building of knowledge.

Some other evaluation procedures also appear to hold promise for utilization and are worth study:

(1) Early identification of potential users of evaluation results and selection of the issues of concern to them as the major focus of study.

Theoretically it is possible for a single study to provide information that can be used by an array of audiences—practitioners, administrators, higher policy makers, professional schools, clients—each of whom had different motivation and capacity to apply the results. In practice, study requirements often diverge. For maximum pay-off, it may be effective to decide in advance where the major potential for utilization lies, and to gear the study to the relevant users.

(2) Involvement of administrators and program practitioners, from both inside and outside the project, in the evaluation process.

Not only does their participation help in the definition of evaluation goals and the maintenance of study procedures, but it may help change the image of evaluation from "critical spying" to collaborative effort to understand and improve. Outside consultants may even become spreaders of the word to other focal sites.

(3) Prompt completion of evaluation and early release of results.

Evaluation reported a year or two, or more, after completion of the program, is often too late to affect decisions, whose schedule is determined by the budgeter's—not the evaluator's—calendar. Long-term follow-up may well be essential but considerations of use may dictate at least preliminary reporting of the direction of results in early phases.

(4) Effective methods for presentation of findings and dissemination of information.

There are at least four sub-items here. One is the clarity and attractiveness of the presentation of evaluation data to non-research audiences. Another is the spelling out of the implications that the study offers for action. This might extend to analysis of the probably consequences of the implied changes for the organization. Third, there may be inventive mechanisms to reach remote audiences impervious to bulky reports and journal articles. And finally, aggressive advocacy by the evaluators for the position derived from evaluation may gain them a hearing in councils of action. This involves the evaluators' abandoning the stance of detached professional appraisal and engaging in the rough and tumble of decision-making both within the organization and in the wider spheres of policy formation.

A first study on utilization of evaluation could select and refine one or two of the notions from this speculative assortment—perhaps the position of the evaluator inside or outside the project staff, an issue with a hardy (mainly oral) tradition, or the inclusion in the evaluation of analysis of alternative program strategies—and investigation of their association with subsequent use of results.

If factors such as those discussed here do in fact increase utilization, there are clear implications for future evaluation practice. If none of these factors has much discernible impact, efforts to apply social science to the solution of social problems must seek new directions. Some critics, for example, have suggested that evaluation be replaced by laboratory experimentation with specific and carefully delimited program components. Although this approach has some appeal, it avoids the effects of the natural setting and the constraints and counterpressures in the larger social system that can nullify program efforts.

What concerns me is the current disenchantment with the utility of evaluation in some influential government agencies and foundations. It is possible that the sins of the program are being visited on the evaluation. Premature disenchantment can clamp limits on creative experimentation in evaluation. Better knowledge of what kinds of evaluation have an impact on decision-making, and under what conditions, should help to encourage more effective development of evaluation practice.

	CHAPTER 26
EVALUATION OF PLANNED EDUCATIONAL CHANGE AT THE LOCAL EDUCATION AGENCY LEVEL	Howard O. Merriman

The advent of planned change in education, with unprecedented support through the expenditure of millions of additional dollars, has brought about not only a need, but a legal requirement for evaluation. In return for Federal support of educational programs, Congress has legislated for an accounting for these funds, not dollar-and-cents bookkeeping, but an accounting for efficacy of the funded program.

This measurement of efficacy, or *evaluation,* is an infant on the educational scene. It lacks an established body of knowledge appropriate to education, sufficient personnel with the necessary competencies and experience, and the techniques and skills to satisfy the legal requirements or needs of the Congress and education.[1]

A traditional view of evaluation is that it ". . . signifies describing something, in terms of selected attributes, and judging the degree of acceptability or suitability of that which has been described . . . (that is) . . . any aspect of the educational scene, but it is typically (a) a total school program, (b) a curricular procedure, or (c) an individual or group of individuals."[2] An explication of evaluation as required by Title I, ESEA, relates that ". . . to evaluate is to judge the worth, rate or value of something. Each decision that is made, each course of action that is chosen, even each word that is spoken follows an evaluation of at least one course of action. Evaluation has taken place anytime something is judged good or bad, better or worse, worth continuing or discontinuing. In education, evaluation provides a basis for making sound decisions about *educational practice and procedures.*"[3] (it. mine)

These guidelines imply the use of evaluation to gather and interpret evidence in support of ingenuity and innovation in reaching educational objectives, such evidence leading to a practical decision, a judgment with the best evidence available. A further clue to the role of evaluation is

that ". . . evaluation is part of the teaching process and should contribute information during the project period as well as at the end . . . (so that) . . . evaluative information may lead to changed methods, or changed objectives, or both."[4]

Title I outlines a complete cycle of educational experimentation and change, with an initial identification of deficiencies in local educational programs, followed by the development and demonstration of effective procedures to alleviate these deficiencies and improve local school practices. Findings of validated programs would then be disseminated.[5] Further testimony concerning the role of evaluation is given by Hastings, who states that "If . . . (we are) . . . to move toward the point of basing decisions . . . on educational purposes and outcome, we need far more evaluative data . . . than . . . in any instance to date." Hastings attributes two general purposes to evaluation: (a) the collection of information to be used as feedback . . . for further revision of materials and methods and (b) to provide information as input for decision-making. . . ."[6]

1. Stufflebeam, D. L. "A Depth Study of the Evaluation Requirement," *Theory into Practice.* Columbus, Ohio: The Ohio State University College of Education. June, 1966, p. 130.

2. Hagen, Elizabeth P. and Thorndike, Robert L. "Evaluation," *Encyclopedia of Educational Research.* New York: The Macmillan Company, 1960, p. 482.

3. *Guide to Evaluation of Title I Projects.* Washington, D. C.: U.S. Office of Education, October, 1966, pp. 2-3.

4. *Guidelines: Special Programs for Educationally Deprived Children: Elementary and Secondary Education Act of 1965/Title I, Section II, Design and Evaluation of Projects.* Washington, D. C.: U.S. Office of Education, 1965, p. 40.

5. *Guide to Evaluation of Title I Projects.* Washington, D. C.: U.S. Office of Education, October, 1966, p. 5.

6. Hastings, J. Thomas. "Curriculum Evaluation: The Why of Outcomes," *Journal of Educational Measurement,* Spring 1966, pp. 27-32.

The Many Faces of Evaluation

It is evident that the query "What is evaluation?" will bring forth differing definitions and characterizations. What is not quite so apparent is that all of these definitions are characterizations of *evaluation*, or at least, components of evaluation. Thus, when Stake in an evaluation report speaks of distinguishing between *antecedent, transaction,* and *outcome* data[7]; Thomas and Kearney of "Identifying target populations, and special educational needs"[8]; Cronbach of "uncovering durable relationships"[9]; the U.S. Office of "feedback" and Mooney "assessing the extent and direction of change"[10]; of letting teachers ". . . say what they see to do and would like to try . . . of recording and data gathering and communicating"[11]; and the others of the various roles and characterizations of evaluation cited earlier in this paper, they are all speaking of activities or components of evaluation that could be categorized in a model-taxonomy of evaluation. The CIPP Model.—To serve as a framework for a study of evaluation, the CIPP Model of evaluation developed at The Ohio State University Evaluation Center is not only useful, but representative of the logical flow of an evaluation effort. The components of the CIPP Model are *Context, Input, Process,* and *Product* evaluation.[12] By limiting the role of evaluation in this paper to its use in project innovations within the local education agency, the relationship of the model components to educational change becomes more apparent.[13]

Evaluation is a way of looking at the world, a means of organizing the realities—in short, an information management system which provides focus to the problems and successes at hand. Much of what evaluation can do for the school administrator or project director-manager has been done before. Few administrators jump into an innovation or change activity without some assessment of context—the extant situation. Educators usually give some thought to the strengths and weaknesses of alternative solution strategies, and through school visits, telephone calls and other informal means, keep "tabs" on "how the project is going." Similarly, it would not be surprising to find that the outcomes of the innovation are measured in some manner. However, it is not an exaggeration to describe these activities as being informal and non-systemized. If one were to list but some of the potential *sources* of information at the disposal of the administrator, (the school, home, community, parents, pupils, teachers, literature, program, and research) and the *types* of information that might be useful to the administrator (attitudes, achievement, socio-economic status, and objectives) it would be apparent that the administrator would necessarily develop a system to

handle the ensuing chaos. And so he does, by giving priority, for example, to (1) information gathered easily, (2) information acquired with least cost, and (3) information acquired with least clutter. But, in so doing, the administrator may lose, among others, (1) a broad base of information, (2) validity and reliability of the information acquired, and (3) source credibility. He is most likely losing more than he is gaining. As an analogy, can one picture the chief executive of a school system arriving at a school board meeting with a shoe box full of bills and another shoe box filled with requests for funds by teachers, principals, aids, etc.? No! He has established an accounting information system, with a budget for fund requests and a statement of expenditures, classified by categories, and certified as reliable and valid by a Certified Public Accountant!

Figure 1 depicts the flow of information with which the school administrator must deal, indicating some of the sources. The decision-maker, the central figure, would utilize the evaluation information system to provide a means of organizing his information to be representative of the appropriate sources, such as teachers, parents and pupils. He would utilize the approach or component (context, input, process, product) to ensure, among other criteria, timeliness, validity, and credibility of the information. He would develop an information system related to his information needs, from data collection through reporting.

Thus, evaluation provides for the administrator a means of looking at, selecting and organizing the pertinent, relevant factors of the total information flow. A description of these processes and typical activities in an evaluation information system appears in Figure 2, page 229.

Evaluation—Systems Analysis

These components of evaluation may be further described in a look at evaluation in a linear sense:

7. Stake, Robert E. "The Countenance of Educational Evaluation," Center for Instructional Research and Curriculum Evaluation, University of Illinois, February, 1966. Mimeograph.

8. Thomas, Alan J. and Kearney, C. Phillip. "An Analysis of the Guidelines," *Theory into Practice*. Columbus, Ohio: June, 1966, pp. 105-109.

9. Cronbach, R. J. "Course Improvement Through Evaluation," *Teachers College Record* 64 (1963): 672-683.

10. Guidelines, op. cit.

11. Mooney, Ross L. "Initiating a Project," *Theory into Practice*. Columbus, Ohio: College of Education, The Ohio State University, June, 1966, pp. 139-143.

12. Conceptualized by D. L. Stufflebeam, Director, The Ohio State University Evaluation Center.

13. For a discussion of evaluation at the local, state, and Federal levels, see (1) Stufflebeam, op. cit.

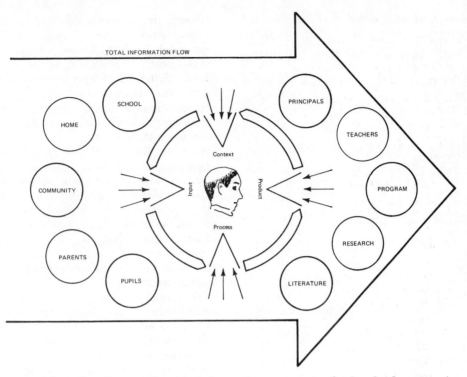

Figure 1. The role of an evaluation information system in the local education Agency.

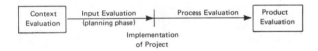

Context evaluation, that is, identifying local educational program deficiencies, is a "snapshot" of pre-project achievement, aptitude, socioeconomic data, attitudes, etc., similar to the *balance sheet* of a business establishment, reporting status at a point in time and space. It is akin to the preliminary phase of systems analysis, a limited systems study. *Product* evaluation, the measurement of outcomes as related to objectives, is a similar *balance sheet,* a static report. Contrasted to these two components are those of *input* (the assessment of potential solution strategies for their probability of effecting desired changes within the given constraints) and *process* evaluation (monitoring activities employed in implementing the planned change). These latter two, *input* and *process,* deal with the dynamic elements of the change activity.

It is important to establish the analogy of *input* and *process* evaluation with the discipline of systems analysis.

In the most general sense systems analysis and operations research can be characterized as the appli-cation of scientific methods and tools to the prediction and comparison of the values, effectiveness, and costs of a set of alternative courses of action involving man-machine systems. . . . Systems studies trace out and assess the impact of a new policy on related activities in order to predict how effective the total set of interacting elements (a system) will be in performing its mission . . . viewing the new along with the old as a part of a set of things which function together. . . . System studies identify systems —limiting elements—a communication bottleneck, outdated information, or an inadequate source of supply.[14]

It is, then, not overly difficult to view evaluation as a specialized flow system, a system of information management for sound decision-making by educators. Lankton testifies to the need for evidence to be used in decision-making.[15] The U. S. Office of Education states that ". . . evaluation is part of the teaching process and should contribute information during the project period as well as at the end . . . (so that) . . . evaluative information may lead to changed methods, or changed objectives, or both. For instance, data on pupil attainment gathered around the mid-

14. Meals, Donald W. "Heuristic Models for Systems Planning," *Phi Delta Kappan,* January, 1967, pp. 199-203.

15. Lankton, Robert S. "Closing the Gap Between Innovation and Evaluation," *NCME Newsletter,* Volume 10, Number 1, January, 1967.

point of the project may show that the original objectives were unrealistic and should be scaled down."[16] Boerrigter indicates that Title I evaluation *should* provide information for improved administration and evidence of adequacy.[17] The static elements, *context* and *product* evaluation, are essentially of a measurement nature, while *input* and *process* are the prediction and monitoring of the potential and real interactions encompassed by the planned change.

A more detailed examination of the CIPP Model illustrates possible operational phases of the components of evaluation, and some of the potential techniques and/or methodology of each phase. It should be noted that these entries are not exhaustive of all techniques or methods. The information system phases for each component make up the horizontal rows of the chart, and are arranged sequentially from left to right.

Information systems for evaluation tend to be particularistic—designed for a specific information need. However, within a component, such as *context,* similar systems may be utilized for like information needs especially when source, sample requirements and criticality are congruent. Further, some systems may be reused, once designed, to provide continual or repeated information flow.

It is convenient to use a "typical" Title I-type problem and project to explicate the model in operation. In an examination of inner-city results from a battery of achievement tests, it is found that the mean scores of inner-city school children on a standardized math test are two and three years below grade level norm. Such a use of assessment procedures can be termed *context* evaluation. Math department personnel are then consulted, who present, from various sources, potential solutions to the problem, such as remedial techniques, curriculum changes, and changes in pupil-teacher relationships. These alternative solutions should be viewed in reference to the barriers to success, viability, sufficiency, economic costs, and other maximum-minimum variates. *Input* evaluation consists of viewing these alternative solutions in reference to barriers to success (i.e., acceptance of solution by teachers, students, etc.), viability (operation of the proposed solution(s) in a non-controlled field setting), sufficiency (ability of solution(s) to overcome the educational deficiency), economic costs (relationship of costs of proposed solutions to expected educational gains—that is, would a four-fold increase in costs which only reduce the gap between ability and achievement by twice be "worth" the increase?) and other maximum-minimum variates. The cycle of *postulating alternatives* and *data gathering-analysis,* with a subsequent valuation of the alternative solution strategies, provides the necessary information for *input* evaluation and

consequently, decision-making about which solution strategy shall be employed. Further, *input* evaluation identifies the potential problem areas and critical occurrences to be monitored during implementation of the solution. Thus, a *process* evaluation design might include monitoring of teacher acceptance of the solution strategy, materials utilization, real practices as related to desired behavior, as well as an on-going evaluation of the solution in meeting objectives sufficiently, or perhaps, viably. Process evaluation is the information management system for decision-making concerning the expansion, contraction, modification, clarification, termination, etc. of the solution strategy. Employment of process evaluation is invited interference, that is, the decision-makers wish to have information during the course of the project in order to modify plans toward a sufficient solution of the problem. The most effective use of process evaluation and utilization of the information in decision-making would ensure maximizing of outcomes, such as, in the case cited, the greatest possible closure of the achievement-ability gap.

The last component in the model, *product* evaluation, consists of the more traditional product measurement, relating outcomes to objectives. The variables tested are dependent upon objectives, such as closure in achievement-ability, improved attitude of students toward a subject matter area, improved school holding power, improved attendance rate—whatever variables can be reasonably expected to change through introduction of the change. Not to be overlooked is the measurement of concomitant variates, which could be adversely affected, that is, increased time, interest and attention given by the student to the mathematics area may be deleterious to his reading achievement.

These are but some of the uses of the components of evaluation, and certainly the future will bring more ingenious and useful approaches and tools.

These needs and demands for evaluation, and the corresponding lack of theory, techniques and tools testify to the infancy of the art. Turnbull discussed the gap between innovation and evaluation,[18] Lankton related problems experienced in Title I evaluation,[19] and Guba, posing the question "How do the (evaluation sections of) Title III proposals . . . stack up?" responded "not very well." In his report to Miller, University of Kentucky, Guba makes recommendations concerning

16. *Guidelines,* op. cit.

17. Boerrigter, Glenn C. "Evaluation of Title I, Elementary and Secondary Act of 1965," mimeograph.

18. Turnbull, Wm. W. Editorial, *NCME* Newsletter, Volume 9, Number 9, September, 1966.

19. Lankton, Robert S., op. cit.

Phase / Component	Identification of Information Needs	Decision Rule Criteria	Information System Specifications	Data Collection	Data Organization & Reduction	Data Storage and Retrieval	Data Analysis	Reporting
CONTEXT — To depict deficiencies in educational opportunities	Socio-economic status Current status Norms desired Mastery desired Cost-Effectiveness	Significant disparity between status and norms or desired mastery level	Source(s) Type of Information Time Requirements Criticality Sample Requirements Quantity Accessibility	Census Data Demographic Study Standardized Tests Pupil Grades Pupil Attendance Dropout Data Attitude Survey Opinionnaire Locally constructed tests	Manual Man-Machine •general programs •special programs	Data Bank Knowledge File Machine Manual	Statistical Analysis Content Analysis Depth Study Case Study	Formal Reports Written Tabular Informal Reports Oral-group Oral-one-to-one
INPUT — To acquire and assess alternative solution strategies	Available solutions to problem Data on prior trials Relationship to context	Feasibility Sufficiency Validity Viability Barriers Tensions Cost-Effectiveness	Source(s) Type of Information Time Requirements Criticality Sample Requirements Quantity Accessibility	Review of literature Interviews: LEA personnel, experts, community leaders, parents, residents Pannels, seminars, group meetings Transfer from other information centers Observations of demonstrations	Manual Man-Machine •general programs •special programs	Data Bank Knowledge File Machine Manual	Statistical, Cost and Case Study Comparison of prior outcomes of alternatives Consultants for feasibility, barriers, tensions Force Field Analysis Educator jury for context, validity	Formal Reports Written Tabular Informal Reports Oral-group Oral-one-to-one
PROCESS — To monitor for •a priori barriers •unanticipated problems •progress	Barriers to success Interactive tensions Problem areas Progress benchmarks	Acceptability Utilization Integration Assimilation	Source(s) Type of Information Time Requirements Criticality Sample Requirements Quantity Accessibility	Logs Observations Interviews Group Interviews Group Debriefing Other Instruments: •Attitude Scale •Acceptance Scale •Facilitant-Restraint Scale •Structured Questionnaire	Manual Man-Machine •general programs •special programs	Data Bank Knowledge File Machine Manual	Content Analysis Statistical Analysis	Formal Reports Written Tabular Informal Reports Oral-group Oral-one-to-one
PRODUCT — To measure outcomes in relation to objectives	Project outcomes •achievement level •attitude •mastery •cost-effectiveness	Mastery level desired Achievement level desired Growth desired Attitude desired	Source(s) Type of Information Time Requirements Criticality Sample Requirements Quantity Accessibility	Standardized Tests Pupil Grades Attitude Scale Attendance Level Dropout Rate	Manual Man-Machine •general programs •special programs	Data Bank Knowledge File Machine Manual	Statistical Analysis •pre-post •experimental-control Population Analysis Accounting	Tabular Statistical

Figure 2. The CIPP Evaluation Model depicting some potential activities within the components of evaluation.

Title III evaluation which may well be appropriate for application to Title I evaluation. These are:

1. Spell out very carefully the objectives for the . . . program at the national level.
2. Provide adequate guidelines for the local proposer on the matter of evaluation.
3. Help the local proposer understand the meaning and utility of each of the four kinds of evaluation: Context, Input, Process and Product.[20]

It is not the purpose of this paper to suggest that evaluation, as herein conceptualized, is a new invention, nor to proffer evaluation as the panacea to the ills of education. Rather, it will provide a way in which to view the complexities of innovating, and some tools and techniques with which to reduce these complexities to a more manageable form. Industry and the military have used such approaches, more familiarly termed "systems analysis." Proponents of the systems approach have suggested its applicability to education.[21] Though one most often thinks of assembly lines and chain-of-command when industrial and military systems are mentioned, the focus of systems analysis is to provide a means to handle the increasing complexity in decision-making and the choice among alternative solution strategies resulting from technological innovation and change.

Change can be local or global; evaluation can be microscopic or macroscopic, applied within the classroom, the school, a school system, and at the state or Federal level. The potential benefits of evaluation in decision-making to the educator must not be overlooked or denied through fear of a "Federal system" of education. As conceptualized, evaluation is neutral, it becomes good or bad only through application—or misapplication.

To summarize, evaluation is a tool of the decision-maker, a way of viewing planned educational change. The CIPP Model is a framework for evaluation of change, and a means of ensuring the efficacy of that change. It is, in short, a systems analysis approach to planned educational change; its purpose, to provide information for sound decision-making; its long-range benefits, to provide improved educational opportunities for youth.

20. Guba, Egon G. *Study of Title III Activities: Report on Evaluation.* National Institute for the Study of Educational Change, October 1, 1966.
21. Meals, Donald W., op. cit.

CHAPTER 27

EVALUATION AT THE LOCAL LEVEL

Robert L. Hammond

Introduction

The need for a systematic approach to the evaluation of innovations has become one of education's most pressing problems. Only by systematic evaluation can education avoid the fads, pressures, pendulum-swingings of educational practice and address itself to the basic question concerning an educational innovation: Is it really effective in achieving its expressed objectives?

At present, there is little or no evidence gathered concerning the effectiveness of educational innovations in meeting their objectives. On what basis, then, are innovations currently adopted or continued in practice? Unfortunately, we often rely on educational ideology or the persuasive claims of advocates or salesmen. Often we claim the merits of an innovation are self-evident. More frequently, we seek the opinions of the consumers, interpreting the enthusiasm of the teachers and students (found in most new programs) as evidence of the complete success of the innovation. Or, conversely, we interpret teacher or student aversion to new programs as evidence of program failure.

Because there are few criteria of educational effectiveness, many suggest that achievement of objectives is difficult, if not impossible, to assess. The procedures, structure, and model described in this paper are proposed as a systematic way to assess the effectiveness of an innovation. Utilizing the basic structure, model, and the consulting, technological and information retrieval services offered by the Center concept, any district can systematically gather valid data needed to decide whether to adopt or continue in practice a given innovation.

Evaluation as a Process

Research has failed to produce adequate guidelines and procedures to be utilized by school districts for the purpose of evaluating both current and innovative programs. The problem is complicated further by the fact that the school districts of the past have not included the process of evaluation as one of the major criteria for curriculum improvement. A lack of guidelines and the reluctance on the part of educators to include evaluation as a major function of curriculum development have produced a situation in which little evidence is available as to what should be evaluated, and how evaluation should take place. The guidelines offered in the literature are usually in the form of recommendations for administering achievement and intelligence tests. With these over-simplified approaches to the problem of evaluation, teachers and administrators are left with the problem of drawing conclusions from inadequate data and the general enthusiasm of teachers and pupils.

Recognizing the need for guidelines and the development of evaluation programs, a team of educators representing elementary and secondary curriculum, administration, guidance, educational psychology, and sociology developed an approach to the problem of evaluation through a ten-month planning period. The results of their efforts described in this paper are not proposed as eternal verities, but as a systematic way in which to assess the effectiveness of both current and innovative programs. The structure and model will undoubtedly undergo modification, or even major changes of form as study progresses.

A Structure for Evaluation

The success or failure of innovations in modern programs of instruction is determined by the interaction of specific forces within the educational environment. The forces affecting innovation are described in terms of specific dimensions and variables operating in a three-dimensional structure (see Figure 1). The interaction of variables

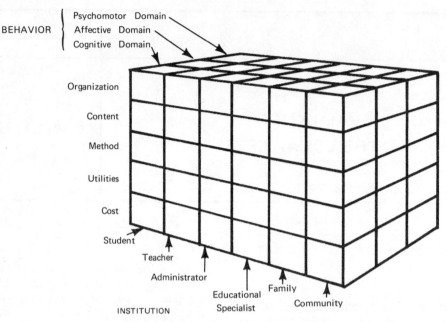

Figure 1. Structure for Evaluation.

from each of the three dimensions produces combinations of variables described as factors to be considered in the evaluation of a given program. The importance of any combination of variables is determined by the nature of the instructional program selected for study.

INSTRUCTIONAL DIMENSION

The Instructional Dimension is that dimension of the model which describes the innovation in terms of specific variables. The first of these variables is that of Organization. Organization is defined as the matrix in which teachers and pupils are brought together so that instruction can take place. The organizational matrix may be divided into two components known as *time* and *space*.

1. *Time* refers to the duration and sequence of blocks of time devoted to the subjects taught. Duration may be defined as the length of any given period. Sequence may be defined as the order in which subjects are taught. Duration and sequence may be thought of in terms of both daily and weekly scheduling. (Example: Science may be taught only twice a week.)

2. *Space* refers to the vertical and horizontal organization of students. Vertical organization serves to classify students and move them upward from the point of admission to the point of departure. Horizontal organization divides students among teachers. Both grouping processes may be homogeneous, heterogeneous, or a combination of the two.

a. Vertical Organization: Vertically, schools may be graded or non-graded, or fall somewhere in between.

(1) Graded: In pure grading, the content of the instruction program and its sequential arrangement are determined by assignment of subject matter to various grade levels, by designation of instructional materials suitable for particular grade levels, and by promotion of pupils upon satisfactory completion of the work specified for each grade.

(2) Non-graded: In pure non-grading, sequence of content is determined by the inherent difficulties of subject matter in the childrens' demonstrated ability to cope with it; materials are selected to match the spread of individual differences existing within the instructional gap; and the children will operate according to their readiness to perceive. Promotion or non-promotion does not exist as such. An important goal is to provide continuous progress of each child.

b. Horizontal Organization: Horizontally, schools may be organized into any one of many alternative patterns. But all of these horizontal patterns are derived from essentially four different kinds of considerations—considerations of the child, of the curriculum, of the teacher's qualifications, and the school's philosophy.

(1) Self-contained: Self-contained classroom is defined as a classroom in which a group of children of similar social maturity, ability, age, etc., are grouped together under the continued guidance of a single teacher.

(2) Departmentalization: The characteristic feature of departmental instruction is that a teacher who is highly trained in a field of knowledge is assigned to teach English, which in the elementary school would include reading, writing, spelling, and literature; other teachers assigned to the Social Studies, in-

cluding history, geography, and citizenship; another teacher to Mathematics; another to Natural Sciences; etc.

(3) Cooperative teaching: Under the general heading of cooperative teaching may be found dozens of different patterns of school and staff organization. Some of these are derived from, or associated with, attempts to achieve greater flexibility in pupil grouping. Others are associated with efforts to eliminate the administrative and instructional characteristics of rigid, lock-step, organizational structure. One of the most important forms of cooperative teaching is the organizational pattern known as team teaching.

The second variable is that of Content. Content is defined as that structure or body of knowledge which is identified with the subject matter of a discipline and controls its inquiries. Content may be described in terms of specific topics to be covered at a given grade level.

A third variable is that of Methodology. Methodology is that process designed to facilitate learning. It may be divided into three levels: teaching activities, types of interaction, and learning principles or theories utilized.

1. *Teaching Activities*

    a. Lecture
    b. Discussion
    c. Question-answer
    d. Committee
    e. Round table
    f. Symposium
    g. Drill
    h. Homework
    i. Review
    j. Individual supervised study
    k. Resource person(s)
    l. Field trips
    m. Inquiry
    n. Debate
    o. Media*

    *Includes: texts, resource books (dictionaries, encyclopedias, library, etc.), workbooks, films, film strips (with and without tapes), tapes/records, television (commercial, educational, closed circuit), laboratories (science, language), programmed teaching machines/texts.

2. *Types of Interaction*

    a. Teacher ⟷ Student
    b. Student ⟷ Student
    c. Media ⟷ Student
    d. Teacher ⟷ Teacher*

    *Principally team teaching.

    (In addition to identifying the interaction participants, there are a number of codes that have been developed to describe the interaction such as: (1) Interaction Analysis—Ned Flanders; (2) Teaching Interaction—Marie Hughes; (3) Classroom Transaction—Stanford University (Sample: Devised and revised by many members of staff).

3. *Learning Theory*

    a. Behavior which represents the achievement or partial achievement of an educational objective should be reinforced.
    b. The introduction of cues which arouse motivation toward the achievement of an educational objective will increase the effectiveness with which that objective is achieved.
    c. Practice in applying a principle to the solution of problems will increase the probability of transfer of training to new problems require the use of the same principle for their solution.
    d. Since learners differ in their capacity to make the responses to be acquired, learning will be most effective if it is planned so that each learner embarks on a program commensurate with his capacity to acquire new responses.
    e. If a pupil has had training in imitation, then he is capable of learning by observing demonstrations of skills to be acquired.
    f. The learner will learn more efficiently if he makes the responses to be learned than if he learns by observing another make the responses or makes some related response.

The fourth and fifth variables are Facilities and Cost. Facilities is defined as that space, special equipment, and expendables needed to support an educational program. Cost is the money required for facilities, maintenance, and personnel to accomplish a given task.

The variables defined in the above represent important categories to be considered in the instructional program. The innovation to be considered may be contained in any one of the variables (e.g., team teaching—organization). Yet all variables must be considered in the analysis of the total program. If innovations are to be adopted on a wide-scale, a complete picture of the program must be studied with its various components carefully analyzed.

INSTITUTIONAL DIMENSION

The Institutional Dimension is that dimension of the model defined by the variables of Child, Teacher, Administrator, Educational Specialist, Family, and Community. Any given innovation will be influenced by the unique qualities of the individuals involved. For the purposes of evaluation, each of the variables is described in terms of sub-variables that may have a direct influence on the given program. The following examples are a sample of these descriptive sub-variables.

1. *Student*

    a. Age
    b. Grade level
    c. Sex
    d. Family variables
    e. Socio-economic variables
    f. Physical health
    g. Mental health
    h. Achievement
    i. Ability
    j. Interest
    k. Relationship to innovation

2. *Teacher, Administrator, and Educational Specialist*

    a. Identification Data

        (1) Age
        (2) Sex
        (3) Race, nationality, religion
        (4) Physical health
        (5) Personality characteristics

b. Educational Background and Work Experience
   (1) Undergraduate major and minor
   (2) Graduate major
   (3) Highest degree
   (4) Educational experience
   (5) Experience outside education
c. Environmental Factors
   (1) Professional salary
   (2) Professional affiliations
   (3) Non-professional affiliations
   (4) Socio-economic status of residence
   (5) Professional and non-professional reading habits
   (6) Leisure activities outside professional work time
d. Degree of Involvement in Program

3. *Family*
a. Degree of Involvement with Innovation
   (1) Have children in school; all affected by the innovation.
   (2) Have children in school; some affected by, some not affected by, the innovation.
   (3) Have children in school; none affected by the innovation.
   (4) Have no children in school (these are treated under descriptive items in the Community variable.)
b. General Characteristics
   (1) Ethnic/national/linguistic
   (2) Size
      (a) Total
      (b) Siblings
      (c) Other relatives present
   (3) Age distribution
   (4) Marital status
   (5) Pattern
      (a) Nuclear
      (b) Extended
   (6) Income
      (a) Approximate level
      (b) Number of wage earners
      (c) Source
      (d) Occupation
   (7) Residence
      (a) Urban
      (b) Suburban
      (c) Rural
      (d) Cost range
   (8) Education
      (a) Approximate formal level
         i. Parents
         ii. Siblings
         iii. Other relatives present
      (b) Informal
         i. Industrial
         ii. Military
         iii. Community service
         iv. Other
   (9) Affiliations
      (a) Religious   (d) Professional
      (b) Political   (e) Other
      (c) Social
   (10) Mobility
      (a) Parents' place of origin
      (b) Length of time in community

(c) Frequency of moving
(d) Extent of traveling

4. *Community*
a. Geographical Setting
   (1) Location   (2) Environment—general
b. Historical Development
c. Population Characteristics
   (1) Demographic data
      (a) Population size
      (b) Population density
      (c) Marriage and divorce rates
      (d) Birth and death rates
      (e) Age distribution
   (2) Ethnic/nationality
   (3) Linguistic
   (4) Change patterns
      (a) Mobility patterns
         i. Immigration
         ii. Emigration
         iii. Migrant-indigenous ratio
      (b) Growth patterns
d. Economic Characteristics
   (1) Commercial/industrial organization and development
   (2) Occupational range
   (3) Sources/range of individual incomes
   (4) Sources/range of tax base
e. Social Characteristics
   (1) Institutions and organizations
      (a) Governmental/political
      (b) Educational
      (c) Religious
      (d) Service
      (e) Social
      (f) Commercial/financial
      (g) Labor
      (h) Professional
      (i) Recreational
      (j) Protection
   (2) Power structure
   (3) Socio-economic stratification

Assessment programs of the past have focused primarily on the child and his response to content in a given subject area. With the changes taking place in instructional programs, more evidence is needed as to the influence of teacher, administrator, parent, and community on a given innovation.

BEHAVIORAL DIMENSION

The Behavioral Dimension is defined by the variables of Cognitive, Affective, and Psychomotor Behavior. Evaluation as a process is best approached through objectives stated in behavioral terms. At this point in the development of the structure for evaluation, three variables for classifying these objectives are recognized. The first of these variables is Cognitive Behavior. Cognitive Behavior includes the recall, comprehension and application of knowledge and utilization of intellectual skills of analysis, synthesis, and evaluation. The best example of tests in this area are the standardized tests of achievement. In the majority of programs this is the only test utilized to describe the success or failure of both current and innovative programs.

The second variable in this Dimension is Affective Behavior. Affective Behavior is defined as the interest, attitudes, values, appreciations, and adjustments of the individual. In recent years we have reached a point in the evaluation process where we are now concerned not only with the knowledge gained, but with the willingness of the student to identify himself with a given subject. Many instructional programs today repel students for reasons other than academic ability. Recognizing this fact, it is important that we look at the reasons for this behavior.

Psychomotor Behavior is the third variable in the Behavioral Domain. It includes those acts which involve neuro-muscular coordination. Handwriting and physical education utilize this variable to draw conclusions about special programs.

A fourth variable, Perceptual Behavior, is now under study at the Center. It is hoped that this area will be adequately defined so that it may be utilized in the evaluation process for the coming year. At this point, it may be classified as experimental.

The structure developed provides a framework to produce factors that have a direct influence on a given innovation. The factors created by the interaction of one variable from each of the dimensions may be studied in any depth desired by a school district. In most cases the study of a given factor will be determined by time, availability of tests and procedures, and the needs of a given school district.

A Model for Evaluation as a Process

Once the forces affecting a given innovation have been identified and placed in a structure which permits an analysis of the interaction of these forces, the next step is that of placing the structure in a working model for evaluation (see Figure 2).

The application of this model in school evaluation programs must be approached with caution through carefully defined steps. Teachers and administrators have not been adequately trained in the skills necessary to evaluate instructional programs. Once these skills have been developed through the cooperative efforts of the school and Center, the school district personnel should progress to the point that they can operate independently. The training period demands the first step toward adequate evaluation be limited to the capabilities of the personnel in the given school district.

Sound evaluation procedures require that the process begin with the current programs. Before attempts at innovation are made, adequate baseline data is required to make those decisions which determine the direction of the change process.

Beginning with the prediction source, the program must be defined in terms of what is to be evaluated. All too frequently, the school district moves into the evaluation process by attacking the total school program. Due to the limited skills of personnel, the evaluation process is doomed before it starts, or more often returns to the use of standardized achievement tests as the only criteria for evaluation. The first step should be one of beginning with a single subject area of the curriculum, such as mathematics, and even then it would be advisable to limit the first phase to a selected number of grades, due to the time factor involved. The nature of the change process involving a given innovation should limit this problem to begin with, as it is assumed that a given innovation would not be applied across all grade levels until verification of intended objectives had been completed.

The second step is that of defining the descriptive variables in the Instructional and Institutional Dimensions. Before moving to step three, all variables with the exception of Cost and those within the Institutional Dimension should be defined.

The third step in the evaluation process is that of stating objectives in behavioral terms. This represents one of the most crucial steps in the evaluation process. Properly stated objectives will:

1. specify the kind of behavior which will be accepted as evidence that the learner has achieved the objective.
2. state the conditions under which the behavior will be expected to occur.
3. specify the criteria of acceptable performance by describing how well the learner must perform.

In the process of stating objectives, the structure for evaluation (Figure 1) will be used to point out a need for objectives in addition to those involving Content, Child, and Cognitive Behavior.

Once the behavioral objectives have been developed, the fourth step in the evaluation process is that of assessing the behavior described in the objectives. The Center will provide information regarding standardized tests, techniques, test research, and the technical help necessary for creating additional instruments and techniques to be used by the classroom teacher. The final phase of step four is the output of factors determined by the current program for innovation under consideration.

With the factors identified, the fifth step is that of analyzing the results within factors and the relationships between factors, to arrive at conclusions based on actual behavior. Once the out-

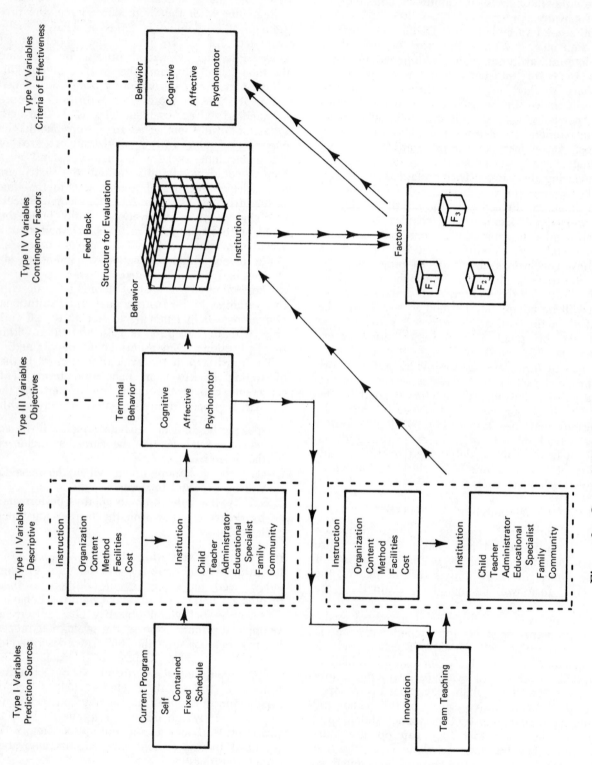

Figure 2. Generalized scheme for evaluation of innovations.

comes have been defined, there is a feedback process to the terminal behavior defined through objectives to determine the effectiveness of a given program in reaching the desired outcomes.

With the current program evaluated through the process described, the school or district is ready to consider change in the instructional program. Change will take place in the form of innovations. The decisions for innovation will be determined by evidence gathered as to what the change process should involve, and most important of all, it will provide data for the school boards, community, and administration to make those important decisions necessary for providing instructional programs which meet the needs of every child.

The Evaluation Center

At present, the majority of school districts do not have access to nor possess the essential tools and trained personnel necessary to adequately assess both current and innovative programs for instruction. The process of bringing research to the classroom demands technical help, the hardware, and training programs that far exceed the budget limitations of most school districts. To meet this need, a model Center was developed through a planning grant under Title III of the Elementary and Secondary Education Act of 1965. The Center was designed to provide school districts with the help needed to train district personnel in the process of evaluation. The basic purpose of the Center is that of cooperating and assisting in the process of evaluation. It *is not* the purpose nor function of the Center to act as an outside evaluation agency. The Center operates on the philosophy that evaluation must be a product of the local district. Outside agencies should serve as consultants to help strengthen and develop the skills necessary to do an adequate job of evaluation. To accomplish this task, a Center composed of three divisions was developed. The three Divisions are those of Field Services, Evaluation Services, and Publications.

THE FIELD SERVICES DIVISION

The major task of the Field Services Division is that of initiating a systematic self-evaluation of innovations within participating school districts. Once the school district has made contact with the Evaluation Center, the Field Services Division will:

1. provide the necessary help to define the innovation in relation to the model provided for evaluation.
2. assist in the accumulation and classification of data relating to selected innovations.

3. provide assistance in designing and implementing in-service training programs for participating personnel within the school districts.
4. provide the assistance necessary in the selection of consultants needed to provide help in specific problem areas for evaluation.
5. provide assistance in the analysis of data in relation to factors identified within the model.
6. assist in the dissemination of the data relating to the evaluation of selected innovations.

As stated previously, one of the primary objectives of the Center is to ensure a continuing program of self-evaluation. To accomplish this task, the Field Services Division will be responsible for training selected personnel within the school districts to carry on the major responsibilities for evaluation. Field Service Specialists and consultants will be utilized to accomplish this task. The Field Service Specialists, with the cooperation of other Divisions in the Center, will provide the necessary leadership to coordinate the activities for in-service training in the evaluation of given innovations.

THE EVALUATION SERVICES DIVISION

The Evaluation Services Division will assume, as its major role, a service function to the Field Services Division and the participating schools.

A general description of its two components best illustrates the responsibilities of the Division. The first: The Evaluation and Assessment Office will be primarily concerned with the refinement of program design into operational terms and the development of instruments and analytical methods. In addition, and of secondary importance, this Office will be expected to continually conduct developmental programs which will yield instruments and techniques useful to the functions of the Center.

The Office of Evaluation and Assessment will provide technical assistance to other Divisions of the Center and to the districts participating in the Project in the following ways:

1. Refine general evaluation problems into specific operational form.
2. Develop and refine assessment methodology and instrumentation for the evaluation programs conducted by the Center.
3. Provide a central source for information concerning assessment techniques in evaluation programs.
4. Direct and conduct analytical studies in support of ongoing evaluation programs.
5. Provide consultative services to local districts in regards to local research and evaluation efforts.
6. Conduct a systems analysis of the operations of the Center and develop improved operations and functioning procedures.
7. Develop techniques which would make the Central Resource Information Bank (CRIB) more useful

in providing a descriptive information framework within which more meaningful evaluations can be made.

8. Prepare descriptive and technical reports and summaries based on the contents of the files created for the Central Resource Information Bank (CRIB).

Through its efforts of screening relevant publications, and reports on its close contacts with retrieval and dissemination centers, regional laboratories, ERIC, and other agencies, the Evaluation and Assessment Office will be more able to design and develop models for the evaluation programs of the Center.

The Office of Information Storage and Processing will be the other major component of the Evaluation Services Division. This sub-division will provide a multiple service function: to the Director and all Divisions of the Center; the participating school districts; and to authorized researchers outside the formal structure of the Project. There will be two main concerns of this Office. The first will be the development and maintenance of an extensive data bank for the accumulation, storage, and ready access to descriptive data pertinent to the EPIC model. In addition to the descriptive data, it is expected that the bank will create readily accessible files on exemplary practices and programs from both within and outside the geographic area of direct concern to the Center. The second major charge to this group will be to provide necessary data processing services to all projects within the Center. This service will include such items as machine-document design, machine-document origination, the conduct of empirical analysis, and assistance in the development of techniques to make data collection and information processing less of a routine burden on the evaluation teams and researchers, as well as expediting necessary summaries.

PUBLICATIONS DIVISION

The Publications Division is the link in the operational chain by which knowledge gained is shared with others in order that more effective educational systems may result. Productive output will begin on the first day of operation with news releases to all appropriate media that operations have begun.

Recognizing the necessity for continuous support from parents and the community, the Publications Division will prepare and traffic news releases, thereby relieving administrators from having to divert their energies into this area of operation.

As soon as the Center Specialists have a flow of materials in and have performed their first evaluations leading to positive conclusions, the Publications Division will launch what should prove to be a most valuable method of sharing information. This will be the Case Study Report, a single sheet printed on both sides, punched for notebook filing. Case Study Reports will be developed under a consistent format giving subject, the number of (or in) classes, stage of project at the time of the review, followed by a full description (whether conclusions have yet been reached or are still pending), comments by the classroom teacher, and comments by the Center evaluator.

These Case Study Reports will be issued under classified and numbered designations with a series for each specific interest group—mathematics, biological sciences, etc., in order that they may be requested by simple number designation. Later reports on the same class would carry the parent number, with a suffix to show a re-evaluation had been effected. These are the basic end products which can be placed in the hands of interested educators everywhere to provide inspiration, guidance, and assurance. These will originate with the Specialists, be processed by the Publications Division writers into the pattern, rechecked with the Specialists, then additionally rechecked with the originating classroom teacher to ensure that the final presentation is truly authoritative and that no distortion or misinterpretation exists in the printed report. Because the Center will be new and the long-range acceptance of its findings will depend upon the validity of its presentations from the start, special care will be taken to ensure that every phase of every presentation is correct.

These printed two-page Case Study Reports will be the items most widely distributed and undoubtedly the most in demand. They adapt themselves as the appropriate items for professional meetings—ranging from single schools to districts to counties to state to national educational conclaves.

Nation-wide notice of availability of each new Case Study Report as it is about to be released will be effected through a monthly publication, which will develop either a feature-type presentation, or a more simple abstract on each one to give the reader an idea of the coverage afforded by each Case Study Report, without going into full details. Again, the Publications Division will blend the ingredients for reaching the audience.

Additionally, the staff members in the Publications Division will capsulize the Case Study Reports (individually) into one-paragraph form for inclusion on what could be termed a "request checklist" or perhaps an "order blank." These will be prepared in a format suitable for use as enclosures in all correspondence from EPIC—

serving as an effective informational tool. These order blanks also will be display table items. They will be updated constantly, in the intervals necessitated by keeping up with the ever-expanding activities.

The monthly publication will be the informational contact tool of the Center, contrasted with the Case Study Reports which will be the end product presentation. It will present information covering all segments of the educational strata, as contrasted with the pin-point approach of the Case Study Reports, which have the distinct advantage of being ready to go into subject-classified notebooks. The commentaries at times may be based on comparisons of some of the Case Study Reports, whereas the individual Case Study Reports themselves will not try to be comparative. The monthly publication will be the "official voice" of the Center and thereby will provide the medium for introduction of new concepts, requests for new or different kinds of participation, a tally of achievements by appropriate groups, etc. It offers the opportunity for personal observations or the sharing of beliefs by the central administrator.

Conclusions and Recommendations

The importance of a sound approach to the problem of evaluation cannot be over-emphasized. Evaluation at the local level has been the problem-child of education—everyone needing and wanting answers to the problem, but no one willing to take on the task of attacking the complex problems involved. This paper represents one approach toward a solution of this problem. The EPIC Center established under a Title III operational grant has two major objectives: (1) To develop and refine programs for evaluation as a process, and (2) The development of a Center to put these programs into action through adequately trained personnel and the hardware necessary to give school districts the help they so desperately need. Those participating within the Center recognize that the implementation of the recommendations presented in this paper require the development of operational procedures not yet defined. The development of these procedures are in progress at the present time. It will be some time before all problems are solved; yet, the many months of effort indicate that there is a solution to each of these problems. With this in mind, the following recommendations are made:

1. Evaluation Centers be established to aid local school districts in the solution of the problems dealing with evaluation of both current and innovative programs on the local level.

2. The structure and model proposed in this paper need to be put into action in pilot programs across the country to bring new ideas and refinement to the processes described.

3. The concentrated support of Federal, state, and local agencies in providing the necessary funds and resources necessary to encourage talented teachers to enter the training programs needed to provide school districts with trained personnel in evaluation.

SELECTED
REFERENCES

Abramson, D. A. "Curriculum Research and Evaluation," *Review of Educational Research* 36 (1966): 388-395.

Adkins, Dorothy C., and Troops, Herbert A. Simplified formulas for item selection and construction. *Psychometrika* 11 (1937): 165-171.

Ahmann, J. Stanley, et al. *Evaluating Elementary School Pupils.* Allyn & Bacon, Inc., 1960.

Ahmann, J. Stanley, and Glock, Marvin D. *Evaluating Pupil Growth.* 2nd ed. Allyn & Bacon, Inc., 1963.

Aiken, W. M. *The Story of the Eight Year Study.* New York: Harper & Row, Publishers, 1942.

Alkin, Marvin C. *Towards an Evaluation Model: A Systems Approach.* Los Angeles, Calif.: UCLA Center for the Study of Evaluation, Working Paper No. 4, December, 1967.

Alpert, R.; Stellwagen, G., and Becker, D. "Psychological factors in mathematics education." Palo Alto, Calif.: School Mathematics Study Group, Stanford University, 1963.

American Association for the Advancement of Science. *Commission on Science Education Newsletter* I (1965): 2-4.

American Association for the Advancement of Science, Commission on Science Education. *An Evaluation Model and Its Application. Science—A Process Approach.* Washington, D. C.: The Association, 1965.

American Educational Research Association. *Perspectives of Curriculum Evaluation.* American Educational Research Association Monograph Series on Curriculum Evaluation, No. 1. Chicago: Rand McNally & Co., 1967.

American Psychological Association. *Standards for Educational and Psychological Tests and Manuals.* APA, 1966.

Ammons, Margaret. An empirical study of progress and product in curriculum development. *Journal of Educational Research* (1964): 451-457.

Ammons, Margaret and Gilchrest, R. S. *Assessing and Using Curriculum Content.* Washington, D. C.: Association for Supervision and Curriculum Development, 1965.

Anderson, Harry E., and Bashaw, W. L. *An Experimental Study of First Grade Theme Writing.* Athens, Georgia: University of Georgia, (no date).

Anderson, J. E. Problems of method in maturity and curricular studies. *NSSE 38th Yearbook, Part I.* G. M. Whipple, ed., 1951, pp. 397-422.

Anderson, R. C. Educational psychology. *Annual Review of Psychology* 18 (1967): 129-164.

Anderson, Scarvia B., et al. "Social studies in secondary schools: A survey of courses and practices," *Cooperative Test Division.* Princeton, N. J.: Educational Testing Service, February, 1964.

———. "Between the Grimms and 'The Group': Literature in American High Schools," *Cooperative Test Division.* Princeton, N. J.: Educational Testing Service, April, 1964.

———. "Evaluation in English," *Conference of California Association of Teachers of English.* Princeton, N. J.: Educational Testing Service, February, 1966.

———. "Noseprints on the glass, or, How do we evaluate museum programs?" *Smithsonian Conference on Museums and Education.* Princeton, N.J.: Educational Testing Service, August, 1966.

Appel, V., and Kipnis, D. Use of levels of confidence in item analysis. *Journal of Applied Psychology* 38 (1954): 256-259.

Applebee, Roger K. "A Record of English Teaching Today," *English Journal,* March, 1966.

Arnstine, D. G. "The Language and Values of Programmed Instruction," *The Educational Forum* 28 (1964): 337-45.

Association for Supervision and Curriculum Development. *Evaluation as Feedback and Guide.* 1967 Yearbook. Washington, D. C.: The Association, a department of the National Education Association, 1967.

Atkin, J. Myron. "Some Evaluation Problems in a Course Content Improvement Project," *Journal of Research in Science Teaching* 1 (1963): 129-132.

———. "Basing Curriculum Change on Research and Demonstration." Excerpt from paper presented at ASCD Convention, San Francisco, 13 March, 1966.

————. "Science Education: 'Process' and 'Content' in Grade Schools." A letter reprinted from *Science* 151 (1966): 1033.

Ausubel, D. P. "An Evaluation of the BSCS Approach to High School Biology," *American Biology Teacher* 28 (1966): 176-186.

————. Crucial psychological issues in the objectives, organization, and evaluation of curriculum reform movements. University of Illinois Bureau of Educational Research, 1966.

Ayres, L. P. History and present status of educational measurements. *NSSE Yearbook*, 1918, *19*.

Bakan, R. The use of a modified multiple-choice item under various conditions. *Journal of Educational Research* 51 (1957): 223-228.

Baker, Eva. *Establishing performance standards.* Los Angeles: Vimcet Associates, 1966.

Baker, E. L. *The Differential Effect of Behavioral and Nonbehavioral Objectives Given to Teachers on the Achievements of their Students.* U.S. Dept. of Health, Education, and Welfare, 1967, Interim Report.

Baker, G. Derwood, et al. *New Methods vs. Old in American Education.* An analysis and summary of recent comparative studies. New York: Bureau of Publications, Teachers College, Columbia University, 1941.

Baker, Robert. "Curriculum Evaluation," *Review of Educational Research* 39 (1969): 339-358.

Barker, Roger, and Gump, P. V. *Big School, Small School.* Stanford, Calif.: Stanford University Press, 1964.

Barker, Roger. Explorations in ecological psychology. *American Psychologist* 20 (1965): 16-26.

Barzun, Jacques, and Graff, Henry. *The Modern Researcher.* New York: Harcourt, Brace & World, Inc., 1957.

Bauernfeind, Robert H. " 'Goal Cards' and Future Developments in Achievement Testing," *Proceedings of the 1965 Invitational Conference on Testing Problems.* Princeton, N. J.: Educational Testing Service, 1966.

Beauchamp, George A. *Comparative Analysis of Curriculum Systems.* Wilmette, Ill.: Kagg Press, 1967.

Berdie, R. F., et al. Testing in guidance and counseling. McGraw-Hill Book Co., 1963.

Berg, Harry D., ed. *Evaluation in Social Studies.* Thirty-fifth Yearbook of the National Council for the Social Studies, 1965.

Berkson, J. Cost-utility as a measure of the efficiency of a test. *Journal of the American Statistical Association* 42 (1947): 246-255.

Berlau, H. "New Curriculum and Measurement of Thinking," *Education Forum* 30(1966): 303-11.

Bellack, Arno A. *Theory and research in teaching.* New York: Bureau of Publications, Teachers College, Columbia University, 1963.

Billings, Neil. *A Determination of Generalizations Basic to the Social Studies Curriculum.* Baltimore: Warwick and York, Inc., 1929.

Biological Sciences Curriculum Study. *Newsletter,* Nos. 19 and 24 (1963, 1965).

Birkmaier, E. "Evaluating the Foreign Language Program," *North Central Association Quarterly* 40 (1966): 263-271.

Black, H. *They shall not pass.* William Morrow & Co., Inc., 1963.

Bliesmer, Emery P., and Yarborough, Betty H. "A Comparison of Ten Different Beginning Reading Programs in First Grade," *Phi Delta Kappan* 46 (June, 1965).

Bloom, Benjamin, ed. *Taxonomy of Educational Objectives, Handbook I: Cognitive Domain.* New York: Longmans, Green & Co., Ltd., 1956.

————, ed. The role of the educational sciences in curriculum development. Chicago: University of Chicago Press, 1964. (mimeograph)

————. Toward A Theory of Testing Which Includes Measurement-Evaluation-Assessment. *Occasional Report No. 9.* Los Angeles, Calif.: Center for the Study of Evaluation, 1968.

Bobbitt, John Franklin. *The Curriculum.* Boston: Houghton Mifflin Co., 1918.

Boersma, Wendell C. *The Effectiveness of the Evaluative Criteria as a Stimulus for School Improvement in Eleven Michigan High Schools.* Doctoral thesis. Ann Arbor, Mich.: University of Michigan, 1967.

Bogatz, Gerry Ann. "Inside the City: Evaluation Report from a Limited School Trial of a Teaching Unit of the High School Geography Project," *Curriculum Studies.* Princeton, N. J.: Educational Testing Service, December, 1966.

————. "Manufacturing: Evaluation Report from a Limited School Trial of a Teaching Unit of the High School Geography Project," *Curriculum Studies.* Princeton, N. J.: Educational Testing Service, February, 1967.

————. "Political Processes: Evaluation Report from a Limited School Trial of a Teaching Unit of the High School Geography Project," *Curriculum Studies.* Princeton, N. J.: Educational Testing Service, April, 1967.

————. "Networks of Cities: Evaluation Report from a Limited School Trial of a Teaching Unit of the High School Geography Project," *Curriculum Studies.* Princeton, N. J.: Educational Testing Service, January, 1967.

Bond, Guy L., and Dykstra, Robert. "The Cooperative Research Program in First Grade Reading Instruction," *Reading Research Quarterly* 2(1967): 5-142.

Braddock, R.; Lloyd-Jones, R., and Schoer, L. *Research in Written Composition.* Washington, D. C.: National Council of Teachers of English, 1963.

Brogden, H. E. An approach to the problem of differential prediction. *Psychometrika* 11 (1946): 139-154.

————. The effect of bias due to difficulty factors in product-moment item intercorrelations on the accuracy of estimation of reliability. *Educational and Psychological Measurement* 6 (1946): 517-520.

————. Variation in test validity with variation in the distribution of item difficulties, number of items, and degree of their intercorrelations. *Psychometrika* 11 (1946): 197-214.

Brogden, H. E., and Taylor, E. K. The dollar criterion—applying the cost accounting concept to criterion construction. *Personnel Psychologist* 3 (1950): 133-154.

Bross, I. D. J. *Design for Decision*. New York: The Macmillan Co., 1953.

Broudy, H. S.; Smith, B. O., and Burnett, J. R. *Democracy and Excellence in American Secondary Education*. Chicago: Rand McNally & Co., 1964, pp. 43-73.

Brownell, W. A. The evaluation of learning under dissimilar systems of instruction. *California Journal of Educational Research* 17 (1966): 80-90.

Bruner, J. *The Process of Education*. Cambridge, Mass.: Harvard University Press, 1960.

Buros, O. K., ed. *The Fourth Mental Measurements Yearbook*. Gryphon Press, 1953.

———. *The Fifth Mental Measurements Yearbook*. Gryphon Press, 1959.

———. *The Sixth Mental Measurements Yearbook*. Gryphon Press, 1965.

———. *Tests in Print*. Gryphon Press, 1961.

Cahen, Leonard S. "An Interim Report on the National Longitudinal Study of Mathematical Abilities," *Mathematics Teacher* 58 (1965): 522-27.

Callahan, R. E. *Education and the Cult of Efficiency*. Chicago: University of Chicago Press, 1962. (Paperback edition, Phoenix, 1964.)

Campbell, D. T., and Fiske, D. W. Convergent and discriminant validation by the multitrait-multimethod matrix. *Psychological Bulletin* 56 (1959): 81-105.

Campbell, Donald T., and Stanley, Julian C. *Experimental and Quasi-Experimental Designs for Research*. Chicago: Rand McNally & Co., 1966.

Carlson, Richard O., et al. *Seminar on change processes in the public schools*. Eugene, Oregon: Center for the Advanced Study of Educational Administration, University of Oregon, 1965.

Carroll, J. B. The effect of difficulty and chance success on correlations between items or between tests. *Psychometrika* 10 (1945): 1-19.

Carroll, John B., and Ellis, Allan B. et al. *Planning and Utilization of a Regional Data Bank for Educational Research Purposes*. Final Report. Cambridge, Mass.: Harvard University, December, 1965.

Cawelti, Gordon. *Guide for Conducting an Evaluation of the Comprehensive High School through Faculty Self-Study*. Chicago, Ill.: Rand McNally & Co., April, 1966.

Chandler, R. E. Two additional formulae for use with suppressor variables. *Educational and Psychological Measurement* 21 (1961): 947-950.

Charters, W. W. *Motion pictures and youth, a summary*. New York: The Macmillan Co., 1935.

Chase, C. I., and Ludlow, H. G. *Readings in educational and psychological measurement*. Boston, Mass.: Houghton Mifflin Co., 1966.

Christal, Raymond E. *JAN: A Technique for Analyzing Group Judgment*. Washington, D.C.: Technical Documentary Report PRL-TDR-63-3, February, 1963. Reprinting January, 1965.

Churchman, C. W., et al. *Introduction to operations research*. New York: John Wiley & Sons, Inc., 1957. (Esp. Part II, "The problem.")

Clark, D. L., and Guba, E. G. An examination of potential change roles in education. Columbus, Ohio, 1965. (multilith)

Cleeton, J. V. The optimum difficulty of group test items. *Journal of Applied Psychology* 10 (1926): 327-340.

Coffman, W. E. Estimating the internal consistency of a test when items are scored 2, 1, or 0. *Educational Psychological Measurement* 12 (1952): 392-393.

Coleman, J. S., et al. *Equality of Educational Opportunity*. Washington, D.C.: Government Printing Office, 1966.

Comley, Robert E. "A correlational study of achievement of students beginning UICSM high school mathematics in 1958 or 1959." Urbana: University of Illinois Committee on School Mathematics, December, 1965.

Connolly, J. A., and Wantman, M. J. An exploration of oral reasoning processes in responding to objective test items. *Journal of Educational Measurement* 1 (1964): 59-64.

Conrad, H. S. Characteristics and uses of item-analysis data. *Psychological Monographs*, 1948, No. 295.

Cook, Desmond. *Program Evaluation and Review Technique: Applications in Education*. Washington, D.C.: U.S. Office of Education Cooperative Research Monograph, No. 17, OE-12024, 1966.

Cook, S. W., and Selltis, C. A multiple-indicator approach to attitude measurements. *Psychological Bulletin* 62 (1964) 36-55.

Coombs, C. H. On the use of objective examinations. *Educational Psychological Measurement* 13 (1953): 308-310.

Coombs, C. H.; Milholland, J. E., and Womer, F. B. *The assessment of partial knowledge in objective testing: PRB technical research note 33*. Washington: Department of the Army, 1955.

———. The assessment of partial knowledge. *Educational Psychological Measurement* 16 (1956): 13-37.

Coombs, C. H.; Bezambinder, T. G., and Goode, F. M. Testing expectation theories of decision-making without measuring utility or subjective probability. *Journal of Mathematical Psychology* 4 (1967): 72-103.

Coughland, Robert. "The Factorial Structure of Teacher Work Values." *American Educational Research Journal* 6 (1969): 169-190.

Court, A. T. Measuring joint causation. *Journal of the American Statistical Association* 25 (1930): 245-25.

Cox, R. C. Item selection techniques and evaluation of instructional objectives. *Journal of Educational Measurement* 2 (1965): 181-185.

Cox, Richard C. *Achievement Testing in a Program of Individualized Instruction: Some Considerations*. Pittsburgh: Learning Research and Development Center, University of Pittsburgh, February, 1967.

Cox, R. C., and Unks, Nancy. *A selected and annotated bibliography of studies concerning the taxonomy of educational objectives: cognitive domain*. Pittsburgh: University of Pittsburgh: Learning Research and Development Center, 1967.

Cox, Richard C., and Graham, Glenn T. The development of a sequentially scaled achievement test. *Journal of Educational Measurement* 3 (1966): 147-50.

Cramer, Elliot M., and Beck, R. Darrell. Multivariate analysis. *Review of Educational Research* 36 (1966): 604-17.

Crawford, W. R. *A validation of the structure and generality of "A Taxonomy of Intellectual Processes."* Unpublished doctoral dissertation. Tallahassee: Florida State University, 1966.

Cronbach, L. J. Psychological issues pertinent to recent American curriculum reform. Paper delivered at the 16th International Congress of Applied Psychology, 1961.

————. "Course Improvement through Evaluation." *Teachers College Record* 64 (1963): 672-683.

————. The psychological background for curriculum experimentation. In *Modern Viewpoints in the Curriculum*, edited by P. C. Rosenbloom, chapter 4. McGraw-Hill Book Co., 1964.

————. Logic of experiments on discovery. In *Learning by discovery*, edited by Shulman and Keislat. Rand-McNally & Co., 1966.

Cronbach, L. J., and Meehl, P. E. Construct validity in psychological tests. *Psychological Bulletin* 52 (1955): 281-302.

Cronbach, L. J., and Gleser, G. *Psychological Tests and Personnel Decisions.* Urbana, Ill.: University of Illinois Press, 1957. pp. 1-77; 98-133.

Cronbach, Lee J., and Suppes, Patrick. *Research for Tomorrow's Schools: Disciplined Inquiry for Education.* New York: The Macmillan Co., 1969.

Damrin, D. E. The Russell Sage Social Relations Test: A technique for measuring group problem-solving skills in elementary schoool children. *Journal of Experimental Education* 28 (1959): 85-99.

Davidson, D., Suppes, P., and Siegel, S. *Decision Making: An Experimental Approach.* Stanford, Calif.: Stanford University Press, 1957.

Davis, F. B. *Educational measurements and their interpretation.* Belmont, Calif.: Wadsworth Publishing Co., Inc., 1965. (Chapters on measurement of change, underachievement and over-achievement.)

Davis, O. L., and Tinsley, Drew. *Cognitive objectives revealed by classroom questions asked by social studies student teachers.* Paper read at the annual meeting of the American Educational Research Association, New York, 1967.

Davis, Robert B. *The Changing Curriculum: Mathematics.* Washington, D. C.: Association for Supervision and Curriculum Development, 1967.

Dershimer, Richard A. Evaluation and Decision Making. Washington, D. C.: American Educational Research Association, 1968. (mimeograph)

Diederich, P. B., et al. Factors in judgments of writing ability. *Educational Testing Service Research Bulletin*, 1961, pp. 15-61.

Dowd, Donald J., and West, Sarah C. An Inventory of Measures of Affective Behavior. In *Improving Educational Assessment and An Inventory of Measures of Affective Behavior*, pp. 98-158. Washington, D. C.: Association for Supervision and Curriculum Development, NEA, 1969.

Downey, Lawrence W. *The Task of Public Education: The Perceptions of People.* Chicago: Midwest Administration Center, University of Chicago, 1960.

Dressel, P. L. "Teaching, Learning, and Evaluation," *Improving College and University Teaching* 13 (1960): 11-15.

Dressel, P. L., and Mayhew, L. *General Education—Explorations in Evaluation.* Washington, D. C.: American Council on Education, 1954.

Dressel, P. L., et al. *Evaluation in Higher Education.* Boston, Mass.: Houghton Mifflin Co., 1961.

DuBois, P. H., and Wientge, K. M. *Strategies of Research on Learning in Educational Settings.* St. Louis: Washington University, 1964.

Dyer, Henry S. "The Discovery and Development of Educational Goals." *Proceedings of the 1966 Invitational Conference on Testing Problems.* Princeton, N. J.: Educational Testing Service, 1967. pp. 12-24.

Easley, J. A., Jr. "Evaluation problems of the UICSM curriculum project." Paper presented at the National Seminar for Research in Vocational Education. University of Illinois, 1966. (mimeograph)

Easley, J. A., Jr., Kendzior, Elizabeth, and Wallace, Robert. "A 'Bio-Assay' of Biology Tests," *American Biology Teacher* 29 (1967): 382-89.

Ebel, Robert L. Content standard test scores. *Educational and Psychological Measurement* 22 (1962): 15-25.

————. Some measurement problems in a national assessment of educational progress. *Journal of Educational Measurement* 1 (1966): 11-18.

Educational Policies Commission. *The Central Purpose of American Education.* Washington, D. C.: National Education Association, 1961.

Educational Testing Service. *A Plan for Evaluating the Quality of Educational Programs in Pennsylvania—Highlights.* Princeton, N. J.: Educational Testing Service, 1965.

Edwards, W. The theory of decision making. *Psychological Bulletin* 51 (1954): 380-418.

Eigen, L. D. Some problems in field testing programs for teaching machines. *Journal of Educational Sociology* 34 (1961): 372-376.

————. The implications for research methodology of some behavioral studies in programed instruction. *Psychology in the Schools* 1 (1964): 140-147.

Eisner, Elliot W. "Curriculum Ideas in Time of Crisis," *Art Education* 18 (1965).

————. "Educational Objectives: Help or Hindrance?" *School Review* 75 (1967): 250-266.

————. "A Response to My Critics," *School Review* 75 (1967): 267-268.

————. Children's Creativity in Art: A Study of Types. *American Educational Research Journal* 2 (1965): 125-36.

————. Instructional and Expressive Educational Objectives: Their Formulation and Use in Curriculum. AERA Monograph Series on Curriculum Evaluation 3. Chicago: Rand McNally & Co., 1969.

Eisner, Elliot W., and Ecker, David W., ed. "Evaluating Children's Art," *Readings in Art Education.* Waltham, Mass.: Blaisdell Publishing Co., 1966.

Findley, W. G. "The Ultimate Goals of Education," *School Review* 65 (1956): 10-17.

Findley, W., ed. *The impact and improvement of school testing programs.* N.S.S.E. Yearbook, 62, II. Chicago: University of Chicago Press, 1963.

Fishbein, M., ed. *Readings in attitude theory and measurement*. New York: John Wiley & Sons, Inc., 1967.

Fischer, J. H. The question of control. *Proceedings of the 1965 Invitational Conference on Testing Problems*. Educational Testing Service, 1966.

Fivars, G., and Gosnell, D. *Nursing evaluation: The problem and the process, the critical incident technique*. New York: The Macmillan Co., 1966.

Flanagan, J. C. *Design for a Study of American Youth*. Boston, Mass.: Houghton Mifflin Co., 1962.

Flanders, Ned A. *Teacher Influence, Pupil Attitudes, and Achievement*. Cooperative Research Monograph no. 12, U.S. Department of Health, Education, and Welfare, Office of Education. Washington, D. C.: U.S. Government Printing Office, 1965.

Florida Educational Research and Development Council. *Plan for Study of the Educational Needs of Florida*. Gainesville, Florida: College of Education, University of Florida, 1968.

Flynn, John P., and Garber, H., eds. *Assessing Behavior: Readings in Educational and Psychological Measurement*. Reading, Mass.: Addison-Wesley Publishing Co., Inc., 1967.

Forehand, G. A. The role of the evaluator in curriculum research. *Journal of Educational Measurement* 3 (1966): 199-204.

Ford, Susan F. A Paramorphic Representation of Counsellors' Judgments. Unpublished doctoral dissertation. Rutgers University, 1969.

Foshay, Arthur W., et al. *Educational achievements of thirteen year olds in twelve countries*. Homberg: UNESCO Institute for Education, 1962.

Fox, David J., et al. Evaluation of ESEA Title I Projects in New York City, 1967-68, Project No. 0368. New York City: Center for Urban Education, December, 1968.

Fraser, Dorothy. *Deciding What To Teach*. Washington, D. C.: National Educational Association, 1963.

Frederiksen, N. Proficiency tests for training evaluation. In *Training Research and Education*, edited by R. Glaser. Pittsburgh: University of Pittsburgh Press, 1962.

Frederiksen, N., and Gilbert, A. Replication of a study of differential predictability. *Educational Psychological Measurement* 20 (1960): 759-767.

Frederiksen, N., and Melville, S. D. Differential predictability in the use of test scores. *Educational Psychological Measurement* 14 (1954): 647-656.

Freeman, L. C., et al. *Metropolitan Decision-Making: Further Analyses from the Syracuse Study of Local Community Leadership*. Syracuse, N. Y.: University College of Syracuse University, 1956.

French, J. W. *The relation of problem-solving styles to the factor composition of tests*. Princeton, N. J.: Educational Testing Service, 1963.

French, Joe. *Guidelines for Evaluating Projects and Programs Under Title II, PL 81-874 and Title I, PL 89-102*. Princeton, N. J.: Educational Testing Service, 1965.

French, W., et al. *Behavioral goals of general education in high school*. New York: Russell Sage Foundation, 1957.

From theory to the classroom. Background information on the First Grade Project in New York City Schools. New York City Board of Education and Educational Testing Service, 1968.

Frymier, J. R. National Assessment. Appendix A, In *Evaluation as feedback and guide*, edited by F. T. Wilhelms. Association for Supervision and Curriculum Development, 1967.

Furno, Orlando F. Sampling survey designs in education—focus on administrative utilization. *Review of Educational Research* 36 (1966): 552-65.

Furst, E. J. *Constructing Evaluation Instruments*. New York: Longmans, Green & Co., Ltd., 1958.

————. Tasks of evaluation in an experimental economics course. *Journal of Educational Measurement* 3 (1966): 213-219.

Gage, H. L., ed. *Handbook of Research on Teaching*. Chicago: Rand McNally & Co., 1963.

Gagné, Robert M. *The Conditions of Learning*. New York: Holt, Rinehart & Winston, Inc., 1965.

————. "The Analysis of Instructional Objectives for the Design of Instruction." In *Teaching Machines and Programmed Learning, II, Data and Decisions*, edited by Robert Glaser, pp. 21-65. Washington: Department of Audio Visual Instruction, NEA, 1965.

————. "Curriculum Research and the Promotion of Learning," *Perspectives of Curriculum Evaluation*. Chicago: Rand McNally & Co., 1967.

————. The acquisition of knowledge. *Psychological Review* 69 (1962): 355-65.

————. The analysis of instructional objectives for the design of instruction. In *Teaching machines and programed learning II*, edited by R. Glaser, pp. 21-65. NEA, 1965.

————. The analysis of instructional objectives for the design of instruction. In *Teaching Machines and Programed Learning, II, Data and Directions*, edited by R. Glaser. National Education Association, 1965.

————. "Curriculum Research and the Promotion of Learning," In *American Educational Research Association Monograph Series on Curriculum Evaluation* 1. pp. 19-38. Chicago: Rand McNally & Co., 1967.

Gagné, R. M., ed. *Psychological Principles in System Development*. New York: Holt, Rinehart & Winston, Inc., 1962. Chapter by Miller, on task description; and by Glaser and Klaus, on proficiency measurement.

Gagné, R. M., and Bassler, O. C. Study of retention of some topics of elementary non-metric geometry. *Journal of Educational Psychology* 54 (1963): 123-131.

Gagné, R. M., and Paradise, N. E. Abilities and learning sets in knowledge acquisition. *Psychological Monographs* 75 (1961).

Geis, Fred, Jr. The Semantic Differential Technique as a Means of Evaluating Changes in "Affect." Doctoral thesis. Cambridge, Mass.: Graduate School of Education, Harvard University, 1968.

Gerlach, V. S., and Sullivan, H. J. *Constructing Statements of Outcomes*. Inglewood, Calif.: Southwest

Regional Laboratory for Educational Research and Development, 1967.

Ghiselli, E. E. Differentiation of individuals in terms of their predictability. *Journal of Applied Psychology* 40 (1956): 374-377.

—————. Differentiation of tests in terms of the accuracy with which they predict for a given individual. *Educational Psychological Measurement* 20 (1960): 675-684. (a)

—————. The prediction of predictability. *Educational Psychological Measurement* 20 (1960): 3-8. (b)

—————. Moderating effects and differential reliability and validity. *Journal of Applied Psychology* 47 (1963): 81-86.

Gibson, J. S. New Frontiers in the Social Sciences. Goals for Students, Means for Teachers. Medford, Mass.: University of Massachusetts, Lincoln Filene Center for Citizenship and Public Affairs, 1965.

Girshick, M. A. An elementary survey of statistical decision theory. *Review of Educational Research* 24 (1954): 448-466.

Glaser, R. Instructional technology and the measurement of learning outcomes. *American Psychologist* 18 (1963): 519-521.

—————. Toward a behavioral science base for instructional design. In *Teaching Machines and Programed learning, II,* edited by R. Glaser, pp. 771-809. NEA, 1965.

—————. The program for individually prescribed instruction. Paper read at the annual meeting of the American Educational Research Association, Chicago, February, 1966.

Glaser, R. ed. *Teaching machines and programed learning, II, data and directions.* Washington, D. C.: NEA, 1965. (Chapters: 7, Lumsdaine; 17, Glaser).

Glaser, Robert, and Cox, Richard. "Criterion-referenced testing for the measurement of educational outcomes." In *Instructional process and media integration,* edited by Robert Weisgerber. Chicago: Rand McNally & Co., 1967.

Glaser, Robert; Damrin, Dora F., and Gardner, Floyd M. *The Tab Item: A Technique for the Measurement of Proficiency in Diagnostic Problem-Solving Tasks.* Urbana, Ill.: University of Illinois, June, 1952.

Glass, Gene V. Design of Evaluation Studies. Paper presented at the Council for Exceptional Children Special Conference on Early Childhood Education, New Orleans, Louisiana. December, 1969.

Godshalk, F. I., Swineford, F., and Coffman, W. E. The measurement of writing ability. *Research Monograph No. 6.* College Entrance Examination Board, 1966.

Goodlad, John I. Curriculum: the state of the field. *Review of Educational Research* 20 (1960): 192.

Goodlad, J. I. *The Changing School Curriculum.* New York: Fund for the Advancement of Education, 1966.

Gorlow, Leon, and Noll, Gary A. The measurement of empirically determined values. *Educational and Psychological Measurement* 27 (1967): 1115-1118.

Goslin, D. A., et al. *The use of standardized tests in elementary schools.* Technical Report No. 2 on the social consequences of testing. New York: Russell Sage Foundation, 1965.

Gosling, George. *Marking English Compositions.* Australian Council for Educational Research, ACER Research Series, No. 81, 1966.

Gough, H. G. Clinical vs. statistical prediction in psychology. In *Psychology in the Making: Histories of Selected Research Problems,* edited by L. Postman, pp. 526-584. Alfred A. Knopf, Inc., 1962.

Greeley, Andrew M. and Rossi, Peter H. *The Education of Catholic Americans.* Chicago: Aldine Publishing Co., 1966.

Greene, William W. "Evaluation of the Anthropology Curriculum Project for grades one and four as measured by selected and prepared testing instruments." Panel report on the Anthropology Curriculum Project. Paper read at NCSS, Miami Beach, November, 1965.

Grobman, Hulda. Student performance in new high school biology programs. *Science* 143 (1964): 265-66.

—————. The place of evaluation in the biological sciences curriculum study. *Journal of Educational Measurement* 3 (1966): 205-212.

Gronlund, N. R. *Measurement and evaluation in teaching.* New York: The Macmillan Co., 1965. "The Gross Educational Product: How Much are Students Learning?" *Carnegie Quarterly* 14, No. 2, Spring 1966.

Guba, Egon G. "Methodological Strategies for Educational Change." Paper presented to the Conference on Strategies for Educational Change, Washington, D. C., November 8-10, 1965.

Guba, Egon G., and Stufflebeam, Daniel L. "Evaluation: The Process of Stimulating, Aiding, and Abetting Insightful Action." Paper delivered at the Second National Symposium for Professors of Educational Research. Boulder, Colorado, November 21, 1968.

Guttman, L. The structure of interrelations among intelligence tests. *1964 Invitational Conference on Testing Problem,* Princeton, N. J.: Educational Testing Service, 1965.

Hammond, Robert L. "Evaluation at the Local Level." *Project EPIC Report.* Tucson, Arizona: Project EPIC, August, 1967.

Hand, H. C. National assessment viewed as the camel's nose. *Phi Delta Kappan,* 1 (1965): 4-12.

Haney, Richard E. *The Changing Curriculum: Science.* Washington, D. C.: Association for Supervision and Curriculum Development, 1966.

Harap, Henry, ed. *The Changing Curriculum.* New York: D. Appleton-Century Co., 1937.

Harris, Chester W. *Some Issues in Evaluation,* paper delivered to the Social Studies Institute, University of Wisconsin, July 2, 1958.

Harris, C. W., ed. *Problems in measuring change.* Madison: University of Wisconsin Press, 1964.

Harrison, G. V. *The Instructional Value of Presenting Explicit Versus Vague Objectives.* California Educational Research Studies, 1967.

Harvey, O. J., et al. "Teachers' Beliefs, Classroom Atmosphere and Student Behavior," AERJ 5 (1968): 151-166.

Hastings, J. T. "Innovations in Evaluation for Innovations in Curriculum." In *Curriculum Development and Evaluation in English and the Social Studies*, edited by E. R. Steinberg, chapter five. Carnegie Institute of Technology, 1964.

—————. *Evaluating Change*. San Francisco: ASCD Conference, March, 1966.

—————. Curriculum Evaluation: the whys of the outcomes. *Journal of Educational Measurement* 3 (1966): 27-32.

Hathaway, S. R. Increasing clinical efficiency. In *Objective approaches to personality assessment*, edited by B. M. Bass and I. A. Berg, pp. 192-203. Princeton, N. J.: D. Van Nostrand Co., Inc., 1959.

—————. Clinical intuition and inferential accuracy. *Journal of Personality* 24 (1956): 223-230.

Havighurst, Robert. *A Study of the Public Schools of Chicago*. Chicago: Board of Education, 1964.

Hawkins, David. "Learning the unteachable." In *Learning by discovery*, edited by E. Keislar and L. S. Shulman, pp. 3-12. Chicago: Rand McNally & Co., 1966.

Heath, R. W. Pitfalls in the evaluation of new curricula. *Science Education* 46 (1962): 216.

—————. Curriculum cognition, and educational measurement. *Educational and Psychological Measurement* 24 (1964): 239-53.

Heath, R. W., et al. *The use of achievement and ability test averages*. (Research Memorandum), ETS, May, 1966.

Heine, Ralph W., ed. *The Student Physician as Psychotherapist*. Chicago: Chicago University Press, 1962.

Helmstadter, Jerry C. An empirical comparison of methods for estimating profile similarity. *Educational and Psychological Measurement* 17 (1957): 71-82.

Henry, N. B., ed. Measurement of understanding. *Yearbook National Society for the Study of Education*, 1946, 45, Part I.

Herrick, V. E., and Tyler, R. W., eds. *Toward Improved Curriculum Theory*. Supplementary Educational Monographs, No. 71. Chicago: University of Chicago Press, 1950.

Herron, J. D. Evaluation and the new curricula. *Journal of Research in Science Teaching* 4 (1966): 159-170.

Herzog, Elizabeth. *Some Guide Lines for Evaluative Research*. Washington, D. C.: U.S. Department of Health, Education, and Welfare; Children's Bureau, 1959. p. 17.

Hively, W. Constructing, evaluating, and revising a program of instruction in algebra for in-service teacher training: a case history and essay on methodology. Minnesota National Laboratory, October, 1964.

—————. Some guidelines for evaluating programs of instruction in mathematics. University of Minnesota. (dittograph)

Hoffman, B. *The Tyranny of Testing*. New York: Crowell Collier and Macmillan, Inc., 1962.

Hoffman, P. J. The paramorphic representation of clinical judgment. *Psychological Bulletin* 57 (1960): 116-131.

Holland, J. L. Creative and academic performance among talented adolescents. *Journal of Educational Psychology* 52 (1961): 136-147.

Holland, J. L., and Nichols, R. C. Prediction of academic and extra-curricular achievement in college. *Journal of Educational Psychology* 55 (1964): 55-65.

Holt, R. R. Clinical and statistical prediction. *Journal of Abnormal and Social Psychology* 56 (1958): 1-12.

Holtzman, W. H. Objective scoring of projective techniques. In *Objective Approaches to Personality Assessment*, edited by B. M. Bass and I. A. Berg, pp. 119-141. Princeton, N. J.: D. Van Nostrand Co., Inc., 1959.

Holtzman, W. H., and Sells, S. B. Prediction of flying success by clinical analysis of test protocols. *Journal of Abnormal and Social Psychology* 49 (1954): 485-490.

Horst, P. The role of prediction variables which are independent of the criterion. In *Prediction of Personal Adjustment*, pp. 431-436. SSRC: 1941.

Hovland, C. Reconciling conflicting results derived from experimental and survey studies of attitude change. *American Psychologist* 14 (1959): 8-17.

Hughes, M. M. *A Research Report: Assessment of the Quality of Teaching in Elementary Schools*. Salt Lake City: University of Utah Press, 1959.

Hunt, D. E.; Hardt, R. H., and Victor, J. B. *Characterization of Upward Bound 1967-68*. Syracuse: Syracuse University, Youth Development Center, 1968.

Hunt, W. A. An actuarial approach to clinical judgment. In *Objective Approaches to Personality Assessment*, edited by B. M. Bass and I. A. Berg, pp. 169-189. D. Van Nostrand Co., Inc., 1959.

Husén, T. *International Study of Achievement in Mathematics: A Comparison of 12 Countries*. New York: John Wiley & Sons, Inc., 1967.

Hutt, M. L. Actuarial and clinical approaches to psychodiagnosis. *Psychological Reports* 2 (1956): 413-419.

Hyman, H. H., et al. Applications of methods of evaluation. Berkeley: University of California Press, 1962.

Hyman, Herbert H., and Wright, Charles R. "Evaluating Social Action Programs." In *The Uses of Sociology*, edited by Lasarsfeld, Paul F., Sewell, William H., and Wilensky, Harold L., pp. 741-783. New York: Basic Books, Inc., 1967.

Ikeda, Hiroshi. *A Factorial Study of the Relationships Between Teacher-held Objectives and Student Performance in UICSM High School Mathematics*. Research Report, No. 10. Urbana: University of Illinois Committee on School Mathematics, June, 1965.

Ironside, Roderick A. "Adult Literacy: Appropriate Measures for Use in Appraisal," *Curriculum Studies*. Princeton, N. J.: Educational Testing Service, March, 1967.

Jackson, P. W. *The Way Teaching Is*. Washington, D. C.: Association for Supervision and Curriculum Development, 1966.

James, H. T. "Wealth, Expenditures and Decision-making for Education." Report to the U.S. Office of Education, Research Contracts Division, Project

No. 1241. Palo Alto, Calif.: Stanford University Press, 1963.

Jenkins, J. J., and Paterson, D. G., eds. *Studies in Individual Differences*. New York: Appleton-Century, 1961. (pp. 17-26; 32-44; 45-58).

Jensen, Gail E. *The Validation of Aims for American Democratic Education*. Minneapolis, Minn.: Burgess Publishing Co., 1950.

Kaplan, A. *The Conduct of Inquiry*. San Francisco: Chandler Publishing Co., 1964.

Karplus, Robert, and Thier, H. D. *A New Look at Elementary School Science*. Chicago: Rand McNally & Co., 1967.

Karlinger, Fred N. "The First- and Second-Order Factor Structures of Attitudes Toward Education," *American Educational Research Journal* 4 (1967): 191-206.

————. Attitudes toward education and perceptions of teacher characteristics: A O study. *American Educational Research Journal* 3 (1966): 159-168.

Kerlinger, Fred N., and Pedhazur. Educational attitudes and perceptions of desirable traits of teachers. *American Educational Research Journal* 5 (1968): 543-560.

Kindred, Leslie. *How to Tell the School Story*. Englewood Cliffs, N. J.: Prentice-Hall, Inc., 1960.

Klein, S. P.; Skager, R. W., and Schultz, C. B. *Dimensions for evaluating art products*. Research Bulletin, Educational Testing Service, March, 1966.

Klein, S., et al. Measuring artistic creativity and flexibility. *Journal of Educational Measurement* 3 (1966): 277-86.

Kleinmuntz, B. *Personality measurement*. Homewood, Ill.: Dorsey Press, 1967.

Klopfer; Leopold, and Cooley, William W. *Use of case histories in the development of student understanding of science and scientists*. Cambridge: Graduate School of Education, Harvard University, 1961.

Kluckhohn, Clyde. "Values and Value-orientations in the Theory of Action: Explorations, Definition and Classification." In *Toward a General Theory of Action*, edited by Talcott Parsons and Edward Shils, chapter four. Cambridge, Mass.: Harvard University Press, 1951.

Knox, A. B. "Developing an Evaluation Plan in Adult Farmer Education," *Agricultural Education Magazine*, December, 1962, pp. 55-62.

Krathwohl, David; Bloom, Benjamin, and Masia, Bertram. *Taxonomy of Educational Objectives, Handbook II; Affective Domain*. New York: David McKay Co., Inc., 1964.

Krathwohl, David R. "The Taxonomy of Educational Objectives—Its Use in Curriculum Building," In *Defining Educational Objectives*, edited by C. M. Lindvall, pp. 38-48. Pittsburgh: University of Pittsburgh Press, 1964.

————. "Stating Objectives Appropriately for Program, for Curriculum, and for Instructional Materials Development," *Journal of Teacher Education* 12 (1965): 83-92.

Kropp, R. P., and Stoker, H. W. *The construction and validation of tests of the cognitive processes as described in the taxonomy of educational objectives.*

Cooperative Research Project, No. 2117. Florida State University: Institute of Human Learning, 1966.

Kropp, R. P.; Stoker, H. W., and Bashaw, W. L. *The construction and validation of tests of the cognitive processes as described in the taxonomy of educational objectives.* (Cooperative Research Project Mimeo) Institute of Human Learning and Department of Educational Research and Testing, Florida State University, 1966.

————. The validation of the taxonomy of educational objectives. *Journal of Experimental Education* 34 (1966): 69-76.

Krumboltz, J. D. *Learning and the educational process*. Chicago: Rand McNally & Co. (Especially Chapter 1, Educational objectives and human performance by Gagné, and Chapter 10, School learning over the long haul, by Carroll.)

Kurland, Norman D. *Developing Indicators of Educational Performance*. Lecture presented at the 31st Educational Conference by the Educational Records Bureau, New York City. October, 1966.

Lachman, R. The model in theory construction. *Psychological Review* 67 (1960): 113-129.

Lado, R. *Language testing: The construction and use of foreign language tests*. New York: McGraw-Hill Book Co., 1964.

Larkins, A. Guy, and Shaver, James P. Hardnosed research and the evaluation of curriculum. Logan: Utah States University, College of Education, 1969. (mimeograph)

Lawrence, G. D. *Analysis of teacher tests in social studies according to the taxonomy of educational objectives*. Claremont, Calif.: On file at Honnold Library, Claremont Colleges, 1963.

Lee, Dorris May. "Teaching and Evaluation," In *Evaluation as Feedback and Guide*, Chapter 4, pp. 72-100. 1967 Yearbook, Association for Supervision and Curriculum Development, a department of the National Education Association, 1967.

Lee, M. C. Interactions, configurations, and non-additive models. *Educational Psychological Measurement* 21 (1961): 797-805.

Lehman, David L. "A New Dimension in the Evaluation of BSCS," *Biological Sciences Curriculum Study Newsletter* 30 (1967): 21-5.

Lennon, Roger T. *Assumptions Underlying the Use* of Content Validity. *Educational and Psychological Measurement* 14 (1955) 294ff.

Levine, A. S. A technique for developing suppression tests. *Educational & Psychological Measurement* 12 (1952): 313-15.

Lindbloom, Charles E. "The Science of Muddling Through," in *Policy Making in American Government*, edited by Edward U. Schreier, pp. 24-37. New York: Basic Books, Inc., Publishers, 1969.

Lindquist, E. F., ed. *Educational Measurement*. American Council on Education, 1951.

Lindvall, C. M. *Defining educational objectives*. Pittsburgh: University of Pittsburgh Press, 1964.

————. "The Task of Evaluation in Curriculum Development Projects: A Rationale and Case Study," *School Review* 74 (1966): 159-67.

Lindvall, C. M., and Cox, R. C. *Evaluation as a Tool in Curriculum Development: the IPI Evaluation Program*. American Educational Research Association Monograph Series on Curriculum Evaluation, No. 5, 1970.

Lisonbee, Lorenzo. "The comparative effect of BSCS and traditional biology on student achievement," *School Science and Mathematics* 10 (1964): 27-32.

Loevinger, Jane. Objective tests as instruments of psychological theory. *Psychological Reports Monographs* 3 (1957): 635-694.

Lord, Frederic M. Sampling fluctuations resulting from the sample of test items. *Psychometrika* 20 (March, 1955): 1-22.

————. The measurement of growth. *Educational and Psychological Measurement* 16 (1956): 421-37. See also Errata, ibid., 17 (1957): 452.

————. Item Sampling in Test Theory and in Research Design. Research Bulletin No. 65-22. Princeton, N. J.: Educational Testing Service, June, 1965.

Lord, Frederic M., and Novick, Melvin R. *Statistical Theories of Mental Test Scores.* Reading, Mass.: Addison-Wesley Publishing Co., Inc., 1968.

Loree, M. Ray. *Relationships among Three Domains of Educational Objectives.* May 11, 1965. (mimeograph)

Lortie, Dan C. "Rational Decision-Making: Is It Possible Today?" *The EPIE Forum* 1 (1967): 6-9.

Lubin, A. Some formulae for use with suppressor variables. *Educational Psychological Measurement* 17 (1957): 286-296.

Lueck, W. R., et al. *Effective Secondary Education.* Minneapolis: University of Minnesota, 1966.

Lumsdaine, A. A., et al. Recommendations for reporting the effectiveness of programmed-instruction materials. 1965. (mimeograph)

Macdonald, J. B. "Myths about Instruction," *Educational Leadership.* 22 (1965): 571-76ff.

Madaus, G. F., and Rippey, R. M. Zeroing in on the STEP writing test: What does it tell a teacher? *Journal of Educational Measurement* 3 (1966): 19-26.

Mager, R., and McCann, J. *Learner-Controlled Instruction.* Palo Alto, California: Varian Associates, 1961.

Mager, R. F. *Preparing Objectives for Programmed Instruction.* San Francisco: Fearon Publishers, Inc., 1962.

Maguire, Thomas Owens. "Value Components of Teachers' Judgments of Educational Objectives." Doctoral Thesis. Urbana: University of Illinois, 1967.

————. Decisions and curriculum objectives: a methodology for evaluation. *Alberta Journal of Educational Research* 16 (1969): 17-30.

Maier, M. S. *Evaluation of a New Mathematics Curriculum.* Princeton, N. J.: Educational Testing Service, 1962.

Marks, M. R., Christal, R. E., and Bottenberg, R. A. Simple formula aids for understanding the joint action of two predictors. *Journal of Applied Psychology* 45 (1961): 285-288.

Maslin, J. "Role-related behavior of the subject and psychologist and its effects upon psychological data," in *Nebraska Symposium on Motivation,* edited by D. Levine, pp. 67-73. Lincoln: University of Nebraska Press, 1966.

May, M. I., and Lumsdaine, A. A. *Learning from films.* New Haven: Yale University Press, 1958.

Mayer, W. V. "The Impact of Testing on School Curricula," *American Biology Teacher,* December, 1964, 784-788.

Mayhew, Lewis B. "Measurement of Non-cognitive Objectives in the Social Studies," in *Evaluation in Social Studies,* edited by Harry D. Berg, chapter fourteen. Thirty-fifth Yearbook of the National Council for the Social Studies, 1965.

McClelland, D. C. *Personality.* Dryden Press, 1951. (Particularly on relation of measuring schemes to theoretical view.)

McCloskey, Gordon. *Education and Public Understanding.* New York: Harper & Row, Publishers, 1959.

McGuire, C. Research in the process approach to the construction and analysis of medical examinations. *20th Yearbook, National Council on Measurement in Education.* 1963, pp. 7-16.

McIntyre, Robert, et al. Planning for the Evaluation of Special Education Programs: A Resource Guide. Washington, D. C.: USOE Bureau of Education for the Handicapped. Contract OEG-0-9-372160-3553(032), 1969.

McKeachie, W. "Procedures and Techniques of Teaching: A Summary of Experimental Studies. In *The American College,* edited by N. Sanford, chapter 8. John Wiley & Sons, Inc., 1962.

McLure, William P. *Statewide Techniques For Survey and Analysis of Educational Needs.* Urbana, Ill.: Bureau of Educational Research, University of Illinois, 1968. (mimeograph)

McNeil, J. D. "Antidote to a School Scandal," *Educational Forum,* 31 (1966): 69-77.

McNemar, Q. The mode of operation of suppressant variables. *American Journal of Psychology* 48 (1945): 554-555.

Mechner, F. J. "Science education and behavioral technology," in *Teaching machines and programed learning, II, data and directions,* edited by R. Glaser. NEA, 1965.

Meehl, P. E. *Clinical vs. statistical prediction.* Minneapolis: University of Minnesota Press, 1954.

————. Wanted—a good cookbook. *American Psychologist* 11 (1956): 263-272.

————. When shall we use our heads instead of the formula? *Journal of Counseling Psychology* 4 (1957): 268-273.

————. A comparison of clinicians with five statistical methods of identifying psychotic MMPI profiles. *Journal of Counseling Psychology* 6 (1959): 102-109.

————. The cognitive activity of the clinician. *American Psychologist* 15 (1960): 19-27.

Meehl, P. E., and Rosen, A. Antecedent probability and the efficiency of psychometric signs, patterns, or cutting scores. *Psychological Bulletin* 52 (1955): 194-216.

Merwin, J. C. The progress of exploration toward a national assessment of educational progress. *Journal of Educational Measurement* 3 (1966): 5-10.

Merwin, J. C., and Tyler, R. W. "What the Assessment of Education Will Ask," *Nation's Schools* 78 (1966): 77-79.

Messick, Samuel. The perceived structure of political relationships. *Sociometry* 24 (1961): 111-116.

Mewborn, A. C. (senior author) and Hively, W. (project director). *Evaluation Manual for a Programmed Course in Algebra for Teachers.* Minneapolis: University of Minnesota Press, 1964.

Michael, D. N., and Maccoby, N. Factors influencing the effects of student participation on verbal learning from films: Motivating versus practice effects, "feedback," and overt versus covert responding. *Student Response in Programmed Instruction: A Symposium,* edited by A. A. Lumsdaine, chapter 18, 1961.

Michael, William B., and Metfessel, Newton S. A paradigm for developing valid measurable objectives in the evaluation of educational programs in colleges and universities. *Educational and Psychological Measurement* 27 (1967): 373-83.

Michigan University. School of Education. *A Study of School Classroom Behavior from Diverse Evaluative Frameworks: Developmental, Mental, Health, Substantive Learning, Group Process.* East Lansing: Michigan State University Press, 1961.

Miller, D. C. *Handbook of research design and social measurement.* New York: David McKay Co., Inc., 1964.

Miller, H. L., and McGuire, Christine. *Evaluating Liberal Adult Education.* Chicago: Center for the Study of Liberal Education for Adults, 1961.

Miller, J. G. "Future Impact of Psychological Theory on Personality Assessments," in *Objective Approaches in Personality Assessment,* edited by B. M. Bass and I. A. Berg, pp. 204-216. Princeton, N. J.: D. Van Nostrand Co., Inc., 1959.

Miller, R. B. "Analysis of Instructional Objectives," in *Training Research and Education,* edited by Robert Glaser, chapter two. Pittsburgh: University of Pittsburgh Press, 1962.

Miller, R. B. "Task Description and Analysis," in *Psychological Principles in System Development,* edited by Gagne, p. 187ff. New York: Holt, Rinehart & Winston, Inc., 1962.

Morrissett, I., ed. *Concepts and Structure in the New Social Science Curricula.* West Lafayette, Ind.: Social Science Education Consortium, 1966.

Morrissett, Irving, and Stevens, W. William. "Curriculum Analysis," *Social Education* 31 (1967): 483-486, 489. (Also in *The EPIE Forum* 1 (1967): 11-15.

Morrison, James W. "Designs and models for community action program evaluation." Prepared for the annual meeting of the Society for the Study of Social Problems, Miami Beach, August, 1966.

Morsh, J. E., and Wilder, E. "Identifying the effective instructor: A review of the quantitative studies, 1900-1952." *USAF Personnel Training Research Center, Research Bulletin.* 1954, No. AFPT-RC-TR-54-44.

Mort, Paul R., and Furno, Orlando F. *Theory and Synthesis of a Sequential Simplex: A Model for Assessing the Effectiveness of Administrative Policies.* Institute of Administrative Research, Study No. 12. New York: Teachers College, Columbia University, 1960.

Munro, T. The interrelation of the arts in secondary education. *The Creative Arts in American Education.* Cambridge, Mass.: Harvard University Press, 1960.

National Council for the Social Studies. *Evaluation in Social Studies.* Thirty-fifth Yearbook. Washington, D. C.: the Council, a department of the National Education Association, 1965.

National Opinion Research Center. *The Public Looks at Education.* Report No. 21. Denver: National Opinion Research Center, 1944.

National Study of Secondary School Evaluation. *Evaluative Criteria.* Fourth Edition. Washington, D. C.: National Study Committee, 1969.

Nedelsky, Leo. *Science Teaching and Testing.* New York: Harcourt, Brace & World, Inc., 1965.

Neidt, C. O. "Changes in attitudes during learning." Report to the U.S. Office of Education, Title VII Project No. C-1139, 1964.

Nerbovig, Marcella H. *Teachers Perceptions of the Function of Objectives.* Doctoral Thesis. Madison: University of Wisconsin Press, 1956. *Dissertation Abstracts* 16 (1956): 2406-2407.

Neuwein, Reginald A. *Catholic Schools in Action: A Report.* South Bend, Indiana: University of Notre Dame Press, 1966.

Newcomb, T. M., et al. *Persistence and Change, Bennington College and Its Students after 25 Years.* New York: John Wiley & Sons, Inc., 1967.

Newmann, Fred M., and Oliver, Donald W. "Education and Community," *Harvard Educational Review* 37 (1967): 61-106.

North Central Association of Colleges and Secondary Schools. *Guide for the Evaluation of Institutions of Higher Learning.* 1965 ed. Chicago: North Central Association, 1965.

Nunnally, Jum. *Tests and Measurements: Assessment and Prediction.* New York: McGraw-Hill Book Co., 1959.

Nuthall, G. A. "A Review of Some Selected Recent Studies of Classroom Interaction and Teaching Behavior," *New Zealand Journal of Educational Studies* 3 (1968): 125-147. Also in AERA Monograph Series on Curriculum Evaluation, Volume 6, *Classroom Observation* (in press).

Oliver, Donald. "The Education Industries," *Harvard Educational Review* 37 (1967): 111.

Oliver, Donald W., and Shaver, James F. *Teaching Public Issues in the High School.* Boston: Houghton Mifflin Co., 1966.

Oppenheim, A. N. *Questionnaire Design and Attitude Measurement.* New York: Basic Books, Inc., Publishers, 1966.

Osburn, H. G. *Item Sampling for Achievement Testing.* Houston: Psychology Department, University of Houston, 1967. (mimeograph)

Osgood, C. E.; Suci, G. J., and Tannenbaum, P. H. *The Measurement of Meaning.* Urbana: University of Illinois Press, 1957.

Oskamp, S. The relationship of clinical experience and training methods to several criteria of clinical prediction. *Psychological Monographs* 76 (1962): whole issue.

Pace, C. R., and Stern, G. G. An approach to the measurement of psychological characteristics of college environments. *Journal of Educational Psychology* 49 (1958): 269-77.

Pace, C. Robert. *When Students Judge Their College*. College Board Review, No. 58, Winter, 1965-66.

Page, Ellis Batten. *Recapturing the Richness Within the Classroom*. Paper presented at Annual Meeting of the American Educational Research Association, Chicago, Ill., February 11, 1965.

————. "The Imminence of Grading Essays by Computer," *Phi Delta Kappa* 47 (1966): 238-43.

Parker, J. "The Relationship of Self Report to Inferred Self Concept," *Educational and Psychological Measurement* 26 (1966): 691-700.

Payette, R. F. Development and analysis of a cognitive preference test in the social sciences. Unpublished doctoral dissertation. Urbana: University of Illinois, 1967.

Payne, Arlene. *The Study of Curriculum Plans*. Washington, D. C.: National Education Association, 1969.

Peak, Helen. "Problems of Objective Observation," in *Research Methods in the Behavioral Sciences*, edited by Leon Festinger and Daniel Katz, pp. 243-299. New York: Holt, Rinehart & Winston, Inc., 1953.

Peckham, Percy D. An evaluation of the Boulder Valley School District ESEA Title III Project: A computerized approach to the individualizing of instructional experiences. Boulder: Laboratory of Educational Research, University of Colorado. No date. Photocopy.

Pellegrin, R. J. "Community power structure and educational decision-making in the local community." Paper read at the National Convention of the American Association of School Administrators, Atlantic City, 1965.

Plumlee, Lynette B. "Estimating Means and Standard Deviations from Partial Data—An Empirical Check on Lord's Item Sampling Technique," *Educational and Psychological Measurement* 24 (1964): 623-30.

Pool, Ithiel de Sola. "Behavioral Technology," In *Towards the Year 2018*, pp. 87-96. Foreign Policy Association, 1968.

Popham, W. J. *The Teacher Empiricist*. Los Angeles: Aegeus Press, 1964.

————. *Educational Criterion Measures*. Inglewood, Calif.: Southwest Regional Laboratory for Educational Research and Development, California, 1967. (a)

————. *Development report: Educational criterion measures*. Inglewood, Calif.: Southwest Regional Laboratory for Educational Research and Development, April, 1967 and August, 1967. (b)

————. *Educational Needs Assessment in the Cognitive, Affective, and Psychomotor Domain*. Los Angeles: Center for the Study of Evaluation, U.C. L.A. Paper presented at three ESEA Title III Regional Workshops, 1969.

Popham, W. James, and Baker, Eva. "The Instructional Objectives Preference Test," *Journal of Educational Measurement* 3 (1965): 186.

————. *Development of Performance Test of Teaching Proficiency*. American Educational Research Association paper dealing with vocational education status report, 1966.

Popham, W. James, and Skager, Rodney. *Instructional Objectives Measurement System. Progress in Evalu-*

ation Study. Third Annual Report to the U.S. Office of Education, Center for the Study of Evaluation, Los Angeles: University of California, 1968.

Provus, Malcolm. "Evaluation of Ongoing Programs in the Public School System," in *Educational Evaluation: New Roles, New Means*, edited by Ralph Tyler, pp. 242-283. Sixty-eighth Yearbook of the National Society for the Study of Education, Part II. Chicago: University of Chicago Press, 1969.

Reder, H. W. *Criteria for Judging the Effectiveness of Training Programs*. Stanford University, 1966. (mimeograph)

Reichenbach, H. *Experience and Prediction*. Chicago: University of Chicago Press, 1938.

Reitman, W. R. Computer models of psychological processes and some implications for the theory and practice of education. In *Needed Research in the Teaching of English*, pp. 98-106. OE-30010 Coop. Res. Monograph No. 11. Washington, D. C.: U.S. Office of Education, 1963.

Restle, F. *Psychology of Judgment and Choice. A Theoretical Essay*. New York: John Wiley & Sons, Inc., 1961.

Rimm, D. Cost efficiency and test prediction. *Journal of Consulting Psychology* 27 (1963): 89-91.

Roper, Elmo. "A Survey of People's Attitudes Towards Our Public School System." *Life*, September, 1950, pp. 24-26.

Rorer, L. G., et al. The optimal use of a fallible predictor. Unpublished manuscript. Eugene: Oregon Research Institute, 1964.

Rosenbloom, P. C., ed. *Modern Viewpoints in the Curriculum*. New York: McGraw-Hill Book Co., 1969.

Rosenshine, Barak. New Correlates of Readability and Listenability. In *Reading and Realism*, Part I, edited by J. A. Figurel, pp. 712-716. Newark, Delaware: International Reading Association, 1969.

Rosenthal, R. *The Experimenter Effect*. New York: Appleton-Century-Crofts, 1966.

Samph, Thomas. The Role of the Observer and His Effects on Teacher Classroom Behavior. Occasional Papers, Volume 2, Number 1. Pontiac, Michigan: Oakland Schools, (no date).

Sandifer, Mary Ruth. *American Lay Opinions of the Progressive School*. Washington: Catholic University of America Press, 1943.

Saunders, D. R. The moderator variable as a useful tool in prediction. Proceedings of the 1954 Invitational Conference on Testing Problems, pp. 54-58. Princeton, N. J.: Educational Testing Service, 1955.

————. Moderator variables in prediction. *Educational Psychological Measurement* 16 (1956): 209-222.

Saupe, Joe L. "Selecting Items to Measure Change," *Journal of Educational Measurement* 3 (1966): 223-28.

Scandura, Joseph M. "Precision in Research on Mathematics Learning: The Emerging Field of Psychomathematics." *Journal of Research in Science Teaching* 4 (1966): 253-74.

Scannell, D. P., and Stellwagon, W. R. "Teaching and Testing for Degrees of Understanding," *California Journal of Instructional Improvement* 3 (1960): 1.

Scheffler, I. "Justifying Curriculum Decisions," *School Review* 65 (1958): 470-72.

Schenck, E. Allen, and Naylor, James. "A Cautionary Note Concerning the Use of Regression Analysis for Capturing the Strategies of People," *Educational and Psychological Measurement* 28 (1968): 3-7.

Schönemann, Peter H. A Generalized Solution of the Orthogonal Procrustes Problem. *Psychometrika* 31 (1966): 1-10.

Schramm, Wilbur. Procedures and Effects of Mass Communication. In *Mass Media and Education,* Part II, pp. 113-138. National Society for Study of Education, Fifty-third Yearbook. Chicago: University of Chicago Press, 1954.

Schutz, R. E. *Measurement procedures in programmed instruction.* Final report, Title VII, Project 909. Tempe: Arizona State University, 1964.

Schutz, R. E.; Baker, R. L., and Gerlach, V. S. *Measurement procedures in programmed instruction.* Tempe: Arizona State University, Classroom Learning Laboratory, 1964.

Schutz, R. E.; Baker, R. L., and Sullivan, H. J. *A guide to the development of instructional materials.* Technical Report: Aerospace Medical Research Laboratory, Wright-Patterson AF Base, Ohio, 1967.

Scriven, M. "The Philosophy of Science in Educational Research," *Review of Educational Research,* 30, 1960, 422-429.

————. *Value claims in the social sciences.* Lafayette, Ind.: Social Science Education Consortium, 1966.

————. *Student Values as Educational Objectives.* ETS conference, New York City, 1965. In *Proceedings,* (op. cit.), 1966.

————. The Methodology of Evaluation. In *Perspectives of Curriculum Evaluation,* edited by Ralph Tyler, Robert Gagné, and Michael Scriven. AERA Monograph Series on Curriculum Evaluation, No. 1. Chicago: Rand McNally & Co., 1967.

Shaw, Marvin E. and Wright, Jack M. *Scales for the Measurement of Attitudes.* New York: McGraw Hill Book Co., 1967.

Shuford, Emir H., Jr.; Albert, Arthur, and Massengil, H. Edward. Admissible probability measurement procedures. *Psychometrika* 31 (1966): 125-45.

Silberman, H., et al. *Use of exploratory research and individual tutoring techniques for the development of programming methods and theory.* Title VII Research Report. Santa Monica: Systems Development Corporation, 1964.

Silverman, Robert E. *The Evaluation of Programmed Instruction: A Problem in Decision Making.* Reprinted from *Psychology in the Schools* 1 (1964): 74-78.

Sjogren, Douglas; England, George W., and Meltzer, Richard. The Development of an Instrument for Assessing the Personal Values of Educational Administrators. Fort Collins: Colorado State University, 1969.

Skager, Rodney W.; Schultz, Charles B., and Klein, Stephen P. Points of view about preferences as tools in the analysis of creative products. *Perceptual and Motor Skills* 22 (1966): 83-94.

Skinner, B. F. *Cumulative Record.* New York: Appleton-Century-Crofts, 1959.

Smedslund, J. Concrete reasoning: A study of intellectual development. *Monographs in Social Research on Child Development,* 1964. (whole issue).

Smith, B. O. Teaching and testing values. *Proceedings of the 1965 invitational conference on testing problems.* Princeton, N. J.: Educational Testing Service, 1966.

Smith, B. O.; Stanley, W. O., and Shores, J. H. *Fundamentals of Curriculum Development.* New York, World Book, Co., 1957 (2nd edition).

Smith, E. R., and Tyler, R. W. *Appraising and Recording Student Progress.* New York: Harper & Row, Publishers, 1942.

Smith, K. U., and Smith, M. F. *Cybernetic principles of learning and educational design.* New York: Holt, Rinehart & Winston, Inc., 1966. (Chapter 15)

Snider, James G., and Osgood, Charles E., eds. *Semantic Differential Technique: A Sourcebook.* Chicago: Aldine Publishing Co., in press.

Snyder, W. R.; Flood, P. K., and Stuart, M. Use of CAI in evaluation of the ISCS Seventh-grade course. In *Intermediate Science Curriculum Study Newsletter.* Florida State University, 1967.

Sontag, Marvin. "Attitudes Toward Education and Perception of Teacher Behavior." AERJ 5 (1968): 385-402.

Southwest Educational Development Laboratory. *CALIPERS: Planning the Systems Approach to Field Testing.* Austin, Texas: Southwest Educational Development Laboratory, 1969.

Squire, J. R. "Evaluating High School English Programs." *North Central Association Quarterly* 40 (1966): 247-254.

Squire, James R., and Applebee, Roger K. *A study of English programs in selected high schools which consistently graduate outstanding students in English.* Urbana: University of Illinois, Cooperative Research Project No. 1994, December, 1965.

Stake, Robert. "The Countenance of Educational Evaluation," *Teachers College Record* 68 (1967): 523-540.

————. "A Research Rationale," *The EPIE Forum* 1 (1967): 4-6.

————. Generalizability of Program Evaluation: The Need for Limits. *Educational Product Report* 2 (1969): 39-40.

Steele, Joe M. Things as they are: an evaluation procedure to assess intent and practice in instruction. Urbana: University of Illinois, 1969. Unpublished doctoral dissertation.

————. Dimensions of the Class Activities Questionnaire. Urbana: CIRCE, College of Education, University of Illinois, 1969. Multilith.

Steinberg, E. R., et al. Curriculum development and evaluation in English and social studies. Cooperative Research Project No. F-041. Pittsburgh: Carnegie Institute of Technology, 1964.

Stephan, F. F. and McCarthy, F. J. *Sampling Opinions, An Analysis of Survey Procedure.* New York: John Wiley & Sons, Inc., 1958.

Stephenson, W. *The Study of Behavior.* Chicago: University of Chicago Press, 1953.

Stern, G. G., Stein, M. I., and Bloom, B. S. *Methods in Personality Assessment*. Glencoe, Ill.: The Free Press, 1956.

Stoker, H. W., and Kropp, R. P. "Measurement of Cognitive Processes," *Journal of Educational Measurement* 1 (1964): 39-42.

Stone, Philip J., et al. *The General Inquirer: A Computer Approach to Content Analysis*. Cambridge, Mass.: The M.I.T. Press, 1966.

Stufflebeam, Daniel L. "A Depth Study of the Evaluation Requirement," *Theory into Practice* 5 (1966): 121-33.

————. *Evaluation Under Title I of the Elementary and Secondary Educational Act of 1965*. Address at Evaluation Conference sponsored by the Michigan State Department of Education, East Lansing, January 24, 1966.

————. Evaluation as Enlightenment for Decision Making. In *Improving Educational Assessment and an Inventory of Measures of Affective Behavior*. Washington, D. C. Association for Supervision and Curriculum Development, NEA, 1969.

Suchman, Edward A. *Evaluative Research: Principles and Practice in Public Service and Social Action Programs*. New York: Russell Sage Foundation, 1967.

Sullivan, H.; Baker, R. L., and Schutz, R. E. *Classroom episodes for teaching psychological principles and concepts of learning*. Tempe, Arizona: Arizona State University Classroom Learning Laboratory, 1966.

Taba, H. *Teaching strategies and cognitive functioning in elementary school children*. Cooperative Research Project No. 2404. San Francisco: San Francisco State College, February, 1966.

————. *Curriculum Development, Theory and Practice*. New York: Harcourt, Brace & World, Inc., 1962.

Taba, H., and Sawin, E. I. "Proposed Model in Evaluation," *Educational Leadership* 20 (1962): 57-59.

Tannenbaum, H. E., and Stillman, N. *Evaluation in Elementary School Science*. USOE-29057 Circular No. 757, 1964.

Taylor, H. C., and Russell, J. T. The relationship of validity coefficients to the practical effectiveness of tests in selection. *Journal of Applied Psychology* 23 (1939): 565-578.

Taylor, P. A. "The Mapping of Concepts." Unpublished doctoral dissertation. Urbana: University of Illinois, 1966.

————. "The Theory of Value and Decision-Making," *Manitoba Journal of Educational Research* 2 (1966): 54-60.

Taylor, Peter A., and Maguire, Thomas O. "A Theoretical Evaluation Model," *The Manitoba Journal of Educational Research* 1 (1966): 11-18. (a)

————. Perceptions of some objectives for a science curriculum. Urbana: University of Illinois, Center for Instructional Research and Curriculum Evaluation, 1966b. (mimeograph)

Taylor, Peter A., and De Corte, Erik. Standards for judging instructional affectiveness: a problem in educational evaluation. *Manitoba Journal of Education* 6 (1970): (in press).

Temp, George. *Statistical Statements in Social Science: Student Response to a Teaching Episode Developed by Sociological Resources for Secondary Schools*. Princeton, N. J.: Educational Testing Service, July, 1966.

————. "Calculus Project Films: Teacher Reaction Survey," in *Curriculum Studies*. Princeton, N. J.: Educational Testing Service, July, 1966.

————. "Problems of Measurement and Sampling in Studies of Lower-Class Deprived Children," *Curriculum Studies*. Princeton, N. J.: Educational Testing Service, February, 1967.

Thistlewaite, D. College press and changes in study plans of talented students. *Journal of Educational Psychology* 51 (1960): 222-234.

Thomas, J. Alan. Cost-Benefit Analysis and the Evaluation of Educational Systems. Proceedings of the 1968 Invitational Conference on Testing Problems. Princeton, New Jersey: Educational Testing Service, 1968.

Thrall, R. M.; Coombs, C. H., and Davis, R. L., eds. *Decision Processes*. New York: John Wiley & Sons, Inc., 1954.

Torgerson, W. S. *Theory and Methods of Scaling*. New York: John Wiley & Sons, Inc., 1958.

Townes, Charles H. Quantum electronics, and surprise in development of technology. *Science* 159 (1968): 699-703.

Travers, R. M. W. *An introduction to educational research*. 2nd ed. New York: The Macmillan Co., 1964. (Chapters 6, 8, & 9)

Traxler, A. E., and North, R. D. *Techniques of Guidance*. 3rd ed. New York: Harper & Row, Publishers, 1966.

Trow, Martin. "Education and Survey Research," in *Survey Research in the Social Sciences*, edited by Charles Y. Glock, Chapter sixteen. New York: Russell Sage Foundation, 1967.

————. Methodological Problems in the Evaluation of Innovation. UCLA: Center for the Study of Evaluation of Instructional Program, CSE Report No. 31, May, 1969. Also in Wittrock, M. C., and Wiley, David, eds. *The Evaluation of Instruction: Issues and Problems*. New York: Holt, Rinehart & Winston, Inc., (in press).

Tucker, L. R. *Factor Analysis of Relevance Judgments: An Approach to Content Validity*. 1961 Invitational Conference on Testing Problems Proceedings. Princeton, New Jersey: Educational Testing Service, 1961.

————. Three mode factor analysis. *Psychometrika* 31 (1966): 279-312.

————. Relations Between Multidimensional Scaling and Three-Mode Factor Analysis. Urbana: University of Illinois, 1969. (photocopy)

Tyler, Louise. Technical Standards for Curriculum Evaluation. Paper presented at Annual Meeting of the American Educational Research Association, Chicago, 1968. (mimeograph)

Tyler, R. W. *Constructing achievement tests*. Columbus: Ohio State University Press, 1934.

————. Characteristics of a satisfactory diagnosis. In *Educational Diagnosis*, edited by G. M. Whipple, pp. 95-112. NSSE 34th Yearbook, 1935.

————. *Basic Principles of Curriculum and Instruction.* Chicago: University of Chicago Press, 1950.

————. "The Development of Instruments for Assessing Educational Progress," *Phi Delta Kappan* 47 (1965): 13-16.

————. "Assessing the Progress of Education," *Phi Delta Kappan* 1 (1965): 1-12.

————. "Assessing the Progress of Education in Science," *The Science Teacher*, September, 1966, pp. 11-14.

————. "The Objectives and Plans for a National Assessment of Educational Progress," *Journal of Educational Measurement* 3 (1966): Spring, 1966.

————. The current status of the project on assessing the progress of education. Prepared for publication in *Educational Horizon*, 1967.

Umpleby, Stuart. "The teaching computer as a device for social science research." CEEL Report X-7. Urbana: Computer-based Education Research Laboratory, University of Illinois. May, 1969.

U.S. Office of Education. Plan for the Use of Educational Specialists in Visits to the Laboratories. Washington: USOE, Division of Educational Laboratories. No date, circa 1968. (photocopy)

Unruh, Glenys, ed. *New Curriculum Developments: A Report of ASCD's Commission on Current Curriculum Developments.* Washington, D. C.: Association for Supervision and Curriculum Development, 1965.

Veal, L. Ramon. "Developing an instrument for measuring composition ability in young children." Paper read at annual meeting of NCME, New York, 1967.

Verhaegen, R. M. *The Effect of Learner-Controlled Instruction in a Tenth Grade Biology Curriculum.* Thesis (M.A.) University of California, Los Angeles, California, 1964.

Walbesser, H. H. "Evaluation as a Guide to Course Improvement," *Science Education News* 1, American Association for the Advancement of Science, November, 1964, 1-2.

————. "Science Curriculum Evaluation: Observations on a Position," *The Science Teacher* 33 (1966): 28-35.

Wallace, C. An abilities conception of personality. *American Psychologist* 26 (1966): 113-116.

Ward, J. H. An application of linear and curvilinear joint functional regression in psychological prediction. Research Bulletin 54-86, AFPTRC, Lackland AFB, Texas. 1954.

Wash, James A., Jr. "An Evaluation of the Sequential Anthropology Curriculum Project." Paper read at annual meeting of AERA, February, 1967.

Webb, E. J., et al. *Unobtrusive Measures, Nonreactive Research in the Social Sciences.* Chicago: Rand McNally & Co., 1966.

Wehling and Charters. "Dimensions of Teacher Beliefs About the Teaching Process." *American Educational Research Journal* 6 (1969): 7-30.

Welch, Wayne W., and Walberg, Herbert J. "A Design for Curriculum Evaluation," *Science Education* 52 (1968): 10-16.

Wessel, N. Y. "Innovation and Evaluation: In Whose Hands?" *Proceedings of the 1966 invitational conference on testing problems. Princeton,* N. J.: Educational Testing Service, 1966.

Wharton, Lyndon B. *Needs Assessment.* Report of Title III E.S.E.A. Springfield, Illinois: Office of the Superintendent of Public Instruction, no date.

Wherry, R. J. Test selection and suppressor variables. *Psychometrika* 11 (1946): 239-247.

Wherry, R. J., and Naylor, J. C. "Comparison of Two Approaches—JAN and PROF—for Capturing Rater Strategies," *Educational and Psychological Measurement* 26 (1966): 267-286.

Whyte, W. F. On the utilization of the behavioral sciences in manpower research. Paper prepared for OMAT Sub-committee on Research Meeting, March 18, 1966.

Wiley, David E., and Bock, R. Darrell. "Quasi-Experimentation in Educational Study," *School Review* 75 (1967): 48-62.

Wilhelms, F. T., ed. *Evaluation as feedback and guide.* ASCD Yearbook, 1967.

Williams, B. R. "Economics in Unwonted Places," *Advancement of Science,* 1 (1965): 20-28.

Williams, J. D. *Teaching Methods Research Background and Design of Experiment.* Arithmetic Research Bulletins, August, 1965. Nos. I, II, and III.

————. "Effecting Educational Change; Some Notes on the Reform of Primary School Mathematics Teaching," *Educational Research* 8 (1966): 191-95.

Williams, J. P. Effectiveness of constructed-response and multiple-choice programing modes as a function of test mode. *Journal of Educational Psychology* 56 (1967): 111-117.

Winter, Stephen S., and Welch, W. W. "Achievement Testing Program of Project Physics," *The Physics Teacher* 5 (1967): 14-18.

Winter, W. D. Student values and grades in general psychology. *Journal of Educational Research* 55 (1965): 331-333.

Wise, John; Nordberg, Robert; and Reitz, Donald. *Methods of Research in Education.* Boston: D. C. Heath & Co., 1967.

Wittcock, M. C.; Wiley, David; and McNeil, John. The connotative meaning of the concept "Public School Teachers": an image analysis of semantic differential. *Educational and Psychological Measurement* 27 (1967): 863-869.

Wolff, Max, and Stein, Annie. *Six Months Later: A Comparison of Children Who Had Head Start Summer, 1965, with their Classmates in Kindergarten.* Washington, D. C.: Office of Economic Opportunity, 1966.

————. *Long-range Effect of Pre-Schooling on Reading Achievement.* Washington, D. C.: Office of Economic Opportunity Project 141-61 Study III. 1966.

Wood, Dorothy Adkins. *Test Construction, Development and Interpretation of Achievement Tests.* Columbus, Ohio: Charles E. Merrill Publishing Co., 1960.

Wrightstone, J. W., et al. *Evaluation in Modern Education.* New York: American Book Co., 1956.

Young, M. *The Rise of the Meritocracy, 1870-2033.* Baltimore, Md.: Penguin Books, Inc., 1958.

DATE DUE
